ROUTLEDGE LIBRARY EDITIONS: WW2

Volume 4

CHURCHILL IN HIS TIME

CHURCHILL IN HIS TIME
A Study in a Reputation, 1939–1945

BRIAN GARDNER

Routledge
Taylor & Francis Group
LONDON AND NEW YORK

First published in 1968 by Methuen & Co Ltd

This edition first published in 2022
by Routledge
2 Park Square, Milton Park, Abingdon, Oxon OX14 4RN

and by Routledge
605 Third Avenue, New York, NY 10158

Routledge is an imprint of the Taylor & Francis Group, an informa business

© 1968 Brian Gardner

All rights reserved. No part of this book may be reprinted or reproduced or utilised in any form or by any electronic, mechanical, or other means, now known or hereafter invented, including photocopying and recording, or in any information storage or retrieval system, without permission in writing from the publishers.

Trademark notice: Product or corporate names may be trademarks or registered trademarks, and are used only for identification and explanation without intent to infringe.

British Library Cataloguing in Publication Data
A catalogue record for this book is available from the British Library

ISBN: 978-1-03-201217-9 (Set)
ISBN: 978-1-00-319367-8 (Set) (ebk)
ISBN: 978-1-03-210012-8 (Volume 4) (hbk)
ISBN: 978-1-03-210013-5 (Volume 4) (pbk)
ISBN: 978-1-00-321320-8 (Volume 4) (ebk)

DOI: 10.4324/9781003213208

Publisher's Note
The publisher has gone to great lengths to ensure the quality of this reprint but points out that some imperfections in the original copies may be apparent.

Disclaimer
The publisher has made every effort to trace copyright holders and would welcome correspondence from those they have been unable to trace.

BRIAN GARDNER

Churchill in his time

A Study in a Reputation 1939–1945

METHUEN & CO LTD
11 New Fetter Lane · London EC4

First published 1968 *by Methuen & Co Ltd*
Copyright © 1968 by Brian Gardner

Contents

	List of Illustrations	vi
	Acknowledgements	vii
	Introductory Note	xiii
1	Prologue: Prophet, Part I	1
2	1939 Naval Person	20
3	1940 Emergency Premier	40
4	1940 Inspired Leader	65
5	1941 Old Soldier	97
6	1942 Political Prey	141
7	1943 Proud Strategist	211
8	1944 Struggling Statesman	232
9	1945 Prophet, Part II	269
10	1945 Victor	289
11	Epilogue: Loser	295
	Sources	315
	Index	337

List of Illustrations

facing page

The Prime Minister in east Scotland, October 1940	32
The King and Queen greet relatives of the men killed in the engagement with the *Graf Spee*	33
Anthony Eden	48
Duff and Lady Diana Cooper	48
Lord Beaverbrook	49
Richard Stokes	49

Between pages 136 and 137

General de Gaulle
Aneurin Bevan
Brendan Bracken
Emanuel Shinwell
Stafford Cripps
The Prime Minister's return from Yalta

Acknowledgements

The author and publishers wish to thank the following for permission to reproduce the extracts listed below:

George Allen & Unwin Ltd for extracts from *Diary of a Diplomatic Correspondent* by G. Bilainkin, and *Voices from Britain* by P. Smithers; the Alliance Press Ltd for extracts from *The Prime Minister* by P. Paneth; Edward Arnold Ltd for an extract from *Two Cheers for Democracy* by E. M. Forster; A. Watkins Inc for an extract from *Drive* by C. Codman (copyright 1957 by T. D. Codman) (Atlantic-Little, Brown and Company); B. T. Batsford Ltd for extracts from *Hitler's Reich and Churchill's Britain* by S. Laird and W. Graebner; J. M. Spaight for an extract from *Victory from the Air* by Auspex (Geoffrey Bles Ltd); A. M. Heath & Co Ltd for an extract from *Ramparts of the Pacific* by H. Abend (the Bodley Head Ltd); the author for an extract from *Lest We Regret* by D. Reed (Jonathan Cape Ltd); the author and Jonathan Cape Ltd for an extract from *Second World War* by Viscount Norwich; Jonathan Cape Ltd for an extract from *From the City, From the Plough* by A. Baron; the Cambridge University Press for extracts from *A French Officer's Diary* by D. Barlone, and an extract from *The Nature of Modern Warfare* by C. Falls; the Carnegie Endowment for International Peace for an extract from *International Conciliation*; Cassell & Co Ltd for extracts from *Secret Session Speeches*, *The Dawn of Liberation*, *Into Battle*, *The End of the Beginning*, *Victory*, vols. I, II, III, and VI of *The Second World War* by Sir W. S. Churchill, *Orders of the Day* by Earl Winterton, *With Prejudice* by Lord Tedder, and *The Reckoning* by the Earl of Avon; A. D. Peters & Co for extracts from *Testament of Adolf Hitler* edited by H. R. Trevor-Roper, translated by François Genoud (Cassell & Co Ltd); Field-Marshal Sir Claude Auchinleck and Mrs R. Connell Robertson for an extract from *Auchinleck* by J. Connell (Cassell & Co Ltd); Laurence Pollinger Ltd for extracts from *This is London* by E. R. Murrow (Cassell & Co Ltd), *Only the Stars are Neutral* and *The Wounded Don't Cry* by Q. Reynolds (Cassell & Co Ltd); David

Higham Associates Ltd for an extract from *Memoirs*, vol. II by Sir B. H. Liddell Hart (Cassell & Co Ltd); Chatto and Windus Ltd for an extract from *War Begins at Home* edited by T. Harrison and C. Madge; the *Chicago Daily News* for an extract from an article by Leland Stowe; William Collins Sons & Co Ltd for an extract from *Wavell* by J. Connell, *Memoirs* by Viscount Montgomery, and *Nine Troubled Years* by Viscount Templewood, for extracts from *The Rommel Papers* edited by Sir B. H. Liddell Hart, *The Turn of the Tide* by Sir A. Bryant, *Trenchard* by A. Boyle, *The Thirties* by Malcolm Muggeridge, *The Private Papers of Hore-Belisha* by R. J. Minney, *Diaries and Letters: 1930–39* and *Diaries and Letters: 1939–45* by Sir H. Nicolson, *Triumph in the West* by Sir A. Bryant; Weidenfeld & Nicolson for an extract from *The Call to Honour: Documents* by General C. de Gaulle (William Collins Sons & Co Ltd); David Higham Associates Ltd for an extract from *Bomber Offensive* by Sir A. Harris (William Collins Sons & Co Ltd); the author for an extract from *So Few Got Through* by M. Lindsay (William Collins Sons & Co Ltd); Constable & Co Ltd for extracts from *The Ironside Diaries* edited by R. Macleod and D. Kelly, *Winston Churchill: The Struggle for Survival* by Lord Moran, and *Personal Experience* by Lord Casey; London Express News and Feature Services for extracts from articles from the *Daily Express* and *Sunday Dispatch*; Odhams Press Ltd for an extract from the *Daily Herald*; Associated Newspapers Ltd for extracts from articles from the *Daily Mail* and *News Chronicle*; the Daily Mirror Newspapers Ltd for extracts from articles from the *Daily Mirror* and *Sunday Pictorial*; the *Daily Telegraph* for extracts from the *Daily Telegraph*; Hugh Cudlipp for extracts from *Publish and Be Damned* (Dakers Ltd); J. M. Dent & Sons Ltd for an extract from *A Village in Piccadilly* by Mrs R. Henrey; Meredith Press Inc for an extract from *As He Saw It* by E. Roosevelt (Duell, Sloane & Pearce Inc); A. M. Heath & Co Ltd for extracts from *The White House Papers*, vol. I by R. Sherwood (Eyre & Spottiswoode); the Beaverbrook Foundations for extracts from *The Private Papers of Baudouin*, translated by Sir Charles Petrie (Eyre & Spottiswoode), and *Behind the Battle* by J. de Courcy (Eyre & Spottiswoode); A. P. Watt & Son for extracts from *The Sound of the Trumpet* and *The Reeling Earth* by S. G. Millin (Faber & Faber Ltd); A. M. Heath & Co Ltd for extracts from *I Was There* by W. D. Leahy (Victor Gollancz Ltd); A. D. Peters & Co for an extract from *And Yet I Like Americans* by J. L. Hodson (Victor Gollancz Ltd); Her Majesty's Stationery Office for extracts from *The Trial of German Major War Criminals: Proceedings of the International Military Tribunal at Nuremberg*, and *Hansard*; Robert Hale Ltd for extracts from *War Reporter* by B. Gray; Hamish Hamilton Ltd for extracts from *The Goebbels Diaries* edited by L. B. Lochner, and an extract from *For What Do We Fight?* by Sir Norman Angell; the Earl of Birkenhead for extracts from *The Life of Lord Halifax* (Hamish Hamilton Ltd); A. M. Heath & Co Ltd for an extract from *The High Cost of Hitler* by J. Gunther (Hamish Hamilton Ltd), and extracts from *Berlin Diary* by W. L. Schirer (Hamish Hamilton Ltd); Laurence Pollinger Ltd for an extract from *What of the Night?* and from *Right Honourable Gentlemen* by V. Adams (Hamish Hamilton Ltd), *European Spring* by C. B. Luce (Hamish Hamilton Ltd), and extracts from *Eclipse* by A. Moorehead (Hamish Hamilton Ltd); the Hamlyn Group for an extract from *Bridge into the Future: Letters of Max Plowman* (Dakers Ltd); William Heinemann Ltd for extracts from *Frankly Speaking* by James F. Byrnes (Harper & Row Ltd); George G. Harrap & Co Ltd for an extract from *With Rommel in the Desert* by H. W. Schmidt, and *Ego 6* by J. Agate; Rupert Hart-Davis Ltd for an extract from *The Initials in the Heart* by L. Whistler, and extracts from *Old Men Forget* by Viscount Norwich, and *Trumpets from the Steep* by Lady Diana Cooper; William Heinemann Ltd for extracts from *Three Years With Eisenhower* by H. C. Butcher, *Crusade in Europe* by General D. Eisenhower, *Stafford Cripps* by E. Estorick, for an extract from *Once There Was a War* by J. Steinbeck, *Concerning W. S. Churchill* by Sir G. Arthur; A. P. Watt & Son for an extract from *Strictly Personal* by W. S. Maugham (William Heinemann Ltd); Miss Nancy Maurice for an extract from *Assignment to Catastrophe*, vol. I by Sir E. L. Spears (William Heinemann Ltd); the *Chicago Sun Times* for extracts from *Ciano's Diaries* edited by M. Muggeridge (William Heinemann Ltd); Hodder & Stoughton Ltd for extracts from *Richard Stafford Cripps* by C. Cooke; Time Inc (New York) for extracts from *Year of Decisions* by H. Truman (Hodder & Stoughton Ltd); the estate of the late Richard Dimbleby for an extract from *The Waiting Year* by R. Dimbleby (Hodder & Stoughton Ltd); Hutchinson Publishing Group Ltd for an extract from *The Tragedy of Winston Churchill* by V. W. Germains (Hurst & Blackett Ltd); Hutchinson & Co Ltd for an extract from *Men, Martyrs and Mountebanks* by B. Baxter, for extracts from *Londoner's Life* and *Off The Record* by C. Graves, *They Left the Back Door Open* by L. S. B. Shapiro (Jarrolds Ltd), *Geoffrey Dawson and Our Times* and *Immortal Years* by Sir E. Wrench, *Why England Slept* by J. F. Kennedy, *My Political Life* by L. S. Amery, *A Penguin in the Eyrie* by H. Bolitho, *Tempestuous Journey* by F. Owen, *The War that Churchill Waged* by L. Broad, *The Business of War* by Sir J. Kennedy and B. Fergusson, *Watchwords* by J. F. C. Fuller (Skeffington & Son Ltd), *Wavell in the Middle East* by H. Rowan-Robinson; Miss Christine Eade for extracts from *Churchill by his Contemporaries* edited by C. Eade (Hutchinson & Co Ltd); Michael Joseph Ltd for an extract from *The Phoney War* by E. S. Turner and two extracts from *War at the Top* by James Leasor and Sir L. Hollis; Youngman Carter Ltd for extracts from *The Oaken Heart* by Margery Allingham (Michael Joseph Ltd); Laurence Pollinger Ltd for an extract from *Someone Had Blundered* by Bernard Ash (Michael Joseph Ltd); *The Listener* for extracts from a leading article, 17 May 1945, p. 540, column 1, and two reports, May 1945 ('Points from the Past Week's Foreign Broadcasts') and September 1944 (B.B.C. War Correspondent Stanley Maxted); Longmans, Green & Co Ltd for extracts from *Broken Images* by John Guest, *The Annual Register* – 1941, and *Benito Mussolini* by C. Hibbert; Macdonald & Co (Publishers) Ltd for an extract from *But For Britain* by H. Fyfe; Laurence Pollinger Ltd for extracts from *The Stilwell Papers* by J. W. Stilwell, edited by T. H. White (Macdonald & Co (Publishers) Ltd); Macmillan & Co Ltd for extracts from *King George VI* and *John Anderson* by J. W. Wheeler-Bennett, *The Blast of War* by H. Macmillan, *Dynamic Democracy* (War Pamphlet No. 15) by F. Williams, *The Portsmouth Letters* by W. M. James, the Literary Executors of the late Richard Hillary and Macmillan & Co Ltd for an extract from *The Last Enemy* by R. Hillary, *Life of Neville Chamberlain* by K. Feiling, *England's Hour* by V. Brittain; the Society of Authors for extracts from *Outside Information* by N. R. Smith (Macmillan & Co Ltd); the Macmillan Company (New York) for extracts from

The Public Papers and Addresses of Franklin D. Roosevelt; the *Guardian* for extracts from the *Manchester Guardian*; Associated Book Publishers Ltd for extracts from *Atlantic Meeting* by H. V. Morton (Methuen & Co Ltd); William Morrow & Co Inc for extracts from *This is Pearl!* by W. Millis; Frederick Muller Ltd for an extract from *What They Said at the Time* edited by K. Freeman; Miss Ann King-Hall for extracts from *Newsletter* and the *National Newsletter* edited by Stephen King-Hall; the *New Statesman* for extracts from *New Statesman & Nation*; The New York Times Company for extracts from the *New York Times* – 1942, 1944, and 1945; Nicholson & Watson Ltd for extracts from *How War Came* by R. G. Swing; The Observer Foreign News Service for extracts from *The Observer*; Odhams Press Ltd for an extract from *Step by Step: Selections from the Writings and Speeches of W. S. Churchill*; Oxford University Press for extracts from *A Diary With Letters* by Thomas Jones; A. & C. Black Ltd for an extract from *Top Secret* by R. Ingersoll (S. W. Partridge & Co); Random House Inc for an extract from *Suez to Singapore* by C. Brown; *Reynolds News* for an article from *Reynolds News*; *The Scotsman* for an extract from *The Scotsman*; Curtis Brown Ltd for an extract from *Hitler and His Admirals* by A. Martienssen (Martin Secker & Warburg Ltd); Southern Methodist University Press for an extract from *Quotemanship* edited by P. F. Boller; the Spectator Ltd for an extract from the *Spectator*; Time Inc for extracts from *Time*; Time & Tide Ltd for an extract from *Cavalcade* by W. J. Brittain; Times Newspapers Ltd for extracts from *The Times* and the *Sunday Times*; Tribune for extracts from *Tribune*; Vallentine, Mitchell & Co Ltd and Otto Frank for an extract from *The Diary of a Young Girl* by Anne Frank; George Weidenfeld & Nicolson Ltd for extracts from *Chips* edited by R. Rhodes James, *Inside Hitler's Headquarters* by W. Warlimont, and *Unity: Documents* by General C. de Gaulle; Ernest Benn Ltd for an extract from *The English: Are They Human?* by G. J. Renier (Williams & Norgate Ltd).

The author and publishers also wish to thank the following for permission to reproduce the illustrations appearing in this book:

Fox Photos Ltd for those facing pages 32, 136 and 48 (bottom right); Imperial War Museum for those facing page 48 (top) and between pages 136 and 137 (bottom right); New York Times Photos for that facing page 137; Radio Times Hulton Picture Library for those facing pages 33 and 48, and between pages 136–137 (top, and bottom left).

The author would like to thank Miss Vanessa Hamilton for copyright research.

Introductory Note

Sir Isaiah Berlin, writing of Winston Churchill's 'inner essence and true nature', has said of him: 'A man larger than life, composed of bigger and simpler elements than ordinary men, a gigantic historical figure during his own lifetime, superhumanly bold, strong, and imaginative . . . a mythical hero who belongs to a legend as much to reality, the largest human being of our time.' One would hesitate to contradict so eminent a person; but if we can slice away the myth, then it might be useful to see how the man stood in reality rather than how he is in legend. Attempts to record history as what really happened instead of – as most history – what readers or the historian want to believe happened, are customarily labelled 'debunking'. In 1964 Kingsley Martin wrote: 'The time for debunking Winston Churchill is not yet, and when it comes it will not succeed as easily as with other great personages. Not that material for criticism is lacking.'

What is needed is not a debunking of Churchill, but a debunking of the Churchill legend. A legend that holds that Churchill in the Second World War was the embodiment of the will of the people, that he led the 'free world' virtually united behind him to final victory. Memory is short. Churchill played a more important part in the winning of that war for the democracies, in spite of his many errors, than any other man – except Adolf Hitler himself. But from 1941 he led an increasingly disunited nation, in full discord with France and the United States; he led it to what he believed in the end was failure; he led it to the chorus of persistent criticism, insults, and personal attacks that any other Prime Minister in any other times might have expected. In 1942 Churchill was compared in the House of Commons and in print to Hitler. These critical voices were too numerous, and many of them too respected, to be considered isolated, solitary, or eccentric.

After a certain amount of myth-slicing it can be seen that Churchill was essentially a lonely figure during the war, as he had been before it. Sir Isaiah's much-praised essay was entitled

Mr. Churchill in 1940. It is true that in 1940, but only then, he did achieve with his speeches a remarkable degree of national communion. Kingsley Martin finished the article, which he had begun with the words above, 'But everything will be forgiven him because of 1940.'

It is forgotten that during those times, Churchill was, contrary to popular understanding, not in as close touch with the people as for instance a typical peace-time premier. During 1943 Churchill delivered only six speeches to the House of Commons (and one to the U.S. Congress), made ten statements or tributes there, and gave four broadcast speeches – and also speeches at the Guildhall, National Liberal Club, Harvard, the Albert Hall, Harrow School, and the Mansion House. This does not compare very well with the average Prime Minister. Answering questions in the House was more of an event than a routine occasion for him. Such questions mainly dealt with minor problems, and not Churchill's part in the war. Debates on the conduct of the Government were extremely infrequent. Nevertheless, Churchill contrived an understanding with the people rare if not unique among the war leaders.

During the war – as the consensus of history will surely reveal – there were five major failures: the loss of initiative that resulted from the United States delaying entry into the war until they were attacked; the lack of a political, as opposed to a purely military, objective of the United States in the later stages, apart from a desire to prevent the re-establishment of the pre-war British Empire; the insistence on unconditional surrender; the failure to offer the under-privileged European peoples any alternative to a brutalizing State despotism, described as Communism, except a return to the old régimes under a League of Nations type of internationalism; and the delivery of the atomic bombs on Japan, which was isolated and ripe for surrender. For two of these blunders Churchill cannot be held responsible; with two others he was oddly unconcerned. He was wrong about many of the lesser problems, particularly concerning strategy. His main contributions were: his speeches, not only to his own countrymen, but also for instance to Congress and to France, which were not unimportant weapons in the bringing down of Hitler; withholding the R.A.F. from probable destruction in the Battle of France; influencing the American decision to beat Germany before Japan; refusing to attempt a premature second front; bringing scientists into government (albeit not always with success); and saving Greece from a far worse civil war than it experienced. He also prevented the military from controlling the war, but at a high cost.

In the Second World War, Churchill enjoyed great and unusual power, but he used it, on the whole, in a way worthy of the fight itself in what was after all modern history's most righteous war; he pronounced fine and noble calls to service; in his hands, power did not corrupt. This does not mean he was 'superhuman'. Churchill made mistakes, had bitter enemies in his own camp, and had glaring faults; he was more human than most of us.

In Churchill's own history, *The Second World War,* we see the man mainly as he saw himself. Here he is as others saw him.

The quotations selected for the anthology proper were all said or written during the war. This is what people thought at the time. It is what was said of the man without the benefits or handicaps of hindsight: from it, it is hoped that a picture may emerge, in fairly close focus, untinted and untouched, of this man as he was during the peak of his career, at the time on which his reputation will always be based. It includes, as it must, an account of the opposition in Britain during the war – an aspect of the war which has been somewhat neglected. This neglect is a pity, for the opposition to Churchill, which kept open the arteries of democracy, was intense and not always unsuccessful in forcing events. It was a compliment to the British system, as Churchill himself, who relished criticism even less than most people, was quick to point out at the end of the war (although he had made strenuous efforts to stifle it in the Press, and, by demanding votes of confidence, to some extent in Parliament).

Here and there I have included a contemporary extract, not immediately concerned with Churchill, so that the broad context of the war will not be entirely forgotten.

Readers should not be misled by the familiar use of 'Winston'. For a quarter of a century Churchill had been known by his first name to many of his countrymen who had never even seen him.

Some of the sayings of Hitler are extracts from those war writings or transcripts which have been credited to him, and which I have no reason to doubt.

Churchill was the greatest and most famous public figure in British history since the Duke of Wellington. Wellington, a careful general, was basically a reactionary and autocratic Tory. Churchill, an impulsive Defence Minister, was basically (for he was steeped in the history of the nineteenth century) a liberal, if not radical, Whig, reluctant to part with imperial responsibilities. Both men shared a conviction that Britain had a special contribution to make to the world. Wellington was a soldier who felt it his duty to be a politician. Churchill was a politician who wanted to be a soldier. It is the political rather than the military sector which the British people have consistently favoured for two centuries. A nation which since Cromwell has always felt uncomfortable with all but its most eccentric military leaders, was led in its most dangerous battle by a war leader in a zip-suit and carpet slippers: a man whose greatest work till then had been in literature. The British saw in Churchill something flattering to themselves. When Wellington died, the vast crowds stood in awe – or instinctively hissed. At the funeral of Winston Churchill, they stood to attention, and bared their heads in the cold morning air.

B.G.

CHAPTER ONE

Prologue: Prophet, Part 1

A political author, 1931:

The true tragedy of Mr Churchill is that whilst he has in reality nothing to *offer* the genuine Labour man, or Liberal, he fails to command the confidence of the genuine Conservative. For the ghosts of the Gallipoli dead will always rise up to damn him anew in times of national emergency ... What sensible man is going to place confidence in Mr Churchill in any situation which needs cool-headedness, moderation, or tact? In this sense of latent distrust is to be found the greatest obstacle to the realization of Mr Churchill's own most coveted ambition. The public looks upon him as a brilliant man but rash, hot-headed, impulsive ... 'Cleverness' and 'wisdom' are not synonymous terms; there is still a broad gulf between the 'man of talents' and the 'man of genius'. One may perhaps feel that at the present time when the Empire is going through the most terrible economic crisis known to history, the facile phrases, glittering hopes, and unbalanced enthusiasm, which issued in the Tragedy of the Dardanelles, are a little out of place.

It is difficult to exaggerate the loneliness of Winston Churchill's position in British politics during the 1930s. From 1924 to 1929 he had held one of the three most important political offices in the land, that of Chancellor of the Exchequer: now he was almost an outcast. It was not only, in a time when social and economic conditions had forced the Conservative Party to the left, that his views were thought to be reactionary – it was also a personal feeling about the man. Churchill, it seemed, had done rather better in politics than his ability warranted. He was unreliable. People were tired of him. He was, it was said, essentially a figure of the past, like Lloyd George and Austen Chamberlain, lingering on in the House of Commons, but out of touch with the times. Many thought they had reasons for personal enmity, for Churchill had always taken an active rather than passive view of government. There was something about Churchill – a kind of irrepressible, occasionally sour, bombast – for which many of his countrymen did not care. There was a widespread feeling in the 1930s that the nation had got wise to Churchill at last – and just in time. He was, it seemed, a political adventurer, a swashbuckler of the most dangerous sort.

Another, also in 1931:

A few misguided bank clerks who parade Hyde Park in black shirts are of no moment... Mr Winston Churchill is in another category. He is intelligent... He is public spirited in the sense that he has no selfishness and is as devoted to his class as a Japanese to his house. He hates popular government, unless it is hedged round by such securities as will ensure the privilege of the ruling order. He is ruthless, and treasures only those prejudices which he chooses to possess. Mr Churchill loves war and loves violence... Devoured by a perpetual *besoin de faire*, unable to satisfy it except in side-shows like Gallipoli, Russian guerrilla wars and the organisation of gentlemen in plus-fours for general-strike-breaking, he is waiting for the day. Will his day arrive?... I do not believe it, since Englishmen still form the backbone of the British army. If a Communistic England is unthinkable, a Fascist England may be called highly improbable. The main obstacle in Mr Churchill's way is that Fascism is a system and that England is England.

Herbert Samuel, Leader of the Liberal Party,[1] 1931:

If indeed the truest patriot is a man who breathes hatred, who lays the seeds of war and stirs up the greatest number of enemies against the country, then Mr Churchill is a great patriot.

Even his friends had little opinion of Churchill's political stature at the time.

Lord Beaverbrook,[2] letter, 7 January 1931:

Winston Churchill is trying to make a corner for himself in Indian affairs. He is now taking up the stand of a veritable die-hard. But he does not carry conviction... He has disclosed too many shifting faces to expect to be regarded as immovable now. His voice lacks that note of sincerity for which his country looks.

It was Churchill's stand on India – a 'jewel of the Empire' with

---

[1] Liberal M.P., 1902–18, 1929–35; Minister, 1909–16; Leader of the Liberal Party, 1931–5; Home Secretary, 1931–2; Viscount, 1935; died 1963.

[2] Canadian financier; Unionist M.P., 1910–16; Minister of Information, 1918; newspaper proprietor; Minister for Aircraft Production, 1940–1; Minister of Supply, 1941–2; died 1964.

which he did not think Britain should part – that brought him most reprehension from liberals. In a typical phrase, he spoke of Gandhi as 'a seditious saint striding half-naked up the steps of the Vice-regal Palace'. For a while, he was able to lead about fifty Conservative M.P.s against Government policy in India. But his supporters dwindled over the years.

As for the Labour Party, Emanuel Shinwell[1] has written: 'Nobody in British politics during the early twenties inspired more dislike in Labour circles than Winston Churchill . . . [in the late twenties] the mention of his name at Labour gatherings was the signal for derisive cheers . . . [in the thirties] there was a general conviction that this was the twilight of his career.'

Lord Beaverbrook, letter, January 1932:

He has held every view on every question. He has been apparently quite sincere in all his views. Perhaps he has convinced himself. But he is utterly unreliable in his mental attitude.

In January 1933, Adolf Hitler became Chancellor of Germany. Churchill became associated with another group of rebels in the House of Commons – those who warned of 'the German menace'. They consisted mainly of a different group to those in the India lobby, and included Austen Chamberlain, Edward Grigg, Lord Winterton, and Brendan Bracken. But as a political ally, he was no longer desirable. Gradually, he became isolated from all but three of those calling for action to meet the growing threat of Hitler.

The sages of the age looked elsewhere for their prognostications about the aspirations of man:

Walter Lippmann,[2] after a speech by Adolf Hitler, 1933:

We have heard once more, through the fog and the din, the hysteria and the animal passions of a great revolution, the authentic voice of a genuinely civilised people. I am not only willing to believe that, but it seems to me that all historical experience compels one to believe it.

During these years, Churchill tended to devote himself to

---

[1] Labour M.P., 1922–4, 1928–31, 1935–; held first junior ministerial post in 1924; Minister of Fuel and Power, 1945–7; Minister for War, 1947–50; Minister of Defence, 1950–1.
[2] Assistant to Secretary of War, 1917; special writer on politics, *New York Herald Tribune*, 1931–67.

personal pursuits: his home, his family, painting, and his biography of his ancestor Marlborough, a considerable literary and historical achievement. He had already had published, in four successive volumes during the twenties, a history of the First World War, which although underrated at the time, was a work of the highest quality. Somewhat unexpectedly in view of a number of slight books which had appeared years previously, Churchill was going to be a considerable figure in the history of English literature, no matter what his place in politics. He derived a great deal from his study of Marlborough's need for allies in Europe. As has been pointed out, Churchill was usually surefooted and confident in Europe, through his knowledge of history, but ignorant of the East, where he made mistakes. It was a decade in which Churchill, rather late in life, came to a full maturity. For this reason, L. S. Amery described Churchill's exclusion from office as 'one of the best things that ever happened for England'.

Lord Beaverbrook, letter, 1 January 1934:

I think Winston Churchill will retire from Parliament. It is really the best thing for him to do.

Ramsay MacDonald's 'National Government', formed in the economic crisis of 1931, was dissolved in October 1935. It was succeeded by the Second National Government, predominantly Conservative but with a few Labour supporters like MacDonald's son and Harold Nicolson, under the premiership of Stanley Baldwin.

Churchill fought this election on the need for rearmament. Although he was willing to serve in the Government, Baldwin excluded him.

Ralph Wigram, British diplomat, after Hitler seized the Rhineland, March 1936:

War is now inevitable, and it will be the most terrible war there has ever been ... I have failed to make the people here realise what is at stake. I am not strong enough, I suppose; I have not been able to make them understand. Winston has always, always understood, and he is strong and will go on to the end.[1]

---

[1] Served at the Paris Embassy and Foreign Office during the thirties; died 1936. His widow married Sir John Anderson, 1941.

PROLOGUE: PROPHET, PART I

A magazine editor, friend of Churchill's son Randolph, 1936:

His greatest love, after his country, is his home, Chartwell, at Westerham, Kent. He gets up at about eight o'clock nowadays. With his breakfast he reads all the newspapers, looking at every page of every newspaper. At about half past nine, if it is fine, he goes out and paints. Sometimes, instead of painting, Winston Churchill will work at the third volume of his life of his ancestor Marlborough. Cigar in hand, whisky and soda on a table near him, he walks about the room dictating to his chief secretary. In the afternoon, as likely as not, he will spend a few hours bricklaying, wearing old kid gloves and still smoking a cigar. Even when he has a lunch appointment in London he stays at Chartwell the previous night, making the fifty-five minutes' journey by a Daimler car given to him by more than a hundred friends on his return from his last visit to the United States, when a taxicab knocked him down. But Winston Churchill often asks himself whether living a life of a country gentleman, however intelligently and with whatever distinction, is the real part for him to play when his country may be in danger.

On 1 May 1936, Churchill wrote: 'Germany is arming more strenuously, more scientifically and upon a larger scale, than any nation has ever armed before ... there are four or five millions of active, intelligent, valiant Germans engaged in these processes, working, as General Goering has told us, night and day. Surely these are facts which ought to bulk as large in ordinary peaceful people's minds as horse-racing, a prize fight, a murder trial or nineteen-twentieths of the current newspaper bill of fare.' But Churchill, so many people declared, was 'a warmonger'.

In 1936 Baldwin, not entirely unaware of the trend in Europe, set up the Ministry for Co-ordination of Defence. It was expected that Churchill, having been First Lord of the Admiralty, and Minister for War and Air, would get the post. He did not; it was 'a heavy blow'. Churchill attacked the Government's defence preparations, or lack of them, more unsparingly than ever. 'Mr Baldwin knew no more than I, how great was the service he was doing me in preventing me from becoming involved in all the Cabinet compromises and shortcomings of the next three years, and from having, if I had remained a Minister, to enter upon a war bearing direct responsibility.'

Churchill was handicapped in his warnings by the unfortunate fact that he was himself partly responsible, when previously in office, for Britain's lamentable air force and military inadequacies.

On 15 March 1937, Stanley Baldwin described Churchill as part of:

the flotsam and jetsam of political life thrown up on the beach.

Baldwin resigned in May 1937, after the Abdication crisis. Throughout the crisis, Churchill had been the King's closest adviser and supporter. This had added to his already considerable enemies – not least *The Times* – and had convinced many that whatever political flair he might once have enjoyed had finally deserted him.

Baldwin's successor as head of the so-called National Government was Neville Chamberlain, brother of Austen, and son of a great Colonial Secretary. Churchill indicated that he would serve under Chamberlain, but the new Prime Minister had other ideas: 'If I take him into the Cabinet, he will dominate it. He won't give others a chance of even talking.' This continued ostracism was a more bitter blow to Churchill than is generally recognized.

Under Chamberlain, the armament situation improved. Churchill acknowledged, as early as 31 May 1937, that 'no one was more active' for rearmament than Chamberlain had been during Baldwin's last administration. But the foreign policy situation – dubbed 'appeasement' – became disastrous, according to Churchill. This did not endear him to those who were unable, or unwilling, to face the realities in Europe. The Beaverbrook Press was campaigning for the idea of 'Splendid Isolation'; this was, as Lord Beaverbrook explained on 9 September 1937, 'a plea for the detachment of Britain from Continental quarrels'.

In February 1938, Anthony Eden, a comparatively young Tory, resigned as Foreign Secretary. 'Greatly to his credit, as I see it,' remarked Chamberlain, who wanted to conduct his own foreign policy. He appointed the equally charming, but more amenable, Lord Halifax to the post.

Neville Chamberlain, letter to his sister, 20 March 1938:

In face of such problems, to be badgered and pressed to come out and give a clear, decided, bold, and unmistakable lead, show 'ordinary courage', and all the rest of the twaddle, is calculated to vex the man who has to take the responsibility of the consequences. As a matter of fact, the plan of the 'Grand Alliance', as Winston calls it, had occurred to me long before he mentioned it. I talked about it to Halifax, and we submitted it to the Chiefs of Staff and the F.O. experts. It is a very attractive idea; indeed, there is almost everything to be said for it until you come to examine its practicability. From that moment its attraction vanishes. You have only to look at the map to see that nothing that France or we could do could possibly save Czechoslovakia from being overrun by the Germans, if they wanted to do it.[1]

In May 1938, Lord Swinton, Air Minister since 1935, was dismissed by Chamberlain as a scapegoat for delays in aircraft production. Even Churchill considered this unfair. He had a motion down which demanded an inquiry into air defences.

Harold Nicolson,[2] letter, 17 May 1938:

We had an excitement yesterday, Swinton sacked. At once I telephoned (or rather got Duncan [Sandys] to telephone) to Winston saying that his motion must be withdrawn. He assented grumpily. But how silly the whole thing is! Here we are at the gravest crisis in our history, with a genius like Winston doing nothing . . .

Doing nothing? Not in an administrative way, but one of the things Churchill had done was to collect around him a nucleus of M.P.s with similar views on the European crisis. They were three: Robert Boothby, Brendan Bracken, and Churchill's son-in-law, Duncan Sandys. Another, larger group of rebels collected around Eden; this group feared association with Churchill, because of the latter's views on India and other matters, which were considered reactionary. It has been said by one of the group that Eden, despite his great reputation for independence and political courage, was reluctant even to be seen talking to Churchill. Among these rebels were L. S. Amery, who brought with him his own 'group' of rebels, Edward Grigg, Richard Law (Bonar Law's

---

[1] In a newspaper article two days previously, Churchill had called for a defence agreement between 'the Powers of the second rank in Europe' and Britain and France. Chamberlain himself attempted to carry out this policy twelve months later. Chamberlain had been Conservative M.P. for a Birmingham constituency since 1918; he had been a good Minister of Health, and twice Chancellor of the Exchequer.

[2] Foreign service, 1909–29; worked for Beaverbrook Press; National Labour M.P., 1935–45; he experienced the ten years of one of Britain's greatest parliaments on the slender majority of 87.

son), Harold Macmillan, Archibald Sinclair (Leader of the Liberal Party), E. L. Spears, and Lords Cranborne and Lloyd.

Neville Chamberlain, 11 September 1938:

I fully realise that, if eventually things go wrong and the aggression takes place, there will be many, including Winston, who will say that the British Government must bear the responsibility, and that if only they had had the courage to tell Hitler now that, if he used force, we should at once declare war, that would have stopped him. By that time it will be impossible to prove the contrary, but I am satisfied that we should be wrong to allow the most vital decision that any country could take, the decision as to peace or war, to pass out of our hands into those of the ruler of another country, and a lunatic at that. I have been fortified in this view by reading a very interesting book on the foreign policy of Canning[1] ... Over and over again Canning lays it down that you should never menace unless you are in a position to carry out your threats.

Having seized Austria in March, Hitler turned more of his attentions to Czechoslovakia, where lived three and a quarter million Germans. At the Nuremberg Rally on 12 September he made a bellicose speech claiming the German-inhabited area of Czechoslovakia.

Richard Hillary:

I was in Rouen on the night of Hitler's final speech before Munich. The hysterical 'Sieg Heils!' of his audience were picked up by the loudspeakers through the streets, and sounded strangely unreal in the quiet evening of the cathedral city. The French said nothing, merely listening in silence and then dispersing with a shrug of their shoulders. The walls were plastered with calling-up notices and the stations crowded with uniforms. There was no excitement. It was as though a very tired old man was bestirring himself for a long-expected and unwelcome appointment.[2]

Some of the statesmen of Europe may not have had a clear idea of what was going on; but the ordinary people of Europe were more wise, and knew.

---

[1] George Canning, nineteenth-century Foreign Secretary. The book was *The Foreign Policy of Canning*, by H. Temperley. Hitler recognized that Chamberlain's journeys were to gain time (*The Kersten Memoirs*, 24 July 1942).

[2] Written in 1941. Author of *The Last Enemy*; served in the R.A.F., shot down, badly burned, 1940; died on active service 1943.

During the Czechoslovakia crisis, Chamberlain flew three times to talk to Hitler.

Harold Nicolson, diary, 22 September 1938:

At about 11.30 Winston Churchill telephones. Would I come up to London for a meeting at 4.30 in his flat? I say that I shall be there. I travel up and go to 11 Morpeth Mansions. Winston has just been to Downing Street. He says that the Cabinet are at last taking a firm stand ... It comes down to this, either Chamberlain comes back with peace with honour or he breaks it off. In either case we shall support him. 'Let us form the focus,' says Winston. We say that indeed we will ... He stands there behind the fire-screen, waving a whisky and soda at us, rather blurry, rather bemused in a way, but dominant and in fact reasonable.

Duff Cooper,[1] after Cabinet, 24 September 1938:

Personally I believe that Hitler has cast a spell over Neville. After all, Hitler's achievement is not due to his intellectual attainments nor to his oratorical powers, but to the extraordinary influence which he seems able to exercise over his fellow-creatures. I believe that Neville is under that influence at the present time. 'It all depends,' he said, 'on whether we can trust Hitler.' 'Trust him for what?' I asked.

At 2 a.m. on 30 September, Chamberlain, Hitler, Mussolini, and the French Premier Daladier, signed the Munich Agreement, which transferred a large slice of Czechoslovakia to Germany, together with most of that country's defences and about a third of its population. On his return to London, Chamberlain waved the declaration at a Downing Street window, and declared to the crowd that it signified 'peace in our time', although as he explained to his colleagues it meant nothing of the sort.

Malcolm Muggeridge, in 1939:

He showed it to them, the very document, pointed to the signature upon it; then told them to go home and sleep quietly in their beds, confident that they were secure against molestation, not just for that night and tomorrow night, but for many nights, perhaps for ever. Peace in our time; peace in his time – not even that. This first ecstasy

---

[1] Conservative M.P., 1924–9, 1931–45; War Minister, 1935–7; First Lord of the Admiralty, 1937–8; Minister of Information, 1940–1; Ambassador to France, 1944–7; biographer of Talleyrand and Haig; Lord Norwich, 1952; died 1954.

soon passed. The Munich Agreement turned out to be scarcely distinguishable from the Godesberg ultimatum, and, as executed, to involve still further concessions to Germany. As Mr Churchill well put it: 'The German dictator, instead of snatching his victuals from the table, has been content to have them served to him course by course.'[1]

On the first day of the House of Commons debate on Munich, Duff Cooper, First Lord of the Admiralty, announced his resignation: 'The Prime Minister has believed in addressing Herr Hitler through the language of sweet reasonableness. I have believed that he was more open to the language of the mailed fist.' Churchill made one of his greatest orations: 'All is over. Silent, mournful, abandoned, broken, Czechoslovakia recedes into the darkness. She has suffered in every respect by her associations with France, under whose guidance and policy she has been actuated for so long ... Do not suppose that this is the end. This is only the beginning of the reckoning.'

Harold Nicolson, diary, 6 October 1938:

Our group decide that it is better for us all to abstain, than for some to abstain and some to vote against. We therefore sit in our seats, which must enrage the Government, since it is not our numbers that matter but our reputation. Among those who abstained were Eden, Duff Cooper, Winston, Amery, Cranborne, Wolmer, Roger Keyes, Sidney Herbert, Louis Spears, Harold Macmillan, Richard Law, Bob Boothby, Jim Thomas, Duncan Sandys, Ronald Cartland, Anthony Crossley, Brendan Bracken and Emrys-Evans. That looks none too well in any list. The House knows that most of the above people know far more about the real issue than they do. It was clear that the Government were rattled by this. In the first place, the P.M. gave a pledge that there would be no General Election. In the second place made the astounding admission that his phrase about 'peace in our time' was made under the stress of emotion. The House breaks up with the Tories yelling to keep their spirits up. But they well know that Chamberlain has put us in a ghastly position and that we ought to have been prepared to go to war and smash Hitler. Next time he will be far too strong for us.

The Times lobby correspondent wrote a favourable account of

---

[1] Hitler's Godesberg ultimatum concerning Czechoslovakia had been due to expire on 28 September. Muggeridge wrote his book *The Thirties* while a recruit in the Army; served in Intelligence; editor of *Punch*, 1951–7.

Duff Cooper's resignation speech. It was not published, and replaced by a piece written by the editor. The correspondent resigned the following day. Politically speaking, Cooper 'dined out' on his resignation speech for the remainder of his career.

Churchill's speech was almost too much for his constituency, Epping. The chairman of the Epping Conservative Association was incensed. He said Churchill was 'a menace in Parliament'. Churchill threatened to resign and fight a by-election. The Association gave him a vote of confidence, but only of three to two.

Chairman of the Chigwell Unionist Association, which was also in Churchill's Epping constituency:

Mr Churchill's castigation of the National Government, which we returned him to support, is a mockery and a shame. In any other Party but the Conservative it would have earned his immediate expulsion.

Adolf Hitler, shortly after Duff Cooper's resignation:

I am fully aware that if one day the place of Chamberlain were taken by such men as Eden, Duff Cooper or Churchill their aim would be to unleash at once a new world war against Germany.

Duff Cooper, who had known Churchill since 1914, became a prominent member of the 'Eden group'. A few weeks after the Munich debate, he pointedly disassociated himself from Churchill in the House. Even at this time, close association with Churchill was considered politically dangerous.

Lord Maugham, the Lord Chancellor (and brother of author Somerset), suggested that agitators like Churchill and Cooper ought to be 'shot or hanged'.

Hitler maintained that the only one of his demands which need concern Britain, was the return of the former German colonies, for which he said he would not go to war.

Adolf Hitler, 8 November 1938:

After all, Churchill may have 14,000, 20,000, or 30,000 votes behind him – I am not so well informed about that – but I have 40,000,000 behind me.

Harold Nicolson, letter, 9 November 1938:

I went to a hush-hush meeting with Anthony Eden. Present: Eden, Amery, ... Harold Macmillan, Spears [etc.]. All good Tories and sensible men. This group is distinct from the Churchill group. It also includes Duff Cooper. We decided that we should not advertise ourselves as a group or even call ourselves a group. We should merely meet together from time to time, exchange views, and organise ourselves for a revolt if needed. I feel happier about this ... Obviously they do not mean to do anything rash or violent. At the same time they are deeply disturbed by the fact that Chamberlain does not seem to understand the gravity of the situation. Unless we pull ourselves together and have compulsory registration in the next few months, it will be too late. It was a relief to me to be with people who share my views so completely, and yet who do not give the impression (as Winston does) of being more bitter than determined, and more out for a fight than for reform. I shall be happy and at ease with this group.

The editor of the left-wing *New Statesman & Nation*, Kingsley Martin, interviewed Churchill in January 1939:

K.M.: The country has learnt to associate you, Mr Churchill, with the view that we must all get together as quickly as possible to rearm in defence of democracy ... Is it in your view possible to combine the reality of democratic freedom with efficient military organization?
W.C.: ... I see no reason why democracies should not be able to defend themselves without sacrificing these fundamental values ... I am convinced that with adequate leadership, democracy can be a more efficient form of government than Fascism. In this country at any rate the people can readily be convinced that it is necessary to make sacrifices, and they will willingly undertake them if the situation is put clearly and fairly before them ... It may be that greater efficiency in secret military preparations can be achieved in a country with autocratic institutions than by the democratic system. But this advantage is not necessarily great, and it is far outweighed by the strength of a democratic country in a long war ... Questions in Parliament and Debates, far from hindering the conduct of the war, frequently assist it by exposing weak points and give opportunities to clear up misunderstandings.
K.M.: Captain Liddell Hart has remarked that to have conscription to combat Fascism is like cutting our throats to avoid a disease.
W.C.: I see no reason why any essential part of our liberties should be lost by preparations for defence ... [but] I do not think we need a great conscript army on the continental model.

While nations busily armed themselves for the war which statesmen said had been averted, there was a sort of political hush in Europe. Where would Hitler strike next, and when?

E. M. Forster,[1] 1939:

I was in London that dark Wednesday night when the news of an agreement between [Hitler and Chamberlain] seeped through. It was good news, and it ought to have brought great joy; it did bring joy to the House of Commons. But unimportant and unpractical people often foresee the future more clearly than do those who are engaged in shaping it, and I knew at once that the news was only good in patches. Peace flapped from the posters, and not upon the wings of angels. I trailed about reading the notices, some of which had already fallen into the gutter. On the Thursday I returned to the country, and found satisfaction there in a chicken run which I had helped build earlier in the week. This post-Munich world may not last long, but we are living in it now, and we have not any other life. We have to make the best of an unexplored and equivocal state, and we are more likely to succeed if we give up any hope of simplicity. 'Prepare, prepare!' does not do for a slogan. No more does 'Business as usual.' Both of them are untrue to the spirit of 1939, the spirit which is half-afraid and half-thinking about something else . . . This decade has lasted long enough, and the Crisis in particular has become a habit, indeed almost a joke. Emotions are no longer deeply stirred by it, and when Germany or Italy destroys an extra country we are upset for a shorter period each time. We are worried rather than frantic . . .

Political commentator, 9 March 1939:

It is interesting to note the political trend in Britain and France as influenced by the waning of the crisis. Neville Chamberlain is now complete master of the field in Britain. Having put over the armament programme, having arranged to finance it and get it under way at its present speed, he now towers above all possible leaders in Britain . . . though Eden did resign once, that act seems to have exhausted his powers of sacrifice. The other Conservatives who opposed Chamberlain over Munich are now eating out of his hand. And why not? What they wanted was a strong Britain. Churchill and Duff Cooper can only be gratified that Chamberlain put as much drive into getting Britain armed as he has. Churchill now is a frequent caller at 10 Downing Street; he has influence with the government and is not entirely out of favour with it.

It was true that even well before the Munich crisis, Churchill had called on Chamberlain to discuss events and plans. But Chamberlain took little notice of what he heard on those occasions.

---

[1] Distinguished novelist and essayist since 1905.

Even convinced anti-'Munichites' could summon up some not-too-grudging praise from prominent Nazis.

R. H. S. Crossman,[1] 18 March 1939:

Goering is too free and easy to be a typical Prussian, but his real courage and capability lift him above the rank of Nazi bosses. Apart from Hitler, he is the only statesman of any calibre in the Third Reich ... Moreover, it was his energy in reorganising the Prussian police and establishing the Gestapo which enabled Hitler to consolidate his position in 1933, and since then the triumphs of Nazi foreign policy would have been impossible without his work ...

Three days previously Germany had extended its 'protection' to the remainder of Czechoslovakia. German troops had marched into Prague.

Neville Chamberlain, 19 March 1939:

As always, I want to gain time, for I never accept the view that war is inevitable.

Chamberlain on Churchill, April 1939:

The nearer we get to war, the more his chances improve, and *vice versa*.

Harold Nicolson, 14 June 1939:

Dine with Kenneth Clark. The Walter Lippmanns are there: also the Julian Huxleys and Winston Churchill as the guest of honour. Winston is horrified by Lippmann saying that the American ambassador, Jo Kennedy, had informed him that war was inevitable and that we should be licked. Winston is stirred by this defeatism into a magnificent oration. He sits hunched there, waving his whisky-and-soda to mark his periods, stubbing his cigar with the other hand. 'It may be true, it may well be true,' he says, 'that this country will at the outset of this coming and to my mind almost inevitable war be exposed to dire peril and fierce ordeals. It may be true that steel and fire will rain down upon us day and night scattering death and destruction far and wide. It may be true that our sea-communications will be imperilled and our food-supplies placed in jeopardy. Yet these trials and disasters, I ask you to believe me, Mr Lippmann, will but serve to steel the resolution of the British people and to enhance our will for victory. No, the ambassador should not have spoken so, Mr Lippmann; he should not have said that dreadful word. Yet supposing (as I do not for one moment suppose)

---

[1] Journalist and University don before the war; 'Psychological Warfare' expert during the war; Labour M.P., 1945–; Minister of Housing, 1964–6; Leader of the House, 1966–8.

that Mr Kennedy were correct in his tragic utterance, then I for one would willingly lay down my life in combat, rather than, in fear of defeat, surrender to the menaces of these most sinister men. It will then be for you, for the Americans, to preserve and to maintain the great heritage of the English-speaking peoples. It will be for you to think imperially, which means to think always of something higher and more vast than one's own national interests. Nor should I die happy in the great struggle which I see before me, were I not convinced that if we in this dear dear island succumb to the ferocity and might of our enemies, over there in your distant and immune continent the torch of liberty will burn untarnished and (I trust and hope) undismayed.' We then change the subject and speak about the Giant Panda.

The nearest equivalent in the Labour Party to Churchill in the Conservative, was Sir Stafford Cripps. He, too, had warned against the dangers of appeasement and had called for rearmament. He had recently been expelled from the Party, with Aneurin Bevan, for his efforts to promote a Popular Front of Labour, Liberals, and extreme left, as the only hope of defeating the National Government in the forthcoming election of 1940.[1] Austere, reserved, vegetarian, and intense, no man could have been more different from Churchill. What relations would develop between the two? It was a question which would have great political relevance three years later.

Stafford Cripps, diary, 22 June 1939:

I saw [Churchill] at his flat for over an hour. He inveighed strongly against the P.M., said he and Eden and others had been ready to join the Cabinet since Hitler went into Prague but would not be admitted as it would stop all possibility of appeasement . . . He agreed on the need of an all-in government, but despaired of any way of getting rid of or convincing Chamberlain[2] . . . It was a most interesting talk in

---

[1] Sir Stafford Cripps: born 1889, son of the Lord President of the Council in the first Labour government; lawyer; K. C., 1927; Solicitor-General, 1930–1; Labour M.P., 1931–50. Under Churchill he was successively Ambassador to Moscow, Leader of the House, Minister for Aircraft Production. Under Attlee: President of the Board of Trade, Chancellor of the Exchequer. Died 1952.

[2] The Popular Front collapsed when rejected at the Labour Party Conference at Whitsun, 1939; Cripps then campaigned for a kind of coalition. At the outbreak of war he applied to rejoin the Party, but was asked to sign a humiliating statement, expressing contriteness; this he refused to do, and he sat as an Independent until March 1945.

which amongst other things he pointed out that but for Chamberlain's switch on foreign policy after Prague's occupation the Popular Front movement would have swept the country and I gathered he would have supported it.

Tom Driberg on a Royal visit to Guildhall,[1] *Daily Express*, 24 June 1939:

There was handclapping as some arrived. I tried to grade the applause. The first to get a three-star burst of clapping was Lord Gort, who strode in with spurs clinking, right hand swinging strenuously, soldierly face glowing. So far as I could judge, the only other 3-star clapping was for Lord Derby, the Bishop of London, the Prime Minister (for whom there were also a few cheers). Loudest cheers, only indubitable 4-star clapping, were for U.S. Ambassador Kennedy. It was his day. Two-star men included Hore-Belisha and Winston Churchill.

Geoffrey Dawson,[2] editor of *The Times*, 3 July 1939:

The *Daily Telegraph* joined in the hue and cry for the inclusion of Winston in the Cabinet in order to impress the Germans. We continued the more effective process of calling attention to the growing strength of the British Army.

But Dawson forgot that he was in no position to gauge such 'effectiveness'. An opinion is not a fact; it was a conceit not unlike him. But whereas the Conservative Party 'establishment' were against Churchill almost to a man, the public were beginning to think otherwise: for someone who was meant to be an adventurer, his warnings had been going on a remarkably long time, and with strange consistency, determination, and integrity. The *Daily Telegraph* had been leading a newspaper campaign for his return to office.

J. B. Priestley,[3] 10 July 1939:

Why is the definite public demand for the inclusion of Mr Winston

---

[1] Wrote the column 'William Hickey' in the *Daily Express*; Independent M.P., 1942–5; Labour M.P., 1945–55, 1959–. Author of a critical biography of Lord Beaverbrook.

[2] One of a supposedly influential coterie at All Souls College, Oxford, of which he had been a Fellow since 1898. Editor of *The Times*, 1912–19 and 1923–41. Supported Baldwin over India and Abdication, Chamberlain over Germany; died 1944.

[3] Author since 1922, and left-wing political writer.

Churchill in the Cabinet being so obstinately resisted? There are three good reasons why he should be included. First, he is a man of outstanding ability and experience, and nobody except the leaders of our present Cabinet believes it to be rich in these qualities. Secondly, the people want him there. Thirdly, his presence will at least do something to show the world, which has no confidence whatever in our statesmen, that we are in earnest.

Sir Thomas Inskip, Minister for Co-ordination of Defence, 3 August 1939:

War today is not only not inevitable but is unlikely. The Government have good reason for saying that.

German troops were entering the free port of Danzig. Now it was known where Hitler would strike next: Poland.

On 3 August Duff Cooper wrote to Baldwin, on the latter's seventy-second birthday, with a curious suggestion:

If the international situation deteriorates, which I believe it will, we shall be compelled to have a Coalition Government. I don't believe that Neville could ever lead such a government, especially after a performance like that of last night. What are the alternatives? – Halifax or Winston. I don't really believe the former is up to it, and the latter has so many and such violent enemies – not only in the House, but there are large numbers of people in the country who admire but don't trust him. It is for these reasons that I am wondering whether after two years' rest you feel you could come back. Men are only as old as they feel, and I can't tell how you feel. Mr G. was in his prime at seventy-two.

If war came, Chamberlain would very probably not last long. It was worrying, for there was no sign whatever of an obvious successor.

American radio correspondent, London, 16 August 1939:

Now let me call your attention to a minor item of news which may have a major bearing on all this. It comes from Hong Kong, and tells of the Japanese army bringing up troops right to the Hong Kong border, and the British sending troops to the border to face them. True, the Japanese gave two days' notice of their troops taking up this position, which they said was necessary in mopping-up operations in conquered Chinese territory. But in the language of power those Japanese troops, appearing just where they have at just this time, are as unmistakable as a fire alarm. They say: Look out, you British, if you get into a war in Europe we shall take Hong Kong, and that is the beginning of the end of British influence in the Far East. Little is being said about the invisible role of Japan in the European crisis . . .

The Town Clerk, Westminster, 22 August 1939:

Gas Helmets for Infants Under Two Years: Parents and guardians residing in Westminster are asked to bring their infants up to two years of age to one of the below-mentioned centres during the week commencing on Thursday, August 24, 1939 – including Saturday and Sunday – between the hours of 10.0 a.m. and 6.0 p.m., to be fitted with helmets for protection against the effects of gas.

On 25 August the Anglo-Polish Treaty of Mutual Assistance was signed in London. Two days later, Hitler confirmed his view that Danzig belonged to the Reich, and must be returned to it.

Malcolm Muggeridge, 1939:

Groping along darkened streets, dimly it was felt that a way of life was failing, its comfortable familiarity passing away never to reappear . . .

At dawn on 1 September German troops invaded Poland. That afternoon Chamberlain sent for Churchill and, bowing to growing public opinion, asked him to join – in an unstated position – the small War Cabinet which he proposed to form. Churchill accepted, 'without comment'. He had spent the previous night on watch for Nazis at his house in Kent, armed, alternating guard with his old Scotland Yard detective (in retirement, but whom he had sent for that day). 'Nobody would have had a walk-over.'

John Gunther[1] broadcast to N.B.C., 1 September 1939:

It's a strange face that London wears tonight. It's a dark face. We're having a black-out here. The streets are black, the houses are black. It began to rain this afternoon, and the streets emptied quickly, as darkness fell; in the length of Piccadilly there were only half a dozen cars. Some workmen were still busy, carrying sandbags into position. The whole town looks sandbagged . . . War began today. You all know that. What may be the second world war began today. You all know that too. But London is quiet; quiet and confident. The British take even such a supreme moment of crisis as tonight with good humour, calmly. A few moments ago I saw something highly typical on the news ticker: 'The Football Association announces that a message

---

[1] His *Inside Europe*, first of a famous series, was published in 1936; he had been a resident London correspondent of the *Chicago Daily News*, for which newspaper he worked from 1922 to 1936.

received stated that the situation at present does not warrant the cancellation of to-morrow's matches.'

On 3 September the British Government presented a two-hour ultimatum to Germany, demanding the recall of German troops from Poland, expiring at 11 a.m.

At 11.15 a.m., Great Britain declared war on Germany. France declared war on Germany at 5 p.m.

L. S. Amery,[1] diary, 3 September 1939:

I think I see Winston emerging as P.M. out of it all by the end of the year.

---

[1] Born in India; at school with Churchill; *The Times*, 1899–1909; Conservative M.P. for the same Birmingham constituency, 1911–45; First Lord of the Admiralty, 1922–4; Colonial Secretary, 1924–9; Secretary of State for India, 1940–5; author and mountaineer; died 1955.

CHAPTER TWO

1939 Naval Person

Reports of 'Mass Observation' social survey, 3 September 1939:

Office-girl, aged twenty-one, in Sheffield:

Glorious morning, mum and dad and self listening to every bulletin. War declared. Funny feeling inside me, and yet all three stood at attention for 'The King', and I know we were all in the same mind, that we shall and must win.

Middle-aged schoolmistress in small country town:

At 11.15 I went up, and we sat round listening to Chamberlain speaking. I held my chin high and kept back the tears at the thought of all that slaughter ahead. When 'God Save the King' was played we stood.

A young wife in Leeds:

The milkman told me about the ultimatum to Germany expiring at 11.0 a.m. We could eat no breakfast hardly and just waited with sweating palms and despair for 11 o'clock. When the announcement was made, 'This country is at war with Germany', I leant against my husband and went quite dead for a minute or two.

Writing soon afterwards to friends in America, a British woman author captured the mood with accuracy:

There was no bravura, no sudden quickening of the blood, no secret feeling of exultation and anticipation of the conflict. *Land of Hope and Glory* sung with feeling made one feel slightly sick. We seemed to me to be going to war as a duty, a people elderly in soul going in stolidly to kill or be killed because we felt it was the only wise course to take. It was insufferably depressing. I began to hope (feeling very glad nobody knew) that the air raid would begin at once and the worst happen quickly... At eleven o'clock the next morning Mr Chamberlain made his famous speech and, still like the family solicitor, so kindly and so very upset, told us it had come. We were at war. Still there was no band, no cheering, no noise; only this breathless feeling of mingled relief and intolerable grief.

After accepting from Chamberlain the office of First Lord of the Admiralty – which he had held in the previous war – Churchill went to the flat of his comedian son-in-law, Vic Oliver, to drink champagne. He then went straight to the Admiralty. He had not appreciated Chamberlain's two-day delay between offering him an appointment and then naming it.

This first day of the second great Anglo-German war was marked by a mysterious, but portentous, air-raid warning. Churchill departed for the shelter armed with 'a bottle of brandy and other appropriate comforts'.

Message flashed from Admiralty to H.M. ships, 3 September 1939:

Winston is back.

One of Churchill's few old friends from First World War days was Violet Bonham-Carter. She visited him at the Admiralty. He greeted her with, 'Well – here we are back in the old premises after a short interval of 25 years.' When she criticized the Government for having 'the old Appeasers', he burst into a vehement defence of Chamberlain: 'No man is more inflexible, more single-minded. He has a will of steel.'

Churchill was thrilled to be back in power after eleven years of rebellious opposition. He immersed himself in naval matters; but he did not confine his interests there. He continued to plead, as he had for so long, with the small European nations to organize themselves for collective security. This advice, which they would have been well-advised to take, caused considerable resentment in those countries, and was used by the Germans for propaganda; the British, the German radio declared, wanted to fight, as always, their battles with the blood of others. He took a close interest in the affairs of the Army, as he had in the previous war when First Lord of the Admiralty. The War Minister was Leslie Hore-Belisha; he was jealous of his responsibility for the Army.[1]

---

[1] President of the Oxford Union, 1919; served on the Western Front, 1914–16; Liberal National M.P., 1923–42, Independent M.P., 1942–5; Minister of Transport, 1934–7; War Minister, 1937–40; Minister of National Insurance, 1945; died 1957.

Churchill did not begin the war with success. He had charge of the largest navy in the world. As he said: 'It would be unjust to the Chamberlain Administration and their Service advisers to suggest that the Navy had not been adequately prepared ... there was no challenge in surface craft to our command of the seas. There was no doubt that the British Navy was overwhelmingly superior to the German in strength and in numbers.' Nevertheless, the war was only two weeks old when the aircraft-carrier *Courageous*, accompanied by two destroyers, was sunk by a submarine in the Bristol Channel, with the loss of over five hundred men. When told the news, Churchill was philosophical: 'We can't expect to carry on a war like this without those sort of things happening from time to time.'

Beverley Baxter,[1] 1939:

On the last Wednesday in September, Mr Winston Churchill as First Lord of the Admiralty, rose to make a full report. We watched him with particular interest for reasons that can be easily understood. For the last four years and longer he had been the *enfant terrible* of Westminster, the principal prosecutor, the outlaw, the advocate, the jury and the innocent spectator. There had been times when his popularity zoomed to the stratosphere, and there had also been notable occasions when the House had treated him with something very near contempt. He and Mr Chamberlain had engaged in a hundred battles, and because of their physical proximity to each other in the House it had been almost a case of hand-to-hand fighting. Yet on the rare occasions that Chamberlain had dropped his cutlass, Churchill had stepped back and waited for his adversary to recover his defence. It was this element of magnanimity which made it possible, when the war began, for the Prime Minister to take Mr Churchill into his Cabinet without loss of face. When Churchill first appeared on the Front Bench as a War Minister, we gave him a hearty cheer, yet for once he failed to respond to the plaudits of that audience which he values and understands more than any other. He seemed repressed and stumbled over his words in replying to routine questions. It is true that Churchill had been at the Admiralty only a few days, but then we did not look upon him as an ordinary man who would take time to play himself in. Therefore, there was some shaking of heads. The old bandit who had been the terror of the mountain passes was cornered at last, and the fire in him was burn-

---

[1] Born in Canada; with Beaverbrook Press, 1920–33; Conservative M.P. from 1935.

ing low. 'He looks older,' said an Opposition Liberal with that instinct for change and decay which characterizes that bench of shadows. His head was thrust forward characteristically, like a bull watching for the matador. He squared his shoulders a couple of times as if to make sure that his arms were free for the gestures that might come. His first few remarks were cautious and exploratory. He was feeling his way and taking the measure of the situation, like a good boxer. Then he risked his first feint. 'It is a strange experience to me,' he said with a sort of philosophical solemnity, 'to sit at the Admiralty again, after a quarter of a century, and to find myself moving over the same course against the same enemy and in the same months of the year –' He paused, and a tense House waited for one of those purple phrases which would crystallize the incredibility of such an experience. Churchill's face assumed an air of innocent perplexity. ' – *the sort of thing one would hardly expect to happen*,' he said. The old master had played an unexpected trick on us. For sheer understatement it could not have been excelled. A roar swept through the House and a smile of satisfaction stretched across Mr Churchill's face.

Naval C.-in-C., Portsmouth,[1] 1 October 1939:

Winston [and] Brendan Bracken came for the afternoon. We did a tour of *Vernon*, Barracks, Dockyard and Eastney. Winston was indefatigable. He must have a tremendous physique. He thinks that bombing will start shortly, perhaps with the first new moon, and said that the Germans now have more planes than we have. He was in grim mood and spoke very earnestly of the tremendous task ahead of us.

American correspondent, Berlin, 2 October 1939:

Just heard the B.B.C. announce that English planes had flown over Berlin last night. A surprise to us here. No air-raid alarm. No sound of planes. But they're all lying these days. The Germans say they've sunk the *Ark Royal* for instance[2] ... The local enthusiasm for peace a little dampened today by Churchill's broadcast last night. I have been wondering about that one tube of shaving-cream my ration gives me for the next four months. My beard will be pink....[3]

Churchill continued to busy himself with all kinds of affairs

---

[1] Admiral Sir W. M. James: Conservative M.P., 1943–5.

[2] The pilot who made the claim was decorated, no doubt somewhat to his later embarrassment.

[3] In the broadcast, Churchill had prepared the public for 'a war of at least three years', and had noted that 'the courage and skill which the Germans always show in war will not free them from the reproach of Nazism, with its intolerance and its brutality'.

outside his immediate ministerial province. He corresponded with Roosevelt, promoted an 'anti-waste campaign', demanded increased war production, and gave speeches on the war in general. He called for 1,000,000 women to work in munitions factories – when there were at the time 1,300,000 insured unemployed.

Cripps, diary, 4 October 1939:

[He] thought it would be a good thing if I could go to Russia, and eagerly threw out the suggestion I might go as Ambassador – which I did not encourage, as it would be, I think, of little help.

Already, Hitler referred to Churchill in his speeches more frequently than to Chamberlain. After a visit by Ribbentrop, German Foreign Minister, to Russia during which Poland had been carved up to the temporary satisfaction of both parties, a 'peace offensive' was launched from Berlin. Lloyd George, and some pacifists and Communists, thought this a reasonable suggestion, and, on 3 October, said as much in Parliament. Lloyd George suggested that a Secret Session should be held, in order to discuss peace terms. He was hotly attacked by Duff Cooper. Later the 'Welsh wizard' addressed a group of members privately and explained that what he had really meant, but had been unable to say, was that peace should be arranged for at least a five-year period, to enable rearming, and then the war could be resumed. On 21 October at a public meeting in Caernarvon, he called for a conference with Hitler.

Hitler, speech to the Reichstag, 6 October 1939:

Why should this war in the West be fought? For restoration of Poland? Poland of the Versailles Treaty will never rise again. This is guaranteed by two of the largest states in the world. Final re-organization of this territory and the question of re-establishment of the Polish State are problems which will not be solved by a war in the West, but exclusively by Russia on the one hand and Germany on the other. The problems awaiting solution there will never be solved either at the conference table or in editorial offices, but by the work of decades ... Mr Churchill and his companions may interpret these opinions of mine as weakness or cowardice if they like. I need not occupy myself with what they think; I make these statements simply because it goes without saying that I wish to save my own people this suffering. If, however, the opinions of Churchill and his followers should prevail ... Then we shall fight. Neither force of arms nor lapse of time will conquer Germany. There never will be another November, 1918, in German history.

1939 NAVAL PERSON

Historians have recently claimed that Britain stumbled unwillingly into war, little if at all aware of any point to it, of any crusading spirit, of a war of 'good against evil': that such ideas were spread about later by Churchill.

Stephen King-Hall,[1] broadcast, 8 October 1939:

There is no compromise possible between our ideas and those of the Nazis as to how human life should be organised, and what are good and bad standards of conduct. As the Prime Minister said: 'It is the evil things that we shall be fighting against – brute force, bad faith, injustice, oppression and persecution.' I will end this talk by saying that it is our inescapable duty to fight those things to the bitter end, for were we not to do so, we should close the history book of liberty in Europe for many years to come.

John F. Kennedy,[2] son of the United States Ambassador, in London, 1939:

To say that democracy has been awakened by the events of the last few weeks is not enough. Any person will awaken when the house is burning down.

Some still clung to the belief that all would be well if only Hitler could be kept talking.

G. Bernard Shaw, 21 October 1939:[3]

As I am a born coward, and dislike extremely all this black-out business and ruinous taxation and the rest of it, I shall still want to know what I am fighting for. Mr Chamberlain has cleared up that question to a certain point. He declares that we are not out for territorial conquest or material acquisitions of any sort. This means that the war is a purely ideological one ... Then why put ourselves in the wrong, and Herr Hitler in the right, by refusing to get together and see whether this permanent ideological Trotskyan war is really unavoidable? If it is, we can fight as easily after a conference as before it. I am too old to

---

[1] Royal Navy, 1914–29; founded his own *News-Letter*, in 1936; Independent M.P., 1939–44; the most impartial and perceptive political journalist of the age, read, alas, by only a few; died 1966.

[2] Kennedy was a student at the London School of Economics. The book he wrote at this time, *Why England Slept*, shows a remarkable understanding of the British political scene of the thirties. President of the United States, 1961–3; died 1963.

[3] Churchill had first met Shaw in about 1901; he was 'one of my earliest antipathies'.

have any conscience in this or any other matter; but I still hate to see people making fools of themselves.

Shaw soon afterwards suggested that Britain was in a position to make peace with Germany. A more sensible appraisal of the facts was put forward by someone less famous, but more aware of the causes and nature of war.

Sir Norman Angell,[1] 1939:

The emergence of this form of nationalist dictatorship is very largely due to the failure of the European nations to create an international society which would ensure, by its collective power, the security of each member. Collective defence not having been realised, dynamic nations have been led to rely each upon its own individual power, thus precipitating competition for strategic frontiers irrespective of the desires of minorities, competition for self-sufficiency and for power preponderance.

Before the war, Churchill had been receiving increasing favour from the Press. This support was now intensified, particularly in Labour newspapers. That Churchill's predictions had come true had strengthened his support in the country; but it had not made him new friends in Parliament.

Reynolds News, 29 October 1939:

His mind is receptive to new ideas. His will is inflexible. Unlike most politicians, he finds easy the transition from the compromises of ordinary times to the need for swift decisions in days of danger ... If any man can rescue British conservatism from the state of political bankruptcy into which it has fallen, then that man is Winston, the least conservative of them all. Of all our leaders of to-day, Churchill and Greenwood are the only politicians whom the British public hears gladly. Chamberlain bosses Parliament – Churchill leads it ... [the people] drove Churchill into the Cabinet against the will of its members. As the grave issues of the times clarify, they will find it necessary to drive out the blunderers, but Winston, an instrument if not the architect of social change, is likely to remain ... an organizer of victory.

Adolf Hitler, to the German High Command, 3 November:

I have led the German people to a great height, even if the world does hate us now. I risk the loss of this achievement. I have to choose between

---

[1] Author of *The Great Illusion*, 1910; Labour M.P., 1929–31; Nobel Peace Prize, 1933.

victory or destruction. I choose victory ... My decision is unchangeable. I shall attack France and England at the favourable and earliest moment.

American columnist,[1] October 1939:

I claim that the damn war hasn't started ... If the issues between England and France on one side, and Germany on the other, are destined to be settled by force, the decision, win or lose, will be reached in a matter of 72 hours – in short, via a true air war.

On 14 October the *Royal Oak* was sunk in the supposedly safe waters of Scapa Flow. Churchill's enemies would have had difficulty in concealing a satisfaction which they might have felt if 786 sailors had not lost their lives.

Sir Samuel Hoare,[2] letter to Lord Lothian, British Ambassador in Washington, 11 November 1939:

Winston has been through a rough sea over the Scapa incidents. Being for the moment the war hero, he has come through it fairly well. I shudder to think what would have happened if there had been another First Lord and he [i.e. Churchill] had been in Opposition. As it is, the Navy have had a shake up, and I am sure that there is no risk of such mistakes being made again.

Churchill admitted that if it were not for his remarkable position in the Government – so recently its main critic, and bearing no responsibility for the arrangements existing at the beginning of the war – Chamberlain would probably have felt obliged to dismiss him.

Liddell Hart,[3] diary, 11 December 1939:

In conferences, Hore-Belisha is rising much in the opinion of some who

---

[1] Major Al Williams, once record-breaking aviator.

[2] Conservative M.P., 1910–44; as Secretary of State for India, 1931–5, and then as Foreign Secretary, 1935, he was one of Churchill's arch-enemies. At this time he was Lord Privy Seal. On becoming Prime Minister, Churchill sent Hoare away as Ambassador to Spain. He was created Viscount Templewood in 1944; died 1959.

[3] Captain B. H. Liddell Hart, a leading exponent of the theory of mechanized war, neglected in his own country; military correspondent of *The Times*, 1935–9; when Dawson refused his criticisms of the defence situation, he published them elsewhere; Personal Adviser to the War Minister, 1937–8; Liddell Hart had tried to interest Churchill in Orde Wingate as early as 1938; knighted 1966.

disagreed with him before the war. He has impressed them more than Winston Churchill, who is too wordy, and whose grasp of problems is uncertain – seeming to be blurred as if he had drunk too much.

Vyvyan Adams,[1] 1939:

When the fascinating game of Cabinet-building is being played and Churchill is mentioned as a possible Prime Minister one of the players will invariably say 'Winston lacks one thing – judgment.' Having uttered this pontifical condemnation he will sit back and hope that the candidate will be ruled out. It is certainly a very serious charge. And it is difficult to refute because the quality which Mr Churchill is said to lack baffles precise definition.

At last on 17 December the First Lord of the Admiralty was able to point to a success at sea. At the Battle of the River Plate, three British warships had driven a German battleship, the *Graf Spee*, into Montevideo, and the Germans blew it up. One of the British ships was almost sunk, but, as Churchill said, the success 'gave intense joy to the British nation and enhanced our prestige throughout the world'. Enemy submarines, which had already enjoyed such dramatic success, continued to prowl the shipping lanes of the Atlantic. By the end of the year 51 British merchant vessels had been sunk by submarine action; surface raiders, of which the *Graf Spee* had been one, had sunk 10. But Churchill's position was fully restored; confidence in him as an expert man of war increased.

Naval C.-in-C., Portsmouth, 1 January 1940:

Two days ago Winston, his wife and that pretty and attractive younger daughter came for the day. We had great fun. Miss Mary broke a lot of hearts. Winston was in great form, and after a thorough inspection of the magnetic mine, we did the Dockyard and then crossed the water to the new Coastal Craft base. The Dockyard men love him, and turned out in their thousands to cheer. I had a brain-wave in the *Hornet* and we all embarked in an M.T.B. and had a full-speed run out to Spithead. Most exhilarating and Mrs Churchill and Miss Mary were obviously thrilled. We also saw the new submarine *Taku* and Winston, of course,

---

[1] President of the Cambridge Union; Conservative M.P., 1931–45; served in the Army throughout the war; wrote under pseudonym 'Watchman'; drowned while bathing in Cornwall, 1951.

had to go all over her and know everything about her capabilities. When they arrived at Admiralty House for tea, R. asked Winston if he would have tea. His reply was typical, 'My doctor has ordered me to take nothing non-alcoholic between breakfast and dinner'. But he only had two small whiskys-and-soda all day. His energy is amazing.

The year began with a further setback at the Admiralty. An American cargo ship was taken by Royal Navy vessels to the Orkneys, for examination. This caused an outcry in the United States. Churchill said that no American vessels would be diverted in that way again.

The first crisis of the war, in London, occurred over the question of the line the French and British forces should take up. Should they wait for Hitler on French territory, or should they advance to favourable positions in Belgium? The C.I.G.S., commander of the British Army, was General 'Tiny' Ironside, a large man with a not entirely undeserved reputation as a good general.

Ironside,[1] diary, 16 January 1940:

The difference between Chamberlain and Churchill during this little crisis is most marked. Churchill, fully seized with the military value of going to Belgium, is enthusiastic and full of energy. Chamberlain negative and angry at Belgium making conditions.

On 6 January Churchill went to France to explain 'mechanical projects', one of which was a machine 'which would cut a groove in the earth sufficiently deep and broad through which assaulting infantry and presently assaulting tanks could advance', an idea typical of his inventive mind.[2] In the morning before he left, he learnt that Chamberlain was going to dismiss Hore-Belisha, the controversial War Minister. It was a strange affair, in which the King had played an unlikely but not unimportant role. Churchill did not support Hore-Belisha. Hore-Belisha declined other ministerial offers, and departed to the back-benches amidst a chorus of Press dissent, but to little support in the House of Commons.

---

[1] General Sir Edmund Ironside, C.I.G.S., 1938–40; transferred to C.-in-C., Home Forces, on 27 May, but sacked (and promoted Field-Marshal) eight weeks later; Baron, 1941; died 1959.

[2] Churchill received £100,000 to develop the machine; 350 firms were involved, in 'the utmost secrecy'; the machines were never used.

British war correspondent,[1] France, January 1940:

One morning very early, we war correspondents went along to an aerodrome where Winston had arranged to make an inspection of men and machines of the R.A.F.... We arrived at the landing ground before Mr Churchill. Our escorts were Army conducting officers. So some stupid R.A.F. officer refused to allow us on the aerodrome ... So, cursing, stamping our feet to keep the circulation going, we stood on the main Arras–Douai road awaiting Winston. The R.A.F. had several high-ups there to greet him when he stepped out of his car. He gave them a perfunctory 'Good morning', walked over to the war correspondents, and asked us how we all were, how we all liked being in France. Some of the gentry in blue uniform didn't look at all pleased. Especially as we walked across the aerodrome with Mr Churchill, and none of the R.A.F. people dared order us off in his presence. How we all admired Winston, that cold and cheerless morning on the plain of Douai!

The same reporter, January 1940:

Mr Winston Churchill ... stood on the terrace at Gort's château, smoking a cigar, as usual, smiling a little sardonically, I thought, while Lord Gort and General Sir Edmund Ironside were decorated by General Gamelin with the Grand Cross of the Legion of Honour. This happened to be the highest decoration the French could confer on our military leaders. Some of us wondered what would happen when the war really began, if the French were giving away the best prizes in the bag during the 'peace'. The ceremony was a little ludicrous ... General Gamelin pinned the huge glittering cross of the Legion of Honour on the breast of each general. At this stage the ceremony became laughable. For Gamelin, who had nearly as many medals on his chest as Goering, couldn't reach to pin on Ironside's medal without standing on tip-toe. And when, according to the ritual of the business, Ironside had to kiss Gamelin on both cheeks, the giant British general had to bend down as if he were saluting a child. I saw Winston Churchill smiling quite openly.

Diana Cooper, wife of Duff Cooper, who had been First Lord of the Admiralty in 1938:

Last night to the Admiralty, where I went to dine with Winston, my dearly-loved First Lord. O what a change was there since my day! Did you ever see my bed? It rose sixteen feet high from a shoal of gold dolphins and tridents; ropes made fast the blue satin curtains; round the walls Captain Cook was discovering Australia. Now all has suffered

---

[1] Bernard Gray, of the *Daily Mirror*; died at sea, May 1941, while based in Malta.

a sea change. The dolphins are stored away and on a narrow curtainless pallet-bed sleeps the exhausted First Lord. My gigantic gold-and-white armoire holds his uniform. The walls are charts. On the top floor, where I had hung chintz curtains spotted with red and blue seahorses to amuse my little boy, the Churchill family is installed. It makes a delightful self-contained flat with dining-room, bedroom, kitchen and their own lovely pictures. Winston's spirit, strength and confidence are a beacon in the darkness, a chime that wakes the heart of the discouraged. His wife, more beautiful than in early youth, is equally fearless and indefatigable. She makes us all knit jerseys as thick as sheep's fleeces, for which the minesweepers must bless her.

The fact that the Coopers had known Churchill for so long meant little, for they had known virtually everybody in public life. It may be that they were not quite as attractive a couple as they evidently thought they were.

During the first quarter of 1940, Churchill's position was being firmly consolidated – to such an extent that it was able to survive the blow to his reputation which was shortly to occur. One of the reasons for this was the fact that the public were being made aware over the radio of what the House of Commons had known for decades – that despite, or because of, a slurred voice and eccentric delivery, he was a most compelling orator.

Sir George Arthur,[1] 1940:

Mr Churchill also revealed himself as the Government's Number One Broadcaster. Lacking the 'Oxford accent' he spoke as a Briton to Britons. 'Monty Viddio' was just what the man in the pub called that South American port. The Churchillian 'Narzi' sounded just as one imagined such an outsider should sound.

The die-hard enemies, resentful and suspicious, mostly Conservative, sat in Parliament and waited. There were enemies, too, elsewhere. A British colonel, to Clare Booth Luce, 1940:[2]

The colonel shook his head dubiously. 'England,' he said, 'mistrusts Churchill. He's the dictator type, and he has an ancestor complex. He'd

---

[1] Biographer and historian; died 1946.

[2] At a luncheon party at Versailles. Mrs Luce, wife of Henry R. Luce, the owner of *Time* magazine, had a rather pronounced distaste for all things English. In 1940 she told Joseph Kennedy: 'Sometimes they are so insolent, so sure of themselves, so smug, I feel as though it would do them good for once to be beaten.' Henry Luce had suffered the misfortune of attending a typically harsh English school in China.

like to be the Duke of Marlborough, if you follow me . . . He's a brilliant hot-head of course – eighteen ideas to the minute in Cabinet meeting, one of them corking, but the other seventeen bloody awful . . . Halifax would be the man if Chamberlain is ever got rid of.' This didn't seem likely to the colonel, 'since', he said, 'one doesn't swap horses'.

But to more acute political observers it was becoming increasingly likely that horses would be swapped. For sooner or later a true coalition government would surely be necessary. And under whom would Labour agree to serve? Not Neville Chamberlain.

Vyvyan Adams, 1940:

Between these two [Halifax and Churchill] I feel almost certain that the succession rests. And I think that Halifax is the more likely. He has offended nobody. Though pained by his surprise at the shortcomings of mankind, his charity is almost too saintly to permit him to utter a sharp rebuke . . . Winston is half a dozen years older than Halifax at an age when such an interval matters . . . I long for Winston's counsel at the Peace. The establishment of a European Order will be a chivalrous and risky enterprise . . . The vision and genius of Winston Churchill would found the kingdom of the just on sure and enduring foundations.[1]

Chamberlain, March 1940:

I would rather have Halifax succeed me than Winston.

On 3 April the Minister for the Co-ordination of Defence, Lord Chatfield, resigned at his own request. He considered he had nothing to do. The office was abolished. Instead, the First Lord of the Admiralty, 'as the senior Service Minister concerned', was made chairman of the Military Co-ordination Committee. In practice, this gave Churchill some power over all three Services, which caused him much pleasure. His closest supporters had always believed he should fill a new post of 'Minister of Defence', with the three Service Ministers under him. This was the next best thing. Chamberlain, at one time a brilliant administrator, and

---

[1] Adams also made a remarkable appraisal of Macmillan, then aged forty-six: 'Macmillan is no ordinary man. He votes as he feels inclined, treating Parliament not as a playground for parties but as an assembly where men must speak and act as they think. A faint intellectual arrogance limits the number of his intimates . . . On the other hand he is quite fearless . . . He has often been expected to join the Labour Party.' (*What of the Night?* p. 152.)

The Prime Minister in east Scotland, October 1940

February 1940: the King and Queen greet relatives of the men killed in the engagement with the *Graf Spee*

no mean committee man, was losing his grip of the conduct of the war. Unknown to anyone, he was suffering from cancer.

In April, Churchill visited France again. This time he was trying to interest the French in his pet scheme of floating mines down the Rhine. The French refused to co-operate in this imaginative venture; the British Cabinet decided to launch it independently.

Ironside, diary, 8 April 1940:

Winston is back from France full of blood and we shall have far more co-ordination of effort. He was like a boy this morning describing what he had done to meet the Germans. His physique must be marvellous, but I cannot think he would make a good Prime Minister. He has not got the stability necessary for guiding the others.

On 9 April German forces invaded Denmark and Norway. The 'Phoney War' was over.

The Norwegians appealed to Britain and France for help. Churchill wrote: 'The whole of Northern Norway was covered with snow to depths which none of our soldiers had ever seen, felt, or imagined. There were neither snow-shoes nor skis – still less skiers. We must do our best. Thus began this remarkable campaign.'

Many thought at the time, and many still do, that the decision to go to Norway's aid was a prime blunder: details had not been prepared, and it was too late for much, if anything, to be done. At the last minute, against the protests of the C.I.G.S., Churchill, as chairman of the Defence Committee, ordered a change of plan after the troops had embarked. The British acted with remarkable, and, in the circumstances, regrettable speed. Four days after the German attack, British troops were landing in Norway. French troops arrived six days later. Difficulties of supply, lack of air support, administrative confusion, allied wrangling, and untrained troops, combined to doom the expedition.

Harold Nicolson, diary, 11 April 1940:

To the House. It is packed. Winston comes in. He is not looking well and sits there hunched as usual with his papers in his hand. When he rises to speak it is obvious that he is very tired. He starts off by giving an imitation of himself making a speech, and he indulges in vague oratory, coupled with tired gibes. I have seldom seen him to less advantage. The majority of the House were expecting tales of victory and triumph, and when he tells them that the news of our reoccupation of Bergen, Trondheim and Oslo is untrue, a cold wave of disappointment passes through the House. He hesitates, gets his notes in the wrong order, puts on the wrong pair of spectacles, fumbles for the right pair, keeps on saying 'Sweden' when he means 'Denmark', and one way and another makes a lamentable performance. He gives no real explanation of how the Germans managed to slip through to Narvik. We have sunk some eight German transports and two cruisers have been damaged. He claims that this has 'crippled' the German Navy . . . It is a feeble, tired speech and it leaves the House in a mood of grave anxiety.

Amery wrote of the Norwegian fiasco:

It must mean the end of the Government and perhaps of Winston as well.

For as 'co-ordinator' of the Services, Churchill had full responsibility for the campaign, although he did not have full power over all the Services. Members of the Cabinet, especially Halifax and Oliver Stanley, the War Minister, were highly critical of Churchill's performance.

Ironside, diary, 14 April 1940:

One of the fallacies that Winston seems to have got into his head is that we can make improvised decisions to carry on the war by meeting at 5 p.m. each day. It is regardless of the enemy and decisions which have to be made at all hours of the day as the enemy reacts. The S. of S. [War Minister – Oliver Stanley] is going to see the Prime Minister today and tell him that war cannot be run by the Staffs sitting round a table arguing. We cannot have a man trying to supervise all military arrangements as if he were a company commander running a small operation to cross a bridge. How I have kept my temper so far I don't know. It seems incredible that these things should happen.

It was a typically British start to a great war. There was chaos. When asked in the House whether Germans were at Narvik, Chamberlain replied: 'No. It must be Larvik' – a port some 800 miles to the south.

Chaos was followed by disaster. A squadron of outdated biplanes, which arrived on 24 April, was out of action by the 26th. British troops, frozen and half-starved, hid in railway tunnels.

Ironside, diary, 25 April 1940:

Winston was a bit wild at the Cabinet, trying to command the troops in the field and railing at us for not having carried out demolitions on the front held by the Norwegians.

On the same day, one of the very few reporters[1] to reach the scene cabled his dispatch, in which he wrote of:

One of the costliest and most inexplicable military bungles in modern British history ... by those high British authorities who thrust 1,500 young Territorials into the snow and mud below Namsos ten days ago without a single anti-aircraft gun or a single piece of artillery.

Ironside, diary, 27 April 1940:

Winston demurred to evacuation and began to mumble about the British being allowed to disperse in the mountains to help the Norwegians to carry on guerrilla warfare. That it was better to condemn the force ashore to fight to the end. I could not find any military reason for doing this. It was all political.

Evacuation began on 28 April while reinforcements from France were still arriving.

Harold Nicolson, diary, 1 May 1940:

The tapers and tadpoles are putting it around that the whole Norwegian episode is due to Winston. There is a theory going round that Lloyd George may head a Coalition Cabinet. What worries people is that everybody asks, 'But whom could you put in Chamberlain's place?'

Later, during the evacuation from Norway, an aircraft-carrier and 2 destroyers were sunk in one afternoon, with the loss of over 1,500 men. Churchill wrote: 'Considering the prominent part I played in these events ... it was a marvel that I survived.' That he did so was, in his own opinion, because of his pre-war record, which was recent enough to separate him from his Cabinet colleagues. Chamberlain took the brunt of criticism over Norway, although it was largely Churchill's rash enthusiasm which had led the Government so far astray. Churchill, however, could at least point to the fact that he had wanted to concentrate forces at Narvik, instead of dispersing them, but had been overruled by the Cabinet.

Cripps, mobilizing opinion for a new Government, met Lloyd George on 2 May. He found him:

most pessimistic and disturbed and generally disgruntled ... Rather to my surprise [he said] Winston could not be P.M., and that it would have to be Halifax.

---

[1] Leland Stowe, of the *Chicago Daily News*.

For years, Lloyd George and his family – his son and daughter were also M.P.s – had stood aloof from the splintered Liberal Party and National Liberal Party in a very splendid isolation, not without its own arrogance *en famille*.

On 6 May the Sadler's Wells Ballet crossed to the Hague, for a tour of Holland and Belgium.

On 7 May Cripps, anonymously in the *Daily Mail*, called for a coalition under Halifax.

The House of Commons met to debate the Norwegian disaster on 7 and 8 May. It was one of the most dramatic debates in the whole history of the British Parliament. Much of it was worthy of the occasion. L. S. Amery was an old friend of Chamberlain. He said:

> We are fighting today for our life, for our liberty, for our all. We cannot go on being led as we are . . . You have sat too long here for any good you have been doing. Depart, I say, and let us have done with you. In the name of God, go!

It was the end for Chamberlain, who made the characteristic mistake of appealing to his 'friends' in the House. Even his friends realized that it was no longer a matter of personal loyalties. But one of the main features of the debate was the dogged and ungrudging support which the Prime Minister received from the First Lord of the Admiralty.

Admiral of the Fleet Sir Roger Keyes[1] spoke in uniform, which he had never done before. He castigated Churchill for Norway, but also seemed to support Churchill for Prime Minister:

> One hundred and forty years ago Nelson said: 'I am of the opinion that the boldest men are the safest', and that still holds good today.

Churchill was no longer an outsider; his chances were suddenly seen to be not impossible after all. As Liddell Hart said: 'It was the irony, or fatality, of history that Churchill should have gained his opportunity of supreme power as the result of a fiasco [Norway] to which he had been the main contributor.' But there was still strong resistance to him. Other critics who played an important part in the debate were Duff Cooper, Stafford Cripps, and, most

---

[1] Hero of the First World War; Conservative M.P., 1934–43; Director of Combined Operations, 1940–1; Baron, 1943; died 1945.

important of all, Herbert Morrison. It was Morrison who announced that the Labour Party would divide the House at the end of the debate, in what would in effect be a vote of confidence in Chamberlain. Lloyd George, at the age of seventy-seven, made a devastating attack on the Government. It was the last great speech of his career. Violet Bonham-Carter described it as, 'the most deadly speech I ever heard from him – voice, gesture, everything was brought into play to drive home the attack'.

Churchill had the unenviable task of winding up for the Government. His loyalty was faultless: 'Exception has been taken because the Prime Minister said he appealed to his friends. He thought he had some friends, and I hope he has some friends. He certainly had a good many when things were going well. I think it would be most ungenerous and unworthy of the British character, and the Conservative party, to turn in a moment of difficulty ... I say, let pre-war feuds die; let personal quarrels be forgotten, and let us keep our hatreds for the common enemy ... At no time in the last war were we in greater peril than we are now ...'

The Government's majority, nominally about 240, was only 81: a major rebuff for Chamberlain. Nearly all the Labour, Liberal, and old Churchill, Eden, and Amery Conservatives voted in opposition. Some members were so carried away that they stood and sang 'Rule Britannia'.

On 8 May a lunch party was held for Lloyd George by some of his supporters, to discuss putting him forward as Prime Minister, eighteen years after he had last held the office. Among those present were Nancy Astor, Mr and Mrs Henry Luce, and J. L. Garvin, editor of *The Observer*. In Parliament, women M.P.s of all parties secretly vowed to get Chamberlain out.

At about 4.30 p.m. on 9 May, four men met in the Cabinet Room at 10 Downing Street.

Lord Halifax, 9 May 1940:

The P.M., Winston, David Margesson [Conservative Chief Whip] and I sat down to it. The P.M. recapitulated the position, and said that he had made up his mind that he must go, and that it must either be Winston or me. He would serve under either ... I then said that I thought for the reasons given the P.M. must probably go, but that I had no doubt at all in my own mind that for me to take it would create a quite impossible position ... Winston, with suitable expressions of regard and humility, said he could not but feel the force of what I had said, and the P.M. reluctantly, and Winston evidently with much less reluctance, finished by accepting my view. So there we left it for the moment, Winston and I having a cup of tea in the garden while the P.M. kept some other appointment.

What had not been discussed, but what was implicit in the situation, was whether Churchill would serve under Halifax. For if he would not, would Halifax receive the necessary support in the House? The waters were clearing at last. In public and parliamentary esteem, Halifax felt himself dispensable: Churchill knew he himself was indispensable.

News Chronicle, 10 May 1940:

Mr Chamberlain's early resignation is now certain. He spent most of yesterday considering his position in the light of the government's debacle on Wednesday night ... neither Labour nor Liberal leaders were prepared to serve under Mr Chamberlain. A new Premier will thus have to be found. He is more likely to be Mr Winston Churchill than anyone else.

The *News Chronicle*, nevertheless, preferred Lloyd George: 'as the War Premier who brought defeat to Germany last time his resumption of office might well be worth a major battle in its moral effect on the German people'.

While the Labour leaders deliberated in the palm courts of Bournemouth, at their Party Conference there, Hitler was acting. From 4 a.m. that morning, German forces had been invading Holland, Belgium, and Luxemburg.

Belgian Foreign Minister, Paul-Henri Spaak, to German Ambassador, Brussels, 10 May 1940:

Mr Ambassador, the German Army has just attacked our country. This is the second time in 25 years that Germany has committed a criminal aggression against a neutral and loyal Belgium. What has just happened is perhaps even more odious than the aggression of 1914. No ultimatum, no note, no protest of any kind has ever been placed before the Belgian Government...

Frances Stevenson, Lloyd George's secretary, diary, 10 May 1940:

L.G. realizes that Churchill must be chosen, and that he himself is out of the running.

Halifax, 10 May 1940:

The P.M. told me that he had a feeling that Winston did not approve of the delay. The P.M. then told us [the Cabinet] that he had decided not to wait, and was seeing the King this evening to advise that Winston should take over.

A message arrived from the Labour Party later in the day saying that they would serve 'under a new Prime Minister'.

King George VI, 10 May 1940:

I saw the Prime Minister after tea ... I accepted his resignation, and told him how grossly unfairly I thought he had been treated, and that I was terribly sorry ... We then had an informal talk over his successor. I, of course, suggested Halifax, but he told me that H. was not enthusiastic, as being in the Lords he could only act as a shadow or a ghost in the Commons, where all the real work took place. I was disappointed over this statement, as I thought H. was the obvious man, and that his peerage could be placed in abeyance for the time being. Then I knew there was only one person whom I could send for to form a Government who had the confidence of the country, and that was Winston. I asked Chamberlain his advice, and he told me Winston was the man to send for. I said good-bye to Chamberlain and thanked him for all his help to me, and repeated that I would greatly regret my loss at not having him as my P.M. I sent for Winston and asked him to form a Government. This he accepted.

The great test of character and strength was about to begin. By the end of the day, Germany had made a dramatic and successful beginning to the military operation that was to bring Britain to its greatest danger. The British, with uncanny instinct, had chosen that same day the person best fitted, of the nearly fifty million in their island, to lead them in the immediate task ahead.

CHAPTER THREE

1940 Emergency Premier

Count Ciano,[1] Rome, 10 May 1940:

The substitution of Churchill for Chamberlain is received here with absolute indifference; by the Duce with irony.

Lady Oxford,[2] letter, 11 May 1940:

Feeling rather lonely, I thought I would chance seeing the P.M. and Mrs Chamberlain, and went in a taxi at ten last night ... They were both rather moved. He said that no one could have been nicer than Winston ... [He said] 'The day may come when my much cursed visit to Munich will be understood. Neither we nor the French were prepared for war. I am not responsible for this lack of preparation, I blame no one. None of us is always wise; I did what I thought right. I am the last person who would claim immunity from criticism.' I looked at his spare figure and keen eye and could not help comparing it with Winston's self-indulgent rotundity. I shall always maintain that tho' Neville has made many mistakes and not chosen the right men in his futile reshuffles, that he has a magnificent character, and less self-love, or self-pity than any man I know.

King George VI, diary, 11 May 1940:

I cannot yet think of Winston as P.M. ... I met Halifax in the garden and I told him I was sorry not to have him as P.M.[3]

Churchill was not the kind of politician to appeal to the King. He preferred his Conservatives to be conventional, loyal party men. Moreover, Churchill came from a different generation. When they

---

[1] Mussolini's son-in-law. Foreign Minister, 1936–43. Tried to lead Mussolini away from Hitler, but achieved no success whatever.

[2] Widow of Asquith, Lloyd George's predecessor as Prime Minister in the earlier war.

[3] Halifax had been given permission to walk through the garden of Buckingham Palace on his way from his flat in Belgravia to the Foreign Office.

had first met, in 1912, Churchill had been First Lord of the Admiralty, the future king a young naval cadet. Churchill was sixty-five; for five months he had been qualified to draw the old-age pension. His political career was meant to have ended a decade before. He was four years older than Stalin, eight years older than Roosevelt, fifteen years older than Hitler.

The German forces rapidly crossed the Low Countries during 11 May. But as yet there was no despair. Far from it. The much-neglected military oracle, Captain Liddell Hart, wrote:

> In regard to Belgium it can safely be said that both her defences and her forces are much stronger than they were in 1914. This became plain to me during a visit I made to that frontier in 1938. A particularly impressive feature was the elaborate scheme of demolitions, whereby every bridge, road, rail or canal, throughout a deep belt of territory behind the frontier, was prepared for blowing up, with a permanent guard on duty beside each of them. These arrangements promise a greater obstacle than the invaders met in Norway ... Moreover, behind the forward zone of delaying action lies a natural defensive front ... So long as these are adequately reinforced, without loss of time, they should be hard to penetrate. The thrusting power of the German Army lies largely in its mechanised forces, and to these the Low Countries offer far less suitable going than the Germans found in Poland.

It was too late now for warnings, and useless to spread gloom. On 12 May the German Army, moving with fearsome speed across Holland and Belgium, also crossed the French frontier. At 5 a.m. the following morning George VI was wakened at Buckingham Palace by a night-duty policeman to take a call from Wilhelmina. The Dutch Queen begged him to send aircraft to defend Holland immediately.

Churchill set about forming his Coalition Government. He said, 'Eleven years in the political wilderness had freed me from ordinary Party antagonisms. I could not be reproached either for making the war or with want of preparation for it. I thought I knew a great deal about it all, and I was sure I should not fail.' The more important posts were filled on 11 May. Apart from Churchill himself, there were only four others in the 'War Cabinet': Chamberlain, Halifax, and the two leading Labour men – Clement Attlee and Arthur Greenwood. First Lord of the Admiralty (Navy) was A. V. Alexander, Eden was War Minister

(Army), and the Air Minister (R.A.F.) was the Liberal Party Leader, Sir Archibald Sinclair. On following days, other appointments were made: Herbert Morrison as Minister of Supply, Duff Cooper as Minister of Information, Ernest Bevin as Minister of Labour, Lord Beaverbrook as Minister of Aircraft Production (an appointment resisted both by himself and his many enemies), and Sir John Anderson, an outstanding former civil servant, as Home Secretary. Sinclair, who had been Churchill's second-in-command on the Western Front in the First World War, and Bevin, held the same posts until after the end of the war against Germany.

It was immediately noticed that the three Service ministers were not in the War Cabinet. Churchill himself was to be 'Minister of Defence'. 'It was understood and accepted that I should assume general direction of the war . . . I had been careful not to define my rights and duties.' Churchill had assured himself of this powerful position because, as he explained, of his experience during the Gallipoli campaign in the First World War when he had been 'ruined for the time being . . . through my trying to carry out a major and cardinal operation of war from a subordinate position'. The clear implication was that the 'fighting ministers', as opposed to those in the home field, would have less responsibility than ever before. But what intrigued – and angered some – much more than this vital arrangement, was that Churchill had included in his administration many of the former 'Munichites'. This puzzled many people at the time; but the 'Munichites' were after all by far the largest section of the largest Party, most of which had little love for Churchill. Moreover, magnanimity was Churchill's greatest quality as a politician.

On 13 May the House of Commons was summoned especially for the formal business of recording a vote of confidence in the new administration. In a rousing speech, Churchill declared: 'I have nothing to offer but blood, toil, tears and sweat.' Later in the war, millions convinced themselves that they had heard Churchill use this sentence on the radio. He continued: 'You ask, what is our policy? I will say: it is to wage war, by sea, land and air, with all our might and with all the strength that God can give us: to wage war against a monstrous tyranny, never surpassed in the dark, lamentable catalogue of human crime. That is our policy.

You ask, what is our aim? I can answer in one word: victory – victory at all costs, victory in spite of all terror, victory, however long and hard the road may be; for without victory, there is no survival.'

Harold Nicolson, diary, 13 May 1940:

When Chamberlain enters the House, he gets a terrific reception, and when Churchill comes in the applause is less ... Winston sits there between Chamberlain and Attlee, and it is odd to see the Labour Ministers sitting on the Government Bench. Winston makes a very short statement, but to the point ... Then Lloyd George gets up and makes a moving speech telling Winston how fond he is of him. Winston cries slightly and mops his eyes.

Lloyd George's speech, 13 May 1940:

May I, as one of the oldest friends of the Prime Minister in this House – I think on the whole that we have the longest friendship in politics in spite of a great many differences of opinion – congratulate him personally upon his succession to the Premiership? But that is a small matter. I congratulate the country upon his elevation to the Premiership at this very, very critical and terrible moment. If I may venture to say so, I think the Sovereign exercised a wise choice. We know the right hon. Gentleman's glittering intellectual gifts, his dauntless courage, his profound study of war, and his experience in its operation and direction. They will all be needed now. I think it is fortunate that he should have been put in a position of supreme authority ... He is exercising his supreme responsibility at a graver moment and in times of greater jeopardy than have ever confronted a British Minister for all time. We all, from the bottom of our hearts, wish him well.

Sir Stafford Cripps, House of Commons, 13 May 1940:

I do not desire to make any criticism of the right hon. Gentleman or his government, favourable or otherwise. The proof of the pudding will be in the experience of its eating. I should like to ask the right hon. Gentleman to consider one point, which I regard as very urgent in view of the situation that is created by the new national government. The whole of our procedure and practice in the House of Commons is built up on the basis of having an effective, organised opposition ... There is a serious danger, if we have a House of Commons with substantially only one party in it, of the House of Commons being no longer interested in votes and being less interested in the administration of the affairs of the country ...

Cripps's speech received little notice. The debate also included a few nostalgic panegyrics to Chamberlain mixed with grudging support to the man who, to many, was still a political ogre or mountebank.

Only James Maxton spoke forcefully against the new Prime Minister:[1]

I cannot see the wonderful motive power that has been produced by the transference of the relative positions of the two right hon. Gentlemen opposite. It is the most amazing thing to me . . . It does not require any great courage to attack the late Prime Minister. He was in an awkward spot and the jackals gathered around . . . I cannot see what has happened to justify any change of attitude on my part. We are in this position today because of twenty-two years of wasted opportunity . . . The only difference is that the Prime Minister cuts out of his speech any reference to the possibilities of peace short of wholesale slaughter. I and my hon. Friends believe that the overwhelming mass of the people of this world, Germany included, are against the slaughter method of life . . .

The House voted 381 in support of the new Government, and none against. It was, of course, a formality. Much of the Government had already been announced, and some new Ministers had been at their desks for two days. Whether Conservative M.P.s would have been so obliging about Churchill had they not been presented with a *fait accompli*, is very doubtful.

A woman author, 1940:[2]

As the guns thunder across the Channel, Winston Churchill offers his supporters the sole reward of 'blood and toil and tears and sweat'. They are brave words, likely to echo permanently through the corridors of time. But the blood and toil, the tears and sweat, are actually being contributed by 'Class 1940' . . . 'In war,' Arthur Greenwood tells the Labour Party Conference at Bournemouth, 'there is no such thing as equality of sacrifice. Nothing man can offer weighs beside human life.' It is not the elderly politicians, whose blood is shed for the crass blunders . . . Youth, and at present youth only, pays the price of such a conflict as this. Only when the summer is well advanced will civilian groups who have not, hitherto, met the direct cost of war, contribute their quota of casualties.

---

[1] Scottish Labour M.P., 1922–46; Chairman, Independent Labour Party, 1926–31; died 1946.
[2] Vera Brittain, a writer deeply influenced by the First World War; author of *Testament of Youth*.

The most active of those M.P.s who were disappointed in the composition of the Government was Stafford Cripps. He, and many others, felt that Churchill had chosen the crucial War Cabinet 'irrespective of their qualifications'. This was true. Churchill, having been outcast for so long, felt a natural insecurity in the House, from which as he knew so well his power would come. As he later admitted, the Cabinet was chosen for political expediency. Cripps himself, however, was offered the Ambassadorship at Moscow. He accepted, 'provided that I was assured there was a genuine desire to treat Russia as a friendly neutral and not in any way with an underlying hostility'.

But what few people seem to have noticed was that not only was the War Cabinet political in nature – it consisted of two men, Chamberlain and Halifax, who were already psychologically under Churchill's sway and in little or no position to cause him serious opposition, and two others, Attlee and Greenwood, noted for their mildness.

The 'Munichites', naturally, thought that the inclusion in the Government of Amery, Cooper, and Eden, was sheer favouritism.

Geoffrey Dawson, diary, 13 May 1940:

Quite a good little warlike speech from Winston and a solid vote of confidence. His new government daily enlarged by new appointments, *not* too well chosen – too many friends!

Although its essentially political nature enforced much deadweight on the Government's strength, there was in it the makings of a great team. This was due, particularly, to the inclusion of Labour men, which had also an important effect in the country at large. This soon became apparent.

Tom Jones,[1] letter, 8 June 1940:

The coming of Winston to the top and the accession of Bevin and Morrison have wrought a profound change in the consciousness of the multitude. At last the country is awake and working.

---

[1] Dr Thomas Jones; close friend of Baldwin and Lloyd George; began life as academic economist; Professor of Economics, Queen's University, 1909–10; Deputy Secretary to Baldwin's Cabinet; Secretary of Pilgrim Trust, 1930–45; died 1955. Father of Eirene White, Minister of State for Foreign Affairs, 1966.

Francis Williams,[1] 1941:

Naturally the appointment of Ernest Bevin, one of the most forceful critics of the previous government's failure to use the abilities and experience of the trades unions, brought a rapid change in attitude and the appointment of Herbert Morrison to the Ministry of Supply hardly less so. The change that came with the new government was not wrought by any basic alteration in the attitude of the trades unions, for they had been ready from the first to co-operate if they should be allowed. It was due to the fact that those now in charge of the mobilisation of the country's industrial resources were anxious for that co-operation, knew and understood the trades union movement, because they were members of it, and shared its appreciation of the value of organised labour as a great and durable weapon of democracy. Mr Bevin in his own person symbolised the thought which the trades unions had devoted to the problems of industrial mobilisation and the speed with which its leaders could act. He assumed office at 2.30 p.m. on May 15. At 11 o'clock the following morning he presented the War Cabinet with his proposals. They included a new Emergency Powers (Defence) Bill to give the government power by Order in Council to require persons 'to place themselves, their services and their property at the government's disposal.'

On 15 May the Dutch Army capitulated, and the Germans crossed the Meuse, endangering the French and British rear. That morning, the French Premier telephoned Churchill in bed: 'We are beaten; we have lost the battle.' On 16 May the French line collapsed. Churchill decided to rush to Paris.

A counter-thrust, to contain the German onslaught and keep the war in north-west France, could perhaps save the situation. But were the French capable of it?

Paul Baudouin,[2] diary, 16 May 1940:

Mr Winston Churchill arrived at four o'clock with a large staff, and the Prime Minister indicated to him the seriousness of the situation in a few words, illustrating his argument with a large map on which the German bulge was marked in red. Mr Churchill was very surprised for he had

---

[1] Ex-editor of the *Daily Herald*. Controller of News and Censorship, 1941–5. Later, Lord Francis-Williams.

[2] Secretary of the War Cabinet in Reynaud's administration; Foreign Minister in Pétain's administration, 1940–1; resigned. His diary of the fall of France is of great historical importance: the most complete of the time.

not realized the gravity of the position. He kept on saying that the further Germans advanced the more vulnerable they would be to a counter-attack. The Prime Minister[1] beckoned to General Gamelin, who, like a good lecturer, took his stand by the map, and gave an admirable discourse, clear and calm, on the military situation. He showed the German thrust, and he explained the position of the French troops as well as their surprise and disorder, while our reserve divisions, capable of taking the field, were very few in number. Paul Reynaud gave me an agonized look, and Churchill asked General Gamelin to go over his explanation again. His ladylike hand marked here and there on the map the positions of our broken units and of our reserves on the move. He explained, but he made no suggestions. He had no views on the future; there was not a word of to-morrow, not even a hope... Seeing that the English Prime Minister did not appear wholly to grasp the seriousness of the situation the Prime Minister took Gamelin's place by the map, but it was not so much a lecture, as a rapid analysis, that he gave, devoid of all illusions. Both by his expression and by his voice he brought Churchill up to date with what was happening, and he made skilful use of metaphor .'The hard point of the German lance has gone through our troops as through a sand-hill.' He pointed out the importance of the battle in progress in the bulge marked in red on the map. He twice said, 'I assure you that in this bulge there is at stake not only the fate of France but also that of the British Empire.' This exposition lasted two hours, and during it, Mr Winston Churchill listened with the keenest attention and a big cigar in his mouth; at the end of it he was clearly persuaded of the gravity of the situation. On more than one occasion he turned to the windows giving out on the park where the affecting sight of the burning archives afforded evidence of the dramatic nature of the hour. After dining at the British Embassy, the British Prime Minister went round at 11.0 p.m. to see M. Reynaud at the Place du Palais Bourbon. He read to him a long telegram which he had sent to the members of the British War Cabinet in London: one sentence in it was painful to us for it spoke of 'a part of the French army being threatened with the fate of the Polish army' ... Mr Churchill was remarkable for his energy and vehemence as, crowned like a volcano by the smoke of his cigars, he told his French colleague that even if France was invaded and vanquished England would go on fighting until the United States came to her aid, which she would soon do and in no halfhearted manner. 'We will starve Germany out. We will destroy her towns. We will burn her crops and her forests.' Until one in the morning he conjured up an apocalyptic vision of the war. He saw himself in the

---

[1] Paul Reynaud: that rare phenomenon, an anglophile French politician; M.P. since 1919; Prime Minister, 1940; Deputy Prime Minister, 1953.

heart of Canada directing, over an England razed to the ground by high explosive bombs and over a France whose ruins were already cold, the air war of the New World against the Old dominated by Germany. He was convinced that the United States would soon come into the war. Mr Churchill made a great impression on Paul Reynaud, and gave him confidence.

Baudouin, the author of this vivid account, a right-wing banker, was described by E. L. Spears, Churchill's personal representative with Reynaud, as 'tall, clean-shaven, blue-eyed and good-looking. His thick fair hair was brushed straight back from his high forehead. His expression was open, though his manner was reserved. At meetings which I attended, his part was strictly confined to taking notes. As far as I remember, he took these on his knee. On the rare occasions when I had to deal with him he was competent and obliging, or seemingly so. It was only gradually that I realised we stood for things as different as night and day.' Baudouin was a protégé of the Comtesse de Portes, the mysterious woman who seems to have held much influence in French politics at the time, and who had indeed 'managed' Reynaud's rise to power and is said to have dominated his premiership. 'She dressed fashionably,' said Spears, 'giving the impression that she attached importance to wearing a recent model whatever it looked like, preferring the tightly fitting kind, showing the figure. She had very good feet and ankles.'

On this visit to Paris Churchill was accompanied by his personal chief staff-officer, Major-General Hastings Ismay, who held the job throughout the war. They communicated with the War Cabinet, in London, in Hindustani, a language known to many who had done service in the British Army but less well known in France. The secrecy was necessary because of a French request for fighter aircraft. The R.A.F. had already lost nearly 300 planes in France. On 16 May the War Cabinet agreed to send over ten more squadrons of fighters. This left twenty-five squadrons in Britain, the number which the Head of Fighter Command, Hugh Dowding, said was essential for the defence of the home country. Churchill had already decided not to go below this figure, 'no matter what the consequences might be'. It was one of the top half-dozen major decisions of the war. But the French continued to call for more fighters until the end.

(*left*). 'The Secretary of State (for War, Anthony Eden) enjoying a joke with men in the desert'

(*below*). Duff and Lady Diana Cooper

(*left*). The Minister of Aircraft Production, May 1940

(*below*). Richard Stokes

Six days after his speech to the Commons, Churchill made his first broadcast to the nation as Prime Minister.

A woman author:

On May 19 Winston Churchill, less cautious, owing to an hereditary belief in British stamina, than the discreet B.B.C. announcers in acquainting us with the fate which looms before us, insists in a broadcast talk that the intensive warfare from which other countries have suffered will be upon us as soon as the situation has 'stabilised' in France ... Martin and I, like other London householders, take the pictures off the walls, store our valuables in the basement, put buckets of sand in the passages, keep the bath filled with water, and make similar preparations now universal, for fighting fires and minimising the effect of bombs. This done, I visit the hair-dresser, deciding that if I must be bombed, I may as well be bombed with neatly arranged hair.

In this broadcast, not as widely remembered as some of his others, Churchill spoke of the times as 'the most sublime' in British and French history. In an effort, perhaps, to raise confidence and morale, he expressed confidence in the stabilization of the front in France: 'I have invincible confidence in the French Army and leaders. Only a very small part of that splendid army has yet been engaged...' Either Churchill thought it best not to tell the people all – although he was later to express pride in always doing so – or his appraisal of German and French strategies, and understanding of Reynaud's report, was not good.

Sir W. M. James:

If ever we needed a leader it is now. The hour has struck and the man has appeared. It was Winston who warned us again and again, it is Winston who has roused the martial spirit of the country by his magnificent oratory, and he is the only Cabinet Minister who has not only experienced and distinguished himself in every form of war, but has been a life-long student of war. He is a gift from the Gods at this moment ... Winston will of course be the Grand Panjandrum for all operations. He has a profound knowledge of war and one cannot imagine him 'sitting back' when important decisions have to be made.

On 19 May General Weygand succeeded Gamelin as French C.-in-C. The Germans poured into France like ants into a garden. The full immensity of the danger was still not apparent. That day, in a message to Gamelin Churchill had referred to 'the tortoise' having protruded its head far from its shell – it was now ready to have it nipped off. The German Army was indeed in a dangerous position – decisive action might have restored some balance. But this was no tortoise; and there were clear signs of poor morale in some sections of the French forces, and a weary defeatism among some of its leaders which had already been apparent during the campaign in Norway. The British, fighting to keep their comparatively small force intact, became increasingly aware of this lack of will in some sectors of the French command. Ironside went to France to see if he could restore some order to confusion. On 20 May he forced a way through the refugee-blocked roads to visit General G. H. Billotte, C.-in-C. of the French armies in the north.

Ironside was horrified, 20 May 1940:

No plan, no thought of a plan. Ready to be slaughtered. Defeated at the head without casualties. *Très fatigués* and nothing doing. I lost my temper and shook Billotte by the button of his tunic. The man is completely beaten. I got him to agree [to a plan] ... There is absolutely nothing in front of them [the French First Army]. They remain quivering behind the water-line north of Cambrai while the fate of France is in the balance. Gort told me when I got back to his Headquarters that they would never attack.[1]

Leslie Hore-Belisha, House of Commons, 22 May 1940:

If we have made errors in the past, they have been errors of inadequate preparation. We have waited until a calamity came upon us before realising its full magnitude. When Norway was invaded we completely underestimated the situation. We sent a small number of troops to meet a large number of troops. Hitler dispatched to that country a far greater army than was necessary to achieve his purpose. He sent 100,000 men or more. But our conception was that we could discharge the task, if we could discharge it at all, with about 4,000 men.

On 23 May 1940, Churchill sent for Lord 'Boom' Trenchard, 'father of the R.A.F.', a Kitchener-like figure, but long since retired and out of touch with the speed of events. He intended asking him to be C.-in-C., Home Forces. The meeting was a disaster. Trenchard was an extremely prickly man, who had come

---

[1] Billotte died next day in a motor accident on the crowded roads, before launching the attack. Also on 20 May, Gort had cornered General Blanchard (First Army) with a map and stubbing it with a pencil had said slowly: '*Il faut tuer les Boches et il faut les tuer ici.*'

to believe the inflated opinions about his powers aired in the Press and elsewhere.

Trenchard, 23 May 1940:

I was more than horrified when Winston and Eden broke off three times to answer the telephone and proceeded to discuss with someone, presumably at the War Office, whether a brigadier in charge of the defences at Boulogne nearly 100 miles away was doing the right thing in resisting the Germans at one end of a quay or another. I heard him give instructions on how the brigadier should fight his battle. It seemed to me that Churchill was acting like a commanding officer instead of a Prime Minister, and I said so. Churchill next made me more annoyed by suggesting that he and I together were responsible for reducing the R.A.F. after the Great War.

With tempers already unsheathed, Churchill then offered Trenchard the job. The old air chief refused to accept it without at least the powers of 'a Deputy Minister of Defence'.

Winston completely lost his temper and became almost as incoherent as myself, muttering something about not having a dictator or a Mussolini at the top, something else about unwarranted attacks on politicians, and something else about making sure of his own powers to curb the stupid generals . . . I said goodbye and left.[1]

Sir Charles Wilson, 24 May 1940:

Winston Churchill is sixty-five. He has just been appointed Prime Minister, and I have become his doctor, not because he wanted one, but because certain members of the Cabinet, who realised how essential he has become, have decided that somebody ought to keep an eye on his health. It was in these rather ambiguous circumstances that I made my way this morning to Admiralty House wondering how he would receive me. Though it was noon, I found him in bed reading a document. He went on reading while I stood by the bedside. After what seemed quite a long time, he put down his papers and said impatiently: 'I don't know why they are making such a fuss. There's nothing wrong with me.' He picked up the papers and resumed his reading. At last he pushed his bed-rest away and, throwing back the bedclothes, said abruptly: 'I suffer from dyspepsia, and this is the treatment.' With that he proceeded to demonstrate to me some breathing exercises. His big

---

[1] On 30 November, 1940, Churchill, in 'cordial mood', offered Trenchard an important job reorganizing Military Intelligence. Trenchard turned it down in order to use all his influence in obtaining a 'bombing strategy'. He died in 1956.

white belly was moving up and down when there was a knock on the door, and the P.M. grabbed at the sheet as his secretary Mrs Hill came into the room. Soon after I took my leave. I do not like the job, and I do not think the arrangement can last.

Max Plowman,[1] letter, Essex, 24 May 1940:

Perhaps Winston will win the war. Perhaps he won't. How anybody could *expect* him to, I don't know, in view of his unparalleled record in losing everything he puts his hand to.

Chamberlain, letter, 25 May 1940:

It is clear as daylight that, if we had had to fight in 1938, the results would have been far worse. It would be rash to prophesy the verdict of history, but if full access be obtained to all the records, it will be seen that I realised from the beginning our military weakness, and did my best to postpone, if I could not avert, the war.

The Cabinet War Room, which under Churchill became the centre of Britain's war operations, had been started underground in 1937 – during Baldwin's premiership of 'unpreparedness'. Referred to as 'Storey's Gate', it was unofficially known as 'The Hole'. General Sir Leslie Hollis has recalled when Churchill was taken there in May 1940: 'No one could say what the news would be within the hour, whether or not England was even then under her first invasion in a thousand years. The little group stood for a moment in silence under the humming fans, each thinking his own thoughts, and then Mr Churchill took his cigar out of his mouth and pointed at the homely wooden chair at the head of the table. "This is the room from which I'll direct the war," he said slowly. "And if the invasion takes place, that's where I'll sit – in that chair. And I'll sit there until either the Germans are driven back – or they carry me out dead." '[2] But during May, Churchill continued to work from the Admiralty. On becoming Prime Minister, he had told Chamberlain: 'No one changes house for a month.'

Reynaud went to London on 26 May to confer with the British

---

[1] Editor, poet, and pacifist author.

[2] Churchill seems to have had a different story for almost everyone on what he would do if the Germans came down Whitehall, but they were all similarly defiant.

about a separate French peace and on agreement with Italy. Baudouin met him at the airport on his return:

At 7.30 p.m. I went to Le Bourget to meet the Prime Minister who had gone to London in the morning, and had conferred with Mr Churchill and the members of the War Cabinet. He told me that it had been a very trying interview, and that he had described the situation to Mr Churchill and his colleagues without minimizing its seriousness. 'The only one who understands is Halifax, who is clearly worried about the future, and realizes that some European solution must be reached. Churchill is always hectoring, and Chamberlain undecided.' Paul Reynaud asked the English to agree to the inter-nationalization of the Suez Canal, Gibraltar, and Malta in order to be able to negotiate with Italy at once. Halifax agreed, but Churchill took refuge behind the War Cabinet which would give its answer on the following day.

That night, the first British troops were evacuated from Dunkirk. Now no one could longer deny the tremendous victory Germany was winning. Two days later, the Belgian King capitulated his army to the German High Command, thus exposing the British left-flank and way of retreat. King Leopold acted on his own initiative; the Belgian Government promptly dissociated itself from the act. It was a desperate blow. The Belgian Army, half a million strong, needed only resolute leadership; but it was understandably disillusioned at lack of allied co-operation (at one time it had received no orders for four days), was threatened on its right-flank by the British retreat, and had little or no air support.

On 28 May Churchill offered Lloyd George a position in the War Cabinet – subject to the approval of Chamberlain. Lloyd George and Chamberlain were among the very few political enemies in Parliament who were also personally hostile. Lloyd George refused. (When, a month later, Chamberlain 'agreed' to his inclusion, he again refused.)

On 31 May, Churchill returned to Paris.

Baudouin, 31 May 1940:

This meeting was affecting, for Mr Churchill twice had tears in his eyes when he was describing the martyrdom of the armies in the north, the terrible suffering of the men, and the loss of material which were saddening England. His voice broke when he told us that in order to save as many English soldiers as possible in order to form a new army he had given the order to embark the wounded last, which to all intents and purposes meant leaving them in the hands of the Germans. He spoke with deep emotion of the common sufferings of France and England. The meeting closed with an impassioned declaration of Mr Churchill in the course of which he re-affirmed the determination of England to fight to the end, and not to accept slavery: he stated that if one of the two comrades fell during the course of the struggle the other would not lay down his arms until his friend was on his feet again. Mr Attlee, the leader of the Labour party, confirmed the determination of England to fight on until victory had been won. M. Paul Reynaud thanked the English ministers for their declarations, and carefully repeated Churchill's statement to the effect that if one of the nations went under the other would continue to fight until the companion who had succumbed was completely restored.

The Dunkirk operation, thanks to a courageous rearguard action, a determined French resistance at Lille, civilian co-operation with ships, and to a miscalculation by Hitler, was proving unexpectedly and dramatically successful. Hitler, believing he needed troops in reserve to finish off France, ordered the German commander, von Rundstedt, not to let his forces closer to Dunkirk than ten kilometres. Von Rundstedt, a very professional military man, went through the remainder of the war in a kind of sour resignation.

The Observer, 2 June 1940:

Tens of thousands more of British and French soldiers were brought safely back from Flanders yesterday. All day long Friday's amazing scenes were re-enacted at South-East ports, at villages and towns on the way to London, at London terminal stations. Several thousand French troops were among yesterday's arrivals. One boat was full of French colonial troops who had been in the midst of desperate fighting up to Friday. Several hundred French artillerymen who had been fighting in the Ypres sector a few hours before were also landed. Again every type of ship brought the Allied soldiers in an almost unending stream. Four warships entered one port within a very short time, their decks crammed. On the other hand, one small ship had not more than thirty troops on board. How rapid the arrival and disembarkation was can be shown by two facts. At one port there was not time to get away some of the unloading ships before others arrived. From the latter troops disembarked over the decks of the empty ships. Once ashore the troops were given sandwiches and coffee or other refreshments. Then they either marched or were taken by motor-bus to railway depots on their way to homes all over England. As they had waited on the beach at Dunkirk these man had endured not only attacks from low-flying planes and shelling, but fire from the German troops drawing ever closer. Some troops waded through water up to their waists, sometimes up to their necks, to get to the waiting boats. One officer said he had been up to his waist for three hours seeing that the men got on board. Other soldiers told of their ordeal going along a long narrow quay which German bombers constantly attacked. All of them, like all those who had preceded them, showed that their spirit was utterly unbroken by the hell through which they had passed. On the carriage doors of the trains which bore them away they scrawled, 'Back to Blighty – but not for long,' and 'Look out, Hitler. We haven't started on you yet.'

On 4 June the evacuation was called off, after more than a million men had been delivered.

Diplomatic correspondent,[1] diary, 4 June 1940:

This evening Churchill made one of the speeches of the war, when he dealt with the fools who have been writing and talking of the evacuation from Belgium and Flanders as 'a defeat turned into victory'. He said that we had lost a thousand guns, all our equipment, in the course of a 'colossal military disaster'. There was a pregnant sentence in which he foretold that if, which he did not believe, England or parts of Britain were subjugated, we should go on fighting from other parts of the Empire until, in God's good time, the new world came to help and re-conquer the old. 'We shall fight on the beaches, in the fields, in the streets and in the hills. We shall never surrender.'

Churchill delivered the speech both in the House of Commons and later on the radio. It was a speech which electrified not only his own country, but the world. With it, Churchill won the complete confidence of the British people, which he had never before enjoyed. Whatever was to happen, Churchill's place in the national life was assured; he would never be in the wilderness again.

News Chronicle, 5 June 1940:

The full gravity of the military position was brought before the House of Commons last night by the Prime Minister in a speech of matchless oratory, uncompromising candour, and indomitable courage. Sometimes he sent a chill through the crowded House, as when he spoke of 'the colossal military disaster' in France and Flanders, and of our determination 'to defend our island home and ride out the storms of war . . . if necessary, for years, if necessary, alone' . . . Always the darkness of the picture he drew was relieved by his faith in the people of Britain – his

---

[1] George Bilainkin, of Allied Newspapers.

confidence that, whatever happened, they would refuse to accept the possibility of defeat. Even if the worst happened: 'We shall defend our island whatever the cost may be. We shall fight on the beaches, we shall fight on the landing grounds, in the fields, in the streets, and in the hills. We shall never surrender.' The House did not cheer . . . [But his] confidence that a German victory was unthinkable – not only to ourselves, but to the United States – was loudly cheered. So was the Premier's determination that the British Expeditionary Force should be rebuilt and re-equipped . . . He paused a moment to bring still nearer to the House the cost of the heroic retreat. Glancing along the Treasury bench, he said in a low voice: 'The President of the Board of Trade is not in his place [Sir Andrew Duncan]. His son has been killed.' He spoke of the epic of Dunkirk as a 'miracle of deliverance' . . . But wars were not won by evacuation.

It was a sombre occasion; the most serious situation that had ever faced a British parliament in war or peace. Some members called for a debate; but it was not possible that night. This angered the Labour M.P. Fred Bellenger; in the Army, he had just returned from Flanders. There were, he said many things he wanted to say. But there was no time . . .

That day the War Office appealed for cigarettes, handkerchiefs, foot ointment and powders, shaving soap, razors and razor-blades . . .

Ed. Murrow,[1] broadcast, 4 June 1940:

I have heard Mr Churchill in the House of Commons at intervals over the last ten years. I heard his speech on the Norwegian campaign, and I have some knowledge of his writings. To-day, he was different. There was little oratory; he wasn't interested in being a showman. He spoke the language of Shakespeare with a direct urgency such as I have never before heard in that House. There were no frills and no tricks. Winston Churchill's speeches have been prophetic. He has talked and written of the German danger for years. He has gone into the political wilderness in defence of his ideas. To-day, as Prime Minister, he gave the House of Commons a report remarkable for its honesty, inspiration, and gravity.

A country-woman, at the village of 'Auburn', somewhere in England, writing to friends in America,[2] 1940:

---

[1] Edward R. Murrow, American broadcaster, who made his reputation with 'This is London' reports in the war. Director, U.S. Information Agency, 1961–4; Hon. K.B.E.; died 1965.

[2] Margery Allingham, author of crime novels; died 1966.

Mr Churchill is the unchanging bulldog, the epitome of British aggressiveness and the living incarnation of the true Briton in fighting, not standing any damned nonsense, stoking the boilers with the grand piano and enjoying-it mood. Also he never lets go. He is so designed that he cannot breathe if he does. At the end of the fight he will come crawling in, unrecognisable, covered with blood and delighted, with the enemy's heart between his teeth. Moreover, he always has been like this as far as anybody remembers, and his family before him. After half a century the country has got into the true with him, but it is its fighting not its normal angle. In handing over his own precious bit and bridle to Mr Churchill the British horse gave himself the master whom he knew to be far more ruthless in a British way than anything possible to be produced elsewhere in Europe. Mr Churchill would ride his horse to the death and die with it as a matter of course, and be sublimely confident of its thanks as they trudged off to join the shades together, and, which is tremendously important, when Auburn and all Auburn kind were quietly depending on his appointment, they knew that as well as, and perhaps a good deal better than, anybody else in the world ... Mr Churchill was safe in the saddle and so at any rate everything was all right now. There were going to be no more strategic withdrawals on the moral front. It was going to be 'do it or bust', and no playing the goat. We'd do the blaming round the fire later, when the books were written and we had the facts. That Sunday evening Mr Churchill made his most needed speech and only part of it was addressed to the nation. The rest was *for* the nation, and that high-pitched stallion trumpet, than which there is no more fearful sound, was far more martial than anything heard in Europe since Queen Elizabeth noised it for her country at Tilbury.[1] To the country he gave what it had been needing so badly since Munich time, trust. Incidentally, too, he gave it authority to do the things it had already decided to do. We could fight them on the beaches, on the roads, in the lanes and in the cities, could we? That was fine. That was grand. It was all right, then. The Miss Ethels and their brothers were not incited but they were sanctioned, and in Britain

---

[1] The only speech comparable in British history to those of Churchill in 1940 was that of Elizabeth I when she addressed her army of some 16,000 men at Tilbury, waiting for the Spanish invasion, in 1588: 'Let tyrants fear. I have always so behaved myself that, under God, I have placed my chiefest strength and safeguard in the loyal hearts and good will of my subjects, therefore I am among you ... I know I have the body of a weak and feeble woman, but I have the heart and stomach of a king, and of a King of England, too. And I think foul scorn that Parma or Spain, or any prince of Europe should dare to invade the borders of my realm ... I will myself take up arms. I myself will be your general.'

sanction makes a lot of difference. The speech was also inspiring, but no man on earth can inspire a country to make a stand like that. No rider whose horse is not straining at the bit can speak with such supreme defiance. It has not been possible to put down all the little scraps of evidence which have made it so clear that the ordinary people knew all this about Mr Churchill, because country people in England so seldom speak unambiguously but rely on the most subtle combination of nods, winks and parables to convey their mind even if they want to, which is not often. I doubt if the ordinary chap cares two penn'orth of gin, as he says, if you know what he thinks or not. He is thinking it. He has got it right and you can work it out for yourself. However, the fact that from the beginning everybody chuckled when Mr Churchill's name was mentioned, and does still, is one piece of evidence ... Mr Churchill has made a lot of fine speeches but it takes more than words to convince the ordinary man and woman personally. For personal conviction one has to know the man, to recognise the mood he epitomises in oneself. When Mr Churchill came into power Auburn said yes, well, now we're for it, and it said it with complete satisfaction.

Diplomatic correspondent, diary, 10 June 1940:

French Embassy staff, all to whom I spoke, say they are surprised by Churchill's 'tactical error', in declaring that, if necessary, Britain would fight on alone. 'This is not exactly encouraging the French to fight on against fearful odds ...'

The French Ambassador was instructed to find out what Churchill had meant; he was informed: 'exactly what was said'. On 10 June Italy, declaring war on Britain and France, invaded the latter.

Meanwhile, a remarkable decision had been taken in Britain and Canada. There were, after Dunkirk, only two fully prepared Divisions in the country: the 52nd Lowland Division and the 1st Canadian Division. Both these were ordered to France, to help the disintegrating French forces. These were disembarking in Normandy while the French front was everywhere collapsing like the crust on an ill-constructed cake. There also remained in France, the 51st Highland Division, the 1st (and only) Armoured Division, and also nine improvised infantry battalions hastily prepared from base and lines-of-communication troops in France. All these continued the fight, and most of them died or were destined to spend the war in prison-camps.

There was a chaotic and tragic meeting of the French War

Cabinet, at Tours, on 12 June. Baudouin noted that Reynaud declared:

England had decided to pursue the struggle to the end; and that we ought to remain by her side whatever happened. Marshal Pétain read a sober declaration which finished on the necessity of asking for an armistice without delay in order to save what was left of France, and to allow the reconstruction of our country. He maintained that any delay would be criminal. Let us think of those who were fighting, and of the millions of civilian refugees who were on the roads. We had already waited too long ... The Prime Minister said that in his eyes the most dangerous aspect of the demand for an armistice was that it would separate France and England, 'but France must never be separated from England and the United States. The Anglo-Saxon world will save France, and it alone can restore her.' On the previous day he had promised Mr Churchill not to take any serious decision before discussing it with him. M. Paul Reynaud would ask Mr Winston Churchill to come to France on the morrow, and to lay his views before the French ministers. The members of the Council approved this suggestion. A lively discussion ensued between the supporters and opponents of an immediate departure for the Breton redoubt. General Weygand and the Marshal declared themselves opposed to this travesty of defence in Brittany. General Weygand said without any circumlocution that this redoubt was a mere fantasy, for there were no troops to defend it. All the ministers spoke in the opposite sense, and most of them at the same time.

Churchill duly made his last desperate mission to France. Could something even now be saved from the wreck? Could not the French spine be snapped straight again?

Paul Baudouin, 13 June 1940:

After a short night's sleep I came downstairs to find M. Paul Reynaud and Leca in the drawing-room on their knees in front of a large map of France which was laid out on the floor; they were both in pyjamas, and were studying the possible lines of defence for the army, as well as the various directions in which the government could withdraw ... At 3.30 p.m. I went with the members of the British government to the Préfecture, and a little later M. Paul Reynaud arrived for the meeting of the Supreme Council. There were present, on the French side, M. Paul Reynaud and myself; and on the English side, Mr Churchill, Lord Halifax and Lord Beaverbrook, accompanied by General Spears. M. Paul Reynaud read the communication which he sent to President Roosevelt last Monday, and he told Mr Winston Churchill that he intended to send a new and pressing message to the President of the

United States. 'Our only chance of victory is the prompt entry of the United States into the war; President Roosevelt must realize this and accept the responsibility. But that in no way modifies the French situation, which is tragic. France has promised England not to make a separate peace, and General Weygand said last night to the council that France has been put in the front of the battle in the common struggle, and has been completely sacrificed. It is now materially impossible to carry on the fight. Will Great Britain release France from her promise? That is the first question, and we ought to examine it at once.' Mr Winston Churchill: 'I fully understand what France has suffered. I am deeply moved by the fact, and I do not under-estimate her frightful sorrows. In England our turn is coming. If our army had not been lost in the north perhaps you would have been able to hold out, for we should have been able to play an important part in the defensive battle which began on June 5, but we were not able to be by your side. Our thoughts are now different from yours, for we have not received such cruel wounds as have been your fate. We have, and henceforth we shall have, only one thought, namely to win the war, and to strike Hitler down. Day after day we shall keep our eyes fixed always on that end. Our determination is to repeat at every hour of the day, "we must fight on". That is why we must ask our friends to do the same. We have no illusions about the strength of Germany; it is powerful and widespread. It is possible that for some time Hitler may be the absolute master of Europe, but that will not last. The French army ought to go on fighting, and if, as General Weygand maintains, its formations break up it should develop and multiply its guerrillas. A guerrilla movement on a big scale will wear out the German army. Whatever happens we are going on fighting until the Nazi régime is totally destroyed. The war will continue until death or victory.' M. Paul Reynaud: 'I did not ask what England is going to do or how she regarded the future. I asked, if a French government said to the English government, "You are going on fighting, but France, on the other hand, can no longer do so, and she cannot be wholly abandoned to German domination. In these circumstances must France, with her pitiful resources, prolong a hopeless struggle which can only render harder and more pitiless the German domination?" Must the French government abandon the soil of France, and leave it all trampled by the rough feet of the conquerors? Surely in such a case Great Britain would not be surprised if France said to her, my sacrifice has been so great and so complete that I ask your permission to withdraw from the struggle by a separate armistice, while maintaining the solidarity caused by an agreement.'

On this day Churchill was at his best: calm, sympathetic, stoical, generous, and without chauvinistic malice or pride. Baudouin's diary continued:

Mr Winston Churchill: 'In any case there shall be no recriminations. In such an assumption recriminations would be vain, and one does not address them to an ally who has been unfortunate. We think that the best thing to do is to inform President Roosevelt and acquaint him with the facts. He, too, must come to a decision.' M. Paul Reynaud: 'Once more I thank Mr Churchill for his promise: France has confidence in Great Britain, for she knows that whatever happens Great Britain will restore her to her power and greatness.' ... Mr Churchill then expressed a desire to speak to Lord Halifax and Lord Beaverbrook, and the meeting was suspended for ten minutes. When it was resumed Mr Churchill said he was glad to be able to tell M. Paul Reynaud that what he had just said about the promise of Great Britain in any event to restore France to her power and greatness could now be considered as confirmed by the British government, since he had obtained the assent of Lord Halifax and Lord Beaverbrook. M. Paul Reynaud: 'I thank Mr Winston Churchill and the two members of the British Cabinet for their common declaration, but I shall wait with anxiety to know if President Roosevelt will take such a step forward as to allow the French government to carry on the war. We will then see how we can co-ordinate our efforts. My profound belief is that we shall finish by fighting the common enemy. I am going to paint for President Roosevelt the exact position of France, and tell him of my country's need of hope if it is to hold out. Has the British Prime Minister any suggestions to make as to the type of argument to employ with President Roosevelt?' Mr Winston Churchill: 'Be very frank and blunt. Tell the President of the problem you have just explained to the British government. You must get a reply out of him almost by return, and you must ask him for all the American air force and the fleet, in short for every help he can give us except an expeditionary force. After he has replied our two governments will examine the position. If America comes in, the final victory is certain.'

The French messages had no effect in Washington. Hull, the Secretary of State, coldly described them as: 'a series of extraordinary, almost hysterical appeals'.

Diplomatic correspondent, 14 June 1940:

My hero, Churchill, does not, in Charbonnière's[1] judgment, come out well. 'You can't acquit him because, if he felt as a member of the Cabinet that the policy of doing nothing was wrong, he had plenty of chances from September onwards to resign from the government. That would have meant the fall of Chamberlain, because Churchill's was a

---

[1] First Secretary at the French Embassy in London.

strong position.' I retorted, 'But Churchill, having been tragically kept in the wilderness so long, has gingered up the Cabinet, effected a metamorphosis.' Now came more frankness. 'We should have said, at the beginning of the war, to you, if you feel that you cannot give us two million men within a year, it means we cannot go on, and the best thing for us to do is to make a separate peace.' I at once felt that not many days will elapse before we are faced with this terrible *dénouement*. I asked how we could justify to historians to-morrow the fact that the two wealthiest, largest empires in the world seemed to have botched everything? There was no reply, and, indeed, there can be no reply.

Churchill's solution to France's misery was a union of the two nations. This plan had been hatched between Charles de Gaulle[1] and the Foreign Office, an unlikely parentage; but then it was an unlikely hour. Churchill himself was not at first entirely enthusiastic: nor, as it transpired, were the French Cabinet – now positively masochistic (apart always from Reynaud) in their desire to prostrate themselves before Hitler. Baudouin, at Cabinet meeting, 16 June 1940:

I then heard that the English had confirmed their refusal to restore to France her freedom of action, but that in return they had put forward a proposal for a close union between France and England with the object, as Mr Churchill envisaged it, of giving to the French that ray of hope of which they had so much need in their existing circumstances. France and England were to form one nation while retaining their separate political organizations. The costs of the war and the reparation of damage would be shared in common. I told M. Reynaud that at any other time this offer deserved to be carefully examined. But that is not the problem at the moment: what we have to decide this evening is whether we are going to ask Germany for her terms for an armistice. M. Paul Reynaud was enthusiastic over Churchill's suggestion for which General de Gaulle had been working in London. I told him that a proposition so fraught with consequences, and with such promise for the future, could not be examined, then accepted or rejected, by a mere Council of Ministers. Moreover, it would do nothing to unravel the knot that was choking the country. This evening the Council had to discuss one problem, and one problem only, was it or was it not necessary to try to stop the war? I went on, 'I entirely approve of your inter-

---

[1] Pre-war advocate of mechanized warfare; commanded 4th Armoured Division, 1940; Under-Secretary for National Defence, June 1940; head of Free French, 1940–4; President of Provisional Government, 1944–6; President of France, 1958–.

view with Mr Churchill at Tours on Thursday last. We must avoid a breach in Franco-British solidarity. Whether he recognizes the fact or not, Mr Churchill on Thursday morally authorized us to ask for an armistice.' The Council of Ministers met again at five o'clock, and the Prime Minister read Churchill's proposition, but without denying its importance the Council considered that it bore no relation to the immediate problems that were calling for settlement.

Joint Declaration for Union, prepared by Churchill to the French Premier, 16 June 1940:

At this most fateful moment in the history of the modern world the Governments of the United Kingdom and the French Republic make this declaration of indissoluble union and unyielding resolution in their common defence of justice and freedom against subjection to a system which reduces mankind to a life of robots and slaves. The two Governments declare that France and Great Britain shall no longer be two nations, but one Franco–British Union. The constitution of the Union will provide for joint organs of defence, foreign, financial, and economic policies. Every citizen of France will enjoy immediately citizenship of Great Britain; every British subject will become a citizen of France.

So much for 'perfidious Albion'. It was the most imaginative gesture of the century. Whether the British Cabinet would have felt able to endorse Churchill's lead is uncertain, but it is more than possible. But what France really wanted was not union with Britain but Britain's fighter planes, and even they would have been too late.

The unfortunate Reynaud resigned. He was replaced by Pétain, who sued for peace the following day, 17 June 1940.

Woman author,[1] June 1940:

The weather is hot and brilliant; as I wait in the Central Lobby of the House of Commons, the high stained-glass windows stand open, showing the fairy-like fabric of carved stone in clear golden sunshine. 'We're in the biggest mess since the Battle of Hastings,' remarks a Welsh M.P. with realistic pessimism. I notice how the coloured reflections from the windows fall upon the sculptured shoulders of former statesmen, not one of whom was confronted with a situation remotely comparable to the present crisis. Big Ben strikes four as solemnly as though it is announcing the hour of doom, and Winston Churchill begins his speech – a speech in the heroic warrior tradition of his ancestors, to whom the sanity of

---

[1] Vera Brittain.

peaceful mediation was an undesirable form of compromise. He speaks of the colossal disaster of the collapse of France and the futility of recrimination, since 'if we open a quarrel between the past and the present, we shall find that we have lost the future'. He reminds the Members of the House again that 'the worst possibilities' are open, and once more records the resolve of Britain and the British Empire to fight on, 'if necessary for years, if necessary alone'. About the severity of the ordeal before us he speaks frankly, but, like every member of the class which has ruled England since the Norman Conquest and has repeatedly carried it into war, he expects the much-enduring British people to stand up to it 'at least as well as any other people in the world'. Finally, the fire of his conclusion reflects his personal belief – not shared by all his countrymen, but entertained by him with dynamic fervour from the time that Nazidom came to power – in the necessity of the war to which England is committed. 'The Battle of Britain is about to begin. Upon this battle depends the survival of Christian civilisation. Upon it depends our own British life, and the long continuity of our institutions and our Empire. The whole fury and might of the enemy must very soon be turned on us. Hitler knows that he will have to break us in this island or lose the war. If we can stand up to him all Europe may be free and the life of the world may move forward into broad, sunlit uplands. But if we fail, then the whole world, including the United States, including all that we have known and cared for, will sink into the abyss of a new dark age made more sinister, and perhaps more protracted, by the lights of perverted science. Let us therefore brace ourselves to our duties and so bear ourselves that, if the British Empire and its Commonwealth last for a thousand years, men will still say, "This was their finest hour".' Two days later, the French plenipotentiaries have been received by the Germans, and David Low, the cartoonist, has published in the *Evening Standard* a drawing of a solitary soldier in a steel helmet, standing on Dover's cliffs and shaking his fist at the blazing vanquished continent. The caption beneath the picture contains only three words: 'Very well, alone!'

CHAPTER FOUR

1940 Inspired Leader

Harold Nicolson, letter, 19 June 1940:

How I wish Winston would not talk on the wireless unless he is feeling in good form. He hates the microphone, and when we bullied him into speaking last night, he just sulked and read his House of Commons speech over again. Now, as delivered in the House of Commons, that speech was magnificent, especially the concluding sentences. But it sounded ghastly on the wireless.

Not to most people. This broadcast of what came to be known as 'The Finest Hour' speech, had an immediate, galvanizing effect on morale, which had been sinking low.

Somerset Maugham, who had just escaped from France,[1] June 1940:

Their confidence was infectious, and if you asked one of them what he thought about France he replied with gay effrontery: 'It doesn't matter; we can lick the Jerries alone.' And at Liverpool, in the officials who came on board, in the porters who took our baggage, in the people in the streets, in the waiters at the restaurant, you felt the same spirit of confidence. Fear of invasion? Not a shadow of it. 'We'll smash 'em. It'll take time, of course, but that's all right; we can hang on.' I found the same spirit in London; I found the same spirit in the country, where the corn in the fields was beginning to turn golden and the apples on the trees already weighed down the branches. Though the collapse of France was a bitter blow and Hitler was announcing that he would sign the treaty of peace in London on August 15th, it was splendidly clear that the people of Britain were undismayed. It was, indeed, a very different England from the England I had left a few weeks before. It

---

[1] Maugham had known Churchill for many years. He had escaped from France in a crowded refugee boat from Cannes to Liverpool, in which he spent twenty days without removing his clothes – an experience which the immaculate Maugham found less than agreeable. He did not care for London in 1940, and eventually left to spend most of the remainder of the war in America.

was more determined, more energetic and more angry. Winston Churchill had inspired the nation with his own stern and resolute fortitude. There was no more half-heartedness. I talked with numbers of people, from privates to generals, from farm labourers to landed proprietors, to poor women and rich, to clerks and financiers; I found everywhere the same sense of the gravity of the situation, the same resolve to continue the struggle to victory, and the same readiness to give everything to achieve it. The British people had realized at last that they were fighting for their existence, and to defend their freedom they were prepared for any sacrifice that was demanded of them.

Count Ciano, Italian Foreign Minister, June 1940:

The fighting spirit of His Majesty's Fleet is alive and still has the aggressive ruthlessness of the captains and pirates of the 17th century. Ambassador Bastianini, who is back from London, says that the morale of the British is very high and that they have no doubts about victory, even though it may come only after a long time.

Mussolini on Churchill, 1940:

He does not have the European spirit, and doesn't really understand anything except the necessity of those English. But he is the man of the moment because he hates the Germans ... He is an obdurate and obstinate old man. In some respects he is like my father.

Even during the fall of France, Churchill was not without his worries on the home front. Increasing pressure was being exerted on him to discard the old 'Munichites'. He rather wanted to do so but did not feel powerful enough to do it. In June he received Cecil King, a director of the *Daily Mirror*.[1] In 1936 the *Mirror* had advocated Churchill as Defence Minister; it had urged his entry into the War Cabinet in 1939; it had backed him for the premiership only weeks earlier. King had written for the *Mirror*:

I was ushered into the presence. Winston was sitting in the Prime Minister's chair in the Cabinet room – in the middle of one of the long sides of the table facing the light and with his back to the fireplace. He was dressed in a very tight-fitting palm beach suit – face bright red with the heat – hair looking scantier than usual – puffing at a cigar. Outside the window paced up and down a man who looked very Civil Service, but might have been a very superior detective. On the walls

---

[1] Cecil H. King, nephew of Lord Northcliffe; Director of Mirror Newspapers 1929–68.

were two maps; one of the western world, the other of the Low Countries and Northern France. I explained that I had come to find out exactly what he did want us to do, as I had had a message through Esmond [Lord Rothermere]. He said he had only been P.M. a month to-day (and what a month!) and already the papers were picking on the Government and demanding Chamberlain's head on a charger ... I said I thought opinion against Chamberlain was high and rising and would continue to rise. He said there was no one in this government he had to accept; that he had heard through a third party that Chamberlain was prepared to take office under him and that he personally was very glad to have him. He was clear-headed, methodical, and hardworking and the best man he had – head and shoulders over the average man in the administration, who were mostly pretty mediocre ... A General Election was not possible during a war and so the present House of Commons, however unrepresentative of feeling in the country, had to be reckoned with as the ultimate source of power for the duration. If he trampled on these men, as he could trample on them, they would set themselves against him, and in such internecine strife lay the Germans' best chance of victory. I said I thought his position in the hearts of the people so unassailably strong that he could take stern measures with these people and get away with it. He asked what was the use of being in the position of a dictator if one could not have the governmental personnel one wanted? And after all, though he did have Chamberlain, Kingsley Wood and Inskip, he also had included every single M.P. who had taken an independent line to Chamberlain – Law, Boothby, Macmillan were all in and Vansittart had been made a Privy Councillor. It was all very well to plead for a Government excluding the elements that had led us astray of recent years, but where was one to stop? They were everywhere – not only in the political world, but among the fighting service chiefs and the civil service chiefs. To clear all these out would be a task impossible in the disastrous state in which we found ourselves. In any case if one were dependent on the people who had been right in the last few years, what a tiny handful one would have to depend on. No, he was not going to run a government of revenge. If the country did not like his government they could form another one and God knows where they would get it from – he wouldn't serve on it. After all, government in these days was no fun – it was listening to a succession of stories of bad news, a heart-breaking job. On the future he said he was convinced there would be widespread air raids in this country as soon as the fighting in this offensive died down. He thought the Germans would try an invasion – he doubted whether they could land more than 20,000 men on account of our Navy, and these would – if necessary – be 'choked in their own blood'. At the same time, did I realise how ghastly our position was? We had won last time after four years of defeats and would do so again. Was this, asked the Prime Minister, a time for political bickering? I said the question was not whether this was a time for bickering, but that the feeling against Chamberlain was very strong, and that a popular newspaper had within limits to reflect public opinion. He said he didn't see the public had any right to take such a line. They had voted for Chamberlain when he was making these blunders: why should they seek Chamberlain's blood when he and they were proved wrong?

Chamberlain remained in the Cabinet. But the *Mirror*, for so long Churchill's ally, was now a potential enemy. It was not to be underrated.

The House of Commons went into Secret Session on 20 June. It discussed the necessity for such sessions, the likely results of a German air bombardment, and the Franco–German armistice. There is no full record of Churchill's speech on that occasion.

Daily Mirror, 20 June 1940:

Even Churchill's eloquence will not succeed in stifling all criticism during to-day's secret session of Parliament; any more than he can stifle it outside Parliament . . . Already here and there, fragments of the old complacency begin to peep out. As when the Petroleum Minister can't see why joy-riders shouldn't waste petrol at race meetings.

Diplomatic correspondent, 25 June 1940:

Hear curious story from diplomatist that 'Newspaper proprietors' saw Churchill a few days ago and said readers' letters had led them to become anxious about the future retention of Chamberlain, and others. Churchill replied that, if they went, he would leave Cabinet too.

Here indeed was the seed of much future discontent. Churchill let the seed grow; by 1942 it had developed into a quite formidable plant. But at the time it was probably the least of Churchill's many grave concerns. The British Army having lost a large quantity of its equipment at Dunkirk, replacements were desperately needed. The United States agreed to sell a vast quantity of supplies, including half a million First World War rifles, for 37 million dollars. But more material of every kind was needed.

Diplomatic correspondent, with Ambassador Kennedy,[1] 11 June 1940:

---

[1] Boston banker; United States Ambassador to the United Kingdom, 1937–41; eldest son killed in action, 1944; father of John F. Kennedy.

I said, 'Is there nothing America can do to expedite supplies?' Kennedy's face had become more and more set, the veins showing on the neck. His answers were frank and considered. He thought for a moment and answered, 'We have little to give you and it's no use pretending that we have. Take planes: we got your orders in January, and you know perfectly well that you can't begin to have mass production on a huge scale in no time. We have no army – only about 200,000 patched-up men, and that means we have no guns or tanks to spare – on a scale that would be worth while. There are only the old things . . . It's no use, as a friend of the democracies, for me to have gone on saying the things people wanted to hear. From the start I told them they could expect zero help. We had none to offer and I know we could not give it, and, in the way of any material, we could not spare it. I could have easily said the usual blah and poppycock, but, what's the bloody good of being so foolish as that? An ambassador's duty is to be frank, not to mislead. I considered that my duty and I discharged it. What the hell are you worth if you just mislead them?' Churchill, according to Kennedy, has much more drive than Chamberlain, but time is running away.

The rifles arrived during July (but with only about fifty cartridges each); they were issued mostly to the Home Guard force, recruited from veterans and others not in the Services.

Before the French Government fell to Germany, it was unable to give a categoric undertaking not to allow the French fleet to fall into German hands. For Britain the matter was more imperative than any other single factor at the time. Only with command of the seas, could the nation survive. Repeated assurances were given by France that the ships would never be used against Britain; but, clearly, France had little intention of scuttling the one element of power which remained to her. The assurances were not enough for Churchill.

The sinking of the French ships in North Africa, at Churchill's command (not without opposition in the Government and Navy), was received by the Vichy Government with astonishment, outrage, and bitterness. Paul Baudouin, now Pétain's Foreign Minister, 3 July 1940:

I had finished my lunch when I was told the stunning news of the ultimatum delivered this very morning by a British Squadron to our ships moored in the roads of Mers-el-Kebir and partly disarmed. A profound anxiety distracts me. Where is this act of the English going to lead us? At 3.30 p.m. there began a meeting at the Marshal's, at which there were present Pierre Laval, General Weygand, Admiral Darlan, and I.

Admiral Darlan told us that at 12.30 p.m. he had received the telegram sent at 8.45 a.m. by Admiral Gensoul, who was in command of the squadron anchored at Mers-el-Kebir. This telegram announced that a powerful English squadron had issued an ultimatum which expired at 3.0 p.m., to Admiral Gensoul either to join the English fleet or to scuttle his ships. The admiral replied that he would answer force by force, and Admiral Darlan approved of this decision. The destruction of part of the French squadron is probably an accomplished fact. We all remained silent, for we were completely overwhelmed. I was overcome by a great feeling of powerlessness, for we are in the most tragic of misunderstandings. To clear up the situation both means of communication and time are essential, and we have neither the one nor the other ... Before dinner I heard of the naval action, and the useless and culpable aggression of England unhinged me. Did not the Marshal, Admiral Darlan, and I give our solemn word? This promise will be kept whatever happens, so why shed blood between the two countries, and that under the amused eyes of the Germans?

4 July 1940:

The night seemed to me frightfully long, and I was heart-broken when I was told at 8.0 a.m. that a cruiser had blown up, and that another, the *Dunkerque*, was in flames. Happily, the *Strasbourg* and some cruisers had been able to get away. The French fleet was unable to make any effective reply, and the death-roll was more than twelve hundred. The crime was committed without running any risks. Furthermore, the British Admiralty most brutally took possession of the French ships which were lying alongside the quay at Portsmouth. The Marshal sent for me at 8.30 a.m., and in his room were Laval and Darlan. The Admiral was not the same man as yesterday, when, soberly and without raising his voice, he told us his sad news. This morning his voice trembled as he confirmed the details of the drama. 'I have been deceived by my brothers in arms. They have betrayed the trust I reposed in them.' The Marshal and Laval remained silent, and the admiral read the instructions which he had just written with his own hand. They were to the effect that last night the cruiser squadron at Algiers passed the night to the south of the Balearic Islands with decks cleared for action. This squadron was to be reinforced by the *Strasbourg*, which had escaped from Mers-el-Kebir, and was ordered, by way of reprisals, to make a surprise attack on the English ships. 'But,' I said at once, 'does this mean war with England?' The Marshal looked at Laval, who said, 'We have made up our minds to reply to yesterday's attack on us by an attack of our own.' I made no reply either to Laval or to Darlan, but I besought the Marshal to reflect upon the catastrophe which he was bringing on France. I saw the Marshal was moved, but he still hesitated, and it was not until half an hour later that he gave way, and agreed with my suggestion not to take any decision in the matter of reprisals.

The possibility of reprisals from the wretched Vichy Government did not alarm Churchill. He had hopes of the forceful general who, having failed to persuade any of his superiors in France to take on the task, was beginning to rally Frenchmen to fight on from England. Charles de Gaulle and his wife were now ensconced in a furnished suburban house at 41 Birchwood Road, Petts Wood.

A French officer in North Africa, diary, June 1940:

De Gaulle seems to be very convincing, very inspiring. Our hearts are filled with hope; we are going to write to de Gaulle to enlist and to fight elsewhere.

This captain in the 2nd North African Division, had just been told about de Gaulle by some villagers while retreating in France. He had not previously heard of him.

The same officer, 4 July 1940:

Great news on the wireless! The British fleet has captured our fleet assembled at Mers-el-Kebir near Oran, under the command of Admiral Gensoul. A few ships tried to escape, in particular the *Dunkerque*. The British shelled and sank it . . . It is pathetic that we and the British have come to this. But one must believe that most of the ships resisted merely for form's sake.

There was a less joyous reaction at the French Embassy in London.

A diplomatic correspondent, with French Embassy official, in London, 5 July 1940:

I said I feared that the thin friendship for the British I had often suspected to be latent in many French hearts would now show itself in a new spirit, 'and perhaps your men will, as an American journalist put it to me, go back to the aircraft factories and build with gusto machines that shall rain bombs on us.' There was no hesitancy about Charbonnière's reply: 'With ten times more enthusiasm than before' . . . The French people, like any other, would not have a foreign nation tell it that it had acted with dishonour. Whatever criticisms the French themselves might, rightly, pass upon the actions of their government, those criticisms would be resented if they came from outside. If the British had waited, just a little longer, and had, meanwhile, desisted from the temptation to make the attacks, it was on the cards that a more representative Cabinet would have been forced to the top. Now everything had been finished, 'by the cold butchery at Oran'. It was impossible to forgive that, no Frenchman could forget it. The British could not allow, they all knew, the French fleet to be used by the Germans against them, but, there were ways and means of achieving their object by the discriminate use of a little tact... I said, 'We have been long enough friends for me to be able to say to you, without offence, that in my heart I wonder if there has been much real affection for the French in this country. In 1923, when you sent coloured troops to occupy German territories, the Great War had been over only five years, and already Members of our Parliament were asking about the relative strength of the British and French air forces. That, I think, showed how strong was the innate suspicion.' Charbonnière agreed, and said, 'The French, at heart, equally little liked the British. They tried to like you because they realized that politically we had to be one; British statesmen also recognized this self-evident truth.'

The best that could be said of the Oran episode was that it left the entire world in no uncertain understanding of Britain's determination: that in waging war Britain could be as ruthless as any power. Churchill said in the House, 4 July 1940: 'It is our inflexible resolve to do everything that is possible in order to prevent [French warships] falling into the German grip. I leave the judgement of our action, with confidence, to Parliament. I leave it to the nation, and I leave it to the United States. I leave it to the world and history.' This speech was the first occasion that Churchill received warm support from the Conservatives; hitherto, 'it was from the Labour benches that I received the warmest welcome when I entered the House or rose on serious occasions'.

Uncommitted nations were watching Britain closely.

Diplomatic correspondent, 4 July 1940:

Maisky's and Churchill's banter a few days ago? The invitation was received in the afternoon and Maisky [Russian Ambassador] went just before dinner, staying half an hour. Churchill teased Maisky about 'Imperialist aspirations' in taking Bessarabia and added, 'But we really don't mind, or care, what you do there.' Maisky laughingly retorted, 'We don't mind if you do; we didn't ask you for permission.'

A joke indeed.

Tom Jones, letter, Cliveden, 13 July 1940:

On Wednesday I had lunch alone at Thames House with L.G. – a lunch sent along by Fortnum and Mason to the fine room overlooking the river. He had lobster and I had sole and salad. He had lots of water and a spoonful of whisky and I had a glass of lager. The object of my visit was to urge him to join the Government. He had already (I knew) had an hour that morning on the same text with Garvin. I found him adamant against going in. It was like calling a specialist in when the patient's case was nigh hopeless. Winston was at the political mercy of Neville with his party majority . . . 'Winston doesn't care either way. He will not smash the Tory Party to save the country, as I smashed the Liberal Party. Winston has intellectual and rhetorical power and resource but he has no psychological insight. He was not a success with the French. He has not big men at his elbow as I had . . . There is no one to stand up to Winston' . . . and so on for over an hour.

Lloyd George, *Sunday Pictorial*, 28 July 1940:

The war is to go on through inconceivable horror until one party or the other wins an incontestable victory – or both parties are so exhausted that the will to continue on both sides fades into an unspeakable weariness that can no longer be lashed by passion, hatred, or ambition into further activity. When, some months ago, there was a temporary lull in the storm, and an opportunity for peace talks presented itself, I was one of the few who thought, at that time, that conversations might serve to avert a catastrophe. I foresaw that catastrophe impending because of the utter unpreparedness of the Allies for so stupendous a struggle. I was then of opinion that a conference – at which non-belligerents like Russia, America and Italy, and perhaps the Scandinavian countries, would be represented – might lead to a better understanding between the angry nations and to the rebuilding of the temple of Peace on a surer foundation than a one-sided victory. I do not propose to discuss now, whether my judgement at that date was sound or not. What I wish to point out is that conditions were then more favourable for a discussion on equal terms than they are to-day, or will probably be a few weeks hence.

Lloyd George was not the only one who believed 'peace feelers' were still Britain's best policy. There were Members of Parliament, and of the Government, who were not totally averse to the idea, which was not only tempting but which could be justified by various arguments of practicality and common sense. Winston Churchill, as is well known, was not among them. German peace overtures via the United States, the Vatican, and the King of Sweden, were rejected. Nevertheless, German embassies in Washington, Madrid (where Churchill sent the arch-appeaser Sir Samuel Hoare), and Berne, were encouraged to believe that peace discussions were not out of the question.

Hitler said in a broadcast, echoing a speech to the Reichstag of 9 July 1940:

> Mr Churchill has just declared again that he wants war. Some six weeks ago he started the war in that sphere in which the British apparently believe themselves particularly strong – the air war against the civilian population, under the pretext of attacking so-called military objectives ... So far I have ordered scarcely any reprisals, but this does not mean that this is or will remain my only reply. It is quite clear to me that our answer, which will eventually come, will bring untold suffering and misery to mankind ... Misery – but not, of course, to Mr Churchill; for by that time he will no doubt be safe in Canada, whither the fortunes and the children of the leading war profiteers have already been removed. This time perhaps Mr Churchill will, by way of exception, believe me when I play the prophet and utter these words: in this way a great empire will be destroyed, an empire which I never intended to destroy or even harm. But it is clear to me that this fight will end only with the complete destruction of one of the two belligerent parties. I know that the party to be destroyed will indeed be England ... In this hour I consider it my duty before my conscience to make one more appeal to England's common sense. I am in a position to do so since I do not come begging as one who was defeated, but merely speak as the victor and in the name of common sense. I see no reason why this fight should continue. I regret the sacrifices which it will call forth ... Mr Churchill may reject my declaration, exclaiming that it results from my fears and doubts of the ultimate issue. If so, I have, at any rate, relieved my conscience before the future ...

But Hitler was not much impressed by the time-gaining manoeuvres in Madrid and elsewhere. Somewhat reluctantly, he had decided on the inevitable consequence of his policy and strategy – the invasion of southern England.

Adolf Hitler, in conference at Berlin, 21 July 1940:

> The invasion of Britain is an exceptionally daring undertaking, because even if the way is short, this is not just a river crossing, but the crossing of a sea which is dominated by the enemy. This is not the case of a single crossing operation as in Norway; operational surprise cannot be expected; a defensively prepared and utterly determined enemy faces us ...

American correspondent, Berlin, 23 July 1940:

> The press campaign to whip up the people for the war on Britain started with a bang this morning. Every paper in Berlin carried practically the same headline: 'Churchill's Answer – Cowardly Murdering of a De-

fenceless Population'. The story is that since Hitler's Reichstag 'appeal for peace' the British have answered by increasing their night attacks – only women and children have been hit. Afraid the German people will swallow this. They are very depressed that Britain will not have peace.

Hitler to General Keitel:

I've proved that I've done everything to come to terms with England. In 1940 after the French campaign I offered an olive branch and was ready to give things up. I wanted nothing from them. On 1 September 1939, I made a proposal to the English or rather I repeated the proposal which Ribbentrop made to them in 1936: I proposed an alliance in which Germany would guarantee the British Empire. It was primarily Churchill and the anti-German crowd around Vansittart who were against the proposal; they wanted war.

Before the invasion could begin, it was necessary to destroy the R.A.F. Germany began the correct tactical move of attacking British airfields in mid-July. It was the start of the Battle of Britain. Independently of this another plan was being developed by the Luftwaffe to bring about Britain's submission through heavy bombing – which would not involve an invasion.

After the fall of France, Churchill, as Defence Minister, completed his domination over the Army. The Navy, which had the least controversial but most vital task – keeping open the sea communications – he was content to leave to A. V. Alexander and Sir Dudley Pound, for the latter of whom he had an especially close regard. The R.A.F., under his old war colleague Sinclair and Sir Charles Portal, was also, he felt, able to do without close supervision, for he agreed in general terms to its strategy of bombing. Three of these four men held the same posts till the defeat of Germany; Pound died in office. The Army, however, was a different matter. The sight of khaki brought out in Churchill many old frustrations and emotions. From an early age he had been fascinated by problems of military strategy and generalship. On the other hand, he had become to believe, first in the Boer War, but much more definitely in the First World War, that generals were almost invariably foolish or dangerous or, as in the case of Haig, both.

Although he believed that the R.A.F. alone was really capable of winning the war, his concentration on the Army was not inconsistent: he believed that only the Army was capable of losing the war on its own.

Churchill always suspected the two senior Services of being hidebound and exclusive. No one believed more in the reality of 'Colonel Blimp' – unless it were Lloyd George. He was fond of reminding generals that 'the high commands of the Army are not a club'. Just as he had previously delighted in the outrage he had caused by being T. E. Lawrence's official guardian, in the Second World War he helped to bring forward such unconventional soldiers as Orde Wingate and Percy Hobart. He said he was more impressed by the officer-like qualities in rankers at Portsmouth than in the cadets at Dartmouth. As Minister of Defence, he turned the Admiralty upside-down when he discovered that three candidates who had humble backgrounds had failed – one, as he discovered on personal interview, had a cockney accent: Churchill ordered them to be given cadetships. Reading in *The Times* that senior officers in an Army command were to take part in cross-country runs, he notified the War Minister: 'Who is the general of this Division, and does he run the seven miles himself. If so he may be more useful for football than war ... In my experience, based on many years' observation, officers with high athletic qualifications are not usually successful in the higher ranks.'

Ironside had given way to General Sir John Dill as Chief of the Imperial General Staff, a very good appointment. Ironside, meanwhile, had been given command of Home Forces, in preparation for the expected German invasion.

General Ironside, 19 July 1940:

> I was summoned to see the Secretary of State at 2.45 p.m. and told that I was to be replaced by Alan Brooke as C.-in-C. Home Forces. Eden told me that the Cabinet wished to have someone with late experience of the war. I told Eden that he needn't worry and that I was quite prepared to be released. I had done my best. In order that the matter should be placed on a good footing, I was to be made a Field-Marshal. And so my military career comes to an end in the middle of a great war ... I don't suppose that Winston liked doing it, for he is always loyal to his friends.

Alan Brooke had commanded well at the decisive flank engagement during the withdrawal to Dunkirk.[1] On the night that he took up his new duties Brooke dined with the Prime Minister:

Just by ourselves at the end of a long day's work ... He was very nice and I got a good insight into the way his brain is working. He is most interesting to listen to and full of the most marvellous courage considering the burden he is bearing. He is full of offensive thoughts, but I think he fully realises the difficulties he is up against. He said that he wondered if England had ever been in such straits since the Armada days. He refers to Hitler always as 'that man'.

Churchill had known Alan Brooke's two brothers well, as a young fellow officer in the last century. Both had died young. 'These connections and memories,' Churchill wrote, 'formed a personal foundation upon which my unbroken wartime association was maintained and ripened.'

Churchill's views, or emotions, about the Army were not entirely based on prejudice. He realized that a war that was likely to be widespread, and in which weapons would be more crucial than sheer manpower, could not be fought successfully by generals at the front. It would have to have overall direction from home, where everything including production and allied diplomacy could be gauged. The generals at the various fronts could hardly be expected to appreciate this, and Churchill did not think the war was a time to humour anyone, particularly generals. All this might have passed without friction, if it had not been for the Prime Minister's close interest in detailed affairs at the fronts.

In command in the Middle East was General 'Archy' Wavell, a much-loved figure in the Army. Wavell was described by Arthur Tedder, Deputy Air C.-in-C., Middle East, in his diary, as 'a nice, solid, sound, honest old thing'. Churchill took a very important view of this command, owing to an obsession with the Suez Canal. Wavell was summoned to London.

Eden, 13 August 1940:

Found Wavell waiting for me at 9.0 a.m. He was clearly upset at last night's proceedings and said that he thought he should have made it

---

[1] Like Alexander, an Ulsterman; Commander, 2nd Army Corps, B.E.F., 1939–40; C.-in-C., Home Forces, 1940–1; C.I.G.S., 1941–6; Field-Marshal, 1944; Viscount, 1946; died 1963.

plain that if the Prime Minister could not approve his dispositions and had not confidence in him he should appoint someone else . . .

On 14 and 16 August there were severe air battles over England, resulting in notable victories for the R.A.F. On 20 August Churchill made yet another magnificent oration, in which, referring to the fighter pilots, he said: 'Never in the field of human conflict was so much owed by so many to so few.'

Churchill was still convinced of the necessity of getting America into the war. Roosevelt was not inclined to agree with him, and isolationism was strong.

Charles Lindbergh, the American aviation hero who was looked upon by many of his countrymen as an infallible sage on many subjects, had broadcast earlier in the year:

> We are in danger of war today, not because Europeans attempted to interfere in our internal affairs, but because Americans attempted to interfere in the internal affairs of Europe. Our dangers are internal. We need not fear invasion unless Americans bring it through their own quarrelling and meddling with affairs abroad. If we desire peace, we need only stop asking for war. Nobody wishes to attack us, and nobody is in a position to do so.

Joseph Kennedy, United States Ambassador to Britain, was an able man in many ways, but he was an appalling ambassador. He had a distaste and impatience of all things diplomatic. It was not so much that he had supported Munich, it was that he so continually justified himself. Wisely concluding that America was not ready to enter the war, he did everything he could to stop her doing so – but, unfortunately, frequently said so. As early as September 1939, the King had felt obliged to write to Kennedy in fairly blunt terms. By now he was almost friendless in Britain.

Diplomatic correspondent, 20 August 1940:

> Kennedy, in morning dress, with red carnation, had just been photographed, occasion being handing to him of £14,000 cheque for war relief. He was cordial, frank, downright; looked sunburned, freckled. 'I have been saying for months', he began, 'that, until the Germans have superiority in the air, and unless they do, there is no chance whatever of their trying invasion. For months your Cabinet has disagreed with me. But yesterday Max [Lord Beaverbrook] rang up to say, "You are right and I agree with you that they won't try it unless they get us

down in the air." Winston, speaking to me a few days ago, said he anticipated invasion right away. I said, "Nonsense, no chance whatever, unless they lick you completely in the air." Of course,' K. went on, 'there is nothing else worth speaking of than the air.' This was after I had said, 'You're more cheerful than when we met on the eve of British operations against the unsurrendered French fleet. I gather you've been visiting some of our camps, factories. How do you feel about them?' 'I don't give a damn for any of these places,' answered the Ambassador. 'They don't count, if the invasion does begin. Navy really doesn't matter much more. If they get your air force whacked, and their own air force remains supreme, there isn't a hope, not a chance in the world . . . Some of you people have been shouting that America should enter the war. If we had entered seven or eight months ago, you would by now have been lost, the slaughter of Britain would have been over, because you know perfectly well we could not have come in to help you soon enough, and we should have now been making preparation for our own effective entry.' Book by his son, Jack, *Why England Slept*, has just gone to Churchill. As soon as the Premier has returned it, I am to have the loan of it. Two copies arrived, by air; one went to Professor Harold Laski, under whom Jack studied at London School of Economics.

A week later:

Kennedy in good spirits, asked me what I thought of his son's volume. I praised it warmly. Of Chamberlain, he said, 'Munich saved the Empire.' He went on, 'When I was in the States with Jack, and heard some professors talking about Munich, I realised that they knew nothing about it . . . Churchill sees now, that, if we had come in, you would have lost the war by this time.'

Kennedy was not basically an anglophobe. He was a Roman Catholic capitalist who saw Stalin as at least as great a menace as Hitler. As a result of consistent misrepresentation, as he thought, in the British Press, he did develop some anglophobia.

On 13 August 1940, Churchill announced the formation of the Home Defence (Security) Executive. This was a committee which was to investigate the possibilities of 'fifth-column' helping the German invaders. It was a time when anyone in Britain with a guttural accent or a foreign-sounding name was likely to be considered a spy. For the first time since May, Churchill came up against severe criticism in the House. The secrecy surrounding the committee – not least the salary of its members – caused resentment. The choice of chairman – Lord Swinton, a former Air Secretary – was also badly received. Churchill, appealing to the

House to support him in not mentioning the affair further, in the public interest, was not impressive.

A. J. Cummings, political commentator, 19 August 1940:

Several members of parliament tell me that in the course of the sharp little interlude in parliament last Thursday over the Swinton Committee, Mr Churchill lost his temper, and his hold on the House, for the first and only time since he became Prime Minister. Nobody will be inclined to rebuke him for an occasional touch of testiness ... The surprising thing about Mr Churchill is that, though anything but a model of human patience, and in spite of the terrible responsibility he now carries, he has not only borne himself (as one would expect of him) with high courage, but has shown high good humour.

The following day, there was criticism of the direction of the war in the House of Commons. The most impressive speech came from Leslie Hore-Belisha, the War Minister who had been sacked by Chamberlain early in the war but not restored by Churchill.

Hore-Belisha, House of Commons, 20 August 1940:

The creation of an army depends upon supply. We cannot hope to defeat the authoritarian powers, who are waging total war and who have the whole of their populations mobilised, unless we rapidly mobilise ourselves. They have great armies, they have great air forces, and they have expanding fleets. In addition, they have kept their industrial organisation concentrated on the war effort. We are not doing that. There is no time to lose. You cannot win a war with 800,000 unemployed. The winning of a war is a conscious process. You must reduce the manufacture of goods which are not necessary, and turn over your production to the war effort. It is no use relying on appeals. You have to do that as a deliberate act. People speak as if you could maintain an export trade in an unlimited manner. Surely, your export trade must be kept at as low a level as is compatible – in addition to your other resources – with paying for the goods you must import. The whole of your industrial machine must be concentrated primarily on the war effort.

Hore-Belisha was to follow Churchill's movements throughout the war with the avidity of a terrier on the scent. There did seem at the time – and to some extent there does still in retrospect – a carping element to much of the criticism of Churchill. Churchill himself thought this. But this was never true of Hore-Belisha; he was meticulous in his objectivity. He never showed the slightest personal animosity to his target, praising as well as criticizing, which is more than can be said of the other critics, mainly drawn from the right of the Conservative Party and the left of the Labour Party. For years before the war the two men had been friends, having met first when Hore-Belisha had been only eleven years old. But the relationship had become tarnished during the 'Sandys Affair' of 1938, when Churchill's son-in-law was supposed to have improperly had secret information about London's defences. Churchill had defended Sandys, and Hore-Belisha had got the worst of it. Churchill was supposed, by the Press, to have been one of his enemies when War Minister, but he had in fact often supported Hore-Belisha in the House. Hore-Belisha's resignation speech, described by Churchill as possessing 'masterly dignity', had been delivered after consulting Churchill's Gallipoli resignation speech.

By the first week of September it was evident to Hitler that the conquest of the R.A.F. was failing. The Luftwaffe was itself in danger. It was decided to switch from the attacks on airfields to the bombing of industrial and other cities at night. The Battle of Britain was nearly over. But the Blitz was about to begin.

Churchill, like Goering, was also a believer in bombing strategy. Over two months previously, on 8 July, he had written to Beaverbrook: 'When I look round to see how we can win the war I see that there is only one sure path. We have no Continental army which can defeat the German military power. The blockade is broken and Hitler has Asia and probably Africa to draw from. Should he be repulsed here or not try invasion, he will recoil eastward, and we have nothing to stop him. But there is one thing that will bring him back and bring him down, and that is an absolutely devastating, exterminating attack by very heavy bombers from this country upon the Nazi homeland.'

In the field of bombing, the R.A.F. had already been mor active than the Luftwaffe.

American correspondent, Berlin, 3 September 1940:

The local papers again rage against the 'British criminals' for having bombed us last night. The *Nachtausgabe* bannerlines: 'New Night Act of the Pirates'. The same paper editorialises: 'Winston Churchill again yesterday gave British airmen the order to drop their bombs on the German civilian population and thus continue their murder of German men, women, and children.' The *Börsen Zeitung* holds that 'last night Churchill continued the series of his criminal blows against the German civil population. Frankly, Churchill belongs to that category of criminals who in their stupid brutality are unteachable.'

In the first two weeks of September there were 10,000 civilian casualties in Britain from air attack; there were 250 service casualties from all causes in the same period. During this month the country waited again calmly for invasion.

Brooke, 6 September 1940:

Told that P.M. had gone to rest. Finally sat down to dinner at 9 ... P.M. warmed up and was most entertaining for rest of evening. First of all he placed himself in the position of Hitler and attacked these shores while I defended them. He then revised the whole of the air-raid warning system and gave us his proposals to criticise. Finally at 1.45 a.m. we got off to bed.

7 September 1940:

All reports look like invasion getting nearer. Ships collecting, dive-bombers being concentrated, parachutists captured, also four Dutchmen on the coast.

6 September 1940:

All reports still point to the probability of an invasion starting between the 8th and 10th of this month.

In a broadcast on 11 September Churchill warned the country of impending invasion.

A woman in London, 12 September 1940:

When the barrage made sustained conversation out of the power of any but the loudest shouters, I turned back to the verbatim report of the P.M.'s broadcast and went through it to see how far the printed word could reproduce the orator's effect and by what means, other than those of voice, manner and, above all, timing, that effect had been secured. In the first place, though there was no announcement: no revelation: no *news* in it, an impression of being taken into the speaker's confidence was given from the outset, by the simple device of quoting figures in such a way as to give them the full status of inside, official information. *You will understand* (our flattered attention is at once roused) *that whenever the weather is favourable waves of German bombers, protected by fighters, often 300 or 400 at a time, surge over this island, especially the promontory of Kent.* Last week's news grows fresh at that 'surge' and 'the promontory of Kent' becomes a strategic point whose importance has hitherto been kept from our knowledge. Relieved from the anonymity of 'certain areas', 'a town on the South-East coast', 'a well-known public building', which dulls the news bulletins from seven in the morning to midnight, we accept the Prime Minister's next disclosures: the Straits of Dover; the Bay of Biscay; the Grenadier Guards, as proof of his well-founded, and nobly expressed conviction that *he*, at any rate, can trust us. The device seems simple enough, but only a great orator has the cunning to use it and the restraint not to repeat it, once it has made its effect. The statement of facts made, a transition to conjecture follows and, as the imagined but not imaginary danger is presented, long successions of monosyllables beat on the ear like the sound of an army marching to drums. *We cannot tell when they will try to come. We can not be sure that in fact they will try at all. But no one should blind himself to the fact that a heavy, full-scale invasion*... As the oration goes on each period closes on this marching rhythm, single notes interspersed with the dissyllable which in music breaks the monotony and gives elastic rhythm to its beat: *Who have been born to value freedom far above their lives*... *He has lighted a fire which will burn*... *until the Old World and the New can join hands*... *A victory won not only for ourselves but for all – a victory won not only for our own time but for the long and better days that are to come.* It sounds simple enough, but how few men can do it, and how few leaders speaking on such an occasion would have had the judgement and restraint to set the prayer 'Let God defend the right' in the heart and not at the end of their oration? And last, but most effective of all, the monosyllable 'I' occurs only four times in all the sixteen hundred words.

Brooke:

15 September. Still no move on the part of the Germans. This coming week must remain a critical one, and it is hard to see how Hitler can now retrace his steps and stop this invasion. The suspense of waiting is very trying, especially when one is familiar with the weakness of one's defences. Our exposed coast line is just twice the length of the front that we and the French were holding in France.

On 17 September with the Blitz well under way, but the R.A.F. still strong and unconquered, Hitler postponed the invasion of England indefinitely. On the same day, Churchill, conscious of a desire for critical debate in the House, appealed to Members of Parliament, in Secret Session, for their co-operation. 'There are some things which it is better for us to talk over among ourselves than when we are overheard by the Germans... I must appeal to the House to show its consideration for Ministers, and for a Government in whom it has recorded its confidence almost unanimously. We are really doing our very best. There are no doubt many mistakes and shortcomings. A lot of things are done none too well. Some things that ought to be done have not yet been done. Some things have been done that had better have been left undone ... The deployment of the enemy's invasion preparations and the assembly of his ships and barges is steadily proceeding, and at any moment a major assault may be launched upon this island ... Upwards of seventeen hundred self-propelled barges and more than two hundred sea-going ships are already gathered at the many invasion ports ... I am confident that we shall succeed in defeating and largely destroying this most tremendous onslaught by which we are now threatened, and anyhow, whatever happens, we will all go down fighting to the end ... I ask the House to assist us in solving these problems, worse than any that have ever threatened a civilized community before, by meeting the wishes of the government in the arrangement of Parliamentary business and in lightening the burden which rests upon the men in charge.' The concessions which Churchill asked, including the abandonment of morning sittings and 'not requiring too many sittings in the next month or two', were granted. But news of a Secret Session caused much unnecessary alarm among the public.

On 3 August Churchill had given his approval to a landing of Free French forces at Dakar on the coast of West Africa. It was a scheme which, being amphibious, was almost irresistible to him. The expedition was the most ridiculous fiasco of the war. At the last minute, surprise having been lost, Churchill got cold feet and wanted to abandon it. About everything possible had gone wrong. There had been incredible muddle. De Gaulle insisted on going ahead. Amid great confusion he tried to land his troops on 23 September and on 25 September. The Vichy French defended furiously, damaging a number of British ships. Churchill personally called off the attack on the afternoon of 25 September, when the whole affair was in danger of becoming a humiliating farce.

Churchill admitted that, 'At home there were many complaints of faulty war direction.' In Australia there was a crisis, for the episode seemed indicative of many of the faults of the First World War and of the confusion at Gallipoli in particular. The Australian Prime Minister, Robert Menzies, was outraged. He sent one of the most curt messages that Churchill received during his premiership.

Menzies to Prime Minister,[1] 29 September 1940:

We are very disturbed in regard to Dakar incident, which has had unfortunate effect in Australia. First, as to matter of substance: it is difficult to understand why attempt was made unless overwhelming chances of success. To make what appears at this distance to be a half-hearted attack is to incur a damaging loss of prestige. Second, as to matter of procedure: it is absolutely wrong that Australian Government should know practically nothing of details of engagement and nothing at all of decision to abandon it until after newspaper publication. I have refrained from any public criticism, but privately can tell you that absence of real official information from Great Britain has frequently proved humiliating. Finally, I must say frankly that Australian Government profoundly hopes difficulties have not been under-estimated in the Middle East, where clear-cut victory is essential.

Churchill retaliated with a few sallies ('I thought indeed that from the way my name was used in the [recent Australian] election quite a good opinion was entertained in Australia of [my] efforts'), but the row was well patched up. As for the House of Commons: 'I decided that no explanations should be offered, and Parliament respected my wish.'

On 21 October Churchill broadcast in French to the people of France: 'Remember we shall never stop, never weary, and never give in, and that our whole people and empire have vowed themselves to the task of cleansing Europe from the Nazi pestilence... Good night then: sleep to gather strength for the morning. For the morning will come.'

After Dakar – a sigh from the past.

Neville Chamberlain was sick and in pain. He retired from the Government on 30 September; Churchill had earlier refused to accept his resignation ('I could ensure him more support politically, than anyone else'). On 17 October he wrote to Baldwin, who was living in Worcestershire, virtually a recluse and even almost ostracized:

In September '38 we only had 60 fire pumps in London, which would have been burned out in a week. Some day these things will be known.

---

[1] Entered Victoria State Parliament, 1928; House of Representatives, 1934; Prime Minister of Australia, 1939–41 and 1949–66.

My critics differed from me because they were ignorant . . . I regret nothing in the past. I do regret that I should be cut off when I feel capable of doing much more were it not for physical disability. But I accept what I can't help and hope I shan't cumber the earth too long. I doubt if I shall ever visit Brum again.[1]

He died three weeks later.

On Halifax's recommendation, Churchill was elected Leader of the Conservative Party on 9 October – perhaps his greatest political mistake, and a quite unthinkable circumstance only eighteen months previously. For some Tories, it was no more than a matter of formal convenience; to them, Churchill would never be the spiritual leader of a party with which he had grappled for so long.

Chamberlain's retirement led to ministerial changes. Sir John Anderson, a most industrious and reliable administrator, was brought into the War Cabinet to overlord all home affairs. 'This enabled me to concentrate upon the military conduct of the war, in which my colleagues seemed increasingly disposed to give me latitude.' It was an important disposition on their part. Herbert Morrison replaced Anderson at the Home Office, a splendid appointment. Morrison, another firm administrator, had been in Ramsay MacDonald's Cabinet of 1931; it was known to very few, even his colleagues, that he suffered from the handicap of total blindness in one eye. London was in the midst of the Blitz. Morrison was a Londoner, with a more intimate knowledge of London's affairs than any other man.

By now, Churchill had settled into his job. His routine was unusual for a Prime Minister, and was accepted by his colleagues with amusement, irritation, or bewilderment. He rose late, doing much paper work in bed; slept in the afternoon; attended the House or meetings; and often reserved the most important conferences, including Cabinet meetings, for as late as 11 p.m., continuing until nearly dawn. This was inconvenient for his colleagues, but it seems to have been an important factor in

---

[1] i.e. Birmingham, of which city, like his father, he had been Lord Mayor. A few months later Nevile Henderson, who had been Ambassador to Berlin and Chamberlain's chief supporter in the appeasement policy, also had cancer diagnosed; he was given six months to live, and died in 1942.

enabling him to master a mass of detail on a great variety of subjects, one of his greatest abilities, and to keep his mind fresh, agile, and constructive.

Apart from Beaverbrook and Smuts, 'he did not have many intimate friends among those with whom he had to conduct the war. He had followers, adherents, assistants, and a few respected colleagues. His intense concentration on the matter in hand left little time in wartime for trivialities or the cultivation of private friendship. He was of an earlier generation than most of those who surrounded him in the Cabinet or even in Parliament... And, of course, having been in the political wilderness for ten years before the war, he was intimate neither with the Conservative nor the Labour leaders.'[1] But there was mutual respect between himself and Attlee and Bevin (who entered the Cabinet in October); charges that Attlee was nothing more than a 'yes-man' have little foundation, and will be answered in time when the relevant records become available. More than anything, Churchill cherished connections with the past. At the time of the ministerial changes due to Chamberlain's retirement, he brought Oliver Lyttleton into the Government, as President of the Board of Trade (Sir Andrew Duncan having taken Morrison's place at the Ministry of Supply). Lyttleton was a businessman, son of a parliamentary friend of Churchill's before the First World War. He was not in Parliament, but Churchill brought him in and made him a Minister right away. This caused some resentment among those who believed war should be conducted as much like peace as possible.

On 15 October, a night of the full moon, a new tactic was employed in the Battle of London. About 480 German aircraft dropped 70,000 incendiary bombs, as well as the high-explosive bombs they had dropped hitherto.

Churchill was 'for' reprisal raids on non-military objectives (as he revealed in *The Finest Hour*). A Gallup Poll in October recorded 46 per cent against retaliatory bombing.

The ministerial changes had not found favour everywhere. The 'men of Munich' were still there. The running battle with the

---

[1] Comments of General Sir Ian Jacob.

Daily Mirror and *Sunday Pictorial* (under the same ownership) continued.

Cecil King, diary, 11 October 1940:

Cudlipp learned at dinner last night that Churchill had brought the *Pictorial* article by Cudlipp to the Cabinet, and the phrase in his speech about vicious and malignant criticism was inserted by general agreement.[1] The drift of the article was that in his recent governmental changes Churchill had shown the same dilatory, short-sighted, party-serving spirit as Chamberlain. Chamberlain, in fact, is dead: long live Chamberlain. And Cudlipp, who signed the article, wound up with a quotation from Churchill's book *World Crisis*, in which Winston says there are good grounds sometimes in peace for a vacillating or cautious policy, but in war decisions must be clear-cut and ruthless, no personal or party considerations must hamper the war effort, and so on. Cudlipp's concluding words were: 'Churchill, you have warned yourself.' Obviously the article was not likely to please Churchill, but I had no idea a storm was at all likely. It just shows what a guilty conscience the old man must have.

12 October 1940:

I was summoned by Cowley (Chairman of the *Mirror*) to the Board Room late yesterday afternoon and found him in consultation with Roome (*Mirror* director), 'Bart' (editor of the *Mirror*) and Esmond Harmsworth. It appeared that in the course of the morning Esmond, as Chairman of the Newspapers Proprietors' Association, had been asked to head a deputation representative of the Press to call on Attlee. He had turned up with Camrose and Southwood and found Attlee and Beaverbrook awaiting them. Attlee told them that the Cabinet had given attention to the Press at a recent meeting, with particular reference to the *Mirror* and *Pictorial*. He said that if criticism of the 'irresponsible kind' inserted in our papers were to continue the Government would introduce legislation making censorship of news *and* views compulsory. The N.P.A. deputation did not take to this suggestion at all kindly and said that compulsory censorship would wreck the Government, and be most damaging to the country's morale. Attlee had various cuttings with him – most of them were from Cassandra's[2] column,

---

[1] Hugh Cudlipp, editor of the *Sunday Pictorial*, 1937–40; Military Service, 1940–6; O.B.E., 1945. He revealed the *Mirror*–Churchill feud in his book *Publish and Be Damned!*. Chairman, Mirror Newspapers, 1963–.

[2] William Connor, the most readable and belligerent columnist of of his day. Knighted 1966; died 1967, on which occasion the *Mirror* reprinted his own ungrudging tribute to Churchill on the latter's death.

but one was from the 'Live Letter Box': the point about the latter being the very trivial technical one that it is illegal for a serving soldier to write to the Press without his commanding officer's permission, which had not been obtained. Attlee described the *Mirror* and *Pictorial* policy as 'subversive' and calculated to cause alarm and despondency at a very critical period. No great stress was laid on the cuttings themselves. The Government had no objection to criticism, said Attlee, but only to irresponsible criticism, and on what constituted irresponsible criticism he was vague or silent. I think if Attlee had told the deputation that if our papers continued their present line they would be prosecuted, the deputation would have cheered. But to threaten a general compulsory censorship would obviously damage the *Telegraph* and *Times* more than the *Mirror*, and was the one and only way of rallying the other papers to our support. Beaverbrook, incidentally, throughout this interview took the part of the honest broker, the friend of both sides.

While the criticism from home hurt, the verbal attacks from the enemy caused no trouble at all.

A woman in Winchester, October 1940:

I tried to listen to the Symphony Concert at eight o'clock. In the middle of *L'après-midi d'un faune* the voice of Haw-Haw filled the air from Milan to Beromünster. There was no getting any other noise. It declared that the Portal family had conspired with the Rothschilds to put Mr Churchill into power in order that the Insurance Companies might wring 100% profits out of the compulsory insurance against air-raids now being forced on the oppressed victims of Democratic Capitalism. Is the sneering contempt in this being's delivery of his lunacies directed against people like myself who are idiotic enough to listen to such poisonous nonsense?

As late in the year as 24 October, Alan Brooke, commanding Home Defence, was expecting an invasion. On 17 October he wrote in his diary: 'Evidence is amassing of an impending invasion.' In the spring of 1941 he was again expecting an invasion, and only then aware, apparently, of the dangers of a parachute attack on London.

All the autumn, the British people had waited for the Germans to parachute into the fields, to swarm over the beaches. But the Germans had not come.

American correspondent, Berlin, 31 October 1940:[1]

---

[1] William L. Shirer; journalist and broadcaster; author of *Berlin Diary*.

Piecing together today – long after the event – stray bits of conversation picked up here and there in Compiègne and Paris, I think the word had come down from Hitler that an invasion of Britain, though it must be quickly and thoroughly prepared, would never be necessary. Churchill would accept the kind of peace which the little Austrian was mulling over in his mind. It would be a Nazi peace, it would bar Great Britain from the continent of Europe at long last; it might be merely an armistice, a breathing-spell during which Germany could consolidate such overwhelming strength on the mainland that Britain in the end would have to bow to the Nazi conqueror without a fight – but it would be a face-saving peace for Churchill. And he would accept it. I believe Hitler really thought he would. And his certainty delayed and slackened the work which was necessary to prepare a devastating invasion force – the construction and concentration of barges, pontoons, shipping, and a thousand kinds of equipment ... The breathing-spell might also be used to settle accounts with Russia. Some observers in Berlin were convinced at the end of June that Hitler was sincerely anxious to conclude peace with Britain (on his own terms, of course) so that he could turn on the Soviet Union – always his long-term objective. Hitler, they believed, felt sure the British would understand this. Had not Chamberlain's policy been to encourage the German military machine to turn east against Russia? The fact that during the last days of June and throughout the first three weeks of July one German division after another was recalled from France and hurriedly transported to what the Germans usually referred to as the 'Russian front' would seem to bear this out. But it is by no means certain ... It may well be that Hitler expected Churchill to make the first move for peace. Didn't an Englishman know when he was beaten? Hitler would be patient and wait and let the realization sink into his thick British head. He waited a month. All through the last lovely week of June and the first three weeks of July he waited. In Berlin we heard rumours that contact had been made between Berlin and London at Stockholm and that peace was being talked but we never had any confirmation of them and in all probability there was nothing to them. On July 19 Hitler spoke out in the Reichstag. He publicly offered Britain peace, though concealing his terms. But the very fact that he devoted most of the session to promoting his leading generals to be field-marshals, as though the victorious war were in truth over, indicated that he still felt certain that Churchill would bid for peace. The Luftwaffe had been established on the North Sea and the Channel for more than a month, but German planes had refrained from any serious attacks on the land of Britain. Hitler was holding it back. I think the prompt and sweeping reaction in England to his 'offer of peace' came as a shock to him. He was not prepared for such a quick and unequivocal rejection. I think he hesitated until the end of July – twelve days – before he accepted that rejection as Churchill's final answer. By then a month and a half of precious time had been largely lost.

On the night of 3 November there was no air-raid alarm in London for the first time in nearly two months.

Harold Nicolson, diary, 5 November 1940:

The Prime Minister makes a statement after Question-time. He is rather grim. He brings home to the House as never before the gravity of our shipping losses and the danger of our position in the Eastern Mediterranean. It has a good effect. By putting the grim side foremost he impresses us with his ability to face the worst. He rubs the palms of his hands with five fingers extended up and down the front of his coat, searching for the right phrase, indicating cautious selection, conveying almost medicinal poise. If Chamberlain had spoken glum words such as these the impression would have been one of despair and lack of confidence. Churchill can say them and we all feel, 'Thank God that we have a man like that!' I have never admired him more. Thereafter he slouches into the smoking-room and reads the *Evening News* intently, as if it were the only source of information available to him.

In the middle of November, the German command changed its tactics yet again. Baffled by the resistance of London, and the size of the city, the Luftwaffe increasingly turned its attention to provincial cities, thus giving London several nights of welcome respite. Churchill considered this a mistake on the Germans' part. He was himself often to be seen visiting ruined and battered areas the day after a raid, encouraging, sympathizing, and producing his silent V-sign gesture, chin thrust forth, clambering over rubble with the aid of a sturdy stick.

Harold Nicolson, diary, 20 November 1940:

He seems better in health than he has ever seemed. That pale and globular look about his cheeks has gone. He is more solid about the face and thinner. But there is something odd about his eyes. The lids are not in the least weary, nor are there any pouches or black lines. But the eyes themselves are glaucous, vigilant, angry, combative, visionary and tragic. In a way they are the eyes of a man who is much preoccupied and is unable to rivet his attention on minor things (such as me). But in another sense they are the eyes of a man faced by an ordeal of tragedy, and combining vision, truculence, resolution and great happiness.

Ed. Murrow, broadcast, 1 December 1940:

There is occurring a certain change in the temper of the House of

Commons. Last week in the debates covering the question of manpower and production one had the feeling that Mr Churchill had lost but little of his hold over the House. At the same time it was clear that many members felt that the able and brilliant commander-in-chief had not surrounded himself with ministers willing to take the drastic steps necessary to reorganize the economy of the country. There is a fairly widespread demand that the government's compulsory powers be more fully used. The training of skilled workers and the slowness with which women have been introduced into industry were severely criticized. So far as the people of this country are concerned, there is every reason to believe that they would welcome a wider and speedier use of the government's compulsory powers. There is widespread realization that the breaking of Germany's counter-blockade is the most urgent of many problems and that it can only be done by increased production. There are still more people willing, anxious, and asking what they can do than there are those who complain that too much is being asked of them ... Others say more bluntly: 'The Americans say this is their war that we're fighting. If we're going to fight it, they ought to help pay for it.' Considerable surprise has been expressed over the amount of looting in bombing areas. It hasn't reached large-scale proportions, but the British are always surprised at any increase in lawlessness. The matter is further complicated by the fact that many of the articles picked up from the bombed houses are of little intrinsic value, a book or a piece of ribbon or a bucketful of coal – that sort of thing. Many people convicted of looting are certainly not criminal types and have not taken the objects for reasons of personal gain. One has a strange feeling, or at least I have, in looking at the contents of a bombed house or shop, that the things scattered about don't belong to anyone. It's as though they, together with the bomb, had just dropped out of the sky. Picking up a book or a pipe that's been blown into the street is almost like picking an apple in a deserted and overgrown orchard far from any road or house.

On 9 December Wavell attacked the Italians in the North African desert. It was the start of a famous victory.

Wavell had been hesitant, cautious, apprehensive about the results of the offensive. This had created a very bad effect on Churchill, who expected his generals to believe in their offensives, and to communicate optimism. There was a bitter row over this. But the battle was successful, and Churchill was generous in his praise. 'I send you my heartfelt congratulations on your splendid victory, which fulfils our highest hopes.' But he did not forget to press Wavell on, unabashed at teaching the most-respected soldier in the Army his business: 'Naturally, pursuit will hold the first place in your thoughts. It is the moment when the victor is most exhausted that the greatest forfeit can be exacted from the vanquished.'

Throughout 1940 Britain had been paying for all its war supplies from America on a cash-and-carry basis – much to the benefit of the American economy. Britain's dollars had nearly all been spent by the end of the year. The United States Treasury was reluctant to face up to the situation until the British Ambassador, Lord Lothian, arrived in New York from London on 8 December. He told the assembled Press: 'Well boys, Britain's broke. It's your money we want.'

This prepared President and public for Churchill's letter at the end of the year, in which he explained that Britain could survive or pay, but it could not do both at the same time.

On 12 December Lord Lothian died. Churchill twice asked Lloyd George, then aged seventy-seven, to take the job. It was an eccentric choice, for Lloyd George was not entirely popular abroad, and his heart was not in the war; on the advice of his doctor, he declined. Churchill then offered the post to Halifax, who had been reasserting himself in the War Cabinet.

Halifax was 'rather shattered' to learn that he was to be demoted and replaced by Eden at the Foreign Office. Nobody at that time really appreciated the importance with which Churchill viewed an Anglo-American alliance. Halifax fought hard against the idea. He even took his formidable wife to 10 Downing Street to argue against it:

Halifax, December 1940:

I have not often assisted at a more interesting interview. Dorothy began, with suitable apologies, by saying that she thought he was making a profound mistake ... although at the present Winston was at the height of his popularity and could do no wrong, he might later on strike a bad patch and there was nobody else at such a time who would be more loyal and perhaps able to help him with certain sections of opinion than I should. It was well done and Winston listened with the utmost attention.

But not done well enough. Lord and Lady Halifax departed for Washington on 14 January. And when 'the bad patch' did indeed come, it was not those 'certain sections' which were to bother Churchill as much as others over which Lord Halifax had no influence at all.

Halifax maintained a rather bemused, but genuine, affection for Churchill, although he did not care for Churchill's way of life; years later he wrote of Churchill 'leaving the room stinking like a third-class smoking carriage' (although it must be doubtful if Lord Halifax had ever travelled in such a carriage).

The only time Halifax had been in the United States was – typically – on the way back from Canada 'in 1905 or 1906'. He became a very able Ambassador. Almost in open defiance of the Press, Churchill appointed David Margesson, a prominent 'Munichite', as Eden's successor at the War Office.

At this time, unlike his opinion at the fall of France, Churchill seemed to think that Britain could win the war alone, providing it could use the United States as its arsenal. In his 'Give us the tools' broadcast, he said: 'This is not a war of vast armies, firing immense masses of shells at one another. We do not need the gallant armies which are forming throughout the American Union. We do not need them this year, nor next year, nor any year that I can foresee.' Churchill had been deeply impressed by the arguments of the R.A.F. For once, Churchill's prophesying was wrong; those 'gallant armies' would have to prove their gallantry in Normandy, on the Gothic Line, at the Ardennes . . .

It was Halifax's task to complete the work, begun by his predecessor, in negotiating Lend–Lease. The war had cost the country 4,500 million dollars cash, and 335 million dollars worth of American shares requisitioned from private people; but the supply was rapidly coming to an end. Roosevelt's problem was to persuade public and Congress.

Roosevelt, Press conference, 17 December 1940:

What I am trying to do is to eliminate the dollar sign. That is something brand new in the thoughts of practically everybody in this room, I think – get rid of the silly, foolish old dollar sign.

Like so much that the President said, it sounded quite easy. A motion for a negotiated peace was rejected in the House by 341 votes to 4.

Anthony Eden, diary, 19 December 1940:

Winston was tired but cheerful. We spoke of the dark days of the summer. I told him that Portal and I had confessed to each other that in our hearts we had both despaired at one time. Winston said: 'Yes. Normally I wake up buoyant to face the new day. Then I awoke with dread in my heart.'

The desert victory continued; supplied by the Royal Navy, supported by the outnumbered but victorious R.A.F., the Army raced on: over two hundred miles in six weeks, with the capture of 113,000 prisoners. At last, at long last, since that September Sunday when Britain had gone to war, there was a victory 'on the map' to bring encouragement and hope.

On 29 December London suffered its worst ordeal of the war: 'an incendiary classic', as Churchill described it, timed to coincide with the Thames dead-low-water hour. Nearly 1,500 fires had to be fought; eight of Wren's greatest churches were destroyed or seriously shattered; a large part of the business centre, the City, fortunately almost deserted of people, was obliterated.

Adolf Hitler, 31 December 1940:

Churchill is the same man who discovered in unrestricted aerial warfare the great secret of British victory. For three and a half months this criminal has been ordering German cities to be bombed by night.

The Battle of Britain had been won, and by diversifying his assault the enemy had tacitly admitted that he had lost the Battle of London. The victories in the air in August and September, in the cities in October and November, and in the desert in December, were the first dim light at the end of the tunnel of the Second World War. In each, morale had played a large part, and for this one man was responsible more than any others. In seven months of concentrated leadership he had personally lifted the nation off its knees, inspiring those in high office who were in daily conduct of the war and ordinary people who had never seen him.

One of the results of Churchill's inspired and invaluable performance of 1940 was that for the remainder of the war anyone criticizing him or his actions was liable to appear unpatriotic – as his most fervent supporters were never slow to point out. This gave Churchill a real advantage over any who disagreed with him.

Meanwhile, the Prime Minister continued with the role which he saw as his most important – Minister of Defence – without a

Ministry, without the skill or ability to co-ordinate the three Services, and with an interest in the affairs of the Army out of proportion to the true role of his office. It was certain to lead to some trouble; and so it did, before all became well in the end.

Adolf Hitler, New Year's Eve, 1940:

It is the will of the democratic war-inciters and their Jewish-capitalistic wire-pullers that the war must be continued... We are ready!... The year 1941 will bring completion of the greatest victory in our history.

The *Annual Register*, 1940:

Whatever might be their feelings with regard to the first half of 1940, the British people had every reason to look back on the second half with pride and satisfaction... Rarely in her history had she shown to better advantage than in raising herself out of the depths into which she had been plunged by the deprivation at a critical moment of French support and assistance... Under the inspiring leadership of Mr Churchill it finally cast off the slough which seemed to have settled on it at the time of the Munich agreement... Whatever might be in store for her in the coming year, there could be no question that a brilliant page of Britain's history had been written in the last seven months of 1940.

CHAPTER FIVE

1941 Old Soldier

Not untypical of the new attitude towards Winston Churchill was that of the King, who had formerly thought of him as the somewhat disreputable usurper of his friend Chamberlain.

George VI, Sandringham, 2 January 1941:

My dear Prime Minister ... I feel that it is wrong for me to be away from my place of duty, when everybody else is carrying on. However, I must look upon it as medicine ... I do hope and trust you were able to have a little relaxation at Chrismas with all your arduous work. I have so much admired all you have done during the last seven months as my Prime Minister, and I have so enjoyed our talks together during our weekly luncheons. I hope they will continue on my return, as I do look forward to them so much.

In his reply Churchill said, flamboyantly but with accuracy, 'This war has drawn the Throne and the people more closely together than was ever before recorded, and Your Majesties are more beloved by all classes and conditions than any of the princes of the past.'

Hector Bolitho, author, diary, 1941:

I lunched at Holland House, which has since been bombed. After lunch, I was sitting next to Mr Churchill: the talk moved to the King and Queen, then at the beginning of their war work and influencing the country with their quiet example. Somebody at the table tried to define their influence and Mr Churchill, with his genius for quickening the occasion with the right phrase, said, 'Yes, they have the rare talent of being able to make a mass of people realize, in a flash, that they are good.'

Jan Christian Smuts,[1] 12 January 1941:

---

[1] Began career with brilliant undergraduate record at Cambridge; lawyer; commanded Boer forces, Cape Colony, 1901; C.-in-C., East Africa, 1916–17; Minister, Union of South Africa, 1910–19; Prime

If Churchill wins this war, the English will revise their opinion about cleverness. They won't think it so clever not to be clever. They won't think it so reliable not to be clever. They thought Churchill unreliable. It was the accepted thing, in the old days, to call Churchill unreliable. If Churchill pulls England out of this mess she's in, he'll be the greatest man in English history.

Meanwhile – there was the *Daily Mirror*.

Cecil King to the Prime Minister, 24 January 1941:

Cassandra is a hard-hitting journalist with a vitriolic style, but I can assure you his attitude to neither you personally nor to Mr Eden is in any way 'malevolent'. Quite the contrary. Though we continue to take an unflattering view of some of your colleagues, our criticisms are only directed to the fact that the nation's war effort is less intense than it might be – less intense than it would be if more young men were employed in positions of real authority.

Prime Minister to Cecil King, 25 January 1941:

There is a spirit of hatred and malice against the government, which after all is not a party government but a national government almost unanimously chosen, which spirit surpasses anything I have ever seen in English journalism. One would have thought in these hard times that some hatred might be kept for the enemy . . .

Cecil King, diary, 30 January 1941:

Winston went into the Cabinet room by another door and was standing up by the fire when I came in. He sat me at the table at his right hand and off we started. Outside, German planes came over singly at intervals (it was a cloudy, misty day) and the guns in St James's Park, heavy and Bofors, banged away. When a plane came very near he stopped his talk and listened and twice seemed on the point of retreating to his shelter, but did not do so. Winston himself looked older and more lined than when I saw him last, but if anything tougher. He started off with a great tirade and returned often to the same theme. The gist of his remarks was that our policy constituted a very clever form of fifth columnism – praising the P.M., pressing for an intensification of our war effort, but at the same time magnifying grievances, vilifying

---

Minister, 1919–24; Minister, 1933–9; Prime Minister, 1939–48; great statesman, who helped to form British Commonwealth and League of Nations, but inflated military reputation based on special conditions of Boer War; stubborn supporter of Passchendaele offensive, 1917; one of the founders of the R.A.F.; suggested he should command the U.S. Army in France, 1918; died 1950.

Ministers and generally creating a distrust by the nation for its leaders. That this 'rocking of the boat' (his phrase) might well have disastrous results for the nation. What were we doing it for, anyway? I protested that we supported him as much as we ever had and that we supported many of his Ministers, but others we thought unworthy of high office and said so. Did this mean, he asked, that we arrogated to ourselves the right of appointing Ministers of the Crown? I said No, but surely loyalty to him as P.M. did not carry with it loyalty to Attlee as Lord Privy Seal? He conceded this point, more or less. He said our papers had been the subject of much discussion, that much research had been undertaken into the ownership of our shares; some of his colleagues were convinced that there was something or someone behind it all. I said there was nothing – there were five executive directors, of whom I was one. As I was more interested in politics than the others, the politics were largely left to me. 'Well,' he said, 'you look innocent enough!' He said he didn't mind attacks on the government; it was the malignancy of the attacks that annoyed him. They had contemplated a prosecution and also denunciation in a speech on the wireless, but had thought these measures out of proportion ... He said he had never taken back what he had said about the appeasers, but that M.P.s who had supported Chamberlain still formed a majority of 150 in the House and that he was not going to fight them as they were too numerous.

In January 1941, Roosevelt sent Harry Hopkins as special emissary to Churchill.[1] The President was a great believer in the usefulness of emissaries. Churchill preferred to be his own emissary, and to work at the summit; but, of necessity, he did his best with Hopkins – and made a quick and important conquest. From Claridges Hotel, Hopkins reported to Roosevelt:

Number 10 Downing St. is a bit down at the heels because the Treasury next door has been bombed more than a bit. The Prime Minister is no longer permitted to sleep here and I understand sleeps across the street. He told me they are building a real shelter for him so that he can sleep in peace near by. Everyone tells me that he works fifteen hours a day and I can well believe it. His man Friday – Brendan Bracken – met me at the door – showed me about the old and delightful house that has been home of Prime Ministers of the Empire for two hundred years. Most of the windows are out – workmen over the place repairing the damage – Churchill told me it wouldn't stand a healthy bomb. Bracken led me to a little dining-room in the basement – poured me some sherry

---

[1] Secretary of Commerce, 1938–40; special adviser to the President, 1940–5; died 1946.

and left me to wait for the Prime Minister. A rotund – smiling – red-faced gentleman appeared – extended a fat but none the less convincing hand and wished me welcome to England. A short black coat – striped trousers – a clear eye and a mushy voice was the impression of England's leader as he showed me with obvious pride the photographs of his beautiful daughter-in-law and grandchild. The lunch was simple but good – served by a very plain woman who seemed to be an old family servant. Soup – cold beef – (I didn't take enough jelly to suit the P.M. and he gave me some more) – green salad – cheese and coffee – a light wine and port. He took snuff from a little silver box – he liked it. I told him the President was anxious to see him in April – he expressed regret that Bermuda would not be the place – the climate was nice – he would bring a small staff – go on a cruiser and by accident meet the President at the appointed place – and discuss our problems at leisure. He talked of remaining as long as two weeks and seemed very anxious to meet the President face to face. We discussed the difficulty of communication with the President at long range – there is no question but that he wants to meet the President – the sooner the better. I told him there was a feeling in some quarters that he, Churchill, did not like America, Americans or Roosevelt. This set him off on a bitter though fairly constrained attack on Ambassador Kennedy, whom he believes is responsible for this impression. He denied it vigorously ... Germany cannot invade Britain successfully. He thinks Hitler may use poison gas, but if they do England will reply in kind killing man for man – 'for we too have the deadliest gases in the world' ... He thinks Greece is lost – although he is now reinforcing the Greeks – and weakening his African Army ... He knows this will be a blow to British prestige and is obviously considering ways and means of preparing the British public for it ... he looks forward with our help to mastery in the air and then Germany with all her armies will be finished. He believes that this war will never see great forces massed against one another.

Later that week, Hopkins continued:

Dear Mr President ... The people here are amazing from Churchill down, and if courage alone can win – the result will be inevitable. But they need our help desperately, and I am sure you will permit nothing to stand in the way. Some of the ministers and underlings are a bit trying, but no more than some I have seen. *Churchill* is the gov't in every sense of the word – he controls the grand strategy and often the details – labour trusts him – the army, navy, air force are behind him to a man. The politicians and upper crust pretend to like him. I cannot emphasize too strongly that he is the one and only person over here with whom you need to have a full meeting of minds. Churchill wants to see you – the sooner the better – but I have told him of your problem until the bill [Lend–Lease] is passed. I am convinced this meeting between you and Churchill is essential – and soon – for the battering continues and Hitler does not wait for Congress. I was with Churchill at 2 a.m. Sunday night when he got word of the loss of the *Southampton* – the serious damage to the new aircraft carrier (*Illustrious*) – a second cruiser knocked about – but he never falters or displays the least despondence – till four o'clock he paced the floor telling me of his offensive and defensive plans. I cannot believe that it is true that Churchill dislikes either you or America – it just doesn't make sense. Churchill is prepared for a setback in Greece – the African campaign will proceed favourably – German bombers in the Mediterranean make the fleet's operation more difficult – convoys must all go around the Cape. An invasion, they feel sure, can be repelled – Churchill thinks it will not come soon, but Beaverbrook and others think it will come and soon. This island needs our help now, Mr President, with everything we can give them. There is no time to be out of London, so I am staying here – the bombs aren't nice and seem to be quite impersonal. I have been offered a so-called bombproof apartment by Churchill – a tin hat and gas mask have been delivered – the best I can say for the hat is that it looks worse than my own and doesn't fit – the gas mask I can't get on – so I am all right... Harry.

And again:

Your 'former Navy person' is not only the Prime Minister, he is the directing force behind the strategy and the conduct of the war in all its essentials. He has an amazing hold on the British people of all classes and groups. He has particular strength both with the military establishments and the working people. The most important single observation I have to make is that most of the Cabinet and all of the military leaders here believe that invasion is imminent. They are straining every effort night and day to meet this. They believe that it may come at any moment, but not later than May 1. They believe that it will certainly be an all-out attack, including the use of poison gas and perhaps some other new weapons that Germany may have developed. The spirit of this people and their determination to resist invasion is beyond praise. No matter how fierce the attack may be you can be sure that they will resist it, and effectively. The Germans will have to do more than kill a few hundred thousand people here before they can defeat Britain.

This visit of Hopkins's succeeded in undoing the bad impression and misunderstandings created – on both sides of the Atlantic – by the Ambassador.

An admiral, Portsmouth, 1 February 1941:

I have an interesting day with the Prime Minister to tell you about. He came with Mrs Churchill, Mr Hopkins, Ismay and Harold Butler yesterday. I met them at Southampton, and we toured the town and the docks. The High Street was impressive, few buildings still stood, but it is not such a striking scene of demolition as King's Road. We lunched in the train to Portsmouth, and after a tour of the Dockyard, the Lord Mayor joined us and we toured the City. The Prime Minister was indefatigable and, as usual, had a rousing reception in the Dockyard. He made a very good speech after tea at the Beach Hotel, the new Civic Centre. Mr Hopkins is a very quietly-spoken man who leaves an impression of considerable latent powers. I had an interesting talk with him in the train. At one stop he decided to stay in the car and have a pause, and I was not surprised as the Prime Minister is quite tireless, and insists on walking as much as possible and going on board any ship he sees. He still looked quite fresh when we said goodbye to him at the station, though he had been on the go since early morning.

Quentin Reynolds, after dinner at Chequers, February 1941:[1]

His conversation was like a chameleon on a rock. It dated back into antiquity; it touched on Greece and that reminded him of a canto in *Don Juan* and he talked of Byron; it somehow stretched halfway across the world to India, and that reminded him of Kipling. 'I've got a lot from Kipling,' he said enthusiastically. 'Ah, there was a singer of songs! But, of course, there was only one. I mean Shakespeare. Do you remember in *Hamlet* when . . .' On and on his sonorous voice rolled. He was acting the part now. He was Hamlet, and not a word in a long passage did he miss . . . 'Rupert Brooke. Do you remember that lovely thing he wrote called *The Fish*? [Churchill quoted at length] . . . He went on, and something Hopkins said awakened a memory of Thomas Moore, and from the store of that incredible memory there came forth stanza after stanza of Moore. And then, amazingly, Bret Harte, and he laughed because neither Hopkins nor I could recall the passage he quoted . . . We went upstairs to the room where a projection booth had been installed. The picture, we all agreed was the best film to come out of the war. *Target for Tonight* is the honest, sincere story of the bomber pilots. Churchill smoked and was as tense as any movie fan when things looked bad for the bomber that was over Germany. He chuckled when the bombs hit the Nazi target; he breathed with relief when the pilots returned safely . . . The Prime Minister walked to the door with me. It was a dark night. The rain still slanted down dismally. 'Sure now you

---

[1] Reynolds, ace war correspondent, of *Collier's Weekly*, was embarrassed to discover that he and the Prime Minister alone were not wearing dinner-jackets. But Churchill observed: 'It's easy to see which two men in the room worked all afternoon.'

won't have a drink before you go?' . . . The car pulled away. I looked back. Just for the moment the Prime Minister had forgotten the blackout. He stood there in the huge Gothic doorway, and the dim light from the hall silhouetted him – sturdy, rock-like, immovable. He stuck his cigar in the corner of his mouth at a jaunty angle. His hands were dug deep into the pockets of his blue 'rompers'.

Hopkins returned to Washington with an unusual souvenir: a bottle of Churchill's pills – presented to him for the good of his health by the Prime Minister. Roosevelt ordered that they should be analysed at the Naval Medical Centre. Hopkins noted in his diary:

I am told by the Navy that the whole prescription is a conglomeration of everything that couldn't do anybody much harm. It couldn't possibly do them very much good either.

Sir Charles Wilson, later the same year:

Whenever we are alone, he keeps asking me to take his pulse. I get out of it somehow, but once when I found him lifting something heavy I did expostulate. At this he broke out: 'Now, Charles, you are making me heart-minded. I shall soon think of nothing else. I couldn't do my work if I kept thinking of my heart.' The next time he asked me to take his pulse I refused point-blank. 'You're all right. Forget your damned heart.'

During 1941, German propaganda directed against Churchill became increasingly wild and frantic.

Dr Robert Ley, Leader of the German Labour Front, wrote in *Westdeutscher Beobachter*, 29 January 1941:

Churchill is an obstinate and senile liar. He is a fraud, predisposed to cruelty and brutality, and with no thought for the lives and property of his fellow men. This criminal tendency runs as an unmistakable red thread through his entire life, and now in his old age it has turned him into a grinning gargoyle.

Two days later Goebbels wrote in *Das Reich*:

It is a tragedy for the British nation that it backs Churchill and has linked its fate with his. Churchill, however, will perish by this war, and the curses of the millions whom he has led astray will follow him to his grave. Churchill wants this war for the sake of war; he fostered and prepared it out of his destructive instinct.

Goebbel's concern for 'the British nation' and for Churchill's political career received the ridicule it deserved in Britain – and the propaganda of the man described by some as 'the master propagandist' was too clumsy to have much effect on his own countrymen, who regarded Churchill with increasing awe as the war progressed. As a propagandist Goebbels had the technique of a sledge-hammer employed to adjust time-pieces.

Later in the year, the German radio broadcast the following revelation:

All the books and articles by Churchill published during the past forty years have attracted the attention of the psychiatrist. They are the documents of a pathological liar. Ever since Churchill personally, through a stooge, has directed the course of the English mouth offensive, Great Britain utters only pathological gibbering lies. We can only welcome this. Our news thereby becomes even more effective.

On 6 February John G. Winant replaced Joseph Kennedy as Ambassador. He got on well with Churchill, despite his quiet, retiring nature. He considered the Prime Minister 'an old-fashioned Whig'. Three months after his appointment there were strong rumours of peace negotiations, especially in America. Winant was said to be negotiating terms. Roosevelt put an end to the rumours at a Press conference.

London columnist,[1] 18 March 1941:

Gloriously sunny day. Went to the Pilgrims' lunch, where the Prime Minister and Winant made speeches. Next day I wrote: Tall and shaggy-haired, like a sensitive protective collie compared with the belligerent bulldog appearance of Mr Winston Churchill, Mr Winant spoke with a sincerity unbelievably rare and utterly opposed to the smart aleck Big-Business-cum-Hollywood grin of Mr Joseph Kennedy, his predecessor. It had seemed almost impossible for anyone to follow adequately the magnificent speech of the Prime Minister in which Mr Churchill's sonorous phrases about the ocean-borne trumpet-call alternated brilliantly with the way in which he was either grinding out his implacable determination to repel the Nazis or light-heartedly disclosing front-page news such as the sinking of three U-boats in one day ... it seemed hopeless to think that the dark young Ambassador could maintain the same standard of oratory. But he did. And when he had finished, a hard-boiled American reporter gulped at me, 'That's a hell of a speech,' while Lord Kemsley said, 'Have you ever heard such sincerity? You could not buy a word from that man with all the money in the world.'

---

[1] Charles Graves, of the *Daily Mail*.

Diana Cooper, Ditchley, where Churchill spent some weekends, letter to her son, 19 February 1941:

On Sunday a flood of Poles rushed in – President Sikorski, the Polish Ambassador and some other sledded Polacks.[1] After lunch the little procession, headed by Winston, followed by the upstanding Poles ... walked off to a private room for a conference on Polish publicity. It took an interminable time and when at last it ended and the Poles were due to move home, the Prime Minister suddenly thought that the President should have a guard of honour. Secretaries and A.D.C.s went tearing round trying to find the Captain of the Guard, but he was sleeping or walking and could not be found, so Winston himself finally roused out some rather raw, inexperienced soldiers, who had never formed a guard of honour before. Meanwhile the patient Poles were sitting on the doorstep waiting for their guard to arrive, and the President said: 'Mr Churchill is so great a man that we must let him do what amuses him.' I tried to remember things that the Prime Minister said that would interest you, but my brain is like a sieve and I can only think of one thing which I thought very touching and disclaiming of his power. When I said that the best thing he had done was to give the people courage, he said: 'I never gave them courage; I was able to focus theirs.' He also talks glibly of the war in 1943 and 1944, which causes me to tingle with terror and tedium. We had two lovely films after dinner and there were several short reels from Papa's Ministry. Winston managed to cry through all of them, including the comedy.

On 10 March there was an unusually heavy air-raid on London. The House of Commons was destroyed.[2]

Smuts, 1941:

Will there be reprisals for the air-raids? Certainly there will. The English themselves may not call them reprisals. No, they're bombing military objectives! They don't like to admit – and, in fact, they don't like – ugly necessities. But do you think Churchill the man to accept the bombing of London without retaliation? The Germans, believe me, will be sorry they ever began to bomb London.

---

[1] Polish General and Head of the Government-in-Exile. At the centre of an incident with Russia, in April 1943, concerning the massacre of Katyn. Churchill was inclined to believe Russian protestations. Relations between the Polish Government and the U.S.S.R. were broken off, and never recovered. Sikorski died at the height of the crisis in a plane crash.

[2] The Commons sat in the House of Lords for the rest of the war.

But at this time Churchill's mind was more occupied with a more vital matter. Would America forego payment of its armaments and materials? Because for Britain this was the most important question of the war.

Dorothy Thompson, a much respected American reporter, explained the underlying political difficulties better than anyone else:

It is in the interest of our mutual understanding of each other, which is one of the most important hopes for our comradeship in arms and in reconstruction, that the position of our isolationists should be understood as objectively as possible. The United States has really come of age only in the last generation. Before the last war we were actually a debtor of Europe. The American struggle through a century and a half has been to get loose from Europe. We are a nation of immigrants – that is to say, a population which, one by one, came to us precisely because it wished to escape from Europe – from its militarism, its poverty, its overcrowding, and its eternal wars. Precisely because each of us is in some way dragged back by Europe – by memories, by relatives near or distant, by inherited traditions – our tendency is to steel ourselves against Europe, as a possibly dividing force. We can all think as Americans, but the moment we start to think in European terms, some of us are bound to think as Germans, others as Scandinavians, and others to remember vividly our British inheritance. Furthermore, the basic Anglo-Saxon elements in our population have been greatly diluted by the immigration of the last sixty years, and, unfortunately, even more diluted in the ranks of the rising class of the twentieth century, namely, the ranks of the workers. The hard backbreaking work in America, on the farms, in the mines, on the railroads, and in the factories, has not been done by those of Anglo-Saxon stock, who have occupied for the most part middle-class professions and positions, but by Germans and Scandinavians, Russians and Poles, Czechs and Finns. The children of these stocks are coming into their own with America's coming of age, and they bring a different mind to things than do the British. In this particular war, the fact that Britain emerges as the defender of these peoples, rather than the defender of her own Empire merely, is perhaps the greatest asset that Britain has with this new America. The American of Polish, or Scandinavian or Czech origin is undoubtedly friendlier to Britain than he has ever been in his life, because for the first time he sees the British cause as the cause of the common people everywhere. But the isolationist spirit – the desire to concentrate on building America itself, as the hope of the world; an almost fatigued impatience with Europe – is very fundamental. It expresses itself in the phrase, 'Why should our boys die on foreign soil?' It is very difficult for me to be tolerant at all of the attitude of Mr Lindbergh who, as much as any man alive, should understand the rapid contraction of the world through the development of aviation. Mr Lindbergh's attitude can only be considered logical if he goes the whole way, recognises that America is part of the world and not off on some other planet, and admits openly that he is pro-German and pro-Nazi, as I think he is.

Dorothy Thompson's usual role was explaining the British to the Americans. This she had been doing with rather an excess of high-pitched emotion (the R.A.F. was 'a kind of order – an order of chivalry'). For this she had received some cutting, almost abusive criticism from a less diffuse reporter, Ed. Murrow.

Ed. Murrow, broadcast, 9 March 1941:

So long as Winston Churchill is Prime Minister the House of Commons will be given an opportunity to defend its traditions and to determine the character of the government that is to rule this country. The Prime Minister will continue to be criticized in private for being too much interested in strategy and too little concerned with the great social and economic problems that clamour for solution.

On 11 March the Lend–Lease Bill was signed by the President. It was a death-warrant for Adolf Hitler.

President Roosevelt, speech, 15 March:

The British people are braced for invasion whenever the attempts may come – tomorrow – next week – next month. In this historic crisis, Britain is blessed with a brilliant and a great leader in Winston Churchill. But no one knows better than Mr Churchill himself that it is not alone his stirring words and valiant deeds which give the British their superb morale. The essence of that morale is in the masses of plain people who are completely clear in their minds about the one essential fact – that they would rather die as free men than live as slaves.

R. D. Holt, formerly Senator for West Virginia, *Scribner's Commentator*, July 1941:

Now that President Roosevelt has committed our country to partnership with England's Winston Churchill, we should come to know better the ideals and the past record of this partner who is to help our President carry the four freedoms throughout the world . . . Prime Minister Churchill has been called the world's greatest statesman. He is pictured as a Sir Galahad who is riding forth to save the world from all evil. He is painted as a devoted lover of liberty and democracy . . . His record is not one which could be called just that.

Holt went on to examine Churchill's career. He noted that from the time of the Mahdi in the Sudan, the Prime Minister always seemed to have been on the side of imperialist reaction. By 1945 this sort of conclusion formed the background to the foreign policy of the United States.

Anonymous American statesman:[1]

There is a growing feeling that American people have been bamboozled ... because of misgivings expressed here, came a series of statements that they [the British] didn't want Americans in the war: 'Give us the tools and we will do the job.' Then came the final step of saying that America must come into the war ... We have consented to measures that will lead to inflation and to bankruptcy for most of us – to a complete change in the American way of living. We have done this and suddenly we find ourselves being criticised for not having done something we have been specifically told by the Prime Minister would not be expected of us. That is generally resented ... There has been a little too much of the argument that this is a 'British problem' and that Americans haven't any business not agreeing with any course that suits Mr Churchill. Many Americans feel that this is not exclusively a British problem ... There is a general impression that British agencies – to put it tactfully – are being a little too active ... There is resentment that British agencies brand as isolationists all Americans who do not clamour for war. The word itself has lost most of its meaning and has become a term of abuse. It is applied to all sorts of people who advocate generous help to Britain but who are opposed to going to war. In many cases this is due to a conviction that we can best aid Britain by staying out – to a deep-rooted conviction that the protection of this country at war would result in a drying-up of the flow of equipment to England.

In March 1941, Churchill was chosen as 'Man of the Year' by *Time* magazine. In its favourite portentous prose, the magazine declared:

He gave his countrymen exactly what he promised them: blood, toil, tears, sweat, and one thing more – untold courage. Those burning words summed up the nature of Britain's war, turned Britain's back on the weaknesses of the past, and set her face toward an unknown future.

Time's latent anglophobia had never before been put so unreservedly aside.

---

[1] As reported by the British writer, John de Courcy; almost certainly Joseph Kennedy.

The latest disagreement between the Army and the Minister of Defence concerned the disposition of troops. Churchill was satisfied that the risk of invasion was small. Few of the military experts agreed with him. He wanted to reinforce the Middle East theatre, which he considered so important. They wanted to keep the troops at home, in defence of England. No one knew of Hitler's decision to call off the invasion six months previously.

The Italians, invading Greece from Albania, had been heavily rebuffed by the modest Greek forces. There was evidence that Hitler intended to go to the aid of his ally there as well as in North Africa – strategically eccentric as such moves might be.

Churchill sent Eden and Dill to the Middle East. Eden, in particular, was keen on Britain moving into Greece. Wavell, commanding in the Middle East, did not like the idea; Dill was uncertain; Churchill had been extremely keen at first, but was beginning to waver.

Major-General Kennedy, Memo. on strategy,[1] 2 February 1941:

> We can hardly be too strong in the British Isles. The front to be protected is big. And the Boche has the initiative in the choice of the point of attack. Our plans must be based on stiff resistance on the beaches and on heavy counter-attack before any forces that may have landed can organize themselves. All our strategy must be directed to safeguarding our sea communications. An immediate measure in which the Army can assist is the seizure of Tripoli. In the Middle East we must not throw away our power of offensive action by adopting an unsound strategy in Greece ... It is essential to cling to the things that matter, and not waste our strength on things that are not vital to our strategy.

Churchill to Eden, 21 February 1941:

> If in your hearts you feel Greek enterprise will be another Norwegian fiasco, do not consider yourselves obligated to it. If no good plan can be made please say so. But you know of course how valuable success would be.

After long talks with Eden, Wavell and Dill began to support the scheme. Churchill, meanwhile, in London, was becoming even more hesitant. Smuts had arrived in Cairo and he gave his

---

[1] Later Sir John Kennedy: Director of Military Operations, War Office, 1940–3; Assistant C.I.G.S., 1943–5. Like Brooke he was an ardent ornithologist.

approval; the opinion of this old warrior of the Boer War impressed Churchill. After giving Eden and Dill several opportunities to back down, Churchill finally took the decision to Cabinet on 7 March. They decided to go ahead, despite the many known dangers and risks, and despite the Prime Minister's earlier opinion that: 'Loss of Greece and Balkans by no means means a major catastrophe for us.' The Cabinet accepted full responsibility.

British and German troops poured into Greece. And neither Hitler nor Churchill had their heart in it; both were caught up with floundering allies.

British intelligence summary, March 1941:

Detachments of a German expeditionary force under an obscure general, Rommel, have landed in North Africa.

The obscure general, immediately recognizable in photographs by his goggles adjusted over the peak of his cap, was to become the most famous of the war: the Desert Fox.

Rommel was not obscure: he had been one of the most successful German commanders in the invasion of France. His Division had been the first to reach the Channel of the spearhead through Rouen, capturing numerous French and British forces. He had arrived at Tripoli on 12 February. Surprising both the British and the High Command in Berlin, he attacked on 30 March. By then, Wavell's forces were already heavily committed to Greece, as well as engaged in Abyssinia. A few days later there was a pro-German *coup* in Iraq. The Vichy French were a threat in Syria. Wavell, a gambler of a general, must have known early on that he had lost. Soon his Army was retreating back down the desert road into Egypt.

On 6 April German forces invaded Greece.

Major-General Kennedy, War Office, 10 April:

Dill asked me if I had seen a telegram that had been sent to Wavell telling him to hang on to Tobruk. I said I had, and that Wavell had replied that Tobruk was not a good position to defend. But Dill said he was referring to a second telegram that had been drafted that afternoon. We had had a lot of trouble while Dill was away over signals being sent without our knowledge. This was another instance. I sent for a copy and saw that it contained the following passage: 'From here it seems unthinkable that the fortress of Tobruk should be abandoned without offering the most prolonged resistance. We have a secure sea line of communication. The enemy's line is long and should be vulnerable provided he is not given time to organize at leisure. So long as Tobruk's garrison includes even a few tanks which can lick out at his communications nothing but a raid dare go past. If you leave Tobruk and go 200 miles back to Mersa Matruh you may find yourself faced with something like the same problem. We are convinced you should fight it out at Tobruk.' I said this was absolutely wrong; that we should not dictate strategy and tactics from London to a commander in the field, and that, if I were in Wavell's place, I should disregard it. Holding Tobruk would be like letting go the anchor of a battleship in the midst of a naval battle. In the desert the game to play was to fall back, as we did originally with the Italians, and choose the moment when the enemy was extended to fall upon him. Dill said he would speak to the Prime Minister again. We went along to his room, where he first spoke to Eden on the telephone in the sense of what I had said, and Eden agreed. He then went back to the Prime Minister's annexe at King Charles Street, and asked him to add a sentence to his telegram to the effect that we left Wavell a free hand and would not dictate the course of action from London. Churchill agreed to this. But, at this point, another telegram arrived from Wavell, in which he said that he intended to stand at Tobruk temporarily. I took it over to King Charles Street, and sent it into the Prime Minister's room. He thereupon cancelled his original telegram and cabled back to Wavell that he cordially 'endorsed his decision'.

Brooke, 27 April 1941:

We had to wait for dinner till 9.50 p.m. He was in great form after his broadcast and kept us up till 3.30 a.m. Kennedy (Director of Military Operations) tried to give P.M. a discourse on strategy in which he contemplated a fairly free evacuation of Egypt! This infuriated the P.M. and we had some trouble calming him down. The Kennedy incident was a very typical one. Poor old John had only intended to express that there might be worse things to lose than Egypt. It was, however, at once taken up by Winston as being a defeatist attitude, and Kennedy was relegated amongst those 'many generals who are only too ready to surrender, and who should be made examples of like Admiral Byng!' The more Kennedy tried to explain what he meant, the more heated Winston got, and I was very thankful when we rose from the dinner table and went into the hall to discuss other matters.[1]

The decision to hold Tobruk was made by Wavell on the spot,

---

[1] Like Brooke, Kennedy was able to somewhat even the score by the publication of his diaries after the war.

after advice from the Chief of Staff, Cyrenaica, Brigadier John Harding.[1]

The campaign in Greece was a disaster; with inadequate air support, and with his resources thinly stretched all round the Middle East, Wavell ordered a withdrawal. It was completed on 1 May. Criticism of the campaign, not surprisingly, was intense. And this time much of it was focused on Churchill himself. There was no one to replace him as Prime Minister – that was agreed – but was he after all really the man to be conducting the military side of the war? After the Norwegian lesson, should he not have foreseen the need for overwhelming air superiority – and if he could not get that air superiority, should he not have kept the Army in Africa? If all this was true, Wavell himself was not blameless. He had, somewhat to the Prime Minister's impatience, insisted on whittling his forces away in East Africa. He now attempted to hold Crete, and to counter-attack Rommel. Churchill told him: 'Crete must be held in force.'

On 'the other side of the hill', German forces were also stretched to near their limit.

Adolf Hitler:

Italy's entry into the war at once gave our enemies their first victories, a fact which enabled Churchill to revive the courage of his countrymen and which gave hope to all the anglophiles all the world over. Even while they proved themselves incapable of maintaining their positions in Abyssinia and Cyrenaica, the Italians had the nerve to throw themselves, without seeking our advice and without even giving us previous warning of their intentions, into a pointless campaign in Greece. The shameful defeats which they suffered ... compelled us, contrary to all our plans, to intervene in the Balkans, and that in its turn led to a catastrophic delay in the launching of our attack on Russia. We were compelled to expend some of our best divisions there. And as a net result we were then forced to occupy vast territories in which, but for this stupid show, the presence of any of our troops would have been quite unnecessary. The Balkan States would have been only too pleased,

---

[1] Later Field-Marshal Lord Harding. He had been assured that owing to dust storms there was absolutely no chance of the C.-in-C. landing at Tobruk that day; he was therefore surprised to see Wavell walk into his office in the afternoon. The mainly Australian garrison held out until relieved eight months later.

had they been so allowed, to preserve an attitude of benevolent neutrality towards us ... Ah! if only the Italians had remained aloof from this war.

Churchill was taking a battering. Major-General Kennedy has said: 'At this time criticism was bitter and general.' The most outspoken critic was the Australian Menzies, then in London, who spoke of Churchill's 'deplorable strategic sense'. The Prime Minister had every reason to rue not having listened to his own misgivings about the Greek campaign. There was no end to the advice he now received.

Major-General H. Rowan-Robinson, military writer, 1941:

At present, the efforts of the fighting forces are co-ordinated, most ineffectively, by the War Cabinet. Mr Churchill is, indeed, Minister of Defence and is in theory responsible for co-ordination; but, without a ministry and a staff to support him and to set the problem before him in every one of its aspects, he is utterly unequal, superman though he is, to the task ... Why was it that we were seven months in Crete without organizing the defence of our aerodromes there and why did we decide, to our heavy loss in warships and troops, to defend the island without aircraft?

Cyril Falls, military historian, 1941:

The government has not grasped the new kind of warfare being waged against us ... if we are to counter it effectively we must adopt not only new methods, some of them foreign to us, but also a new outlook, which is still more so ... our system of planning does not correspond to the demands of the present circumstances.

And, once again, there was the old charge that Churchill was harbouring second-raters in the Government.

Military commentator:

A series of defeats which seemed to be due to bad judgment brought the worst weeks the nation had yet passed through. They did not cause depression; they roused anger. Everyone felt we could do better if our course were more skilfully directed. We were changing it too often without good cause. We were losing the advantage of what we had gained by turning our attention elsewhere before we had consolidated our gains .... Churchill was defending the futile effort to defend Crete, for which he took 'the fullest responsibility' ... This revelation as to Churchill's exercise of supreme power in deciding our war strategy and tactics caused painful anxiety. As head of the government and representative of the nation he was trusted implicitly, but the knowledge that he was conducting operations and accepting responsibility, which it was thought, should rest on the General Staff or the commander in the field, sent cold shivers down many spines ... For the first time the government which had been pushed into office by the nation just a year before began to look as if it might be pushed out ... The Prime Minister was told bluntly by the *Daily Mail*, sedately by *The Times*, that the British people would not stand any more 'magnificent evacuations', now that Crete had followed Norway, Dunkirk, and Greece. The *Daily Herald* warned its readers: 'If we don't do better, we may lose the war' ... Churchill's detachment from home affairs and his rather ill-tempered defence of his decision to fight in Crete stirred up afresh the suspicion that he was trying to run the war personally and alone. *The Times* told him he could not win it alone. He needed the help, it urged, of the keenest brains the Empire can produce to draw up long-term strategic plans. 'You are the inspired and inspiring great leader of a democratic people,' it assured him, 'but you are,' it gave him warning, 'trying to do too much yourself.'

Sunday Times, 27 April 1941:

Mr Churchill is not only Prime Minister, but the nation's leader. His position is unchallenged. The people trust him and look to him for guidance. Whatever he asks, they will do. No other British war statesman has ever had the nation so unitedly behind him – not Chatham, not the younger Pitt, not even in the last war Mr Lloyd George ... strong in their support, he can afford to discharge that responsibility with firmness and, whenever necessary, with ruthlessness ... to purge out whatever may still impede our war effort.

On 1 May Churchill did make some adjustments to the Government, in answer to the general demand. The most important was that Oliver Lyttleton was to go out to Cairo, as Minister in the Middle East – to relieve the C.-in-C., too late for Wavell, of all the political burdens of that region which had encumbered him.

The changes were not considered enough.

New Statesman & Nation, 3 May 1941:

That the Prime Minister is bearing too great a burden upon his shoulders because of the inadequacy of his team is common ground with all Members. None would deny, either, that the production of war material is being hampered by failure to co-ordinate the activities of the many departments involved.

Sunday Times, 4 May 1941:

Mr Churchill's own position remains supreme in an exceptional degree. The nation trusts and follows him as its war leader. Familiar as he has long been with all three Services, and bearing as he does a great part of the direct daily responsibility for guiding and co-ordinating them, he is necessarily the head of all our war-effort on the fighting side. But that very fact renders it impossible for him to be personally much concerned in the civilian side of war planning; and it is there that the need for stronger, prompter, and longer-sighted ministerial decisions seems not infrequently to reveal itself. The new changes do not directly solve the problem.

Next week a promised debate on the Balkan campaign took place in the House of Commons. For the first time, Churchill as Prime Minister was to be the object of considerable criticism in the place which he respected above all others.

Before the debate, there was a not unexpected contribution from the Prime Minister's most avid critic of all.

Adolf Hitler, 4 May 1941:

Churchill is the most bloodthirsty of amateur strategists that history has ever known ... running all over Europe to look for a country to become a battlefield.

The House began its debate on the vote of confidence for which Churchill asked on the Government's action in 'sending help to Greece', on 6 May 1941.

Most of the members who spoke, and those did so at great length, expressed the opinion that the vote was unnecessary: the Prime Minister had overwhelming support without it having to be demonstrated. They were, however, glad of the opportunity of airing their own views on strategy, some of it eccentric. In his maiden speech, Professor Savory said:[1]

In my lifetime, I cannot remember any Minister who has inspired such confidence and enthusiasm as our present Prime Minister. Nearly 50 years ago, I had the honour of sitting under the clock behind the Bar and listening to the father of the right hon. Gentleman making his onslaught on Mr Gladstone and the Home Rule Bill of 1893. For a long time, I have felt that the Prime Minister is the one man who should be at the head of affairs in this country. He has genius and the power of inspiring enthusiasm. Looking back on the past, I find that I have to go over the whole period of the 19th century to find a statesman who can be compared with him.

---

[1] Savory, member for Queen's University, caused a considerable stir by his very long and lucid maiden speech.

Hore-Belisha could be expected to be less fulsome. He concentrated his criticism on supply priorities and on the information services. As usual, his points were constructive:

The army must have more mobility and more armour. If there are 10 Bren-gun carriers in a battalion there should be 30. Speed and protection are being shown to be everything. We should henceforward devote as much attention to the production of tanks as we have to aeroplanes. The necessary priorities should be given. The Germans conquered Cyrenaica without air superiority. They conquered with tanks. At least the armoured divisions of our army, and preferably all divisions, should have air support as an integral part of their establishment. The army must have dive-bombers and specialized ground straffing machines such as the Germans have.

When he had been War Minister, Hore-Belisha had struggled for air support for the Army. He continued:

The Greek expedition in the form in which it was sent could hardly have been dispatched if true information had been known. Finally, it is plain that unless we remedy drastically what is wrong with our information service or with the interpretation of it, graver calamities may ensue. Information, indeed, is the weak spot in our strategical armour. It has been proved to be so throughout the war. Because of its defects our plans have proved again and again to be abortive. It was the same story in Norway last year ... the Prime Minister has assumed a great and particular responsibility for strategy ... It might be said of him, as he said of Jellicoe, that he is almost the only man who can lose the war in an afternoon ... Have we gauged accurately the power of our enemy?

Emanuel Shinwell was more combative, but less constructive. He accused Churchill of resenting criticism to such an extent that he had called for the Vote of Confidence purely out of wounded pride.

There never was any apparent need for a Vote of Confidence. Those who criticize, do not seek the government's downfall ... Why should my right hon. Friend the Prime Minister challenge us with this motion? Does he regard criticism as unseemly? ... That this challenge should have been inspired by my right hon. Friend the Prime Minister is an example of what happens when one is transferred from the ranks to the general staff ... I wonder what my right hon. Friend would have said about the present situation if he had remained in the ranks. I imagine the questions, the sarcasm, the eloquence, the sweeping gestures ... Even the Prime Minister must submit himself to the will of the nation, and he and his Cabinet must at least occasionally divest themselves of preconceived notions. That is the way to raise morale; that is the path to victory. Many can provide their own inspiration – they require no external prompting.

Others spoke of the need for a programme of clear-cut war-aims, of failures in war production, and of the passivity of concentrating troops in Britain instead of sending them to the battlefields abroad (of which Shinwell, also, had spoken). On the following day, Lloyd George made a powerful and cutting contribution. He attacked the Government on clumsy planning in manpower and production. He spoke for over half an hour, and he ended by placing the blame on Churchill for trying to do too much himself, to the detriment of domestic affairs.

We have a very terrible task in front of us. No one man, however able he is, can pull us through. I invite the Prime Minister to see that he has a small War Cabinet who will help him – help him in advice, and help him in action.

Churchill ended the debate with a careful review of the war to date, and a long explanation of the Greece campaign. After rebuking Hore-Belisha for his 'temerity yesterday to raise the subject of our admitted shortage of tanks', he added: 'My right hon. Friend played a worthy part in bringing in compulsory service. I should not have referred to this matter if he had not endeavoured to give the House a sort of idea of his super-prevision and super-efficiency and shown himself so aggressive when, I think, with all good will, he sometimes stands in need of some humility in regard to the past.'

Hore-Belisha:

I think that what the right hon. Gentleman is doing in indulging in petty recriminations is quite unworthy of the great purpose that we have in common. I made no reproach whatever against the Government for any lack of tanks. I suggested, and I think the House concurred with me, that the same priority that has been given to aircraft should now be given to tanks, because the Germans achieved their victory in Libya without air superiority. If I am responsible for the present tank position, I will willingly accept, although I could never claim some part in the credit of the advances of General Wavell. I have never claimed that at all. The point is that my right hon. Friend has been in office for 20 months. I have been out of office for 16 months.

During that period he has enjoyed unprecedented powers. With the abrogation of trade union regulations, with the full support of every party, which I never enjoyed, and indeed some of those supporting him now were opposing me, in my own proposals, and to reproach one who has been out of office 16 months is irrelevant.

When the House divided, there were 477 votes in favour, including Hore-Belisha but not Shinwell; 3 voted against – W. Gallacher (Communist), D. N. Pritt (Socialist), Dr A. Salter (Independent).

New Statesman & Nation, 10 May 1941:

On the immediate questions of the war the debate left a disturbing impression of indifferent capacity and tactical optimism... the Premier's own speech was rather a great dialectical triumph than an informative answer to critics. The great ovation accorded him after his speech was a recognition of his oratory, but the uneasiness about innumerable aspects of our war effort was by no means allayed. The Prime Minister dealt quite inadequately with the factual side of the case presented by Hore-Belisha, Shinwell and Lloyd George.

The periodical pointed out that Lloyd George had been dismissed with a reference to Pétain, though 'there was nothing defeatist' in Lloyd George's speech; that Hore-Belisha had been referred back to his own past; and that Shinwell had not received any serious reply at all.

J. L. Garvin, 11 May 1941:

As vividly as at any hour of his life Mr Churchill revealed himself again last week as an incomparable orator equal to every kind of invocation, exposition, or debate... However matchless this Prime Minister may have become in his present resources of expression and delivery, words alone could never do it. They are but a vehicle for the glow of his nature, the fibre of his heart, the equability of his courage, the force of his mind, the massive impact of his entire composition. The result was not only an elemental vote of confidence but a following scene that will live always in parliamentary history... Mr Churchill had sat down amidst storms of cheers. It did not end there. As the Prime Minister walked out most Members stood in their places to cheer him again. Others, with the same fervour or more, made a lane for him as he reached the Bar and passed out of the House. Never before had Mr Churchill found himself embarrassed in the House of Commons by a manifestation like this.

On 24 May, H.M.S. *Hood*, the largest warship in the world and the pride of the Royal Navy, was sunk by gunfire from the

Bismarck, with the loss of over 1,500 men. As Churchill said, 'her loss was a bitter grief'. The damaged *Prince of Wales* did not continue the engagement (there were unfounded rumours of mutiny, which persisted long after the war); but three days later there was some revenge when the *Bismarck* was caught and sunk.

The evacuation of Crete was completed on 1 June.

Daily Mail, 2 June 1941:

We have been in the island since November. What was done in those seven months which failed to prevent another evacuation after a twelve-days' campaign?

Daily Herald, 4 June 1941:

Our first reaction to the bloody fiasco of Crete was bewilderment. Our second was anger.

Seldom, if ever, had a British Prime Minister, or a Minister of Defence, in war been concerned in so many disasters in so short a time.

Hore-Belisha, House of Commons, 10 June 1941:

It would be helpful for the future if we were to ask ourselves whether at Dakar, in Cyrenaica, in Greece, and now in Crete the forfeits which we have incurred have not been at least in part due to an imperfect assessment of possibilities, and indeed of probabilities, and consequently to ineffective preparation. Except in the case of Greece, these are all areas in which the initial advantage and the opportunity of exploiting them have been with us. In Greece there was a period of six months to prepare before the arrival of the Germans ... Summarizing the position then, before the invasion of Crete was launched, it must have been obvious to the responsible authorities, firstly, that the Army had been driven out of Greece because of a lack of aeroplanes or because operational use of aerodromes could not be made; secondly, that experience had shown that the army, despite its valour, could not hold its ground without such support; and thirdly, that the preliminaries to an airborne attack on Crete were in train. Every one of these lessons was discarded. No adequate measures for defending aerodromes were instituted in an island of which we had been in occupation for seven months ...

Churchill replied with his customary ploy of involving Hore-Belisha in the responsibility. 'The right hon. Member for Devonport has made today a very cogent and moderate, well-informed and thoughtful contribution to the debate, but he used a different mood and tone in a speech which he recently delivered in the country,[1] and that at any rate makes it necessary for me to say that the state in which our army was left when the right hon. Gentleman had ended his two years and seven months' tenure of the War Office, during the greater part of which he was responsible for production and supply, was lamentable. We were short of every essential supply ... I think it is only fair, when he himself comes forward and sets himself up as an arbiter and judge, and speaks so scornfully of the efforts of some others who have inherited his dismal legacy, I think when he speaks in this way – he has a great responsibility in the matter – it is only fair to point out to him that he is one of the last people in this country entitled to take that line.' After this exchange, Churchill summoned Hore-Belisha to him in the Smoking Room. 'If you fight me I shall fight you back,' he said. Hore-Belisha accepted the challenge.

Lord Winterton,[2] diary, 10 June 1941:

The Prime Minister was good in reply, though, as usual, he answered few of the real criticisms and, as usual, attacked Leslie Hore-Belisha for his alleged negligence as War Minister.

Wavell launched his counter-attack in the desert on 15 June. It was a total failure. Relations between Churchill and Wavell had steadily deteriorated for more than a year. There was some past history between the two, but this did not affect Churchill's decision to replace Wavell, in whom he had lost confidence weeks before. As with Greece, he had listened to Dill's persuasiveness and tolerated Wavell, although even Dill had admitted to him that on occasion Wavell was 'inclined to be lethargic'. Moreover, he had been impressed with the great esteem in which everyone seemed to hold Wavell. When Dill eventually said, 'Back him or sack him', Churchill replied: 'It is not so simple as that. Lloyd George did not trust Haig in the last war – yet he could not sack him.' On 21 June after the débâcle of the last counter-attack, Churchill felt strong enough to do what his judgement had told him to do long

---

[1] At Edinburgh, 6 June 1941.
[2] Conservative M.P., 1904–51. Served with T. E. Lawrence in Arabia. Chancellor of Duchy of Lancaster, and Paymaster-General, under Chamberlain.

before – he sacked Wavell: 'a new eye and a new hand are required'. Wavell, dispirited and utterly exhausted mentally, asked for home leave. This was not granted him – 'I can't have him hanging about in London living in his club' – although causing dissension was not in Wavell's character; he was sent to India as C.-in-C. There, Churchill assumed, he would be able to ponder 'under the pagoda tree'. The famous old one-eyed soldier had been put away to rest – so it was thought. General Sir Claude Auchinleck, of whom Churchill had recently formed a good opinion, was sent to take up the command.

Journalist, diary, July 1941:

There is a murmuring campaign against the Prime Minister over Wavell and his alleged insistence on complete control of all three fighting services.

Dill told the Prime Minister:

After the war he may write – he writes well – and goodness knows what he may say.

In fact he wrote practically nothing about it, except: 'Winston has always disliked me personally.' But after the war Churchill expressed (to his son Randolph) his regret about Wavell. Churchill never did enjoy wielding power in that way, to cut off a great soldier's career in the middle of a war: but he was not the man to flinch from it for long. Wavell, although too resigned to be an outstanding field general, was a man of very fine character, and had the power to inspire intense devotion among many of those who worked with him. Churchill knew this; but after the deed was done, there were few repercussions. The Prime Minister felt stronger than ever, in the event of future confrontations with the Army.

Political commentator, early 1942:

General Wavell was in the public estimation one of the very big men of the war and a man in whom they had confidence. Since it was abundantly clear that development of the Middle East war was imminent and that India was at this stage unlikely to come into the picture as an important scene of operations, his services did not seem likely to prove more valuable in India than they would have been in the Middle East generally. General Wavell is a curious man, rather silent and exactly the opposite kind of character to Mr Churchill. He is the rigidly professional soldier of very correct views . . . Mr Churchill always finds it extremely difficult to deal with a man who cannot talk a lot and who seems unable to put his case explicitly. He is inclined to think that anybody who cannot talk must be stupid. General Wavell, however, is very far from being a stupid man, as can be seen from his literary as well as his military achievements . . . His apparent difference of opinion with the Prime Minister over the Middle East operations was a misunderstanding, although perhaps a bitter one, rather than a quarrel. Our big Libyan offensive of 1940 was not planned throughout . . . Then came the big campaigns of 1941 . . . The whole thing was shockingly badly handled from beginning to end. General Wavell, who was the only soldier who had yet earned any sort of reputation in this war, was then transferred to India. He was an expert on the Middle East and had been a great friend of Lawrence. It is very questionable whether it was preferable for General Wavell to conform to Downing Street's opinions rather than Downing Street to General Wavell's. At the same time Oliver Lyttleton was appointed a member of the War Cabinet resident in the Middle East – presumably to keep an eye on the soldiers. Mr Lyttleton is a man with a brilliant record in business.

Harold Nicolson, diary, 18 June 1941:

Trenchard admires Winston but regrets that there is nobody to control him. He thinks the Cabinet such little men. And in truth, when we discuss it, there emerge the great figures of the past – Curzon, Balfour, Carson, Birkenhead, Smuts, Kitchener. None of them would have been so frightened of Winston as the whole Cabinet are today.

The day after Churchill dismissed Wavell, Hitler's armies rolled into Russian-held territory, and his air force caught a large proportion of the Russian air force on the ground. The British had been expecting this attack for some weeks, but Stalin had not heeded Churchill's warnings.

When Hitler made his fatal error of the war – committing himself to the probability of having to fight on two fronts of the Reich – it was not immediately evident to his enemies.

The Scotsman, 23 June 1941:

Molotov professes to believe that Hitler will suffer the same fate as Napoleon suffered when he marched on Moscow. Napoleon took from June to September to reach Moscow. It was the retreat and the Russian winter that brought disaster. The speed of war has changed. Hitler has a magnificent war machine, and the performance of the Russian Army in the recent war with Finland gives no ground for high confidence in Russia's resistance to Germany's Panzer divisions and dive-bombers.

Could Hitler defeat Russia before Britain and America were ready to strike him from the West? It was the beginning of the greatest controversy in which Churchill was involved during the war, and the one which brought him most critics: the question of the Second Front.

In a broadcast, Churchill reminded his countrymen that, 'No one has been a more consistent opponent of Communism than I have been for the last twenty-five years – I will unsay no word that I have spoken about it.' But he said that such considerations were overruled by circumstances. 'Any man or State who fights against Nazism will have our aid.' Hitler and most of his sycophantic advisers, however, were loath to believe that the arch-enemy of Communism really meant what he said.

Count Ciano, Rome, 18 July 1941:

Hitler went to war believing that the struggle against Bolshevism might lead the Anglo-Saxon countries to end the conflict. Von Ribbentrop did not agree; in fact, he was convinced that Churchill is ready to make an alliance even with the devil himself if he can only destroy Nazism.[1]

Professor Gerbrandy, Prime Minister of the Netherlands, London, *Free Europe*, 11 July 1941:

Mr Churchill is a statesman in the highest sense of the word, because he sees the connection between the interests of his own country and the interests of the world. His outlook is world-wide.

Major-General Kennedy, after meeting of Defence Committee, 25 June 1941:

[Churchill] had also attacked Dill upon his refusal to agree to the despatch of 100 more cruiser tanks to Egypt, by direct convoy through the Mediterranean, over and above the considerable number that we had already planned to send. Dill felt that, with the Germans racing towards Moscow, invasion of the United Kingdom might be the next item in Hitler's programme after a quick victory over Russia and that it would therefore be wrong to send these tanks away. Churchill had said, 'You would see Tobruk brought down, with all those Australians there, you would see the whole position in the Middle East crumble, rather than send the tanks' ... On the following day Dill told me that the Prime

---

[1] Ribbentrop was well informed. At a private dinner party at Chequers, four weeks previously, Churchill had said: 'If Hitler invaded Hell, I would make at least a favourable reference to the Devil in the House of Commons.'

Minister had once again been in one of his worst moods. He had attacked Dill afresh about the cruiser tanks for Egypt. Dill said, 'I just smiled and sat silent. Then the Prime Minister said, "Well, I won't send them – not because of the reasons you have given, but simply because the Navy can't take them." 'Well,' I remarked, 'it doesn't matter what the reason is, so long as he does not send them.' 'That is exactly what I feel,' said Dill. He repeated that he was prepared to resign on this issue, and that, if the Prime Minister refused his resignation, he would appeal to the War Cabinet. He added that he had twice before offered to resign. The Prime Minister had also spoken at length of the premature offensive in the desert earlier in the month. He was still bitterly disappointed and angry at its failure.

Journalist, diary, 30 June 1941:

Everyone is terribly depressed about the war. All these astrologers ought to be suppressed for their wishful thinking. People are getting so much on edge that they complain of the Prime Minister's perpetual smile. I don't blame them. It is now suggested that one reason for our rout in Libya is that Rommel had air-conditioned tanks...

The same, 2 July 1941:

Everyone is very gloomy. The Prime Minister says that now the recession of our hopes is only equalled by the situation at Dunkirk...

Since the start of the war and before, parliamentary circles had been split between 'tank' lobbyists and 'air' lobbyists. The hero of the latter was, of course, Lord Beaverbrook, who had cut much red-tape and trod on many toes in getting aeroplanes built; but the former, with Hore-Belisha in the van, were constructive and persistent.

Political commentator, 1941:

There was something a little ominous in one statement that was made on behalf of the government in the debate on production in the House of Commons on July 9. 'From now on,' said Mr Harold Macmillan, the Parliamentary Secretary to the Ministry of Supply, 'the special bias in favour of the Ministry of Aircraft Production is not likely to develop.' Does that mean that tanks are to be given priority over bombers? And how does such a policy tally with what Mr Churchill said in his broadcast of June 22, the day when Germany attacked Russia? 'We shall bomb Germany by day as well as by night in ever increasing measure,' said Mr Churchill, 'casting upon them month by month a heavier discharge of bombs and making the German people taste and gulp each month a sharper dose of the miseries they have showered upon mankind.' *That* can't be done if tanks are to be trumps ... for heaven's sake let us not lose perspective in this vital business. To do so might mean losing the war.

The Observer, 13 July 1941:

The House of Commons has never listened to a more impressive series of complaints than in the debate on production. It is a thousand pities that the newspapers were too small to give it more than skeleton form. Members from the army gave a pitiful account of the deficiencies of material, while employers and Labour members, from their respective angles, illustrated the waste and dislocution too prevalent in factories. Sir John Wardlaw-Milne's estimate that only 75 per cent of full efficiency was being attained might be said to represent a fair average of the purport of the other speeches. Among the factors stigmatized were an excess of official forms, incessant modifications of design, incompetent management, and departmental competition for supplies. Several members urged a Ministry of Supply to cover the needs of all the services as the fundamental remedy.

The creation of an overall Ministry of Supply, or Ministry of Production, was continually pressed on Churchill; he was slow to react. At that time, the Ministry of Supply did not have power over aeroplane or naval production; it was, in effect, only concerned with the Army. On 29 June Beaverbrook – formally Minister of Aircraft Production – had become Minister of Supply. He devoted himself to turning out tanks, as he had formerly turned out planes.

None of the three Ministers concerned with Supply (Aircraft Production, Admiralty, Supply) could function properly without the co-operation of the Minister of Labour, the all-important Ernest Bevin. Bevin had an extreme distaste and suspicion of all Press lords, in particular Lord Beaverbrook. Lord Beaverbrook, on the other hand, was accustomed to getting his own way, and did not greatly care for compromise.

He frequently appealed to the Prime Minister, sometimes flaunting resignation. Churchill, however, had gained considerable respect for Bevin's importance – he was both efficient and popular. The mutual respect between Churchill and Bevin was unexpected and commendable.

Charles Rollo, *Current History and Forum*, June 1941:

Asked to name the likeliest successor to Winston Churchill, descendant of the Duke of Marlborough, countless Britons would point to the son of a country labourer, a one-time farmhand, cart driver and union organizer, whose name is Ernest Bevin – 'Ernie' to his friends, the workers... Bevin organized the 'Council of Action' to put an end to the war against the Bolsheviks that Churchill was backing. Bevin won; the war was stopped. Churchill had his revenge in 1926 when he smashed the General Strike of which Bevin was a leader. It is characteristic of the two men that these and other encounters, so far from leading to bitterness, resulted in a mutual respect that became a firm friendship when both started the fight for a bold stand against the dictators after Hitler's rise to power. Today they make a fine working team. 'Whatever Mr Churchill may have been in political life,' Bevin has said, 'I have never met a man of greater resource, greater courage, greater determination in a crisis and greater loyalty to his colleagues.'

Quentin Reynolds, 1941:

The man in the street listens with intense excitement to the magnificent speeches of Winston Churchill and the man in the street wants to believe in the Prime Minister. But, asks the man in the street, is Churchill going to realize that this war belongs to the Ernie Bevins of England, not to the old gang? There is so much that is progressive and magnificent about Mr Churchill's Cabinet that the man in the street hates to see it held back by the legacies of failure whom Churchill still tolerates.

But not all the 'failures' were Chamberlain men. What some people had forgotten when criticizing Churchill's government was that because a man had been anti-appeasement, it did not necessarily follow that he would make a good minister; that this was so had been shown with Boothby, Duff Cooper, and Harold Nicolson. The Duff Cooper affair was particularly embarrassing to the Prime Minister; Cooper was not at all suited to ministerial office, as he had already shown before the war. As Minister of Information, he had formed a squad of investigators who were to go around questioning private citizens. The *Daily Herald*, under Percy Cudlipp, brother of Hugh Cudlipp of the *Mirror* group, blasted at these investigators and called them 'Cooper's Snoopers'. Big advertisements were put into the newspapers defending the scheme. It was no use; the Press still lashed at it. Frank Owen of the *Evening Standard* put his political writer, Michael Foot, to work.[1]

---

[1] Frank Owen: Liberal M.P., 1929–31; editor of the *Evening Standard*, 1938–41; *Daily Mail*, 1947–50.

Michael Foot: President of the Oxford Union, 1933: Labour M.P., 1945–55, 1960–; acting editor of the *Evening Standard*, 1942; editor of *Tribune*, 1948–52, 1955–60.

Duff Cooper's reputation never really recovered – and yet no one in the country, unless it was the Prime Minister himself, had a more impeccable anti-appeasement record. On 21 July 1941, he was replaced at the Ministry of Information by Churchill's most reliable ally, Brendan Bracken. Cooper was sent off to investigate the situation in the Far East. Dill had been trying to get Churchill to send forces and material there, in case of Japanese aggression; he was particularly concerned about Singapore. Cooper took with him his wife Lady Diana. It took three months for Cooper to submit his report, which Churchill considered far too long.

As for Churchill, the Press wanted to like him. But he would not give private interviews. Fleet Street begged him in vain to hold regular and frequent Press conferences in London, as the President did in Washington. The answer from 10 Downing Street was always the same: the Prime Minister made his reports, regularly, to the House of Commons: he was too busy for Press conferences. Even the ace American correspondent Quentin Reynolds only got to see him after a personal plea by Harry Hopkins. No Prime Minister of modern times had been so difficult for the Press to make contact with.

On 23 July the new desert commander was summoned to London. The Prime Minister had detected 'a certain stiffness' in the replies he had received to his flow of advice, suggestions, opinions, and commands.

Auchinleck, letter, August 1941:

Last Saturday I had a long day with Winston at Chequers as we were more or less alone and together, from 11.30 in the morning till 6 p.m., when Anthony Eden arrived. We went for quite a long walk in the grounds after lunch and then sat on the lawn. It was a most perfect summer afternoon... Winston was most affable and terribly interesting. He is a very attractive personality and really amazing for his age. He never seems to tire. I do not know how he does it. He went off for a snooze about 6.30 but was down for dinner... After dining we had a Chiefs of Staff meeting which started at 10.30 p.m. and we were not in bed before nearly 3 a.m.! When I went off Winston was still listening to martial music on the gramophone! Next day I meant to go off early but didn't get away till twelve noon... Winston turned out his guard of Coldstream Guards (about a Company) for me to inspect before I went!

Auchinleck was not the only commander in the Middle East to receive the Prime Minister's close attentions. Admiral Sir Andrew Cunningham, naval C.-in-C., became 'seriously annoyed' at the professional advice given him. When Cunningham tried to get his responsibilities clarified, Churchill replied with further questions and promptings. Cunningham did not reply.

While the politicians, the journalists, the strategists and the generals ranted at the Prime Minister, to the troops and the public he was still the inimitable leader of 1940, if not anti-establishment, at any rate somehow not of it.

On 25 July Churchill, with Alan Brooke, visited an Armoured Division on Salisbury Plain:

> to say a few words to them to let them know that he realized the losses they had sustained in having to send some hundred and fifty tanks to the Middle East. Everywhere he had an astounding reception. He drove in my car between troops lining both sides of the road, all of them cheering him as he went and shouting, 'Good old Winnie!' His popularity is quite astonishing.

Many people felt sympathetic towards Churchill, in what they considered the backbiting of Fleet Street and Westminster. They knew little of the arguments about strategy, and nothing of the rows with the Army.

In July 1941, Roosevelt again sent his special emissary to see Churchill – mainly to arrange the forthcoming Atlantic Conference. But since the first mission, several points of difference had arisen. There was trouble over the exact uses of Lend–Lease raw materials. And there was disagreement between the American and British Chiefs of Staff about the Middle East. The Americans were not happy about so much material being wasted, as they thought, for the possession of arid areas of desert. Hopkins told the British, at 10 Downing Street:

> Our Chiefs of Staff – the men who make the big decisions on all matters relating to defence – believe that the British Empire is making too many sacrifices in trying to maintain an indefensible position in the Middle East. At any moment the Germans might take Gibraltar and seal up the Western Mediterranean. They might block the Suez Canal. They might concentrate enough air and armoured forces to overwhelm the British Armies in the Middle East. Our Chiefs of Staff believe that the Battle of the Atlantic is the final, decisive battle of the war and everything has got to be concentrated on winning it.

Hopkins repeated the proposal that the President and Prime Minister should meet at sea. Churchill reacted with speed. In two weeks, he was on his way.

H. V. Morton,[1] on the Atlantic Meeting, August 1941:

We dined in high spirits that evening, sensing that we were bound on a good adventure. Whether we were conscious that we were moving on the stream of history, I don't know. I suppose that realization comes later. No one, I think, was more cheerful or more conscious of the adventure, and maybe of the history, too, than the chief traveller. We could hear this resonant House of Commons voice raised cheerfully from time to time in the next coach. He admired the golden harvest fields as we flew north. I saw him sitting in the parlour car, and I thought that we should have brought a painter with us. It was an admirable picture. Mr Churchill had changed into a peculiar garment well known in Whitehall and Downing Street called 'the P.M.'s siren suit' or, less reverently, 'the Teddy Bear'. It is a garment of battle-dress design, made of wool almost Air Force blue in colour and fitted with a zip-fastener from neck to waist. It can be put on in a second and discarded as rapidly. Mr Churchill wears this siren suit during his nocturnal hours of working, during air raids and when he summons a War Cabinet in the middle of the night. It is a garment which has absorbed a great deal of its wearer's personality, and is already acquiring a definitely historical appearance. Should it outlast the War, or should someone with a sufficiently high sense of his duty to posterity preserve it when it is worn out, then the suit is clearly destined for a glass case in years to come. With this garment making him seem rounder, plumper and more of a character than ever, Mr Churchill sat with a shaded reading-light at his elbow. He had ceased to draw on a cigar which had gone out. He wore a pair of reading glasses. On chairs round about him were despatch cases and boxes which gushed a river of papers and documents. While he picked up one of them, read it, discarded it or made a note in the margin, he was dictating to two secretaries who sat near with note-books on their knees.

The same, a few days later:

Although Mr Churchill was not always visible to the ship, evidence of him was bellowed all over the battleship by loudspeaker. Men in the engine room, sailors on the mess decks, Marine sentries and others smiled with delight as they heard unaccustomed orders shouted such as 'Will Mr Martin please go at once to the Prime Minister on the bridge?'

---

[1] Morton, at this time working for the *Daily Herald*, was one of the most famous travel writers in the language; he was specially picked to record the Atlantic Meeting.

or 'The Prime Minister requests the presence of Brigadier Dykes upon the bridge.' Hearing such orders the crew caught a reflected glory and knew that this voyage was like no other.

The two men met on 9 August. On Sunday the 10th, they attended Divine Service on Churchill's ship, H.M.S. *Prince of Wales*.

H. V. Morton:

Then the first of the hymns chosen by Mr Churchill went roaring out over the silent bay: 'O God our help in ages past' ... The British and Americans stood together in close ranks, their caps off, their heads bent over the hymn sheets. It was difficult now that the little white caps had been doffed to say who was American and who was British; and the sound of their voices rising together in the hymn was carried far out over the sea. In the long, frightful panorama of this War, a panorama full of guns and tanks crushing the life out of men, of women and children weeping and of homes blasted into rubble by bombs, there had been no scene like this, a scene, it seemed, from another world, conceived on lines different from anything known to the pageant-masters of the Axis, a scene rooted in the first principles of European civilization which go back to the figure of Charlemagne kneeling before the Pope on Christmas morning. The service continued. Captain Leach read the Lessons, and the second of Mr Churchill's hymns was announced – 'Onward, Christian Soldiers'. The deep voices rose again through the still morning and the other ships far out in the bay must have heard it clearly and have recognised it as they sang. I watched the two men in the seats of honour, the tall man and the smaller man in blue, who together represented the people of Britain and the United States; and I wondered what was passing through their minds, at that moment. Churchill was affected emotionally, as I knew he would be. His handkerchief stole from its pocket ... The voices were lifted in a majestic hymn, the choice, not of Mr Churchill, but of President Roosevelt. When the Prime Minister, on the preceding day, hymn-book in hand had consulted the President in his cabin aboard the *Augusta* on the order of the service, Mr Roosevelt had said, 'But you must have "Eternal Father, strong to save".' Now, as the voices rose and fell, a situation that was almost intolerable in its uncalculated emotionalism reached breaking-point.

The Atlantic Charter, bursting with admirable sentiments, hopes, promises, and resolutions, was signed on 12 August. At the end of the war, and after it, Churchill was frequently referred to the Charter by those critics who suspected him of supporting undemocratic régimes. In 1950 Churchill provided this answer: 'Considering all the tales of reactionary, Old World outlook, and the pain this is said to have caused the President, I am glad it should be on record that the substance and spirit of what came to be called the "Atlantic Charter" was in its first draft a British production cast in my own words.'

The most important aspect of the document was that the United States devoted themselves to 'the final destruction of the Nazi tyranny', without actually going to war with Germany – but even this had been fairly clear since Lend–Lease. Apart from that, the Charter, so highly considered at the time, had little if any effect on the world.

H. V. Morton:

I remembered Mr Churchill's words to me one night as he left the ship. 'I have an idea that something really big may be happening – something really big.'

King George VI, diary, 19 August 1941:

The Prime Minister came to lunch. He gave me a very full account of his meeting and talks with F.D.R., and also those with the U.S.A. Service Chiefs. F.D.R. told him that at the moment he would not declare war but that he would wage war with us, against Germany, as evidenced by taking over all convoy work to Iceland. W. was greatly taken by him, and has come back feeling that he knows him. He had several talks with him alone, when W. put our position to him very bluntly. If by the Spring, Russia was down and out, and Germany was renewing her blitzkrieg here, all our hopes of victory and help from U.S.A. would be dashed if America had not by then sent us masses of planes etc...

In September 1941, Stalin asked Churchill for a Second Front, to relieve pressure on Russia, and to sell him tanks and planes. Churchill explained that resources and manpower were so stretched that a Second Front in Europe was out of the question for the time being. He agreed to supply one half of the total of tanks and planes asked for: 'We hope the United States will supply the other half.' He added: 'You used the word "sell". We had not viewed the matter in such terms and have never thought of payment.' But when pressed for a Second Front, Churchill, understandably, reminded the Russian Ambassador: 'Remember that only four months ago we in this island did not know whether you were not coming in against us on the German side. Indeed, we thought it quite likely that you would. Even then we felt sure we should win in the end . . . you of all people have no right to make reproaches to us.'

Eden, diary, 5 September 1941:

To celebrate this [agreement on aid to Russia] Winston insisted on a restaurant dinner and carried Max [Beaverbrook] and self off to Ritz. Very good dinner, oysters, partridge, etc., and good talk. Winston at top of his form. Talk much of past events, some long past. Winston said that he would like best to have F.E. [Lord Birkenhead] back to help him. Not F.E. of last years, but F.E. about '14 or '15. Max told Winston that if he had played his cards well when he was at Admiralty early in last war, especially with Tory Party, he could have been P.M. instead of Lloyd George. Winston agreed. He described as toughest moment of his life when he learnt that Lloyd George did not propose even to include him in his Cabinet.

Hardly a day seems to have passed in the Second World War when Winston Churchill was not referring to the First.

Meanwhile, Beaverbrook had been to Moscow. As often with him, personal contact ruled his motives. He now became a strong supporter of aid in every form to Russia.

On 19 September German forces in Russia, still advancing, took Kiev. On 19 October a state of siege was pronounced in Moscow. But the British Chiefs of Staff were still worried about invasion.

Brooke, 26 October 1941:

I found that the only other guest was Lindemann.[1] Dinner lasted on till about 11 p.m. by the time we had finished having snuff, etc. After dinner the P.M. sent for his dressing-gown to put over his 'siren-suit'. The dressing-gown is a marvellous garment, rather like Joseph's many-coloured robe. We then proceeded upstairs where he had a small cinema. There we watched Russian and German films till about midnight. We then came down and spent from midnight to 1 a.m. with [a lecture] which I had to give. The P.M. then dismissed Lindemann and told him he wanted to speak to me. He proceeded to discuss impending operations in North Africa and Mediterranean and all the hopes he attached to them. From that he went on to discuss defence of this country against invasion and the strength of the forces left for this purpose. I told him of the forces I had, of being very short of tanks if we went on sending them to Russia as proposed. He assured me that I should have some 4,000 tanks in this country by the spring. Finally at

---

[1] Later Lord Cherwell: personal scientific adviser to the Prime Minister, 1940–5; Paymaster-General, 1942–5 and 1951–3.

2.15 a.m. he suggested we should proceed to the hall to have some sandwiches, and I hoped this might at last mean bed. But, no! We went on till ten to three before he made a move for bed. He had the gramophone turned on, and in the many-coloured dressing-gown with a sandwich in one hand and watercress in the other, he trotted round and round the hall, giving occasional little skips to the tune of the gramophone. On each lap near the fireplace he stopped to release some priceless quotation or thought.

Report to the President of the Secret Committee, National Academy of Science, Washington, 6 November 1941:

A fission bomb of superlatively destructive power will result from bringing quickly together a sufficient mass of element U–235. This seems as sure as any untried prediction based upon theory and experiment can be.

Despite all setbacks, Britain at least seemed somehow to have retained her traditional control of the Mediterranean. On 8 November all the merchant ships in an Italian convoy were destroyed. How Churchill was envied, despite all his troubles, by one of his dictator opponents!

Count Ciano, Rome, 10 November 1941:

Mussolini was discouraged, and is right in considering yesterday the most humiliating day since the beginning of the war. 'I have been waiting for a piece of good news for eighteen months now, and it never comes. I, too, should be proud to send a telegram like the one Churchill has sent his admiral, but for too long a time I have been vainly trying to find the opportunity.'

Auchinleck's attack began on 18 November in heavy rain. He heavily outnumbered Rommel in tanks; in aircraft he had a superiority of more than three to one. He achieved surprise, and when the battle was not going well, he took over command in the field himself. Rommel was pushed back. It was essential to keep the sea-flank of the advance protected; but at the end of the year the Royal Navy suffered fearful losses in the Mediterranean from newly arrived German submarines, and not a few from Italian 'human-torpedoes'. This gave Mussolini something to rejoice over at last. Malta was attacked almost ceaselessly from the air. By the end of the year, despite all his efforts and those of the British forces which he deployed in that area, Churchill knew that the Axis powers had mastery in the Mediterranean.

In November 1941, Brooke was again at Chequers. After dinner the Prime Minister took Brooke to his study and told him that, as Dill was a tired man, he had made up his mind to relieve him and make him a Field-Marshal.

He then went on to say that he wanted me to take over . . . and asked me whether I was prepared to do so. It took me some time to reply, as I was torn by many feelings. I hated the thought of old Dill going and our very close association coming to an end. I hated the thought of what this would mean to him. The magnitude of the job and the work entailed took the wind out of my sails. The fact that the extra work and ties would necessarily mean seeing far less of you [his wife] tore at my heart strings. The P.M. misunderstood my silence and said: 'Do you think you will be able to work with me? We have so far got on well together.' I had to assure him that these were not my thoughts, though I am fully aware that my path will not be strewn with rose petals. But I have the greatest respect and real affection for him, so that I hope I may be able to stand the storms of abuse which I may well have to bear frequently. He then went on to explain the importance he attached to the appointment, and the fact that the Chiefs of Staff Committee must be the body to direct military events over the whole world. He also stated that his relations with me must from now on approximate to those of a Prime Minister to one of his Ministers. Nobody could be nicer than he was, and finally, when we went to bed at 2 a.m., he came with me to my bedroom to get away from the others, took my hand and looking into my eyes with an exceptionally kind look, said: 'I wish you the very best of luck.'

Alan Brooke took over from Dill as Chief of the Imperial General Staff on 1 December. Dill was worn out, and he had reached the retiring age of sixty; his wife was dying in the most trying circumstances; his general state of exhaustion had brought on an attack of shingles.

The replacement of Dill, who was a good soldier, by Brooke, did nothing to ease relations between Defence Minister and Chief of Imperial General Staff: if anything, they became worse. Haunted by memories of the First World War, and Lloyd George's inability to remove the unsuccessful Haig, Churchill was as determined as ever to keep his generals under firm control: never for a moment would he allow them to think they were their own masters. The irony of the situation was that Britain was blessed with the finest collection of generals it had ever enjoyed – men who also had learnt the lessons of the former war. The first row with Brooke occurred less than a week after the new appointment. Portal had tried to stop the Prime Minister from committing himself to a promise to transfer planes from North Africa to Russia at the end of the Libyan offensive.

This produced the most awful outburst of temper. We were told that we did nothing but obstruct his intentions, we had no ideas of our own and, whenever he produced ideas, we produced nothing but objections, etc. etc. Attlee pacified him once, but he broke out again; then Anthony Eden smoothed him temporarily, but all to no avail. Finally he looked at his papers for some five minutes, then slammed them together, closed the meeting and walked out of the room. It was pathetic and entirely unnecessary. We were only trying to save him from making definite promises which he might find hard to keep later on. It is all the result of overworking himself and keeping too late hours. Such a pity! God knows where we should be without him, but God knows where we shall go with him!

When the Chiefs of Staff met next morning they were greeted with a memorandum from Churchill. No doubt he saw it as his duty as Defence Minister to probe the advice tendered to him by his Service chiefs, testing their plans by making them oppose him.

Although the war was going so ill for Britain, and for her Russian ally, the country was not at this time without her admirers.

General de Gaulle, London, 25 November 1941:

England has had the incomparable merit and the magnificent courage to confront, alone, destiny at its most threatening ... We shall not cease, till the last evening of the last battle, to stand faithful and loyal, at the side of old England.[1]

L. S. Amery, broadcasting to Germany the day before Churchill's sixty-seventh birthday, 29 November 1941:

He is today the spirit of old England incarnate, with its unshakeable self-confidence, its grim gaiety, its unfailing sense of humour, its underlying moral earnestness, its unflinching tenacity.

Some – mostly the very young – saw Churchill as an independent, almost non-political leader.

---

[1] But after the last battle? De Gaulle, Paris, 16 May 1967: 'Despite or perhaps because of their great battles of former times, I am speaking of course particularly of France and Germany, these countries are inclined to support rather than oppose one another.'

Richard Hillary, New York, 1941:

Was there perhaps a new race of Englishmen arising out of this war, a race of men bred by the war, a harmonious synthesis of the governing class and the great rest of England: that synthesis of disparate backgrounds and upbringings to be seen at its most obvious best in R.A.F. Squadrons? While they were now possessed of no other thought than to win the war, yet having won it, would they this time refuse to step aside and remain indifferent to the peacetime fate of the country, once again leave government to the old governing class? I thought it possible. Indeed, the process might be said to have already begun. They now had as their representative Churchill, a man of initiative, determination, and no Party. But they would not always have him; and what then? Would they see to it that there arose from their fusion representatives, not of the old gang, deciding at Lady Cufuffle's that Henry should have the Foreign Office and George the Ministry of Food, nor figureheads for an angry but ineffectual Labour Party, but true representatives of the new England that should emerge from this struggle?

Diana Cooper, Singapore, October 1941:

... Maybe Winston thinks Duff comfortably out of the way here – no necessity to find him another job that way and quite easy to stop any trouble.

Churchill had always put the Middle East before preparations to combat, or moves to deter, Japan in the Far East. 'I confess that in my mind the whole Japanese menace lay in a sinister twilight ... if Japanese aggression drew in America I would be content to have it. On this I rested.'

But rumours of the Japanese spreading their war with China were mounting.

Sunday Times, 7 December 1941:

A naval attack on the Dutch East Indies would not, however (except by the furnishing of raw materials and liquid fuel) aid the Japanese to crush China, and the presence of a powerful British fleet at Singapore and the menace of American naval action are enough to make them hesitate long before launching out into a hazardous operation 2,000 miles from home. The critical area, therefore, seems to be Indo-China and the neighbouring lands to the west ... The control of Thailand would give the Japanese an incomparably better position in south-eastern Asia than they at present possess, and would enable them to strike south, west or north-west whenever they thought the occasion was favourable. It is not, however, likely to become so for a long time.

General de Gaulle at St James's, Spanish Place, 1941

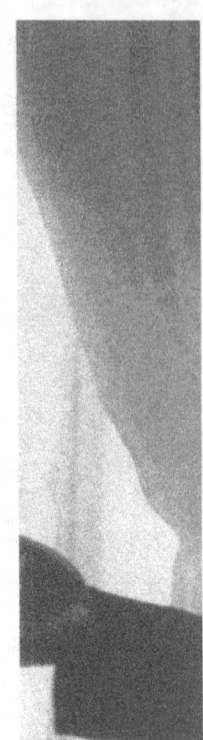

Aneurin Bevan

Emanuel Shinwell

'Brendan Bracken announces our victories to the Press'

Stafford Cripps in India, April 1942

Inside No. 10 on returning from Yalta, February 1945.
Left to right: Sir John Anderson, Sarah Churchill, Clement Attlee, Sir Charles Portal, Herbert Morrison

The Japanese struck at 8.10 a.m. that day. And they struck east – at Pearl Harbor.

At Singapore were the *Prince of Wales* and the *Repulse*, two of the finest ships left to the Royal Navy. They were there, against Admiralty advice, on the insistence of Churchill.

Admiral Sir Tom Phillips took his two battleships from Singapore on 8 December, just after the Japanese had begun their invasion of Malaya. Without fighter escort – the R.A.F.'s pitiable resources became over-stretched in the first few hours of invasion – it was a calculated risk. The skies cleared. Phillips maintained radio silence, thus preventing any chance of fighter protection being called. After twenty-four hours, the Japanese found him.

I can see one plane release a torpedo. It drops nose heavy into the sea and churns up a small wake as it drives straight at the *Prince of Wales*. It explodes against her bows. A couple of seconds later another explodes amidships and another astern. Gazing at her turning over on the port side with her stern going under and with dots of men leaping from her, I was thrown against the bulkhead by a tremendous shock as the *Repulse* takes a torpedo on her portside stern. With all others on the flag deck I am wondering where it came from, when the *Repulse* shudders gigantically. Another torpedo. Now men cheering with more abandon than at a Cup Final. What the heck is this? I wonder. Then see it is another plane down. It hits the sea in flames also. There have been six so far as I know. My notebook, which I have got before me, is stained with oil and is ink-blurred. It says: 'Third torp.' The *Repulse* now listing badly to starboard. The loud-speakers speak for the last time: 'Everybody on main deck.' We all troop down ladders, most orderly except for one lad who climbs the rail and is about to jump when an officer says: 'Now then – come back – we are all going your way.' The boy came back and joined the line. It seemed slow going. Like all the others I suppose I was tempted to leap to the lower deck, but the calmness was catching. When we got to the main deck the list was so bad our shoes and feet could not grip the steel deck. I kicked off mine, and my damp stockinged feet made for sure movement. Nervously opening my cigarette case I found I hadn't a match. I offered a cigarette to a man beside me. He said: 'Ta. Want a match?' We both lit up and puffed once or twice. He said: 'I'll be seeing you, mate.' To which I replied: 'Hope so, cheerio.' We were all able to walk down the ship's starboard side, she lay so much over to port. We all formed a line along a big protruding anti-torpedo blister, from where we had to jump some twelve feet into a sea which was black – I discovered it was oil. I remember jamming my cap on my head, drawing a breath and leaping. Oh, I forgot – the last entry in my notebook was: 'Sank about 12.20 p.m.' I made it before leaving the flag deck. In the water I glimpsed the *Prince of Wales*'s bows disappearing.

An author who analysed this disaster wrote: 'There is absolutely no escape from the conclusion that the prime responsibility for their loss was his . . . He was far from alone in his utter and complete underestimation of the Japanese. He was almost alone – in his erroneous and antique conception of naval strategy, his misunderstanding of the uses and limitations of capital ships. Among politicians, Service chiefs and practical men of affairs in high positions he must have been utterly and completely alone in his time in that curious mystique of the battleship he created for himself – in the way in which he seemed to credit battleships with almost magical powers . . . He wanted the ships sent to Singapore. The Admiralty opposed him. So did everyone in a position to formulate an informed opinion and possessing the right to express it. It was not a question of hidebound traditional strategists opposing a novel conception or an unconventional move: it was a question of hard-headed men, who knew first-hand the conditions and requirements of war at sea in their time, knowing that what they were hearing was a proposal to send ships to certain or near-certain destruction.'

The war had not been on sixteen months. But during that time, the Royal Navy, believed in 1939 to be one of the most important single factors of power in the world, had lost about a third of the most famous battleships and carriers with which it had begun the war.

Within forty-eight hours of the Japanese attack, Churchill had spoken in Parliament; had arranged to visit Roosevelt in Washington; had wired encouragement to Chiang Kai-shek in China; had wired President de Valera in Dublin about the vital use of Irish ports: 'Now is your chance. Now or never! A nation once again! I will meet you whenever you wish.'[1]

---

[1] The request had been rebuffed several times before. There was a bad history between the two, but that did not worry Churchill at the time. De Valera had been the butt of one of Churchill's most abusive invectives, when the former was at the League of Nations before the

A newspaper reporter, Singapore, 13 December 1941:

Raffles Hotel still has dancing every night, but there are not so many dancers.

The Japanese, with efficiency and speed that at first astonished and then bewildered their British opponents, advanced down the Malayan peninsula. Their aircraft were superior to anything that had been imagined (although details of them had been available in the United States for twelve months). Their training and equipment – they wore rubber shoes and sped down roads on bicycles – were unconventional and successful. The unfortunate Wavell, like some character who had strayed by mistake from the stage of a Greek tragedy, found himself again trying to prop up the pillars of a weak, ill-constructed, and far-spread defensive structure, with the minimum of resources.

Sir Charles Wilson, at sea, 20 December 1941:

He is a different man since America came into the war. The Winston I knew in London frightened me. I used to watch him as he went to his room with swift paces, the head thrust forward, scowling at the ground. the sombre countenance clouded, the features set and resolute, the jowl clamped down as if he had something between his teeth and did not mean to let go. I could see that he was carrying the weight of the world, and wondered how long he could go on like that and what could be done about it. And now – in a night, it seems – a younger man has taken his place. All day he keeps to his cabin, dictating for the President a memorandum on the conduct of the war. But the tired, dull look has gone from his eye; his face lights up as you enter the cabin. A month ago, if you had broken in on his work, he would have bitten off your head. And at night he is gay and voluble, sometimes even playful.

On 22 December the Japanese began their assault on the Philippines. On Christmas Day at 3.15 p.m., the British C.-in-C., Hong

---

war and Abyssinia was spurned. They had also been opponents at the time of Irish independence. De Valera did not bother to answer Churchill's plea, and he turned down one from Roosevelt. When Wendell Wilkie had approached de Valera on the matter earlier in the year, he had admitted he would not help Churchill even though he knew his cause was in the right. Wilkie 'did not conceal his contempt'. Although Churchill was sympathetic to Ireland ('There should always be a candle burning in the window for the wandering daughter') he never forgave de Valera, in spite of his magnanimity.

Kong, ordered all commanding officers to break off the fighting and to capitulate to the nearest Japanese commander.

For the Minister of Defence, 1941 had been a disastrous year. No man in British history, holding so much military and naval responsibility, had led his forces through such a succession of disasters. But there were few people as contented that Christmas as Winston Churchill. The Japanese had succeeded in bringing about the prime objective of his own war policy, which he himself had failed in doing. He knew for certain all would be well. Although he had his faults as a strategist, Winston Churchill was no mean prophet. That was the advantage of having a sense of history. It was a sense in which his own generation were strong.

Smuts, 1941:

> I am not worried about the war; it will be difficult but we shall win it; it is after the war that worries me. It will take years and years of patience, courage, and faith.

CHAPTER SIX

1942 Political Prey

The New Year of 1942 came to Winston Churchill aboard a train hurtling through the snow-covered landscape of Vermont, *en route* from Ottawa to Washington. He joined the correspondents in the dining-car for a midnight toast.

C. V. R. Thompson, *Daily Express*, 2 January 1942:

Then Churchill walked to the door of his car. At the threshold he turned round to face us again. He raised his hand paternally. 'God bless you all,' he said, and then added, 'May we come through the year with safety and with honour.'[1]

In 1942 Churchill had to re-establish himself. In 1940 he had been supreme; in 1941 almost everything had gone wrong. Throughout the past year criticism had been mounting. There were many who believed that Churchill would – at the very least – be forced to give up his close direction of the war as Minister of Defence.

1942 saw Churchill's critics and enemies combined in their most powerful assault on him of the war. There were mixed together military setbacks, old jealousies, frustrations, and the scars of long political feuds. The critics felt the time was at last opportune to topple the man who, in 1940, had seemed impregnable in general estimation; Churchill could be the figurehead, while someone else got on with running the war. Some felt the public were ready for it.

It was a curious underestimation, both of the man himself and, to a lesser extent, of the public trust in him.

In the fore were two publications: the *Daily Express*, which criticized Churchill on a point of policy – the delay in a Second Front; and *Tribune*, which attacked the man himself.

Already criticism in Press and Parliament in Australia had

---

[1] Churchill gives an almost identical version of this occasion and toast in *The Grand Alliance*, written some seven years later.

brought about the temporary residence in London of Robert Menzies in 1941. Menzies had sat in the War Cabinet for two months, during which he had been the most determined critic of the Prime Minister's wide powers. Australians had not seen Menzies' long absence in a favourable light; on his return to his country, he had resigned. John Curtin was now Prime Minister. He was, if anything, even more critical of Churchill than Menzies had been; but he preferred to mount his pressure from a far distance. As the débâcle got even worse in Malaya, the Australian Government became infuriated. The Australian Commissioner in Singapore reported a 'landslide collapse of whole defence system. Expected arrival of modern fighter planes in boxes requiring weeks of assembly under danger of destruction by bombing cannot save the situation ... Need for decision and action in matter of hours, not days.' The British in Malaya, in fact, were not only outwitted and outmanoeuvred – they were handicapped by bureaucratic bumbling to a degree of which only the British can be capable. Curtin took the extraordinary step of writing a signed article in the *Melbourne Herald*, in which he made the important statement: 'Without any inhibitions of any kind, I make it quite clear that Australia looks to America, free of any pangs as to our traditional links with the United Kingdom.' The Anglo-Australian relationship was never to be the same again. Australia had gone to Britain's aid in the First World War, and again to the Middle East (where her interests were most threatened) in the Second World War. It seemed in Australia that Britain was not prepared to do the same when her turn came. The fact of the matter was that the British Cabinet and Chiefs of Staff did not consider a Japanese invasion of Australia a probability: Australians, nearer to the scene, felt not only anger but – in Government circles anyway – not a little panic.

Australian author, 1942:

Proud of their English heritage and culture, proud of their full membership in the nations which make up the British Empire, the Australians nevertheless resent and dislike the rudeness and lack of tact of the type of Englishman who knows that he feels he belongs to the 'ruling classes' ... Australians do not approve of the slogan of 'No recriminations' so often heard in the British Parliament, and they would feel more secure if they felt that the appeasers, the Sir John Simons, the Sir Samuel Hoares, were out of the government before the peace is made, and they say so with extreme frankness.

Goebbels, diary, 25 January 1942:

> The Australians are extremely angry ... I am issuing orders to continue to probe this open wound and to rub salt in it.

In Washington, also, there was depression at the British failure in the Far East. The British were always supposed to have had a greater presence in that area than any other power; now they were being brushed aside like some third-rate power.

General Joe Stilwell,[1] Washington, 1 January 1942:

> Talked with the Chief of Staff for an hour on this and that. Trouble with unified command in Far East. Not as between British and ourselves, but among the British! The 'Senior Service' [Royal Navy] sits disdainfully aloof. Nobody can command *them* – it isn't done. The arrogant Royal Air Force will have none of it. Only the ground forces cooperate. George [Marshall] finally got them together by going to Churchill, whom he caught in bed.

But the Americans, also, had nothing but reverses. The Japanese invasion of the Philippines was going well, despite the numerically strong and American-equipped and trained Philippine Army. The American commander in the Philippines was General Douglas MacArthur, the acknowledged expert on military affairs in the Pacific. He had a magnetic personality, and a tremendous reputation as a soldier. Despite the latter, he waited for the invaders inland, and when outmanoeuvred by them, he slowly withdrew to defensive bastions on Luzon – where defeat was inevitable, instead of remaining in the field, where defeat was probable but not inevitable.

At the Washington conference, Churchill was meanwhile seeking agreement for three major decisions: an American invasion of North West Africa (which had already been foreseen by the President); delay of a cross-Channel invasion until 1943; and joint Anglo-American commands in the war against Japan. A joint

---

[1] Commander-Designate of invasion of North Africa, 1942; Deputy Supreme C.-in-C., Far East, till recalled in November 1944. The war's greatest believer in 'attack – all the time'.

declaration was prepared by the twenty-six nations at that time involved in the war against the Axis powers – first dubbed, the 'United Nations'.

During Churchill's absence Aneurin Bevan acquired virtual control of the left-wing weekly *Tribune*. Bevan had admired Churchill in the thirties, but he had now come under the influence of Richard Stokes who detested Churchill.[1] Bevan almost immediately wrote an editorial critical of Churchill: 'My declaration of war', as he said to his managing editor. Bevan, at the time, was the friend of Lord Beaverbrook.

Tribune now became a centre of expression for Churchill's critics. Bevan became the recipient of confidences on the conduct of the war from officers and civil servants who called at the paper's offices or otherwise met him. Some of this Bevan dared not use, because of the laws of libel: scandals concerning Ministers were involved, which have not yet been printed.

Attlee beseeched Churchill to come home and face the House of Commons.

The *Daily Express* mounted its campaign for a Second Front in 1942, with an article by the most forceful journalist of the time, Frank Owen, on 5 January:

Where is there one place in Europe that you would land and create a Second Front? The answer is: 'There are 10,000, and you do not have to land from the sea ... The Tower of Evil stands there, just over the way, casting its darkness over the Continent, a veritable "network of fortifications", vast, strong, menacing, held by determined and still undismayed soldiers. But it is not undamaged. It is not impregnable. And it no longer goes unchallenged.'

Thus began the long and unlikely relationship of the extreme left-wing *Tribune*, its staff, Lord Beaverbrook, and the Independent–Conservative *Express* newspapers. Ten days later a new writer was introduced to the readers of the *Daily Express*. He also called for a Second Front to aid the Russians in 1942. His name was Michael Foot. He had been on the staff of *Tribune*, and had writ-

---

[1] Bevan: son of a coal-miner; Labour M.P., 1929–60; Minister of Health, 1945–51; Minister of Labour, 1951; died 1960.

Stokes: wealthy businessman; Labour M.P., 1938–57; Minister of Works, 1950–1; died 1957.

ten for the *Evening Standard*, of which he was shortly to become acting editor.

But in editorials, the *Daily Express* continued energetically to support Churchill as leader, although harping on his past performance rather than the present. Beaverbrook was attempting, as Minister of Supply, to get his view across to the Cabinet personally. He had no success. He succeeded only in antagonizing still further such staunch Churchill supporters as Ernest Bevin.

Beaverbrook's position was not easy. For while he strenuously objected to what he believed was neglect of the Russian ally, with whom he had enjoyed prestigious personal contact, he more than anyone else understood Churchill's reliance on the Anglo-American alliance, to create which, and to avoid friction in, had been Churchill's basic war policy since he had become Prime Minister.

Political author, 1942:

There were, and still are, powerful people at work telling an anxious public that Britain had not done enough to help Russia, and it is certain that if the worst comes to the worst they will go further and say that Russia would have survived if we had created some kind of diversion ... the obvious fact that no one in the world is more eager to beat the Germans than Mr Churchill [has] helped to overcome these criticisms; but they are still being propagated and a large number of well-meaning people accept the view that a continental landing should be attempted. It is by no means unlikely that in the near future we shall see another big political campaign to force the government into a continental adventure this year. Some of Mr Maisky's utterances have been so unconventional as to suggest an appeal to the people over the head of the government ... The light-hearted way in which inexpert critics are prepared to plunge us into military adventures without knowing whether there is the slightest hope of success is appalling.

With the power of Parliament decreased by the size of the Coalition, the Press played an increasingly important role.

Since 1939 the *Daily Sketch* had been campaigning for closer co-operation between the three Services. The *Daily Herald* had been prominent in criticism of production and manpower disorganization, inefficiency, waste, and call-up of skilled workers. All this had irritated the Labour members of the Cabinet, particularly Ernest Bevin, quite as much as it had irritated Churchill.

In January, 1942 Cassandra wrote in the *Daily Mirror*:

Bungling and mismanagement [of the Army] are on a scale that cannot be concealed and is obvious to all ... Hundreds of thousands of loyal and intelligent civilians are now being drafted into the Army. Most of them find themselves in circumstances where they are forced to put their initiative and commonsense into cold storage for the duration. At the top you have the military aristocracy of the Guards regiments with a mentality not very foreign to that of Potsdam. In the centre you have a second class snobocracy. And behind it all the cloying inertia of the Civil Service bogged down by regulations from which they cannot extricate themselves.

Executives of the *Mirror* were once again called to 10 Downing Street and personally berated by the Prime Minister. This did not deter them.

Harold Nicolson, diary, 14 January 1942:

Meeting of the National Labour Executive. Kenneth Lindsay[1] says that we must concentrate on a long-term policy – the relations between the State and the individual and the State and industry. Frank Markham[2] says that, on the contrary, we must concentrate on winning the war. In order to do this, we must get rid of Churchill who will never win the war. Others say that Winston is not an organiser and is no judge of men. His faith in Beaverbrook is lamentable. The latter thinks only of the sensational and the dramatic: for instance, he did produce a lot of tanks, but only at the expense of their own spare-parts, and the result was that most of our tanks in Libya went out of action. Kenneth Lindsay says that Shinwell is the only man in the House prepared to make a stand against Winston, and Cripps is the only possible alternative Prime Minister. Stephen King-Hall says that the mistake is for Winston to be both Prime Minister and Minister of Defence, and that he neglects production in one capacity and confuses strategy in the other. They all feel that he must be brought down, and yet they all agree (a) that there is no apparent successor, and (b) that his fall would give an immense moral shock to the country. I am disgusted by all this, since they are only thinking in political and departmental terms, and have no conception of the effort of will involved. Winston is the embodiment of the nation's will.

It was at this moment, with rumours of his impending downfall widespread in Westminster and Fleet Street – but not among the

---

[1] Nationalist and Independent M.P., 1933–50.
[2] Later Sir Frank Markham: Labour M.P., 1929–31; Nationalist M.P., 1935–45; Conservative M.P., 1951–64.

public at large – that the Prime Minister returned from Washington.

Sir Charles Wilson, diary, 17 January 1942:

As the train carried the Prime Minister towards London he sat for a time with his white hands laid out on his thighs, his head poked forward, absorbed in thought. The five weeks that he had been out of the country had not been wasted, he felt; the close friendship he had established with President Roosevelt had smoothed out every difficulty. When, however, he picked up a pile of morning papers, he was pained to find that the country did not share his satisfaction. On the contrary, public opinion seemed to be baffled by the way things had gone wrong; the nation was frankly puzzled and worried ... 'There seems to be plenty of snarling,' he said in a tired voice.

Tribune, 23 January 1942:

The question is beginning to arise in the minds of many: is he as good a war maker as he is a speech maker? During 1940 his speeches were a tonic and a definite material contribution to the armament of Great Britain. Whatever happens to him now, history will give him high place for what he did then ... But we are not the spectators of history. We are its victims and architects and it is from that angle that we are compelled to view Mr Churchill and his government at the present time ... People will expect to hear from him the outline of a plan which will use all our resources on a world scale. In particular we shall want to hear how far Russia fits into his intentions ... Churchill obviously has no plan as will be revealed [in the debate] next week. But a plan we must have.

The Times also wrote – with an excess of tact and delicacy – of the dangers when a Prime Minister, having made himself responsible for the direction of military affairs, was not able to call to account the Minister of Defence for the way in which they had been carried out. *The Times*, however, did not even refer to Churchill by position or name. *Tribune* roundly declared that it would have 'no part or lot in such cowardly obscurantism'.

An important factor in the growing opposition was the position of Stafford Cripps. He had been deeply impressed, and inspired, by his experience of the war in Russia. He had become associated with widespread public sympathy for Russia, and his personal popularity was suddenly extremely high. He had asked Churchill to be relieved of his post in Moscow, for he wanted to return to parliamentary life. This was somewhat ominous; for, as Churchill wrote: 'there were some who appeared to regard him as worth running as an alternative Prime Minister, and in these circles it was said that he would lead the new group of critics of the government, which it was hoped to organise into an effective parliamentary force'. Cripps arrived in London on 23 January. Churchill lost no time. He had him to lunch on the 25th, and offered him Beaverbrook's post at the Ministry of Supply. Cripps in the Government was obviously a better proposition, from all Churchill's points of view, than Cripps out of it. Cripps said he would think about it.

The *Manchester Guardian* and the *News Chronicle* had both campaigned for Cripps's inclusion in the War Cabinet. Churchill was well aware of all this. He was, as he said, 'well informed about the Left Wing ideas'. He personally liked Cripps.

The public still knew nothing of the mounting pressure to oust Churchill.

An article in the Swedish newspaper *Dagens Nyheter*, 23 January 1942:

The British people's love for Mr Churchill is so deep that even bad reverses in the Far East were softened by the joy of his safe return. In that country trust in the head of the government does not have to be artificially cultivated. The man who for a long time was not considered capable of holding the highest responsibility has now become the heart in a world war of defence. That heart beat no less calmly and strongly when he stood alone before a continent that had bowed to German arms than it does now when President Roosevelt stands at his side ... After the splendid success Mr Churchill had on his American visit, his prestige and confidence in victory are higher than ever.

Goebbels, 24 January 1942:

Even though, in my opinion, the recurring rumours of a government crisis are grossly exaggerated, nevertheless one cannot overlook the fact that the English people are very restive and apprehensive, and that Churchill must work very hard to dispel the unrest and worry. But I suppose he will succeed once again, all the more so since England has nobody to put in his place.

Two American reporters,[1] talking in London, 1942:

---

[1] Stephen Laird and Walter Graebner, *Time–Life* correspondents in Berlin and London respectively. Their remarkably perceptive conversation was recorded in London, and published as a book.

S.: How united is the British nation behind Churchill?

W.: The vast majority of the British people are one hundred per cent behind Winston Churchill, but this is partly due to the fact that the British people will support any Prime Minister so long as he does nothing that is too shocking. Neville Chamberlain, for example, though the rest of the democratic world thought that he should have been kicked out right after Munich, enjoyed the support of the country through the whole winter and spring of 1940. Even after the Norway fiasco, when scores of M.P.s hurled abuse at him and he was unable to defend his policy, Parliament gave him a sizeable vote of confidence.

S.: Perhaps the reason for the unity behind Churchill is that the extant world situation has united workers and business interests to defeat Hitler.

W.: The Tories and the Labour Party came together because of the terrible fright after the fall of Norway, when it was pretty obvious that Britain would soon be in a very bad way. Chamberlain, as you know, tried to bring Labour into the Government several times before but they always said no – so long as Chamberlain was there. Churchill's great power and hold on the people rests as much on his romantic eloquence as on his solid wartime achievements. By words alone he can rally a worried, disgruntled nation or Parliament behind him. All Britishers now think Churchill is the symbol of their determination to beat Hitler, and to fight with their backs to the wall – to the death if necessary. Many people however wonder whether the nation will not soon demand a more *offensive* spirit in British strategy. Already the press is clamouring for Churchill to do something to take the pressure off the Russians. If he doesn't and if the Russians fall, an anti-Churchill movement might begin to snowball. Churchill would have a difficult time stopping it, especially if America criticized him for not being more aggressive.

S.: Is there important opposition to Churchill now?

W.: There is still opposition to Churchill in many quarters and even in Parliament, although it is never evidenced by the vote. Churchill usually makes an appeal for unity in Parliament because of the good effect it will have abroad. Invariably the whole House will go down the line and support him unanimously, but, at the same time, there is an undercurrent of opposition. One of Churchill's strategies when he fears that a debate might go against him is to place the issue on a 'Vote of Confidence' basis. So the House not only expresses its opinion on the subject that was debated but on Churchill as the leader of the Government. If Churchill lost the Vote of Confidence he and his Government would have to resign. Inasmuch as the nation and Parliament want Churchill retained as Prime Minister the House has no alternative but to vote 'yes' regardless of whether the members approve or not. On the several occasions that Churchill has used these tactics many members of the House have been thoroughly annoyed.

S.: What's the opposition to Churchill based on?

W.: The main criticism of Churchill has been on his Home Front policy. That is, people think that he should pay more attention to such things as propaganda, A.R.P., allowances to soldiers' families, food administration and so on. The plain truth, however, is that Home Front matters seem to bore Churchill. He likes to think of twenty divisions here and a Battle Fleet there. Most other things just leave him cold. The most that he has been able to do – and of course it is considerable – is to make various tours through the blitzed areas. But very few will criticize Churchill openly except in the House of Commons. It is so much in vogue to say that Churchill is a great man and a great leader that criticism by the masses is almost unknown. However, if one hints that perhaps Churchill isn't all that he's supposed to be, a great many people respond immediately and will begin to tell all kinds of things that they dislike about him. The press sometimes criticizes Churchill but only after first publishing an introductory eulogy such as: 'We realise that Churchill is a great war leader, that he has united the country, that he saved the nation last summer . . . but –' The criticisms then follow. What do the Germans think of Churchill?

S.: The German Propaganda Ministry has never been able to create a widespread anti-English or anti-Churchill feeling among the people. It has given up trying to work up an anti-English sentiment and sticks to trying to make Germans hate Churchill and Roosevelt. I doubt very much whether this campaign has been successful.

German propaganda in 1942 tended to concentrate on the rumours of Churchill's drinking habits. He was usually referred to, both on the radio and in print, as a drunkard.

Hitler, broadcast, 30 January 1942:

That twaddler, that drunkard, Churchill, what has he achieved in all his lifetime? That mendacious creature, that sluggard of the first order. Had this war not come, future centuries would have spoken of our age, of all of us and also of myself, as the creators of great works of peace. But had this war not come, who would speak of Churchill? True – one day they will speak of him – as the destroyer of an empire which he, not we, have ruined. One of the most abominable characters in world history, incapable of a single creative action, capable only of destruction . . .

Bodensee Rundschau, 3 March 1942:

In the last war our nation lacked unity and our brave soldiers had to fight against a superiority of numbers and material. Today it is ridiculous to imagine that Hitler will be defeated by the drunkard Churchill and the madman Roosevelt.

Owing to their somewhat noticeable lack of detachment, such utterances had little effect on anyone except sycophants at Hitler's headquarters. Churchill, however, was able to hand out as good as he took. His most notable epithet for Hitler and his colleagues was 'that gang of bloodthirsty guttersnipes', which had the added attraction of being unusually apt.

Sir William Beveridge,[1] top letter in *The Times*, 26 January 1942:

The whole people, with exceptions probably still insignificant, want Mr Churchill as Prime Minister to lead them through war to victory. A growing, and by now, I believe, a considerable proportion of the people feel that they need a different government, which means a changed Prime Minister ... Mr Churchill should be willing to resolve, as he alone can resolve, the dilemma of the British nation, by remaining Prime Minister, but revising some of his views and deciding to change both the structure and some of the personnel of his government. He carries in his hands more fates than almost any man whom it is easy to call in mind from any age of history. Will he not resolve our dilemma and complete the tasks which he has so marvellously begun? To learn by experience is an addition to wisdom, not a confession of failure.

On the following day Churchill faced the House in what was likely to be a severe test of his leadership.

Churchill's major critics in Parliament were: Bevan, Stokes, and Shinwell, leading a left-wing Labour group; a right-wing group of former Baldwin and Chamberlain men; and thirdly, independent of any group, Hore-Belisha. In Churchill's exchanges with Stokes and Bevan, there was a personal unpleasantness absent from other duels throughout his long parliamentary career. The flashes of mischievous humour which from time to time laced even his most bitter exchanges, to the delight of generations of members, were absent. During the war, one member observed:[2]

Nobody who has watched Mr Bevan and his evolutions in this House

---

[1] Senior civil servant in the First World War; Director, London School of Economics, 1919–37; Liberal M.P., 1944–5; Baron, 1946.
[2] Eleanor Rathbone.

can doubt that he entertains a malicious and virulent dislike of the Prime Minister.

Churchill recognized in Bevan a parliamentarian and speaker of his own quality. But both were opinionated men of strong will, and inflexible integrity. Bevan always denied a personal basis to the feud. But Churchill once told A. P. Herbert: 'Well, all I can say is that when I look across the Chamber I see in those eyes the fires of implacable hatred.' Churchill was a great admirer of Pitt – Bevan of Fox.

Churchill had decided to challenge the mounting criticism with a vote of confidence in the House: 'It is because things have gone badly and worse is to come that I demand a vote of confidence.' He noted also the wave of criticisms in the newspapers. His opening speech was frank and forthright: 'We have had a great deal of bad news lately from the Far East, and I think it highly probable, for reasons which I shall presently explain, that we shall have a great deal more. Wrapped up in this bad news will be many tales of blunders and shortcomings, both in foresight and action. No one will pretend for a moment that disasters like these occur without there having been faults and shortcomings.'

Was it important at that juncture in the war to place responsibility for the blunders? Perhaps not. But some members were determined to do so. And they were determined to place it upon the Prime Minister. Churchill tried to make the main aspect of the vote the question of the distribution of forces and equipment between North Africa, the Middle East and Russia on the one hand, and the Far East on the other. He felt he was on strong ground: 'The first obvious fact is that the Far Eastern theatre was at peace and that the other theatres were in violent or imminent war.'

F. W. Pethick-Lawrence,[1] House of Commons, 27 January 1942:

I would almost say a smoke-screen has been put over events in the Pacific deliberately to hid them from the British public . . . The British public is also very much alarmed at the disharmony which has arisen between His Majesty's Government in this country and His Majesty's Government in Australia, widely supported, as it appears to be, by the Australian Press and public.

---

[1] Later Lord Pethick-Lawrence: Old Etonian; Labour M.P., 1923-31, 1935-45; Secretary of State for India, 1945-7.

Sir Herbert Williams:[1]

I cannot vote for the government. Obviously, there have been too many mistakes... You have one man dominating the Chiefs of Staff, who are, after all, only employees whom he can sack at any moment... We are facing the most critical moment in the history of our great Empire, and those with strong views have to say what they think. I do not want to change the Prime Minister. I want, as somebody said, a changed Prime Minister. He must remember that he must not resist criticism... I was at a certain gathering of politicians the other day – all Conservatives – and offered to donate ten shillings to a certain benevolent fund if anyone present, unaided, could write out the names of our present War Cabinet. No one could do it. It is a startling thing to say but I cannot find any member of the House who can give the names of the War Cabinet. It is tragic... He is the only person in this country who is satisfied with his own team... Within a reasonable distance of time, it will not be this government that will crash, but he himself will crash, and he will have brought the trouble on himself.

Williams was well known to be an enemy of Churchill. He had, nevertheless, touched on the crux of the problem: the feeling that Churchill, especially in the Service ministries, had surrounded himself with comparatively weak men in order to get his own way. And there was more than ever before a demand for a Minister of Production, as it was felt that Churchill still had a tendency to neglect home affairs; almost every speaker in the debate called for this new post, or mentioned disappointment at the performance of British tanks.

Tributes were showered on the Prime Minister. But almost every speaker had some critical point to make.

Graham White:[2]

There is a growing feeling in this country, among civilians and Service men alike, that they would like to have a much clearer idea of the kind of peace for which we are fighting.

The criticism of the lack of 'war aims' was continually arising; but for most people the aim of the war was the laudable one of destroying Nazi power and ambitions. The Army Bureau of Current Affairs, set up partly in answer to this call, was a source of

---

[1] Conservative M.P., 1924–9, 1932–45; supporter of Chamberlain.
[2] Liberal M.P., 1922–4, 1929–45.

continual embarrassment and irritation to the Army, and was suspected of left-wing political bias.

A year later, Goebbels was to write in his diary:

> The English are making the same mistake, no doubt at Churchill's instigation. They refrain in every way from saying anything tangible about their war aims. I can only add, thank God; for if they were to put up a peace programme on the lines of Wilson's Fourteen Points they would undoubtedly create great difficulties for us.

Harold Nicolson, diary, 27 January 1942:

> [Churchill] says that we shall have even worse news to face in the Far East and that the Libyan battle is going none too well. When he feels that he has the whole House with him, he finds it difficult to conceal his enjoyment of his speech, and that, in fact, is part of his amazing charm. He thrusts both his hands deep into his trouser pockets, and turns his tummy now to the right, now to the left, in evident enjoyment of his mastery of the position. Herbert Williams and [others] attack the government. But the House is not with them. Winston has won in the very first round, and the future rounds will be dull and sad. My God, my love and admiration of Winston surge round me like a tide!

The January 1942 Debate continued with Sir Archibald Southby:[1]

> Let the Prime Minister choose the best men for the various jobs and then leave those men to do their own work... The plain fact is that the Prime Minister cannot be Prime Minister and at the same time Minister of Defence. What is almost more serious is the interference which I believe exists with the expert Service chiefs. I have said on more than one occasion, and I still say, that the difficulties in which we find ourselves are due to faulty strategy. The whole of our war effort should be based fundamentally on sea-plus-air power. [He attacked Churchill for having sent battleships to the Far East without air support.]

Sir Percy Harris:[2]

> I think that all of us who were present during the period when the Prime Minister was absent felt that during his absence the machinery of government was not effective for its purpose. There was a general feeling that there was no one with the real authority to handle the ever-changing position.

---

[1] Royal Navy, 1901–20; Conservative M.P., 1928–47.
[2] Liberal M.P., 1916–18, 1922–45. Harris at this time was Chief Whip of the Liberal Party and its Deputy Leader under Sinclair; died 1952.

Mr Hore-Belisha:

The country requires that he should have regard solely to the public interest in selecting his colleagues and in maintaining them.

Harold Nicolson, 28 January 1942:

Wardlaw-Milne[1] makes an impressive speech attacking the government over Malaya. But the whole thing seems to me unreal since our misfortune is due entirely to the collapse of the American Navy. It is difficult for Winston to say this, and indeed he slid over the point neatly in his speech yesterday. But it is really absurd to expect our people at Singapore to have taken measures of defence on the assumption that the command of the sea would pass suddenly to the Japanese. And even if they had, we could not have provided sufficient to meet such a disaster. Shinwell makes a vicious speech. Randolph Churchill intervenes to defend his father. He attacks most cruelly those who had abused him ... He is amusing and brave. Bob Boothby says to me, 'I am enjoying this very much, but I hope it does not go on for long.' I have a dreadful feeling that Randolph may go too far. I see his little wife squirming in the Gallery, and Winston himself looks embarrassed and shy. But I am not so sure that it has done Randolph harm.

When the House divided the count was 464 to 1. The sole 'No' came from James Maxton, who had been demanding an early Second Front. But there had been several abstentions. And the message from the House of Commons had been very plainly expressed, by speakers from all parties, over three days: change your team – or next time, we will be less amenable in the lobbies.

Harold Nicolson, diary, 29 January 1942:

Third day of the Vote of Confidence debate. Winston winds up. He is very genial and self-confident. He does not gird at his critics. He compliments them on the excellence of their speeches. When he reaches his peroration he ceases to be genial and becomes emphatic. He crouches over the box and strikes it. 'It only remains for us to act. I offer no apologies. I offer no excuses. I make no promises. In no way have I mitigated the sense of danger and impending misfortunes that hang over us. But at the same time I avow my confidence, never stronger than at this moment, that we shall bring this conflict to an end in a manner agreeable to the interests of our country and the future of the world. I

---

[1] For many years a merchant in India, where he rose to high legislative position; assumed mother's name of Wardlaw, 1922; Conservative M.P., 1922–45; 'Munichite'; tried to muster right-wing critics of Churchill in 1942; died 1967.

have finished.' (Then that downward sweep of the two arms, with the palms open to receive the stigmata.) 'Let every man act now in accordance with what he thinks is his duty in harmony with his heart and conscience.' Loud cheers, and we all file out into the thin and stifling lobby. It takes a long time to count the votes, and finally they are recorded as 464 to 1.[1] Huge cheers. Winston gets up and we rise and cheer him. He turns round and bows a little shyly. Then he joins Mrs Winston, and arm-in-arm and beaming, they push through the crowds in Central Lobby. As I pass the tape I find it ticking imperturbably. It tells us that the Germans claim to have entered Benghazi, and that the Japs claim to be only eighteen miles from Singapore. Grave disasters indeed. At the same time we have released the news of the sinking of the *Barham*. A black day for a vote of confidence.

Sir Charles Wilson, diary, 29 January 1942:

As the P.M. prepared for bed tonight he expressed his feeling of relief at the rout of his critics: 'H— is a silly bastard. There are about half a dozen of them; they make a noise out of all proportion to their importance. The House knows this, but unfortunately people abroad take them too seriously; they do a lot of harm. You know how they voted? Four hundred and sixty-four to one.' His voice rose as if he would like to annihilate his detractors.

Count Ciano, Italian Foreign Minister, diary, 28 January 1942:

I have read Churchill's long address attentively. It is clear that times are bad for them, too, and that many disappointments are in store for the future. But it does not seem that he has faltered in his decision to carry on the struggle to the end.

Sir Evelyn Wrench,[2] Bombay, diary, January 1942:

We were very much impressed by Winston's speech, and delighted to see that he got that wonderful vote of confidence, 464 to 1; it will do a lot of good in India here, where they were inclined to think that he was losing his grip.

Two years later, Wrench explained its importance by recalling that 'British stock was at its lowest, and Indians who, two or three years earlier, had loudly proclaimed their loyalty to the Crown, now joined in the gleeful chorus of those who foretold the downfall of the Empire – if the British *raj* was down and out, let it go'.

---

[1] Two Independent Labour Party members, as well as Maxton, acted as tellers in the Division.

[2] Founder of the English-Speaking Union, 1918; editor of the *Spectator*, 1925–32.

There were four possible contenders for the premiership in 1942: Cripps, Eden, Bevin, and Morrison. Of them, two – Eden and Bevin – were definitely not interested, and the other two, if interested, were not willing to show their interest until sure of substantial support. It may be that Beaverbrook saw himself as a possible contender also; he was not without his admirers, and he undoubtedly had some of the qualities for a war leader. One of the most fantastic rumours of the war had occurred in 1940, when it was whispered about in Fleet Street that Beaverbrook would become Prime Minister in a new government.[1] A poll conducted by the British Institute of Public Opinion gave the following order of preference if a successor to Churchill proved necessary because of, for instance, Churchill's death or injury: Eden (nearly 40 per cent), Cripps, Bevin, Attlee, Beaverbrook, Morrison.[2] Shinwell received one per cent of the poll. But none could approach anywhere near Churchill in general esteem and popularity. He had three unassailable advantages: in 1940, a memory which thrilled the public, he had shown himself the guardian of the national will to an extent that brought pleasure even to political philosophers; he had an obsessional love of the House of Commons, which he fondled with obvious and delicate care; and he had no clear rival. Most people were prepared to go on waging war with the man they knew, whom many loved, in the siren suit, with the cigar, the V-sign, and the grin. His removal would have been resented by a majority (perhaps smaller than was thought). The House of Commons knew this, and most members acted accordingly.

On 29 January Cripps – having heard in the House the extent of the criticism of Churchill – declined the offer of the Ministry of Supply. He said he was not prepared to work under Beaverbrook – whom Churchill wanted as Minister of Production – without a place in the War Cabinet. His refusal gave him, as he intended it should, the freedom to express in public his pleas for closer cooperation with Russia, and criticisms of the direction of the war. The whole idea of the Minister of Production, as an 'overlord'

---

[1] *Off the Record*, by Charles Graves, pp. 147, 173.
[2] In a different poll, inquiring about those who ought to be in a reconstructed War Cabinet, Beaverbrook received 60 per cent.

minister, was to keep the War Cabinet small, and Cripps's demand was a disappointment to Churchill. The Prime Minister was meanwhile having extreme difficulty in defining with Beaverbrook what the latter's precise duties would be – 'my patience . . . may be deemed considerable'.

To Churchill's chagrin, Cripps was given an opportunity by the B.B.C. to air some of his views. And in answer to a question, while speaking on a public platform, as to why he was not in the Government, he replied: 'Ask Churchill.' This seemed somewhat disingenuous, as he had already declined a job; because of this Churchill suggested that the correspondence between the two, about the Ministry of Supply, be published. Cripps refused.

Cripps did not confine his critical attitude to domestic affairs and strategy. Perhaps over-impressed by articles in the Press, he tried to discover what was wrong with the Services, particularly the Army, by having frank discussions with dissatisfied commanders. One of those he saw was General Sir Frederick Pile, C.-in-C. of Anti-Aircraft Command – one of the few senior officers who favoured a Second Front in 1942. Pile wrote later: 'I had acquired a great admiration for Sir Stafford's brain and integrity. I was afraid, however, that he was lacking in guile and would probably be shot down.'[1] Whether, in fact, Churchill saw Cripps as a subject to be 'shot down' as a German aircraft by one of Pile's guns is doubtful.

Tribune, 30 January 1942:

It would be an excellent thing for Mr Churchill to make certain changes in his team, but it would be a profound mistake to suppose that from this alone any fundamental improvement would result . . . This is no National Government and Churchill is no National Leader. He struts in that guise but in fact he insists that the war shall be conducted in accordance with the principles of the Tory Party. The British Empire is finished. Nothing can save it. Who wants to? Not the millions who suffered under it. They rejoice to see it go . . . We shall need a different spirit than the one which breathed through the speech of the last Imperial spokesman – Winston Spencer Churchill.

But Bevan had misjudged the public mood at this particular

---

[1] *Ack-Ack*, pp. 260–3. Churchill had a personal liaison officer with Anti-Aircraft Command – his son-in-law, Major Duncan Sandys.

time. His editorials, although much discussed by journalists and politicians, had little influence. No matter what *Tribune* thought about it, the public really did look upon Churchill as a national, not a Conservative, leader. And the citizens of Empire were discovering that the replacement of British rule by Japanese rule brought with it little about which to rejoice.

Next week, *Tribune*, more shrilly, kept up the attack:

It is time the country faced up to the position. We don't blame Margesson [War Minister]. He merely took the job Churchill gave him. Margesson's absurdity for the job is the measure of Churchill's failure as Defence Minister. That failure is costing us precious lives and will cost us more yet.

On 4 February Churchill at last announced the formation of the long called-for Ministry of Production, with Beaverbrook at its head. But Beaverbrook continued to nag about his responsibilities.

Goebbels, diary, 5 February 1942:

Churchill's preparations for the East Asia conflict are being revealed more and more as amateurish. Parliament would undoubtedly have sent him flying long ago if there were an adequate successor. But look as you will far and wide, there is none to be discovered.

Stafford Cripps, *Tribune*, 6 February 1942:

This is indeed a total war [in Russia] total in its suffering and total in its effort. Has it been total in the same intense degree so far as we in England are concerned and the part that we have played?

On 8 February Cripps spoke to a large crowd in Bristol:

There seems to be a lack of urgency in the atmosphere of this country. It is almost as if we were the spectators rather than the participants. Perhaps I might compare it to the difference between a keen and enthusiastic supporter of a football team and one of the members of the team. After the match, the supporter goes home and thinks it all out, not as part of his own active effort, but as something he has seen and studied... We must treat the Soviet Union as our allies in a single war ... if we give to Russia all the support we can, then, in my view, there is every chance of Germany being defeated by this time next year.

Goebbels, diary, 11 February 1942:

The Fuehrer regards the [imminent] fall of Singapore as a very serious thing for the English. He believes a crisis may possibly arise for the British Empire. Churchill's position may be badly shaken. I am not prepared as yet to believe it... Week by week the Tories are becoming more and more distrustful of the Churchill policies. This distrust has been especially fed by the silly declarations of Cripps. The Fuehrer agrees that Cripps is a real treasure for us, to be guarded carefully. His latest effusions have created such a sensation in neutral countries that we may in future expect all sorts of good things from this fair-haired boy.

The *Daily Express* returned to the call for a Second Front on 12 February, eulogized Churchill on 17 February, and warned of the dangers in delaying a Second Front on 19 February.

On 17 February Churchill had the appalling task of explaining to the House of Commons the escape of the *Gneisenau, Scharnhorst,* and *Prinz Eugen* from Brest: and of announcing the fall of Singapore, which had occurred two days before, considered by generations of Englishmen to be an impregnable bulwark of British might and a symbol of British prestige and power. The latter, and worse announcement, he shied from, saying that he could add nothing to what was appearing in the Press.

A debate was immediately demanded. But Churchill declined to arrange one for the present. Among those who protested were Sir John Wardlaw-Milne and Aneurin Bevan. But Churchill insisted that a time-lag was necessary, in order to avoid 'rattling' in the Press. He also pleaded weight of work: 'I must ask the House to realise the enormous burdens falling on me, not by my work as Minister of Defence, but by repeated and constant attendance on this House, which I never expected I should have to face, but which I will face.'

Such appeals brought little sympathy. The burden of trying to do too much was just what his critics had for so long been concerned about. There was no doubt that when the debate sparked off by the fall of Singapore eventually came, it would be a difficult one for the Prime Minister.

Mussolini, on the surrender of Singapore, to his Foreign Minister, 16 February 1942:

I should like to know the effect four British officers, presenting themselves with a white flag of surrender, has had upon those whimsical Orientals. If it had been us, no one would have attached any importance to it, but they were British.

The importance of the scene was, in fact, to extend far beyond the Second World War: Australia, outraged, and New Zealand, astonished, would look to America for future support; China and Japan could afford to hear the roar of the British lion with a somewhat deaf ear. For this incalculable disaster for British prestige, dignity, and power, Winston Churchill was not without his responsibility.

Sir Henry 'Chips' Channon,[1] 17 February 1942:

The House of Commons was restless, crowded and angry, yet it does not seem to know its own mind... Never have I known it growl at a Prime Minister. Can he ever recover his waning prestige? He is such a *Schwärmer* that he basks only in approval; smiles and praise encourage him; criticism irritates and restricts him. Today the august assembly nearly blew up. It was a disgraceful scene which lasted an hour and there was no dignity or force; all sense of reality seemed to have left the elected representatives of the people. We have the first dictator since Cromwell, and much as I distrust Winston (and I fear that he has the evil-eye, or ill-luck; certainly nothing that he has ever touched – Dardanelles, Abdication, India Bill, has come off well), I have even less faith in the Commons – a more moribund collection of old fogies and nit-wits I have never met.

Count Ciano, diary, 18 February 1942:

What once appeared fantastic now seems possible. The Japanese victories are shattering British resistance.

Count Ciano, diary, 20 February 1942:

Ribbentrop prophesies that Great Britain will ask for an armistice in order to save what can still be saved.

But the lion was not entirely stuffed with cotton wool, even if his roar had been overrated – as the Japanese armies were at length to discover.

The war, therefore, had begun for the British in the East just as it had found them in the West: unprepared, clumsy, ignorant, and beaten at every level. But this time there could be no Dunkirk.

On 19 February ministerial changes were announced. They went some way to answering the critics. Cripps was in the War Cabinet as Leader of the House of Commons, a clever ploy by Churchill, which gave his potential rival the task of preserving governmental goodwill in the House. Attlee, who had previously had the job, had been against the appointment; he now became

---

[1] Conservative M.P., 1935–58; died 1958.

Deputy Prime Minister, which could mean a lot or a little. Beaverbrook was out. He was said to be suffering from ill-health, and indeed his health had not been improved by his hard work, his continual arguing, and his various worries. Beaverbrook's asthma had taken a remarkable turn for the worse. Sir Charles Wilson considered that Beaverbrook's real trouble was a lack of confidence in his ability to do the job. Churchill put it down to the fact that he 'sought in his heart that relief from burdens and anxieties which many others of my colleagues also desired'. Harold Macmillan, who had been Beaverbrook's Parliamentary Secretary, has said that Beaverbrook definitely resigned through illness and overwork. Churchill himself, alluding perhaps to a particular fracas in Cabinet, referred to 'what I can only call a nervous breakdown'. In any event, Beaverbrook's tantrums and resignation could not have come at a worse time for the Government. His position in the War Cabinet had become almost impossible. Bevin and himself were hardly on speaking terms; his own newspapers were pressing for a Second Front in defiance of Cabinet policy; he could not agree about the powers of the new Ministry of Production. At one Cabinet meeting he had become angry, offered his resignation (a not unusual occurrence), got up and left the room. Perhaps somewhat to Beaverbrook's surprise Churchill accepted the resignation. The Prime Minister had become disturbed at the disunity and friction which Beaverbrook had brought to the Cabinet since his visit to Moscow. He had demanded, said Churchill, 'ever wider and more untrammelled powers'. He had made another enemy when he said in Cabinet of Attlee, 'Why, I've even less say than that miserable little man.'

Beaverbrook went off to America with vaguely defined duties. From Florida he continued to direct his campaign on behalf of Russia. No doubt he watched, from across the Atlantic, the fortunes of his old friend in consolidating his position.

Cripps – austere, principled, independent – was likely to prove just as difficult a Cabinet colleague for the Prime Minister. In his first speech to the House as a member of the War Cabinet, he promised that a new seriousness and austerity would be brought to public life. It was a role which seemed to come to him all too easily: 'We are not engaged in a war in which we can have slogans either Business as Usual or Pleasure as Usual.'

Lord Beaverbrook, Miami, a few weeks later:

> The way of freedom for Russia is the road to liberty for all of us in this world of grief and woe. Among the free peoples of Britain, the Empire, and the United States, who have had to bear such grievous misfortunes and who have been compelled to suffer all the vexations of defeat and retreat, the cry goes up now for offensive action. This is the proper mood for great nations who are resolved to stay great... Attack by sea, attack by air, attack in the field... Too often he [Churchill] has been criticized and condemned by those who know nothing of his difficulties. Too often he has been held responsible for issues that did not concern him. Too many times he has been told to guide the airplane by those who have never flown... let us cherish our leader – Churchill.

Clearly, Lord Beaverbrook was never to be numbered among the critics of Churchill as war leader.

Within five weeks of the Cabinet reshuffle, Cripps was sent on a mission to India. It was not a success, through no fault of his; discomfort in the War Cabinet continued. The only question was how long would Sir Stafford, still highly critical of the way the war was being conducted, wait before resigning.

Churchill's old friend, Oliver Lyttleton the businessman, was brought back from Cairo to fill the vacant post at the new Ministry of Production ('I had known him from childhood in his father's house').

Also sacked from the War Cabinet were Sir Kingsley Wood, Chancellor of the Exchequer, and Arthur Greenwood, the respected but un-warlike pride of the Labour Party. Outside the Cabinet, there was a new War Minister: Sir James Grigg (replacing David Margesson), who had previously been the senior civil servant at the War Office – an unprecedented promotion (if promotion it were). Whether he would prove a more forceful rider than his predecessors, of the Prime Minister's favourite hobby-horse, remained to be seen. To placate the Australian demands, R. G. Casey was made a Cabinet Minister, with responsibility to the Middle East. But the effect was spoilt by the extraordinary way in which the appointment was made – Churchill omitted to discuss it with or even inform the Australian Prime Minister, who took it as a snub.

Admiral James, letter, 1942:

It is doubtful if the Prime Minister, when he went to the House, had any intention of giving way to the demands that he should reconstruct and reorganise his Cabinet. The view in London is that some of the newcomers to the Cabinet insisted on Beaverbrook giving up his office. I shall always remember Beaverbrook's generosity over our Allied Club. There is no doubt that he is a man who gets things done, a human dynamo, but many people criticise the 'current' he uses. But whatever course these debates take, even the most casual reader of the political news can see that the last thing the Commons want is to turn out the Prime Minister. They know, just as every man, woman and child knows, that there is no one else who can see us through these tremendous times. A few people have short memories, but the vast majority of our people have not forgotten the time when the Prime Minister, by his splendid oratory, welded the nation together and inspired the people to work and fight as they had never done before. On the other hand, it is not only the Commons who have felt for some time that the Prime Minister has been shouldering a burden too heavy for any man, and that he should have a stronger team to help him. But if the Prime Minister, who always looks very robust, and whose vitality and youthfulness has surprised everyone here on more than one occasion, does not want strong, masterful men at the council table, he will not have them, and I prophesy he will go his own way till the end, perhaps giving way a little here and there to appease the critics.

The new Minister in the Middle East proved to be competent and useful – from Churchill's point of view.

Casey,[1] diary, later in 1942:

I have become aware in the last month or so that when W.S.C. starts a telegram with the words 'Pray be so good as to . . .' it means he has something on his mind about you or 'us' that he is not happy about, and you'd better watch out. He has an unmistakable telegraphic style, which is as different from the orthodox official telegram as chalk from cheese.

The debate Churchill had promised on Singapore took place on 24 January. He still could not bring himself to announce the city's surrender: 'I have no news whatever from Singapore to give to the House . . . I am therefore unable to make any statement

---

[1] In Australian Foreign Service 1924–31; Member of House of Representatives, 1931–40, 1949–60; Minister to the United States, 1940–2; Minister, War Cabinet, in Middle East, 1942–3; Minister for External Affairs, 1951–60; Life Peer, 1960; Governor-General, 1965–.

about it.' The Press had already announced the surrender nine days before.

But because of his ministerial changes, the Prime Minister found a slightly more favourable House than he had done on the 17th. He was complimented for his responsiveness to parliamentary opinion. But one source of irritation to some, and of genuine concern to others, remained – the Minister of Defence himself. Churchill said: 'It is my practice to leave the Chiefs of Staff alone to do their own work, subject to my general supervision, suggestion, and guidance.' And that was the way it was to be. It was clear that if he had to give up defence, he would give up the premiership too. In a thrust at Lloyd George, he said: 'It is now the fashion to speak of the Lloyd George War Cabinet as if it gave universal satisfaction and conducted the war with unerring judgment and unbroken success. On the contrary, complaints were loud and clamant. Immense disasters, such as the slaughter of Passchendaele . . . befell that rightly famous administration. It made numerous serious mistakes. No one was more surprised than its members when the end of the war came suddenly in 1918.'

Long and critical reviews of recent events and strategy were made by James Griffiths, Sir Archibald Southby and J. H. Martin. Demands were made for commissions of inquiry into the escape of the German warships from Brest, and the loss of Malaya.

Clement Davies:[1]

We are asking that the Minister of Defence should be responsible to somebody. To whom is he responsible? To the House? If we ask a question about Singapore we are told that it is not in the public interest to tell us . . . That is why we have been asking that the Minister of Defence should be separated from the dominating personality of the Prime Minister.

Richard Stokes:

When this Prime Minister took over, he abolished Service Ministers attending the Cabinet and himself became Minister of Defence. He is now, therefore, in a position to go to the Service Ministers and discuss the strategy of the war and then go to the Cabinet and, as Minister of Defence, report, with himself in the chair as Prime Minister, the result of his consultations with the Service chiefs.

---

[1] Liberal M.P., 1929– ; Leader of Liberal Party, 1945–56.

Stephen King-Hall expressed what many people felt:

> When the downfall of France came it really roused us to survival. At that time the Prime Minister was the epitome of the nation. We felt very near to him ... They were dangerous times, but they were great times, and I feel that we are in dangerous times now, although there is no greatness at the present time. There is a sort of apathy, a sense of frustration.

Goebbels, 1 March 1942:

> The *Manchester Guardian* now admits that morale in England was about as low as possible before the reshuffling of the Cabinet. I am now convinced that a crisis of dangerous proportions existed during these days in London. One never learns about such things until much later. That's the way it was, too, during World War I. The English people show fantastic national discipline, especially in wartime. Anything they want to keep to themselves simply doesn't get out.

A typical example of the German propagandist's wishful thinking, and lazy logic (he had been reading all about the recent 'crisis of dangerous proportions' in the London Press).

There had also been a debate in the House of Lords.

Admiral of the Fleet Lord Chatfield, who had been in Chamberlain's War Cabinet, House of Lords, 25 February 1942:

> Mr Chamberlain took the office of Defence Minister, and kept in the War Cabinet the three Service Ministers. The organization was a perfectly sound one but when two months later in May 1940, there was a change of government, changes of great importance were made. The new Prime Minister became the Minister of Defence, he became Chairman of the Chief of Staff's Committee, and he removed from the War Cabinet the Service Ministers ... [he was] not only the advocate of the decisions that he had made, but also, as Prime Minister, the final arbiter of whether his decision was to be agreed to or not ... The Prime Minister emphasised yesterday, that he took personal responsibility for whatever occurred ... I would say to you that there is no man who can hold that single responsibility in a war of this nature, safely ... I can assure Your Lordships that I have had representations made to me by those who work in Whitehall that the hours they have to work are perfectly intolerable. It does not lead to efficiency, as the noble Lord said. Nobody is at his best in the Middle Watch ... I believe it is the height of inefficiency and bad administration to work such hours, which really cannot be necessary, and it only wants a certain amount of sacrifice on the part of different people in order to get a proper working arrangement, efficient in all respects.

Lord Hankey also spoke critically of Churchill's personal conduct, in particular the late hours of Cabinet and defence meetings. Hankey was a member of the Government, as Paymaster-General. He had been in Chamberlain's War Cabinet. A week later, he was out of office.

Criticism of Churchill had not been confined to England. The more anglophobe sections of the American Press had not been blind to their opportunities.

Goebbels, 2 February 1942:

> In the United States a lot of criticism is at present directed against Churchill. We take no note of this criticism because we don't want this tender plant of disagreement between the two allies to die prematurely.

Early in March, the Japanese completed their conquest of the Dutch East Indies. At about the same time, MacArthur left his remaining troops, besieged and doomed, and sailed for Sydney.

The start of the Japanese war had not deterred Churchill from his view that the Middle East was still vital. Although he knew that the war could not be won there, he was convinced that it could be lost there. And there was another reason for his interest in that area. Lord Moran has written: 'My diary for 1942 has the same backcloth to every scene: Winston's conviction that his life as Prime Minister could be saved only by a victory in the field.' Auchinleck was now receiving a similar bombardment of advice, urgings, and exhortations as Wavell had done before.

Brooke, 2 March 1942:

> Found P.M. had drafted a bad wire for Auchinleck in which he poured abuse on him for not attacking sooner. Without it being possible for him to be familiar with all aspects of the situation . . . he is trying to force him to attack at an earlier date than is thought advisable and, what is more, tried to obtain his ends by an offensive wire. Thank Heaven we were able to stop the wire and re-word it.

'It is very exhausting,' Brooke wrote on 24 March, 'this continual protecting of Auchinleck . . .'. Rommel had launched his second counter-offensive at the end of January and had regained much of the ground lost in the previous year. In an advance of nearly three hundred miles, he captured practically all the stores

Auchinleck had been gathering for his own offensive. Auchinleck came to the conclusion that 'to meet German armoured forces with any hope of success our armoured forces as at present equipped, organised, and led must have at least two to one superiority'. He said he could do nothing till July. There were at this time over 630,000 British and Dominion servicemen under his command. Churchill told him, 'You have substantial superiority in the air, in armour, and in other forces over the enemy.'

Major-General Kennedy, March 1942:

Winston is very touchy about the offensive and defensive spirit, and any hint of the latter always rouses him even when quite fair. It is a fault on the right side.

Hitler, meanwhile, was continuing with his conquest of Russia. He already had Leningrad; he was almost within sight of Moscow.

Goebbels, diary, 1942:

The debate in England still revolves around the argument that a victory must be won at least in one theatre of war, and that this theatre is Libya. Churchill has now become a collector of deserts.

Churchill was, however, becoming increasingly interested in the bombing of Germany – in which he had harboured high hopes from the beginning.[1] On 23 February Sir Arthur 'Bomber' Harris took over Bomber Command.

The controversy over area bombing as oppcsed to the bombing of selected military targets continued, mostly behind the scenes, for four years. Opposed to Churchill, Harris, and Cherwell, on strategic grounds, were Professors P. M. S. Blackett, H. Tizard, and S. Zuckermann. The first 'area-raid' had taken place as long before as 16 December 1940. In 1940–41 such bombing had lost more members of the R.A.F. than it had killed Germans. Since 14 February 1942, Bomber Command had been directed to attack

---

[1] In June 1938, Cordell Hull, United States Secretary of State, urged other nations to join with the United States in the formulation of rules of warfare, particularly the abolition of bombing. On 16 June 1938, Chamberlain was asked in the House to support this by stopping bombing on the North–West Frontier. He said he wouldn't. On 22 February 1945, Churchill gave an almost identical answer when asked to consider the abolition of bombing after the war.

residential areas in certain industrial cities. This was a week before Sir Arthur Harris had taken up his command as C.-in-C., Bomber Command. Harris therefore had nothing to do with the policy; he carried out his orders – fully believing in the effectiveness – with vigour. Harris was the man for the job. He had only sixty-nine *heavy* bombers, but he set about improving that immediately. During March a bitter row took place between the scientists as to whether a bombing offensive was feasible and useful. Lord Cherwell (Frederick Lindemann) and Sir Henry Tizard had been engaged in an absurd academic feud since the 1920s. On 30 March Cherwell told Churchill: 'Investigation seems to show that having one's house demolished is most damaging to morale.' This shaft of scientific inspiration led him to advocate the bombing of built-up areas. Tizard did not disagree with the premise, but he insisted that could not be done with the forces available. Cherwell, who was also a strong opponent of an early Second Front, had the ear of Churchill. Two months later, over 1,000 bombers raided Cologne.

Brooke, March 1942:

The last day of the first quarter of 1942 – fateful year in which we have already lost a large proportion of the British Empire and are on the high road to lose a great deal more of it. During the last fortnight I have had for the first time since the war started a growing conviction that we are going to lose this war unless we control it very differently and fight it with more determination ... There are times when I wish to God I had not been placed at the helm of a ship that seems to be heading inevitably for the rocks. It is a great honour to find myself entrusted with such a task, and the hope of saving the ship a most inspiring thought and one that does override all others. But, may God help me and guide me in my task!

Diana Cooper, London, March 1942:

Winston dresses night and day, and I imagine in bed, in the same little blue workman's boiler suit. He looks exactly like the good little pig building his house with bricks. On his feet he bears inappropriately a pair of gold-embroidered black slippers that I gave him – more suited to the silk-stockinged leg of William Pitt. Over all this, if chilly, he's got a quilted dressing-gown, once Pooh-Bah's of *The Mikado* fame, woven in bright spectrum colours. New neighbours dropping in think, I imagine, that it is ceremonial dress, as he never excuses its eccentricity.

After his successful handling of the political crisis, Churchill felt strong enough to tackle the Press – and this time more firmly.

The *Daily Worker* had already been banned for opposing the war.

The *Daily Mirror* had begun an attack on the generals. It was at a time when the War Office was striving to restore morale to the British soldier after his many defeats in battle.

Daily Mirror, March 1942:

> The accepted tip for Army leadership would, in plain truth, be this: – All who aspire to mislead others in war should be brass-buttoned boneheads, socially prejudiced, arrogant and fussy. A tendency to heart disease, apoplexy, diabetes and high blood pressure is desirable in the highest posts.

It would have been relevant journalism if it had been printed twenty-five years before. A brilliant and bitter cartoon of Philip Zec brought matters to a head. Ministers had become increasingly and unusually sensitive to criticism, particularly those who had held high public office before, like Bevin. Morrison issued a warning to the Press; abuse in wartime of freedom of speech and expression would not be tolerated. He reminded Fleet Street of Regulation 2D, which gave the Home Secretary very wide and immediate powers. The regulation had only been approved by the House of Commons, at a time of extreme national crisis, by the small majority of 38. There were many protests at this latest threat. There was a Press Freedom meeting at Central Hall; Rose Macaulay, T. L. Horobin, M.P., and Michael Foot spoke at it. The House debated the matter on 26 March.

Wilfrid Roberts:[1]

> The crime of the *Daily Mirror* is to criticize the government, and all I ask on this point is that, if the crime is against the government, the government should not judge that crime, but that the normal processes of law should be invoked ... The crime of the *Daily Mirror* is to have been too critical. But a newspaper reflects the opinion of the public who read it.

Sir Irving Albery:[2]

> The press today is looking to the House, to uphold the liberty of the press ... the right hon. Gentleman the Prime Minister hardly ever intervenes in a Debate of this kind without showing and expressing his reverence for, and his desire in every way to uphold, democratic traditions in the House of Commons and in the country. I believe in the

---

[1] Liberal M.P., 1935–50.   [2] Conservative M.P., 1924–45.

main that he sincerely expresses these sentiments, but at the same time the House of Commons would be glad to see him take some action to assist towards that end.

In his contribution, Aneurin Bevan made an unexpected admission:

I do not like the *Daily Mirror*, and I have never liked it. I do not see it very often. I do not like that form of journalism. I do not like the striptease artists. If the *Daily Mirror* depended upon my purchasing it, it would never be sold . . . [But] one never knows now what it is possible to write because of the effect it might have on the morale of the country. I have to edit a page every week. I do not know what to do under this kind of censorship.

Others who spoke of the alarm at the Government's threat were A. P. Herbert and Hore-Belisha.

During the course of his speech, Morrison revealed that it was a Cassandra article which had really riled the Government.

Herbert Morrison:

I resent allusions that either the government or I have the slightest desire to interfere with the legitimate and proper liberty of the press. Let it be remembered that under the procedure of Regulation 2D, if I had prosecuted the House would not have been able to say anything about the matter. I could have prosecuted, I could have gone for the heaviest penalties I could get, and the House could not have debated the propriety of my action.[1]

Within a few days of the debate William Connor, 'Cassandra', joined up in the Army. (He eventually joined the staff of an Army newspaper, whereupon a Conservative M.P., Henry Longhurst, a golf reporter, dutifully rose in the House to question why Connor 'should now be writing the same sort of thing in an Army newspaper'). Hugh Cudlipp, the editor who had previously been in trouble, was already in the Army. The record of the British newspapers in the Second World War was in sharp contrast to their

---

[1] In 1943 Morrison was heavily criticized for releasing the British Fascist leader, Sir Oswald Mosley, and his wife, who had been detained under the special powers of Regulation 18B. Churchill encouraged the move. 'Nothing can be more abhorrent to democracy than to imprison a person or keep him in prison because he is unpopular' – but Morrison had to face Cabinet and Parliamentary critics alone, which he did not appreciate.

miserable performance during the earlier war. If the Cabinet had suppressed Press criticism, it would have caused an uproar far greater than anything the Press was causing in its censure.

With the Germans renewing their advance in Russia, the 'Second Front Now' movement was gaining all the time. Encouraged by Beaverbrook, Roosevelt dispatched Hopkins on another mission. His object was to persuade Churchill to agree to a 'limited invasion' in the autumn of 1942. Beaverbrook remained in the United States, at Roosevelt's request: 'I need you here – there is no one else I can talk to when we get word in the course of the next few days.' Beaverbrook was acting as one of Roosevelt's principal advisers on the Second Front dialogue, and was virtually a presidential aide[1] – not, presumably, what Churchill had intended by 'vaguely defined duties'.

Brooke, 10 April 1942:

A very busy day which started with usual Chiefs of Staff meeting, mainly concerned in trying to save India from the Japs; a gloomy prospect with loss of command of sea and air . . . In evening another C.O.S. meeting to discuss Joint Planning Staff report on Marshall's scheme for invasion of Europe.[2] Then out to Chequers for dinner and the night. Harry Hopkins and Marshall there, also three Chiefs of Staff. We were kept up till 2 a.m. doing a world survey but little useful work. This was followed by a film which lasted till 2.45 a.m. Marshall's face was a study. He was evidently not used to being kept out of his bed till the small hours of the morning and was not enjoying it much . . . I wonder how he would like to work permanently with Winston or to be kept out of bed three or four nights a week.

The same, 14 April 1942:

Back to Downing Street for a Defence Committee attended by Hopkins and Marshall. A momentous meeting at which we accepted their proposals for offensive action in Europe in 1942 perhaps, and in 1943 for certain. They have not begun to realise all the implications of this plan and all the difficulties that lie ahead of us. The fear I have is that they should concentrate on this offensive at the expense of all else. We have therefore been pressing on them the importance of providing American assistance in the Indian Ocean and Middle East.

---

[1] *The Roosevelt Letters*, Volume III.

[2] Staff Officer in France, First World War; Army Chief of Staff, 1939–45; Secretary of State, 1947–9; Secretary of Defence, 1950–5.

It was to the 'in 1942 perhaps' that the American Chiefs of Staff harnessed such hopes, and that was to cause further trouble later in the year.

Harold Nicolson, diary, 15 April 1942:

We are addressed by Harry Hopkins in the large Committee Room. He is very astute and makes a good impression. The implication of what he said was that we should be mad to get rid of Winston, since he is the only man who really understands Roosevelt. It was cleverly done. He talks of Anglo-American relations and says that there are many people in the U.S.A. who say that we are yellow and can't fight. It is true that we have been beaten in everything we do.

Harold Nicolson, diary, 22 April 1942:

Malcolm [Macdonald] had been lunching today with Winston. He said that the latter has no illusions at all about the decline in his popularity. 'I am like a bomber pilot,' he said. 'I go out night after night, and I know that one night I shall not return.' Malcolm is in fact rather appalled by the slump in Winston's popularity. A year ago he would have put his stock at 108, and today, in his opinion, it is as low as 65. He admits that a success will enable it to recover. But the old enthusiasm is dead for ever. How foul is public life and popular ingratitude!

But not all politicians have a good gauge of public opinion, and this was a pessimistic view.

Harold Nicolson, diary, 21 April 1942:

Secret Session in the House. I am not allowed, even in my diary, to give all the details of what passed, but I can at least give the outline. Cripps, on his return from India, was received with a cheer stronger than that accorded to Winston. The latter when he rose (and after all the strangers had been spied and harried from the House) adopted his stolid, obstinate, ploughman manner. He tells of Singapore, where the conduct of our large army does 'not seem to have been in harmony with the past or present spirit of our forces'. He tells us of the Naval position in the Indian Ocean, and how the ships came to be lost.[1] He tells us of the Middle East and what happened at Alexandria.[2] He tells us of our present dangers and prospects and dwells at length upon the heavy sinkings which we are sustaining in the eastern Atlantic. It is a long and utterly remorseless catalogue of disaster and misfortune. And as he tells us one thing after another, gradually the feeling rises in the packed

---

[1] The *Prince of Wales* and the *Repulse*.
[2] The *Queen Elizabeth* and *Valiant* had been sunk by Italian one-man torpedoes in Alexandria Harbour on 8 December.

House. 'No man', Members begin to feel in their hearts, 'no man but he could tell us of such disaster and increase rather than diminish confidence.' He has the psychological force of a supreme specialist who tells one that there are signs of tuberculosis, that one may become very ill, but that cure is certain. And as this feeling rises, there rises with it a feeling of shame at having doubted him. He ends without rhetoric, but with a statement about our aircraft production which is encouraging. The House gives him a great ovation and the debate thereafter peters out. I go to the St George's Day pageant organised by the *Daily Express* at the Albert Hall. Winston is there in the royal box. He gives the V-sign to an audience which does not greet him with any tumultuous applause.

Beaverbrook, New York, 23 April 1942:

Ever since my journey to Russia in October last I have been in favour of a second front . . . Stalin has pledged his word to make war and peace with Great Britain and America. He will respect his promise. Stalin accepts the Atlantic Charter . . . He did so in my presence. He expressed no dissent, but entire agreement . . . Our own great leader, Mr Churchill – I read in all the newspapers and I am told here and there wherever I go, that he will fall before the summer is out. You must help me to kill that bad rumour. Such a disaster we cannot contemplate in Great Britain . . . We place our faith in him.

Yes; but who was spreading the rumour? In what British newspapers, apart from the *Daily Express*, had it appeared? The *New York Times* heralded this speech as the 'return of Lord Beaverbrook to politics and opposition politics at that'.

That Beaverbrook protested his loyalty, both in letters and his newspapers, may have caused Churchill more alarm than comfort. Beaverbrook had obsessional tendencies about bringing down governments, although he had seldom had as much to do with such occurrences as he liked to believe.

In April, Hitler and Mussolini met to discuss their good fortune, and to ponder further plans. Mussolini's Foreign Minister was more weary of the war than ever.

Count Ciano, Salzburg, 29 April 1942:

The winter months in Russia have weighed heavily upon him [Hitler]. I see for the first time that he has many grey hairs. Hitler talks with the Duce, I talk with Ribbentrop, but in two separate rooms, and the same record is played in both . . . When Russia's sources of oil are exhausted she will be brought to her knees. Then the British Conservatives, and even Churchill himself, who, after all, is a sensible man, will bow in order to save what remains of their mauled Empire. Thus spoke Ribbentrop. But what if all this doesn't happen? What if the British, who are stubborn, decide to continue? What course must be followed to change their minds? Aeroplanes and submarines, says Ribbentrop. We turn back to the 1940 formula. But this formula failed then ... I am little convinced by it, and say so to Ribbentrop.

On May Day, 1942, *Tribune* opened its second offensive of the year against Churchill. The article was written under pseudonym by Frank Owen, who had recently been editor of Beaverbrook's *Evening Standard*. It has been said that much of the factual material for the article was supplied by Lieutenant-General G. le Q. Martel, of the Royal Armoured Corps, in which Owen was then serving.

There is something to be said for Mr Churchill's Government and it has been exhaustively said. The eager Parliamentary Private Secretaries, the brackenised B.B.C., and the 2D-ed press raise a symphony of praise to the head of the least successful War Administration in Britain for 170 years ... The form has become stereotyped. It opens with the familiar picture of June, 1940, 'when we stood alone and almost with bare hands'. Thus does Churchill wash his own hands of anything that occurred before June, 1940. The recital proceeds via the Battle of Britain and the Blitz, dips into the Atlantic, skirts Libya, by-passes Crete, and comes briefly to the Hitler assault on Russia in June, 1941. We travel on to the Atlantic Charter and dwell on its profound significance, which is necessary, since nobody whatever now remembers one word of it. Then comes the Jap swoop on Pearl Harbour and the long sad story of Malaya, Singapore and Java, mingled with references to our misfortunes at sea in that area. Ah! How could the most far-sighted statesman – or most crapulous critic – have foreseen this melancholy concatenation of disasters? Particularly painful to one who boasts so often that he never boasts at all, and who had so confidently counted on another year of piling up the Allied strength until in 1943 we could begin to march across the sunlit uplands towards the beckoning crest of Final Victory. Such is the Blenheim version of the Churchill Saga. It falls on the fed-up ears of millions of Britons – just as I imagine the Hitler saga now numbs the ears of millions of Teutons. These reminiscences bear no more relevance to our present discontents than would the testament of the late Mr Chamberlain explaining Munich and *his* struggle. What is to be said *against* the Churchill Government? Quite a lot also, though little will be published if Churchill has his way. We shall do here what we can. But first let us point out that the history of this war, and of Mr Winston Churchill's part in it, did not begin in

June or May, 1940, when he became Prime Minister. Churchill has been a member of the British War Cabinet since the first days of the war. He joined Mr Chamberlain as First Lord of the Admiralty on September 3rd, 1939, and from that day forward he was accorded by his colleagues the leading military role in their counsels. The British nation has had nearly three years of Churchill war-making . . . I make these open charges: (1) That it was Churchill, the then First Lord of the Admiralty, who by his wirelessed orders sent the British warships off on a fool's errand to the north while the German warships forced the south Norway fiords; and (2) it was Churchill who held back the British Admirals from breaking into Trondheim while there was still time to eject the newly-landed Germans. No wonder Churchill, on the dramatic Norway debate which killed Chamberlain and made himself king, defended the British Government with all his fire and skill. No wonder that Churchill has ever since discouraged recriminations about Norway and refused all other inquiries into our naval and military reverses . . . Churchill always had a ludicrously romantic conception of the real value of the French Army. The fellow's head is stuffed with the same nonsense about Napoleon and his tradition as it is about Marlborough. Churchill, the Modern War Lord, has never yet grasped the elementary fact that an army is just as good (or bad) as the social foundations on which it rests. The shrilling bugles go to his head! He hears the deep drums – and he is drunk! He sees the proud fluttering flags – and he could weep! He often does! About the solid industrial base of modern armies and the inter-relation of those economic forces which comprise it the British War Premier and Minister of Defence knows less than his Minister of Information. Before the Battle in the West opened Churchill took the same view as those wooden-headed, iron-sided English generals who were daring Hitler to 'come on'. He had the same penetrating vision as General Gamelin himself . . . As for the Maginot Line – it was IT! The Maginot was the *ne plus ultra* of 1940. Two or three times in the winter of 1939–40 the then First Lord of the Admiralty had felt it his duty to visit both the British and French zones fronting the enemy and there to poke his nose into the defences. (Mr Hore-Belisha, then War Minister, showed unusual restraint in refraining from returning the call by inspecting the Scapa Flow defences, which stood in equal need of scrutiny.) From all these operations Churchill returned without expressing the least anxiety about the impregnability of the Western Front. It is a matter of Cabinet history, incidentally, that Hore-Belisha finally inflamed the hostility of the generals by giving voice to *his* doubts. So we come to the Battle of Flanders, Dunkirk, and the Battle of France. None will ever deny or denigrate Churchill's personal services in those black days. He had no choice than to order the evacuation of the British Army. When the Army returned to these shores it was destitute of arms. The whole country was bare of arms. I declare that Churchill, after nine months in the War Cabinet, must bear some responsibility for that. Nevertheless his spirit and voice magnificently rallied the country in its desperate plight. The man was great in our hour of defeat, and if none of his present political lackeys will write that on his tomb, I will take time off to do it. I say now that we cannot fight a war for a world on grateful memories. Nor do I personally hold so poor a view of my countrymen as to suppose that if Churchill had failed to promise that Britain would fight on the beaches we should all have surrendered to the first Nazi on Dover Pier. History will write that if Winston Churchill saved Britain in June, 1940, Britain also did a bit towards saving Winston Churchill and party. But I concede him his ancient glory. I am concerned here, along with millions of my fellow citizens, only with the man's capacity to carry the war forward.

On 3 May *Tribune* continued its series on the Prime Minister. This time, it examined the humiliation of the Greek campaign.

The tanks and troops which should have been in Tripolitania went to Greece. After 22 days the Balkan War was over and 15,000 British and Imperial troops were prisoners or dead. The equipment of as many more remained in the hands of the enemy. Crete remained, and Churchill was going to hold that at all costs. It was held by about 28,000 Allied troops, many of whom had been evacuated disarmed from Greece. After four days the island was taken by parachutists and airborne troops, though the final agonies were prolonged for another week. The attack was supported by overwhelming bomber forces, and when a British fleet made a desperate (and successful) effort to break up a sea descent, they lost heavily. Churchill might have learned from this Cretan experience that warships cannot operate in narrow waters without air support – but he didn't ... Thus did the modern Marlborough throw away his country's finest opportunity in the three years' war. It is claimed now for him that the Greek campaign held up Hitler's attack on Russia for five vital weeks. A triumphant British move into Tripoli and up to Tunis would have exercised Hitler a great deal more.

Author, 10 May 1942:

The Prime Minister made his great radio speech, warning the Germans that if they used poison gas on the Russian front the R.A.F. would make immediate reprisals on German territory ... There was vigorous optimism in his voice, but Londoners had no illusions about the seriousness of his warning. They realised that a heavy gas attack on London was a growing possibility. Madeleine continued to take our young son to the Green Park every afternoon. He amused himself all alone, making sand castles, plotting imaginary gardens, or watching the duck and drake ... the daily frequenters of the Green Park formed a little coterie of their own. They sat in deck chairs in what they liked to call 'The Lake District' – that is to say that little stretch of green grass protected from the wind between the sump and the palisades of the A.R.P. shelters ... From time to time somebody was lucky enough to obtain five or six pounds of horse meat from one of the Belgian shops in Soho, after hours of waiting in a queue. She might share out some of this ... The Prime Minister's speech brought a grim change to these feminine meetings. Those who had never troubled to carry their gas masks decided not only to bring them, but also to organize a rehearsal during which each would wear hers while knitting, so that Bobby should get used to the sight of these terrifying appendages.[1]

Tribune, 15 May 1942:

For three weeks *Tribune* has been publishing a series of articles by Thomas Rainboro'. These articles have been highly critical of Mr Churchill's military conduct of the war. They have aroused widespread controversy: indeed, no articles published since the war began have created more interest. In the first place we give readers of *Tribune* an assurance that the pen-name of Thomas Rainboro' covers the identity of a publicist with unrivalled knowledge of the matters about which he writes; that he is at the same time a brilliant writer the readers of his articles will know for themselves. We have to answer the question, why it is that we publish at this time such a forthright criticism of Mr Churchill's military strategy. We do so in the first place because we consider that public opinion in this country is dangerously ill-informed. The normal sources of information which were available during the last war, and certainly in times of peace, are dried up or choked. The national Press of Great Britain is more closely allied to governing circles than ever it was in British history. An over-centralised Press, dominated by a small number of Press lords with axes to grind, with personal ambitions to be satisfied, conceals from the public a great deal of constructive criticism which should be heard. At the same time a new instrument of mass suggestion has been created. The wireless – always a dangerous weapon in the hands of dictatorial governments – is more especially so in war-time. Only the official voice is heard on the air. Only the official case is put. Only the apologists of official policy, or a few lukewarm, tepid and fearful commentators are permitted to have access to the

---

[1] It was Churchill's idea that Britain should retaliate, and his suggestion to Stalin that this should be announced: 'I have been building up an immense store of gas bombs for discharge from aircraft.' The author was Robert Henry, who wrote a number of books about wartime London.

microphone. Mr Churchill can put his case to Great Britain, but his critics cannot. This is an extremely dangerous situation. At the same time the House of Commons, where there are a small number of public-spirited Members of Parliament who raise their voices from time to time, is cut off from the British people, both by limitation of newspaper space, and by the deliberate act of those who control the newspapers. Journals like *Tribune* have therefore a duty to perform to enlighten the people of Great Britain in the views of those who disagree fundamentally with the way in which the country's affairs are being managed. On Sunday night Mr Churchill made another brilliant speech which has been acclaimed as a great success. How long can we afford a succession of oratorical successes accompanied by a series of military disasters? The people of Great Britain are living in a dream land: a dream land produced by rhetoric by wishful dreams and by the absence of mental astringency to correct their delusions. A corrective must be found for this mood. Thomas Rainboro's articles constitute one of those correctives. That is why *Tribune* published them and will continue to do so. The lesson of the war is surely this, that military decisions have been made by a hand-to-mouth process, in which the individual initiative of the Prime Minister appears as a series of brilliant illuminations, which are only afterwards revealed as more or less unfortunate improvisations. This kind of war cannot be fought that way. The higher direction needs planning and thinking out ahead. No one man can do this.

The final 'Rainboro'' article was a call for a Second Front:

On Sunday, Churchill, after carrying out a campaign of intimidation against the Second Fronters without recent parallel in British politics, joined the second front. He welcomed the 'aggressive military spirit of the British people' which for several by-elections he had denounced as ill-informed and ill-conditioned armchair strategy. No doubt the temporary success of his broadcast owes something to this. He had better be careful. If he merely gave out words to conceal his intention to act, the retaliation will be swift. And will he act before 1943? Churchill has made up his mind to win this war. He is going to end the job that Marlborough was not allowed to end, the War of Succession. He is going to be the hero-victor of 1943. Nothing is to be allowed to interfere with that purpose and that project. Therefore no risks until overwhelming strength is ours. It is not a dishonourable ambition. The question is: is it a reasonable proposition? If we could go on piling up arms and men till 1943 and then crack Hitler on the snout, it would be admirable. But what is Hitler going to be engaged on till 1943? War is not an addition sum but an equation in time. Have we time to afford Churchill's strategy?

In the same issue, *Tribune* published an answer to 'Rainboro''.

Why Mr Churchill? An answer:
(1) Because, as he recently stated, 'he had not noticed there were many candidates for the post of Premier' when it fell vacant.
(2) Because he was then the obvious man for the job.
(3) Because if there was a better man, or any other man, why did he not come forward?

Mr Churchill has remained:
(1) Because at the greatest crisis this country has ever faced, he had the power to draw us together and hold us fast until we were comparatively safe.
(2) Because he has had the gift of keeping together those of widely differing political views, in the country, the Government and the War Cabinet.
(3) Because in this gargantuan task he has done his utmost (can one man do more?) to weld the peoples of the anti-Axis nations together.
(4) Because he has gained, and held, the affection and respect of a big majority of those who placed him in power – in spite of the mistakes he, and perhaps anybody, has, or would have, made.

Mr Churchill will go and, I prophesy, go voluntarily:
(1) When he sees another man ready and willing to take on his unenviable task.
(2) When the country shows that it wants this man and is as ready to trust him as it was Mr Churchill.

I am a lowly member of the Labour Party, but I would like to pay this tribute to a man who, I am convinced, has done his utmost for his countrymen.

On 19 and 20 May there was a further debate on the progress of the war. Criticism of Churchill was severe. It was the same sort that had faced him in the January debate. It seemed that the victory he had won then would have to be won over again.

Sir John Wardlaw-Milne:

Leadership? Apart from the personal leadership to which I have already paid tribute, where is the leadership in this government? What are the government? One man... It is such a responsibility that I do not believe any one man can carry it. I say quite frankly that it is the Prime Minister I am criticizing... As Prime Minister and Minister of Defence he is trying to carry too heavy a burden, and the country, with all its belief in him, which many of us share, with all its trust, with all its gratitude, is beginning to feel that it would be well if he were to share that burden with somebody else.

John McGovern:[1]

I had a letter the other day from a man who listened to the last speech of the Prime Minister dealing with the war. He said, in his letter: 'I listened to it in the very same pub that I listened to his speeches twelve months ago. Twelve months ago, you could have heard a pin dropping on the floor, everybody anxious to listen, but there was talk, laughter and jokes being expressed, and the proprietor had to turn off the wireless because no one seemed interested in the speech.' The letter said that all sorts of disrespectful remarks were being made about the Prime Minister. I do not know whether the Government and the Prime Minister realize it or not, but that is the feeling in the country. Everybody is asking when this government is to come to an end.

Richard Stokes:

I said eighteen months ago that the Prime Minister is a great leader, but that strategically nobody ought to follow him. I hold to that opinion, and everything that has happened since bears it out. I hold the view sincerely that unless we can get a change on the question of the strategic control, we not only will not win the war, but will lose it. We shall not even avoid defeat.

Hore-Belisha, who opened the second day of the May debate, said:

I do not think you can divorce the almost unending and unbroken sequence of strategic disasters from this mixture of the political and military elements in your war-machine ... Who decided to send an army to Greece without adequate air-support – an impossible operation? ... When a man of great political experience and dialectical skill sits with Service men who are not accustomed to the careful use of language and the deployment of argument, you do not know whether the substance that comes out of these discussions is diluted or undiluted. Who decided to defend Crete? Who decided that Crete was defensible when the mainland had gone? Who decided that Singapore should be defended? ...

Cripps, as Leader of the House, was in the difficult position of having to deal with the debate on behalf of the Government: it can be assumed that he was not in total disagreement with some of the critical things that had been said.

---

[1] Labour M.P., 1930–50; imprisoned while a Member during protests in the thirties; forcibly carried out of the House of Commons in July 1931; died 1968.

One of Churchill's defenders was A. P. Herbert:[1]

If the Prime Minister butts into strategic affairs, it is not very surprising. He has been a fighting soldier. He has been First Lord of the Admiralty, he was the first Air Secretary, he has been Secretary of State for War, and Minister of Munitions. By the way, I think I may say to the right hon. Gentleman the Member for Caernarvon Boroughs (Lloyd George) that we were very glad in the last encounter that the political leader butted into strategic affairs; if he had not done so, we should not have had the convoy system, and many other things. But with the present Prime Minister, being the man he is and having had the experience he has, if he does 'butt in', I am sure you will not stop him butting into strategic affairs by juggling with Generals and committees and putting a new General here and a new committee there. This is a question of personality. You have to face that; either you have faith in him and let him have the machinery he can work with, or you must say frankly that you do not want him any more. I hope that will not be the answer. Certainly, it will not be mine.

Beverley Baxter also spoke in support:

No one, not even his most loyal supporters, would say that the Prime Minister has not made mistakes. They are clear to the eyes of us all, but he has never wavered in his broad conception of aid to Russia and the development of the alliance of the English-speaking peoples. He never allowed events in the forefront to rob him of the vast horizon of his own conception. We are reaping to-day the harvest of the Prime Minister's faith, and that harvest spells victory.

Harold Nicolson, diary, 20 May 1942:

The House is in a bad mood and the debate consists of one long stab and dig at Winston. The difficulty is that serious people do not like getting up to defend Winston on strategical grounds. The critics always know some small detail which sounds damaging and which can only be answered by disclosing information of value to the enemy. Hore-Belisha makes a particularly damaging attack. Cripps winds up well and strongly, but I fear that Winston's position in the House (in spite of his triumph in the Secret Session) is not a strong one. This fills me with dismay.

Goebbels, 21 May 1942:

Churchill's conduct of the war was attacked with exceptional vehemence during the House of Commons debate. He is coming under crossfire from all parties. It is nothing short of an enigma how this man can still be so popular.

---

[1] Sir Alan Herbert: author; Independent M.P., 1935-50.

An enigma to a Nazi: less so to others.

New York Times, 21 May 1942:

History will say greater things of Mr Churchill, but perhaps the best current tribute is that without leadership of the kind he has given there would be no debate to-day in the Commons – certainly not the clamour of a militant England impatient to invade Europe.

An important supporter of Churchill was J. L. Garvin, who had been editor of *The Observer* since 1908, and who had originally preferred Lloyd George for the premiership in 1940. Lord Astor (the title had been granted to his father by Lloyd George) was proprietor of *The Observer*. Astor wrote a letter to *The Times*, joining those who condemned Churchill for jealously retaining the Ministry of Defence. Garvin attacked Astor's argument in Astor's own newspaper. Even Garvin – who had one of the most fantastic contracts ever known in Fleet Street – could not do that. Within a few weeks, he was writing for one of *The Observer*'s most habitual foes, Lord Beaverbrook's *Sunday Express*.

Beaverbrook, letter to Henry Luce, 21 May 1942:

The Prime Minister's position today is unchallenged. It is true that those who in the House of Commons formerly were careful to distinguish between him and his government have now come into the open in criticism of him. But the agitation to remove him from his position as Minister of Defence finds no support outside a small group of Tories.

Beaverbrook must have forgotten another 'small group': that of the *Tribune* Socialists and Liberals. By June, Beaverbrook was back in England. Despite his assurances to Luce, Beaverbrook tried to persuade Bevin that Churchill was on the way out. Bevin was disgusted and retorted that he would report the conversation to Churchill. Beaverbrook replied blandly that the Prime Minister would never believe it – although in this he may have been mistaken. Bevin said of Churchill's relationship with Beaverbrook: 'He's like a man who's married a whore: he knows she's a whore but he loves her just the same.'

The *Daily Express* was now organizing meetings, promoting a Second Front and the dismissal of the 'Men of Munich' from the Government, at which members of the *Tribune* group like Shinwell, Owen, and Foot spoke. The fact that the *Express* and its proprietor had themselves supported the Munich agreement left neither abashed. It was Lord Beaverbrook who once said, 'I *always* dispute the umpire's decision.' Beaverbrook said the Army was equipped and ready. But Members of Parliament and war correspondents were continually pointing out that the desert war had proved the inferiority of British equipment to German – particularly in certain kinds of aircraft and tanks (for the production of both of which Lord Beaverbrook had at some time been responsible, although the inferiority of the tanks was based on military decisions taken by the Army before the war).

Major-General Kennedy, 25 May 1942:

The parliamentary debates on the Combined General Staff and the higher direction of the war have fizzled out ... In the end Winston has been left supreme, and stronger than before, and it has been demonstrated again that all the other politicians are pigmies compared with him, and that his hold on the country and his place in the eyes of our allies, are such that a change in leadership at this time is unthinkable. And there is no doubt that, despite his strategical vagaries, he is a great leader.

But Kennedy was assuming too much. There was still one more parliamentary challenge for Churchill to overcome in 1942.

Stephen King-Hall made a succinct and brilliant analysis of the situation on 28 May 1942:

The Prime Minister has said on various occasions that he is not prepared to remain Prime Minister and abandon his function of advising himself as Minister of Defence ... If the military disasters which have overtaken us in the Far East are to be attributed to the quality of function exercised by Mr Winston Churchill, and if further disasters of this kind are likely to come upon us, then it is not a new Minister of Defence, but a new Prime Minister, whom we need. The question, therefore, is whether or not it would be advantageous to our war effort if at the present time the House of Commons withdrew its support from the Prime Minister. [I have] no hesitation in saying that to do so would be a most foolish move. We are now on the eve of tremendous happenings, and the war seems bound to reach a crisis between now and September. The effect on public opinion in the U.S.A. of losing Churchill would be deplorable. Millions of people in the occupied territories would be staggered and depressed. The enemy would exult ... Also, one cannot altogether exclude from the question the choice of a successor. Some might say Cripps. As a matter of fact fewer would say Cripps than would have said it a month ago ... Clem Attlee? To be truthful, we believe he would make quite a good Prime Minister, but our view is shared by no one, perhaps not even by Mr Attlee himself. Mr Anthony Eden? His time will come, but not yet. Mr Bevin? The Tories would not support him though in some respects he has the Tory mind if only they knew it. And that's about the lot. Oh! We had nearly forgotten Sir John Anderson. He must not be thought of as Prime Minister, for if he went to No. 10 Downing Street there would be no one left to undertake the really hard slogging and laborious tasks.

Despite Churchill's parliamentary reports, there was still a feeling that scandals were being hushed up: that commanders on the spot were being left to take responsibility for failures that were not theirs.

Author,[1] 1942:

Never was so much withheld from so many, as in this age of our Ministry of Information. The denial of information, under Mr Churchill's leadership, has become more habitual than before. More than once in this war, Mr Churchill has spoken of military disasters, which befell us, as the gravest in our history. Yet for the first time in our history, enlightenment about them is refused! Information about Hong Kong, Singapore and Tobruk has been denied. In the case of Dunkirk, alone, have the Commander's dispatches been issued. We know *what* happened; we may not know *why* it happened. If you read these dispatches, you will find no justice in the relegation of Lord Gort, the Commander. He was made a 'scapegoat'.

By no means the least of Churchill's trials was the proud French general in London, whose embarrassment at the débâcle in France was equalled only by his own high opinion of himself and his 'destiny':[2]

Mr Churchill said: 'I want a great France with a great army. That is indispensable for peace, order and security in Europe. For thirty years I have never had any other policy towards France and I remain faithful to it to-day.' 'It is true,' answered General de Gaulle, 'that you have always followed that line of conduct. You personally had the merit of remaining faithful to it at the moment of the armistice. You were almost

---

[1] Douglas Reed: correspondent of *The Times* in Berlin and central Europe, 1929–38; author of *Insanity Fair*.
[2] Note taken by General de Gaulle himself of interview with Churchill, 10 June 1942.

alone in continuing to play the card of France and you showed, at that moment, great foresight. The card of France was then called de Gaulle. Our two names are from that time forth attached to that policy. If you renounced it, that would be bad for you as well as for us – all the more so since, at present, the enterprise is beginning to succeed. Free France has become the symbol and soul of the resistance. On these bases I too am faithful to you. But I have very few resources with which to bear the responsibility for the interests of France. This involves great difficulties for me. I ask you to help me to overcome them. I agree that, on the whole, you are not ill-disposed to us. But there are grave exceptions. Also American policy towards us is atrocious. Do you know that, for Memorial Day, the American Government invited the Vichy military attachés and did not invite our officers?' 'Yes,' said Mr Churchill, 'the Americans do not wish to give up their policy with Vichy. They imagine that Vichy will one day be so tormented by the Germans that it will resume the war at the side of the Allies . . . All these affairs,' he said, 'are not of major importance. What is big and important is the war. We shall be in France perhaps next year. In any case, we shall be there together. We have still to overcome great obstacles, but I am sure that we shall win. We are getting stronger and stronger. In 1943 and 1944 we shall be getting stronger still. We shall build so many aircraft, ships and tanks that we shall get the upper hand. If you have difficulties, remember that I too have them. For example, I recently had difficulties with the Australians. They were afraid of being invaded. They got excessively alarmed. They wanted me to send them ships. I hadn't got any . . .' As he saw the General out, Mr Churchill said: 'We must see each other again' . . . 'I shall not desert you,' he said in conclusion, 'you can rely on me.' Mr Churchill saw the General out as far as the Downing Street door.

Churchill and Roosevelt conferred, with their staffs, in Washington, June 1942. Brooke, and his diary, were there.

I found it difficult at the first few meetings to be able to appreciate the degree of importance to attach to the President's military suggestions and I did not know how Marshall would react. With the President and P.M. planning on their own in the White House, it made it difficult at first to carry on business with Marshall. However, I finally got on sufficiently intimate terms with him to be able to discuss freely with him the probable reactions of both President and P.M. to the plans we were discussing . . .[1]

---

[1] Brooke wrote later: 'These remarks of mine about my early relations with Marshall are interesting. His relations with the President were quite different from my relations with Winston. The President

The main source of discussion and contention at Washington was that old problem, the Second Front. Churchill fought hard, and with success, for his theory that all North Africa should be in allied control before an invasion of France.

Sir Charles Wilson, diary, Washington, 21 June 1942:

Went to the White House this afternoon when the P.M. sent for me. Found him pacing his room. He turned on me: 'Tobruk has fallen.' He said this as if I were responsible. With that, he began again striding up and down the room, glowering at the carpet: 'What matters is that it should happen when I am here.' He went to the window. 'I am ashamed. I cannot understand why Tobruk gave in. More than 30,000 of our men put their hands up. If they won't fight – '. The P.M. stopped abruptly. He forgot all about me, lost in thought. After a little, he fell into a chair. He seemed to take a pull at himself. 'It was the President who told me; he was very kind. He only asked, "What can we do to help?"'

Strategically, except in the Prime Minister's view, the fall of Tobruk did not matter at all. But since its previous siege and relief, the place had assumed a great importance to the public – as besieged places are inclined to do.

Sir Charles Wilson, diary, 23 June 1942:

Winston's buoyant temperament is a tremendous asset. I sat up on the night of Tobruk and last night till he went to bed, thinking he might want me. But he isn't made like that. There is never any danger of his folding up in dirty weather. My heart goes out to him. I do like a really full-sized man. With our military prestige at zero here, he has dominated the discussions. All day and half the night, they have gone on since the news of Tobruk came through. Winston has battled with the Americans: he has not allowed the facts, damaging as they are, to handicap him. At this game, there is no one here of his own weight. He has made use of the crisis as an argument for postponing the Second Front; without any help from anyone, he has sustained the theme that only an invasion of North Africa can relieve the crisis.

---

had no great military knowledge and was aware of this fact and consequently relied on Marshall and listened to Marshall's advice. Marshall never seemed to have any difficulties in countering any wildish plans which the President might put forward. My position was very different. Winston never had the slightest doubt that he had inherited all the military genius of his great ancestor, Marlborough. His military plans and ideas varied from the most brilliant conceptions at the one end to the wildest and most dangerous ideas at the other.'

The war seemed to be bringing nothing but disaster: Norway, France, Greece, Crete, Dakar, Libya, the *Hood* and several aircraft carriers, Hong Kong, the *Repulse* and the *Prince of Wales*, Singapore, Burma, the *Scharnhorst* and *Gneisenau* breaking the blockade, and now the fall of Tobruk. Only the Americans, now regaining control of the Pacific, were doing well. Was Britain really that bad at war? At by-elections the electorate was recording its discontent. Perhaps it really was the leadership.

On factory walls around the country 'Second Front Now' was being painted. The feeling of discontent with Churchill was spreading outwards from the confines of Parliament, the top of the Services, some circles in London, and Welsh and Scottish Communists, to men and women in the Services and to civilians. But it was still, almost certainly, a minority.

On 1 July Beaverbrook came out strongly in support of Churchill retaining the Ministry of Defence (the *Daily Express* did not return to the theme of a Second Front until 28 September). On that day, 1 July 1942, Churchill was to suffer what was partly a calculated insult from his Tory enemies, and partly an expression of deep concern at his premiership – a vote of censure which had no chance of success. It was Wardlaw-Milne who moved the vote of censure. He explained that he had tabled the motion with the one object of winning the war in the shortest possible time. He described Churchill's dual role of Prime Minister and Minister of Defence as 'the first vital mistake that we have made in the war'. The motion was as follows:

That the House, while playing tribute to the heroism and endurance of the Armed Forces of the Crown in circumstances of exceptional difficulty, has no confidence in the central direction of the war.

Lord Winterton:

If, whenever we have disasters – because they are disasters – whenever we have defeats, we get the same answer from many members of this House, and from the press outside, that whatever happens you must not blame the Prime Minister, we are getting very close to the intellectual and moral position of the German people 'The Fuehrer is always right' ... Assuming that we suffer – as I hope we shall not, but it looks as if we may – from a major disaster in Egypt and we lose the Suez Canal, and there is another debate, are we to be told: 'Whoever is responsible, the Prime Minister cannot be held to be responsible'? We all agree that the Prime Minister was the captain-guard of our courage and constancy in 1940. I think that not even to the right hon. Gentleman and member for Caernarvon Borough (Lloyd George) does this country, both the present generation and posterity, owe more than it does to the Prime Minister. But a lot has happened since 1940. If this series of disasters goes on, the right hon. Gentleman, by one of the greatest acts of self-abnegation which any man could carry out, should go to his colleagues – and there is more than one suitable man for Prime Minister on the Treasury Bench now – and suggest that one of them should form a government, and that the right hon. Gentleman himself would take office under him. He might do so, perhaps, as Foreign Secretary, because his management of our relations with Russia and with the United States has been perfect.

Clement Davies said:

Every man must judge for himself, or his own conscience, but if there is one man in this country who, on a two years' record of that kind, can say 'I have complete confidence in that government' I am sorry for that man.

John McGovern:

It is a fact that the Prime Minister is exercising a tremendous dictatorship ... From my own experience he is the most arrogant and intolerant member of this House. He walked out when the Noble Lord [Lord Winterton] was speaking. The Noble Lord said he hoped that he was not going out, as he had one or two things to say. He never even turned his head; he marched off. I say that that is the attitude of a man with a dictatorial mind, and so far as I am concerned, if I had to choose between Hitler and the Prime Minister I should not know exactly on which the choice had to fall.

Harold Nicolson, diary, 1 July 1942:

To the House for the first day of the debate on the Vote of Censure. Wardlaw-Milne is an imposing man with a calm manner which gives the impression of solidity. He is in fact rather an ass, and the position he has acquired as one of the leaders of the back-benches has caused his head to swell badly. He begins well enough, but then suddenly suggests that the Duke of Gloucester should be made Commander-in-Chief. A wave of panic-embarrassment passes over the House. For a full minute the buzz goes round. 'But the man must be an ass.' Milne pulls himself together and recaptures the attention of the House, but his idiotic suggestion has shaken the validity of his position and his influence is shattered. Roger Keyes seconds. He is a very dull speaker, and most people troop out to luncheon. Keyes denies that the P.M. ever interfered with Service chiefs. In fact he complains that he never overrides their advice. They are all for caution, and the result was that when we might have won the battle of the Mediterranean, we hesitated and fumbled, and now it was too late. Winterton rises to speak, and the P.M. strolls out deliberately with bowed shoulders. Bob Boothby makes an admirable speech supporting the government, but I notice that in *The Times* it is not even mentioned. The debate goes on till after midnight.

Aneurin Bevan, 2 July 1942:

It is the duty, as I understand it, of Members of Parliament to try and reproduce in the House of Commons the psychology which exists in the country, and there can be no doubt that the country is deeply disturbed by the movement of events at the present time ... I do not know whether hon. Members have received many letters in the last few days, but if they have they will have realised that there are far more people supporting the Motion outside the House than are represented by the names on the Order Paper ... It seems to me that there are three things wrong. First, the main strategy of the war has been wrong; second, the wrong weapons have been produced; and third, those weapons are being managed by men who are not trained in the use of them and who have not studied the use of modern weapons ... No one was more Maginot-minded than the Prime Minister himself ... Why is the strategy wrong? I say, first, that it is because the Prime Minister, although possessing many other qualities, sometimes conceives of the war, it seems to me, in medieval terms, because he talks of it as if it were a tourney ... Get at the enemy where he really is 21 miles away, not 14,000 miles. Get him by the throat[1] ... Send some politicians out ... Send some of us, and let us risk our lives. When the troops land in Europe, and you go to rouse Europe, as Europe can be roused, send some of us out with the landing troops ... The fact of the matter is that the British Army is ridden by class prejudice. You have got to change it, and you will have to change it. If the House of Commons has not the guts to make the government change it, events will. Although the House may not take any notice of me to-day, you will be doing it next week: remember my words next Tuesday and Wednesday ... Therefore you have to change that business: you have to purge the army at the top.

For the occasion, the Government had assembled in the House several members in uniform, some of whom had not been seen since the war began.

---

[1] Bevan's arguments were not unconfused. He had earlier accused Churchill of First World War attitudes, but was now voicing them himself.

Captain John Profumo:

May I, as a serving officer, tell the House – and I can do so quite honestly – that there is a great concern in the Forces about our present situation, but there is far greater concern about the habitual critics, who, after reverse or set-back, like lean and hungry dogs smell around for a bone to pick...

The most authoritative voice raised in dissent was that of Leslie Hore-Belisha. He concentrated on the superiority of enemy equipment, and on miscalculations. He also hinted at the need for an end to squabbles between the Services:

I want to ask the Prime Minister whether he intends to do anything in that direction before it is too late. The principal justification for a Minister of Defence, in my judgment, is that you should integrate these arms. If you allow these old differences to be perpetuated neither your Navy, your Air Force nor your Army can exert the influence upon which you rely... Think what is at stake. In a hundred days we lost our Empire in the Far East. What will happen in the next hundred days? Let every member vote according to his conscience.

Cripps had told Churchill that the House would expect a reply from the Prime Minister himself. (In May, Cripps had been left with the unenviable task.)

Churchill dwelt on the fall of Tobruk and other problems with some frankness: but when the War Office suggested that he should make it plain that Auchinleck was never ordered to hold Tobruk, he declined to do so. The Prime Minister concluded his defence with a typical blend of humility and bravura: 'I ask no favours either for myself or for His Majesty's Government. I undertook the office as Prime Minister and Minister of Defence, after defending my predecessor to the best of my ability, in times when the life of the Empire hung upon a thread. I am your servant, and you have the right to dismiss me when you please. What you have no right to do is to ask me to bear responsibilities of Prime Minister but clamped on each side by strong men... But there is a larger issue than the personal issue. The Mover of the Vote of Censure has proposed that I should be stripped of my responsibilities for Defence in order that some military figure or that some other unnamed personage should assume the general conduct of the war, that he should have complete control of the Armed Forces of the

Crown ... It is a system very different from the parliamentary system under which we live. It might easily amount to or be converted into a dictatorship ...'

Thus did Churchill neatly pass back the whispered charge that foolishly had been brought against him – of dictatorship. He continued: 'The setting down of this Vote of Censure by members of all parties is a considerable event. Do not, I beg you, let the House underrate the gravity of what has been done. It has been trumpeted all round the world to our disparagement ... If those who have assailed us are reduced to contemptible proportions and their Vote of Censure on the National Government is connected to a vote of censure upon its authors, make no mistake, a cheer will go up from every friend of Britain and every faithful servant of our cause, and the knell of disappointment will ring in the ears of the tyrants we are striving to overthrow.'

To vote for the motion, then, was an act not only of disloyalty to the Government but to the very nation itself. The motion was defeated by 476 votes to 25. Among the twenty-five were Fred Bellenger, Clement Davies, Admiral of the Fleet Sir Roger Keyes, Captain A. Cunningham Reid, and Sydney Silverman.

Churchill had the massive support for which he had asked. He was not to be 'clamped on each side by strong men'. And he would continue to direct the war according to his own lights, despite all fears as to his headstrong ideas about strategy, and his conflicts with the Services.

In one matter, at least, Churchill was wrong. The world, far from seeing the debate as a sign of weakness, saw it as a sign of strength. In the midst of a death-struggle, a combatant had sat back and indulged in the niceties of democratic procedure. The friends of Britain recognized her most famous and admired qualities – and rejoiced: the enemies of Britain marvelled – and feared.

Harold Nicolson, diary, 2 July 1942:

The second day of the Vote of Censure debate. Aneurin Bevan opens with a brilliant offensive, pointing his finger in accusation, twisting and bowing. Then comes Walter Elliot and then Hore-Belisha. Winston sits there with a look of sullen foreboding, his face from time to time flickering into a smile. He rises stockily, his hands in his trouser pockets. He makes a long statement which really amounts to the fact that we had more men and more tanks and more guns than Rommel, and that he cannot understand why we were so badly beaten. He gives no indication of how the battle of Egypt is likely to go. In the end, after one hour and thirty minutes, he is quite fresh and gay. He gets his vote of confidence by 476 to 25, plus a great ovation afterwards. But the impression left is one of dissatisfaction and anxiety, and I do not think it will end there. The only thing he could do is to bring back Wavell as C.I.G.S. I feel deeply sorry for him. Every weapon he uses smashes in his hands.

But Churchill was more firmly in power than since 1940. His critics had spoken, they had been given their chance: they had been completely shattered. Never again, till the end of the German war, was any attempt made to marshal a parliamentary opposition to Churchill. It was useless. In future, criticism was from individuals, not groups, and on particular issues – such as the bombing offensive – but not on the general direction of the war. This was not necessarily clear at the time.

Raymond Daniel, London correspondent of the *New York Times*, 4 July 1942:

It is difficult to tell whether the week's parliamentary jousting between the government and a small handful of constant critics has strengthened or weakened Prime Minister Churchill's hand ... The next time there is a severe reverse for British arms the Prime Minister will have to answer for his intransigence ...

Next day, the same newspaper obliquely criticized Churchill for the internment of friendly refugees, many of them Jews.

The reaction on the German radio was hardly convincing, 3 July 1942:

It is very encouraging to know that Churchill will remain at the head of the British direction of the war. His speech yesterday again confirmed the fact that we are dealing with a political gambler and military amateur who is ultimately responsible for Britain's defeats.

An article in *Das Reich*, broadcast by Luxemburg Radio on 10 July 1942:

We must count in England's favour that the British people is better than its present leaders and does not deserve a charlatan like Churchill. But this does not alter the fact that he represents English policy and is our opponent, responsible for the conduct of the war. We would have wished for a worthier enemy. He is a nonentity; one need observe him only for a short while in order to see through him completely. And that imitation of an Englishman had to oppose us in this of all wars! That he should have the right in the name of part of the world to stand against the Fuehrer is as humiliating for us as it is for the English.

Harold Nicolson, diary, next month:

I dine at Pratts and find 'Pug' Ismay next to me ... He says that Winston has the deepest veneration for the House of Commons. One day Pug found him in distress at having to prepare a speech. He said to him, 'But why don't you tell them to go to hell?' Winston turned round on him in a flash and said, 'You should not say those things: I am the servant of the House.'

Two American journalists in London, 1942:[1]

W.: I think Churchill runs England.

S.: Since this isn't a dictatorship, what are the forces that lie behind Churchill?

W.: Churchill is responsible to the House of Commons, hence could be removed from power overnight if the House voted against him on any point of major policy ... However, Churchill, through his great powers of oratory and because of the admiration that most members of the House have for his abilities, has been able to get away with 'murder'. It's only in recent months that the opposition even within the Conservative party has become vocal.

S.: Do you feel this is an indication of how fast Churchill will lose power after the war has been won.

W.: I don't believe that Churchill will last very long after the war. Some people even think he will be forced out long before the war is over. After Crete the opposition was mounting rapidly, and it was checked only by the German invasion of Russia.

S.: Whom does the opposition favour?

W.: Some want Lloyd George to be Prime Minister because they think he would have the support of the masses, that he is extremely forceful, understands politics, and could profit from his experience in the last war. They feel that despite his eighty years he is remarkably fit mentally, and would look into the question of the Home Front – mainly production – more than Churchill has done. Some people thought that Churchill, perhaps realising that Lloyd George might lead an opposition movement, tried his very best to kill it in a recent debate by referring to Lloyd George in the same breath with Pétain. However I don't mean to suggest that Lloyd George represents the spearhead of any opposition move.

S.: In other words the opposition is Conservative rather than Labour?

W.: Yes, the opposition is within the Conservative party. It is not Labour, it's not Liberal – though both parties might give the same

---

[1] Stephen Laird and Walter Graebner.

support to another Conservative Premier as they're giving to Churchill. On the other hand, no possible successor to Churchill has emerged within the Conservative Party. People talk about Eden as the man the Conservatives are grooming as the next P.M., but those in the 'know' think that he lacks the necessary requisites for the job.

Harold Nicolson, diary, 15 July 1942:

If the Russians collapse, they and their friends here will say it was due to Churchill's refusal of a second front. I very much fear that Churchill's own position will not survive a Russian defeat.

On 18 July Hopkins, with Marshall, returned to London to press for a landing in France during 1942. Churchill was still adamant that the risk of defeat – which would have a cataclysmic effect on the war – was far too great.

Major-General Kennedy, July 1942:

In a telegram which Dill sent us just before Marshall's arrival, he mentioned that Marshall had been studying Sir William Robertson's[1] *Soldiers and Statesmen*, and that he had sent him a copy of Volume I of this work, in which he had marked Chapter 3. We looked it up, and found that this is the chapter in which Robertson emphasizes the importance of concentration upon the decisive point, and in which he states his view that the Dardanelles attack was an unjustifiable diversion of effort from the Western Front. The Americans had evidently drawn the deduction that, in July 1942, France was the decisive front, and that new operations elsewhere must, therefore, be wrong. In this same chapter, Robertson also lays stress on the duty of Service advisers to state their opinions whether asked for them or not. The Dardanelles Commission had supported this view when they pointed out that Mr Churchill had obtained the support of the Service Chiefs to a lesser extent than he himself had imagined, because they had not spoken out. Brooke told me, on 18th July, that he had discussed this telegram with Churchill, whose hackles were up over the reference to the Dardanelles. He had said to Brooke that he would make short work of Marshall if he tried to lay down the law on the lines advocated by Robertson. One of my officers told me he had been unable to get a copy of *Soldiers and Statesmen* from any of the libraries – there had been a run on it by Ministers, who were said to be walking about with copies under their arms.

---

[1] C.I.G.S. in the First World War.

The same, 17 July 1942:

Winston certainly inspires confidence. I do admire the unhurried way in which he gets through such a colossal amount of work, and yet never seems otherwise than at leisure. He was particularly genial and good-humoured today. I can well understand how those around him become devoted to him – and dominated by him. I remember Dudley Pound once saying, 'You cannot help loving that man', and I can quite see the truth of this sentiment. There is one thing that Winston's enemies and critics must admit – he has only one interest in life at this moment, and that is to win the war. Every waking moment is devoted to that. He lives his peculiar life, indoors, and rarely going out. Yet this seems to suit him well, and he shows little sign of wear and tear, and he looks in better health than some of the other politicians who work less than he does. Of course he has not the worry of departmental life, with its constant interruptions and distractions, and he can arrange his routine as he wishes. It is an extraordinary *tour de force* all the same.

The London conference with the American delegates was a complete victory for Churchill over the American Chiefs of Staff. The invasion for 1942 was abandoned, in face of steadfast British refusal to have anything to do with it. The invasion of West Africa was decided upon. The deciding factor had been the President's concurrence, on this occasion, with Churchill. The Prime Minister noted with satisfaction: 'All was therefore agreed and settled in accordance with my long-conceived ideas.' It was not the last of the victories of Churchill and Brooke over the American Chiefs of Staff.

It was left to Churchill to tell Stalin.

The *Express* newspapers had been pondering on the utterly remote possibility of a General Election. On 21 July Rupert De la Bère asked the Prime Minister in the House of Commons whether he could make a statement regarding the Government's intentions as to holding a General Election before the end of 1942.[1] Churchill replied: 'It would be most unusual and in my view contrary to the best precedents for any statement to be made forecasting the advice which in hypothetical circumstances should be tendered to the King in respect of a Dissolution of Parliament.'

---

[1] Later Sir Rupert De la Bère: Conservative M.P., 1935–55; Lord Mayor of London, 1952.

De la Bère:

Is it not essential whilst perils press to reason calmly about holding a General Election? Would the Prime Minister impress on Lord Beaverbrook the necessity for calm reasoning?

The Prime Minister:

I must embrace this opportunity of testifying my admiration for the principles of free speech and a free press.

On 3 August Churchill flew to Cairo to study the command situation in Egypt. From there he was to go to Moscow, to break the news to Stalin about there being no Second Front till 1943, and then to return home again via the Middle East. In Cairo, he sacked the unrepentant Auchinleck. Suggestions that Wavell should be brought back from defending India against the Japanese to face Rommel once more, were dismissed with scorn. But Wavell was ordered to accompany Churchill to Moscow; he spoke fluent Russian. It was decided that Alexander should have overall command in the Middle East, and Montgomery should command the Eighth Army (a last-minute choice, as the original one was killed in the air on his way to Cairo). Both Alexander and Montgomery had served with Brooke in France, and their coolness in the retreat had greatly impressed him.[1] Churchill knew little of Montgomery, but he had a great admiration for the handsome Anglo-Irishman, 'Alex': 'cool, gay, comprehending all, he inspired quiet, deep confidence in every quarter'.

In Moscow, Churchill had a rough time with Stalin, whom he had not met before. 'I pondered on my mission to this sullen, sinister Bolshevik State I had once tried so hard to strangle at its birth.'

---

[1] Later Field-Marshal Earl Alexander of Tunis: commanded Irish Guards, 1928–30; First Corps, 1940; G.O.C., Burma, 1942; C.-in-C., Middle East, 1942–3, and allied armies in Italy, 1943–4; Supreme Commander, Mediterranean, 1944–5; Governor-General of Canada, 1946–52; Minister of Defence in Churchill's peace-time premiership, 1952–4.

Later Field-Marshal Viscount Montgomery of Alamein: commanded Royal Warwickshire Regiment, 1931–4; Fifth Corps, 1940; Eighth Army, 1942–4; C.-in-C., Allied Forces, France, 1944; 21st Army Group, 1944–5; C.I.G.S., 1946–8; Deputy Supreme Commander, NATO, 1951–8.

During the conference, Stalin accused Churchill of cowardice, deceit, and of protecting Britain from the brunt of the war – all palpably untrue. Averell Harriman went with Churchill, as Roosevelt's representative and observer.[1]

Harriman to Roosevelt, 13 August 1942:

Last night the Prime Minister and I had an extended meeting with Stalin. Also present were Molotov, Voroshilov, and the British Ambassador. British and American strategic plans for the rest of 1942 and 1943 and their effect on the Russian military situation formed the centre of discussion. It is my belief that, considering all the circumstances, the discussion could not have been better developed nor more satisfactory conclusions reached. Churchill explained ... the reasons for its postponements in full detail and told of the plans for and proposed strength of the major trans-Channel operation. At every point Stalin took issue with a degree of bluntness almost amounting to insult. He made such remarks as – that you cannot win wars if you are afraid of the Germans and unwilling to take risks. He ended this phase of the discussion by stating abruptly but with dignity that although he did not agree with the arguments he could not force us to action ... Thereupon Churchill described the bombing campaign against Germany and expressed the hope that participation by the U.S. Air Force would produce a substantial increase in this bombing. This produced the first agreement between the two men. Stalin took over the argument himself, saying that homes as well as factories should be destroyed. Churchill agreed that civilian morale constituted a military objective, but that the destruction of the homes of workers was only a by-product of near misses on factories. Now there began an easing of the tension and an increasing understanding of common purpose. Stalin and Churchill, between them, soon had destroyed most of Germany's important industrial centres. With great adroitness, Churchill seized the opportunity presented by this friendlier interchange to bring the discussion back to the Second Front. He said he wished he had the same power that Stalin exercised over the Press, which further relieved the tension ... Churchill drew a picture of a crocodile, pointing out that it was as well to strike the soft underbelly (the Mediterranean) as the snout (Northern France).

Surprisingly, Churchill and Stalin parted on fairly good terms. As Churchill said, with justification: 'I am sure that the disap-

---

[1] Wealthy businessman, who held ministerial rank from 1941 as presidential adviser and representative to Presidents Roosevelt, Truman, Kennedy, and Johnson.

pointing news I brought could not have been imparted except by me personally without leading to really serious drifting apart.' It was a triumph of tact and diplomacy. Churchill built the Grand Alliance in 1942, with Hitler's help, and by his frequent travelling he strove to keep it together for three and a half years.

From Moscow, Churchill returned to Egypt. Alexander and Montgomery had only just arrived to take up their commands. Montgomery was already more firmly in control than any previous desert commander.

Brooke, Cairo, 18 August 1942:

Determined at last to have a good night's sleep, I slept solidly from midnight to 8.30 a.m. Whilst dressing the P.M. blew into my room in his dressing-gown and told me he had been thinking over the urgency of the attack against Rommel. He then started producing all the old arguments that I have so frequently battled against for speeding up the date. I had to point out that it was exactly two days ago that Alex had taken over and Monty arrived, that there was a mess to put right, etc. I know that from now on I shall have a difficult time curbing his impatience... I found P.M. was again toying with the idea of stopping on here till the 30th. This is because there is an indication of a possible attack on the 26th and he would like to be here for it. I had to be as firm as I could with him and told him he would put himself in an impossible situation if he stopped on and would be accused of taking control. (It would be far worse than his Antwerp visit in the last war, but I did not say so and only implied it.) I told him we must arrange to start next Saturday or Sunday at latest. I think I have brought him round, and hope he will not slip back.

The same, 19 August 1942:

Back to the Embassy to read recent telegram about Dieppe raid and to pack for our departure for desert. Alex came along with us. We left Embassy at 3.15 p.m. and motored the whole way out, only reaching Eighth Army H.Q. at about 7.40 p.m. Then Monty gave us an excellent appreciation of the situation and an outline plan of what he proposed to do if Rommel attacked before he was ready and also his plans for the offensive. He is in tremendous form, delighted at being out here, and gave me a wonderful feeling of relief at having got him out here. We dined in their Mess and I slept in an ambulance converted into a caravan for Alex. Very comfortable. Very lovely night with the sound of the waves only a few yards away. On the way to bed P.M. took me down to the beach where he was transformed into a small boy wishing to dip his fingers into the sea. In the process he became very wet indeed!

Smuts, in Cairo, 1942:

I am tired. At the Embassy in Cairo, Churchill and I had rooms next to each other, and at all hours of the night he came in with a thought, a cable, just to talk. Churchill doesn't let one sleep, that is why I am tired. But what a man! What a demigod! The more I see of Churchill, the more I think him a demi-god.

The Prime Minister arrived back in London on 24 August.

Meetings of the War Cabinet during August were marked by increasing differences between the Prime Minister and Stafford Cripps. The dialogue between the two was, as Churchill later remarked, 'stern'. By now both men had the greatest respect for each other. But the situation was clearly impossible. Cripps, however, agreed to stay until after the new offensive in North Africa, appreciating that a public show of disagreement would affect morale at a critical time.

By mid-1942 Churchill was deep in arguments over the nature, scope, and date of the American landing in North Africa – codenamed 'Torch'. General Eisenhower, who was to command the operation, and his staff, were installed in London.[1] They were getting a taste of the Prime Minister's unconventional habits and demands.

Captain H. C. Butcher, Naval Aide to Eisenhower, 26 August 1942:

The P.M. is perfectly nonchalant while entertaining guests. General Clark reported that the P.M. had inadvertently pushed a highball glass off a side-table, but went right on talking, not even glancing around to see where the glass and contents had fallen. During the evening, he asked a servant to bring him his change of socks – he took off his shoes, the socks he was wearing, put on the other pair, and replaced his shoes without the slightest embarrassment.

---

[1] General Dwight D. Eisenhower: collected a vast amount of varied administrative and staff experience in the U.S. Army from 1915 to 1940; drafted plans for industrial mobilization; C.-in-C., Allied Forces, North Africa, 1942–4; Supreme Commander, western Europe, 1944–5; Supreme Commander, NATO, 1950–2; President of the United States, 1953–61.

The same, 31 August 1942:

The C.G. got to bed the earliest of any night since he has been in London – 10.30 – all set for a good night's sleep, of which he has had but few lately. About 11 he was already sound asleep when my phone rang. It was the secretary of the P.M. wanting to know if the General could go to 10 Downing later 'that evening' if the P.M. so desired. Had to alert Ike and, of course, he said 'yes'.

Smuts, 1 September 1942:

In England, now, Churchill is all-powerful only to the extent that he is permitted to be all-powerful. And there is a parliament which, in effect, does nothing but criticise him. The Members of Parliament don't deliberate. They don't make plans and decisions. They are there to represent people whose lives are affected by the dictator's plans and decisions, to say whether the people like them or not.

But the stock of the 'dictator' was higher now than it had been all year.

Frank Wolstencroft, President of the Trades Union Conference, 2 September 1942:

Well played, Churchill; I say, well played in the greatest test of all times. Well played, in spite of hard knocks and body-bowling from some of our so-called home supporters as well as from our opponents. I wish you the best of luck in your thankless task. May Heaven be good to you! May you retain your health, strength and vigour until victory is assured. I thank God that in our hour of need the nation found a man with courage and faith in our people to see it through. Opposed to you in politics, I nevertheless express to you the gratitude of the working people for the magnificent example you have set of grim resolution and unflinching devotion to duty.

A rare tribute indeed from a Socialist leader to a Conservative considered to be far to the right of centre. But Churchill and the coalition lost four by-elections during the year.

Sir Charles Wilson, September 1942:

Brendan Bracken: 'I want you, my dear Doctor, to keep an eye on your patient. There may be trouble ahead. The Prime Minister must win his battle in the desert or get out.
Wilson: I fancy the P.M. has too much on his hands to mope over things...
Bracken: ... There is a good deal going on under the surface. I'm afraid of that fellow Cripps. I think he means business. If he pulls out, there'll be the hell of a row.

Wilson: I thought it was Trenchard who was making trouble.
Bracken: Oh, he will make a bit of a stink, but he can't bring the Prime Minister down.

Trenchard was obsessed by the bombing-strategy controversy. He believed that Churchill was not nearly convinced enough of the importance of putting everything into Bomber Command.

Emanuel Shinwell, speech at Bedford, September 1942:

If we have reached the sorry pass that there is only one man in the country who is regarded as able to preside as head of the government, it is doubtful whether it is any longer a country worth asking anybody to fight for.

Shinwell courageously said that he refused to believe the notion that Churchill was indispensable. Not many agreed with him.

Butcher, London, 5 September 1942:

Churchill agrees to the military layout [for invasion of French West Africa] 'as you propose it'. He volunteered that since the British have troops trained for landing, he would be willing that they wear the American uniform and added, 'they will be proud to do so'.

The same, 9 September 1942:

As Ike and Clark had anticipated, the P.M. now is insistent upon settling a date for the attack. When the P.M. questioned him, Ike declared, 'November 8 – sixty days from to-day'. The P.M. was disappointed; he is so anxious to see the operation under way . . . The P.M. seeking haste, again suggested that British soldiers, more advanced in their training than Americans, be used in American uniforms and reiterated that he would be 'proud to have 'em wear 'em'. But Ike said that the sham would soon be discovered and would undermine confidence in the whole American operation. Thought the P.M. was disappointed at his decision. Asked Ike if the P.M. had mentioned the fine reportorial job he had done in speaking in Commons during the day. 'Did he? He read most of it to us.' While the P.M. was directing his dinner conversation for a moment to General Clark, Ike seized the opportunity to release a suppressed yawn, only to have the P.M. turn suddenly toward him and catch him at it. Not for this reason, but because the P.M. wanted to talk foreign affairs with Mr Eden, who came in at 11, the two Americans were released much earlier than anticipated. Seems there is a long hallway from the drawing-room to the front door, along which guards are stationed. At past dinners, the P.M. had followed his two guests to the door, and, as each new thought struck him, held his guests until it was completely discussed, mostly by the Prime Minister.

Anticipating that some such afterthoughts might hold them again (not that they dislike talking with the P.M. – in fact, their comments have all been to the contrary – but both were anxious to get home to bed), Clark, with his long strides, paced the escape down the narrow corridor. They felt as if they'd almost run out of 10 Downing.

In the speech referred to above – one of his periodic 'Reports on the war situation' – Churchill had said: 'In the debate on the Vote of Censure on 2 July, some of the opposition speakers seemed to think that the fall of Cairo and Alexandria was only a matter of days. "Wait till Monday", "Wait till Tuesday", it was said. Well, we have waited.'

But no one was waiting for Montgomery's offensive with greater impatience than the Prime Minister.

Rommel, 9 September 1942:

I know Churchill is supposed to have said that he will only be able to hold Egypt a few months longer, but I'm more inclined to think that he's considering launching a new offensive with superior forces in four to six weeks' time. A victory for us in the Caucasus is the only thing that would stop him.

Harold Nicolson, diary, 9 September 1942:

Guy Burgess[1] has heard from his friends who are in close touch with Cripps that the latter is so discontented with the conduct of the war that he proposes to resign. He has already sounded *The Times*, and possibly Kemsley's papers, to see if they will give him press support. Guy and I agreed that Cripps's attitude was probably wholly disinterested and sincere. He really believes that Winston is incapable of dealing with the home-front and that his handling of the minor problems of production and strategy is fumbling and unprecise.

Stafford Cripps was only waiting for the outcome of the North African offensive, to free himself at last and to end his difficult position in the War Cabinet. Contrary to the rumours at the time, his disagreement with Churchill was less over the Second Front, than on the organization of the direction of the war, details of administration, and the feeling that not enough was being done to prepare for peace. There was not enough planning. But the main trouble was that Churchill preferred to run the war, irrespective of Sir Stafford Cripps.

---

[1] At that time in the Secret Service. Defected to Russia, 1951.

Cripps to Prime Minister, 21 September 1942:

In my view the present method of conducting affairs is unsatisfactory and is too much on a 'hand-to-mouth' basis . . . problems of strategy are conceived by the War Cabinet hurriedly, without sufficient information and often in isolation . . . Under such conditions it is not right, in my view, that the War Cabinet should appear to carry responsibility for the conduct of the war, since it is not in a position to discharge that responsibility . . . As you have stated, if you are to run the war, you must run it your own way . . .

Cripps was not the kind of man to sit comfortably in the War Cabinet as conducted by Churchill – a Cabinet in which as Attlee had once to remind the Prime Minister, a monologue was not a discussion. Churchill replied that he was 'surprised and somewhat pained to receive your letter'.

Montgomery's refusal to precipitate his offensive brought the inevitable crisis.

Brooke, 23 September 1942:

Many troublesome things on foot . . . After lunch P.M. sent for me to discuss a wire he wanted to send to Alexander. I tried to stop him and told him that he was only letting Alex see that he was losing confidence in him, which was a most disconcerting thing before a battle. He then started all his worst arguments about generals only thinking about themselves and their reputations and never attacking until matters were a certainty; of never being prepared to take any risks, etc. He said this delay would result in Rommel fortifying a belt twenty miles deep by forty miles broad; that we should never get through owing to a series of Maginot defences. I had a very unpleasant three-quarters of an hour. However, I succeeded in getting a very definite tempering down of the message.

Sir Charles Wilson, 30 September 1942:

Brendan Bracken came to see me today. He says that if Rommel is victorious the position of the Prime Minister will become very difficult. 'You see, Charles, important changes in the direction of the war would then be inevitable, and Winston will never submit to any curtailment of his powers. If we are beaten in this battle, it's the end of Winston.'

Harold Nicolson, diary, 29 September 1942:

Aneurin Bevan stands me a drink. He bewails the government and says that we shall lose the war if Churchill stays. This is all very difficult to answer. I agree that very serious strategic and supply mistakes have been made . . .

But Bevan and the other independent critics were now isolated.

Beaverbrook, letter, 29 September 1942:

Churchill remains predominant. He has no rivals. And his critics serve only, in the main, to fortify him in the affection of the public. For when the people compare the critics with the object of their criticism they have no doubt which they prefer.

Cripps to Prime Minister, 3 October 1942:

You have not convinced me that the changes which I have suggested in the central direction of the war are unnecessary. I firmly believe that alterations of that nature are essential if we are to make the most of our war potential.

During the time of suspense, while waiting for the new desert offensive, Churchill was encouraged by Smuts, who was on one of his periodic wartime visits to London. Churchill always paid great attention and respect to the South African leader, another source of contention with the Australians.

Except for three days, it rained all the five weeks I was in England. I spent two week-ends at Chequers and one, with Lloyd George, at Churt. It was on a Sunday morning at Chequers I prepared that speech I made to the two Houses of Parliament . . . A lot of things have been improved in London – for instance, St Paul's – by the Blitz. There was not much rest in a Chequers week-end. Churchill takes no more exercise in the country than in town; but he has to get away from the underground offices in Downing Street where they work nowadays. Churchill's working-times – quite logical for him – are not restful for other people. He sleeps between two and six, both a.m. and p.m., in order to break up the day's work. He works privately between 6 a.m. and 11 – in bed. He sees people officially between 11 and 1, both a.m. and p.m. He sees other people between 6 p.m. and 9, and then he dines. He keeps six secretaries going, and he keeps everyone else going. One doesn't mind. As I have told you before, Churchill is a demigod, and one has to accommodate oneself to demigods . . . At Churt I said to Lloyd George: 'Why didn't you go into the War Cabinet when they asked you?' 'Because it wasn't a War Cabinet,' he said. 'It was a Churchill Cabinet.' I wonder if England would have stood without Churchill. Look what a fall France had – the greatest since Babylon – because they had a Pétain instead of a Clemenceau. The English are a better-balanced people than the French, but they too needed a leader. And, thank God, they had one. Yes, thank God. The English and all of us may thank God there was a Churchill in England . . . After the war? If the English think they are going to have a softer life after the war, they are mistaken.

Montgomery, making full use of Auchinleck's preparations,

struck at Rommel's defences on 23 October, a month later than Churchill had been promised. At first, there was no sign of an immediate, dramatic success.

Montgomery, from diary, 29 October 1942:

During the morning I was visited at my Tactical H.Q. by Alexander and Casey, who was Minister of State in the Middle East. It was fairly clear to me that there had been consternation in Whitehall when I began to draw divisions into reserve on October 27 and 28, when I was getting ready for the final blow. Casey had been sent up to find out what was going on – Whitehall thought I was giving up, when in point of fact I was just about to begin. I told him all about my plans and that I was certain of success; and de Guingand spoke to him very bluntly and told him to tell Whitehall not to bellyache.[1]

Rommel, to his wife, 23 October 1942:

Dearest Lu, Who knows whether I'll have a chance to sit down and write in peace in the next few days or ever again. To-day there's still a chance. The battle is raging. Perhaps we will still manage to be able to stick it out, in spite of all that's against us – but it may go wrong, and that would have very grave consequences for the whole course of the war ... the enemy's superiority is terrific and our resources very small.

Hitler did not share Rommel's view of the importance of the campaign, but he did not relish defeat anywhere.

At 11.30 p.m. on 29 October Churchill sent for Brooke (when in London, Brooke hardly dared have an early night):

He ... was specially nice. Referring to Middle East he said, 'Would you not like to have accepted the offer of Command I made to you and be out there now?' I said, 'Yes', and meant it. And he said, 'Smuts told me your reasons, and that you thought you could serve your country best by remaining with me, and I am very grateful for this decision.' This forged one more link between him and me. He is the most difficult man I have ever served, but thank God for having given me the opportunity of trying to serve such a man in a crisis such as the one this country is going through.

Verbatim note by de Gaulle's staff, 30 October 1942:

Marshal Smuts asked General de Gaulle not to attach too much importance to Mr Churchill's changes of mood. 'I have known him a long

---

[1] Major-General Sir Francis de Guingand: Montgomery's Chief of Staff, 1942–5; previously he had been Wavell's Chief of Intelligence, and had forecast disaster in Greece.

time,' he said. 'I met him (when he was still almost a child) when we took him prisoner in the Boer war. He's a very good fellow at heart.'

De Gaulle had complained to Churchill about not receiving enough of the right sort of aid for French resistance in occupied France. During 1942 resistance movements had grown to some strength in Europe, often with post-war rather than war aims. Britain was usually quick to make contact and give such help as seemed practical. Germany's occupation of many countries was marred by savagery and cynicism; the Nazis' herding and methodical destruction of European Jews brought them the lasting contempt of mankind. The Japanese, who attempted to excuse their actions through a religious code, also brought, through their cruelty, a peculiarly horrible odour to the Second World War.

Partly to give encouragement to the conquered people, Churchill was in favour of armed raids on the coasts. As early as August 1940, he had stated: 'We must develop the storm troop or Commando idea.' Earlier in 1942 the Canadians had attacked at Dieppe with nearly 5,000 men, almost one in five of whom had been killed. It had been a 'trial-run' for the invasion, on Churchill's decision; a frightful and costly fiasco. The raid had been a help in warning the Americans of the dangers of premature operations in France.

Even in late 1942 preparations to combat a German invasion of England had not been put aside. From Memo. prepared for Chiefs of Staff by committee on plans for German invasion, October 1942:

The elimination of Churchill must be an essential feature of any attack on British morale. It would no doubt have an infuriating and therefore temporarily invigorating effect on the population, but that would wear off. And there is no other statesman who could possibly take his place as the focus and fountain-head of British morale.

On 2 November after heroic fighting by Australian, New Zealand, and British troops, Montgomery broke through. The 'Desert Fox' was beaten at last – near an insignificant, dirty little village called Alamein.

Brooke, 4 November 1942:

P.M. delighted. At 3.30 p.m. he sent for me again to discuss the project of ringing church bells. I implored him to wait a little longer till we

were quite certain we should have no cause for repenting ringing them
... At 11 p.m. sent for again by P.M. who was busy dictating messages
to Roosevelt, Stalin, Dominions, Commanders, etc. He was in a great
state of excitement ... The Middle East news has the making of the
vast victory I have been praying for. A great deal depends on it.

And four days later there was more excellent news. The American landings in Vichy-held North West Africa had taken place in some confusion, but without serious setback. It was an occasion of some importance; for the discharging of American troops on to a remote African shore was the entry of American ground forces into the Second European War.

An American soldier:

Midnight. The stars are out, but it's dark as hell on deck. The engines are down to a slow throb ... The net flattens hard against the ship's side, reducing finger and toe holds to next to nothing. A steel helmet well heated by the subtropical sun, a slippery tommy-gun, a saturated uniform, trench coat, and full infantry pack are not conducive to speed, but it didn't take us long to scramble up the dune to the crest tufted with coarse grass. Beyond and behind its comforting protection stretched a wide field. It presented a curious appearance. Standing and sitting in small groups, the French officers and coal-black enlisted men of the Fedala garrison. Their rifles were stacked in neat array and most of them were smoking *jaunes*.

It was not like that everywhere. American and French troops had a number of fierce and bloody engagements; American and British paratroops captured vital centres, and soon much of Morocco and Algeria was in allied hands. But German troops were also arriving, in Tunisia.

Not the least effect of the offensive was that three days after the initial landings, German troops entered unoccupied France and took over the Vichy State.

On 13 November Tobruk was retaken by Montgomery's advance.

On 22 November Stafford Cripps resigned from the War Cabinet. But Churchill prevailed upon him to remain in the Government, and he became Minister of Aircraft Production. There he was able to practise the efficiency that he had been preaching in the Cabinet. It was a successful move, which suited both Churchill and Cripps. It came as a kind of tidying-up at the end of the year. Cripps carried out his duties ably and with impeccable loyalty until the end of the war.

Daily Mail, 23 November 1942:

Ministerial changes announced today will come as a considerable surprise to the public generally ... Sir Stafford Cripps, the supreme individualist, has obviously never been really happy as a member of the War Cabinet, and there have been persistent reports of differences on policy between him and other members of that body. In his growing absorption in post-war problems, moreover, he may well have found himself at variance with Cabinet members of all parties.

Cripps was replaced in the War Cabinet by Herbert Morrison, Home Secretary – a man, it is worth noting, with whom Churchill had never been able to get on.

At the end of 1942, Churchill, despite the efforts to remove him, was still in power. On 29 November he broadcast to the world: 'The dawn of 1943 will soon loom red before us, and we must brace ourselves to cope with the trials and problems of what must be a stern and terrible year. We do so with the assurance of ever-growing strength, and we do so as a nation with a strong will, a bold heart, and a good conscience.'

Brooke, 30 November 1942:

Cabinet meeting from 5.30 to 8 p.m. and now we are off for another meeting with P.M. from 10.30 p.m. to God knows when, to discuss more ambitious and impossible plans for the re-conquest of Burma.

It is now 1 a.m. and I am just back from our meeting. With today I complete my first year as C.I.G.S.; not that I think I shall complete a second one. Age or exhaustion will force me to relinquish the job before another year is finished. It has been quite the hardest year of my life, but a wonderful one in some ways to have lived through ... By the end of the third week I thought I was finished and that I could never compete with the job ... The P.M. was desperately trying at times, but with his wonderful qualities it is easy to forgive him all ... And now, at last the tide has begun to turn a little, probably only a temporary lull, and many more troubles may be in store. But the recent successes have had a most heartening effect, and I start on a new year with great hopes for the future.

During December Churchill unexpectedly began pressing a Second Front for 1943 on the Chiefs of Staff. As this seemed to contradict his previous support for an assault on continental Europe from North Africa, Brooke was irritated even more than usual.

Brooke, 15 December 1942:

We finished off our paper refuting P.M.'s arguments for a Western Front in France (1943) and pressed for a Mediterranean policy aiming at pushing Italy out of the war and Turkey into it. By this means we aim at relieving the maximum possible pressure off Russia. Clark Kerr, the Ambassador in Moscow, gave us an hour on his views of Stalin's reactions if we do not start a Western Front in France. He urged that such a course might well lead to Stalin making a separate peace with Hitler. I refuse to believe such a thing possible.

The same, 16 December 1942:

At 6 p.m. we had a C.O.S. meeting with P.M.; Anthony Eden also there. All about policy for 1943. As the paper we put in went straight against Winston, who was pressing for a Western Front whilst we pressed for amphibious operations in the Mediterranean, I feared the worst. However, the meeting went well from the start and I succeeded in swinging him round. I think he is now fairly safe, but I have still the Americans to convince first and then Stalin next.

Churchill was indeed 'safe' on that subject.

Brooke, 22 December 1942:

Roosevelt has sent message to Winston suggesting a meeting in North Africa somewhere near Casablanca about January 15. We shall consequently soon be travelling again.

1942 had been a desperate year for Winston Churchill. It had been soured by the pin-pricks of his critics and generals almost as much as by the efforts of the enemy. On 15 December he was asked in the House why the new British tank had been named the Churchill tank: 'I had no part in that decision, but I can well believe that the fact that it was called by this particular name afforded a motive to various persons to endeavour to cover it with their slime.' It had not been a happy year. But the Prime Minister was undaunted. Rommel had been beaten at last; Churchill's favourite policy of capturing all North Africa had been successfully begun; at Midway the domination of the Japanese in the Pacific had been broken; and at Stalingrad a German Army, futilely obeying until the last minute a message from Hitler forbidding surrender, was being ground to pieces. It was, as Churchill said, 'The end of the beginning'. He had come through the year with safety and with honour.

CHAPTER SEVEN

1943 Proud Strategist

Sunday Dispatch, 11 January 1943, announced the possibility of:

One little bomb that would destroy the whole of Berlin . . . a bomb that would blast a hole twenty-five miles in diameter and wreck every structure within a hundred miles . . . The explosive in this bomb would be the energy contained in the uranium atom.

Churchill and his party arrived at Casablanca on 13 January. Roosevelt arrived the following day. For the Prime Minister, it was a satisfying moment. 'It gave me intense pleasure to see my great colleague here on conquered or liberated territory which he and I had secured in spite of the advice given him by all his military experts.'

Harold Macmillan, now British political adviser in North Africa and the Mediterranean, was at the conference. He took a somewhat sardonic view.

Letters, January 1943:

[Churchill's] villa was guarded by a guard of Marines, but otherwise things were fairly simple. His curious routine of spending the great part of the day in bed and all the night up made it a little trying for his staff. I have never seen him in better form. He ate and drank enormously all the time, settled huge problems, played bagatelle and bezique by the hour, and generally enjoyed himself. The only other member of the Government present was [Lord] Leathers, Minister of War Transport, and the P.M. had nobody except his secretaries and so on. The whole affair, which lasted for nearly a fortnight, was a mixture between a cruise, a summer school and a conference. The notice boards gave the time of the meetings of the various staffs, rather like lectures, and when they got out of school at five o'clock or so, you would see field-marshals and admirals going down to the beach for an hour to play with the pebbles and make sand castles. Then at night came the meetings of the Emperors and the staffs and great discussions and debates.

Macmillan, like Lyttleton, Alexander, and Casey, was the kind of man whom Churchill cherished, and who usually did well under his patronage: elegant, witty, handsome, and a veteran of the trenches of the First World War.

The Casablanca discussions centred around the question of whether to cross the English Channel and get to grips with Hitler, or whether to cross from North Africa to southern Europe – i.e. an invasion of Sicily and then Italy. Churchill told Eisenhower: 'General, I have heard here that we British are planning to scuttle [the cross-Channel operation]. This is not so. I have given my word and I shall keep it. But we now have a glorious opportunity before us; we must not fail to seize it. When the time comes you will find the British ready to do their part in the other operation.' But Marshall was becoming more tired of Churchill's delays, and of Europe generally, every day. He wanted to concentrate on the Pacific. At length it was agreed that Sicily should be taken, and that Britain should attempt greater activity in the East.

It was at Casablanca that Roosevelt suggested the policy of 'Unconditional Surrender'. Churchill agreed, but tried to exclude Italy. Roosevelt's son has written: 'For what it is worth, it can be recorded that it was Father's phrase, that Harry [Hopkins] took an immediate and strong liking to it, and that Churchill, while he slowly munched a mouthful of food, thought, frowned, thought, finally grinned, and at length announced, "Perfect!" '

Finally, the Americans reluctantly agreed to delay the invasion of France until 1944.

Brooke, 20 January 1943:

It has been one of the most difficult tasks I have had to do, and at one time I began to despair of our arriving at any sort of agreement. Now we have got practically all we hoped to get when we came here. They are difficult, though charming people to work with. Marshall's thoughts revolve round the creation of forces and not on their employment. King's [U.S. Navy] vision is mainly limited to the Pacific . . . although he pays lip service to the fundamental policy that we must first defeat Germany and then turn on Japan, he fails to apply it in any problems connected with the war. Arnold [U.S. Air Force] limits his outlook to the air and seldom mixes himself with other matters. But as a team they are friendliness itself, and, although our discussions have become somewhat heated at times, yet our relations have never been strained.

After the conference, Churchill went off to tour the Mediterranean. He visited Cairo, Turkey, Cyprus, Libya, and Algiers. On 3 February he spoke to the Eighth Army at Tripoli.

James Agate, famous critic, February 1943:

When a man tells me that a good writer or a good speaker quotes either to show off or to save himself trouble I recognise the ... well, unthinking mind. A few days ago we had an example of quotation at its finest – Mr Churchill in his speech to the Eighth Army congratulating them on their 1400 mile trek. He said that they had, 'Nightly pitched their moving tent a day's march nearer home'. Are we to think that the Prime Minister was flaunting his familiarity with the works of James Montgomery? Or that he could not have put the same thing in his own words? No. Mr Churchill is the greatest orator this country has possessed in living memory. He has a genius for coining apt, memorable, witty, and moving phrases. But he knew that no words which he could have invented would have stirred those boys like the words of the old hymn ...

Despite hopes to the contrary, the Germans were foolishly holding Tunisia; it was evident that a major campaign would have to be fought in order to get them out.

In 1943 Churchill attended five major conferences abroad.

Admiral James, 4 February 1943:

The all-round depreciation in our situation has not unnaturally caused great anxiety in the country, and this has been reflected in Parliament. There is a growing feeling that the running of this gigantic war is too much for one man, even Winston, and that we should have a War Cabinet of men of proved capacity to help him, men who have no other job. The critics quote Lloyd George's War Cabinet in support of their contention. But the Prime Minister thinks otherwise, and he is virtually dictator, as there is absolutely no one else to take his place and lead us to victory. He has a real sense of humour and I am sure has a silent chuckle when he reminds the House that he is entirely their servant ... He has been again to confer with Roosevelt, and it is when he is away from the country that one feels that no one is at the helm, and if, as has just happened, we have set-backs when he is away, the demand for a War Cabinet is a very natural one.

On his return from North Africa, Churchill ('more tired by my journeyings than I had realised'), went ill with pneumonia. The doctors persuaded him – after some effort – to read only 'the most important and interesting' documents, and a novel: for the latter, he chose *Moll Flanders*, 'about which I had heard excellent accounts'.

In February 1943, the Beveridge Report for Social Security in Britain was completed. It was a noble document to produce in the midst of a death struggle with three great world powers. Churchill's attitude was: 'We must not forget that we are a parliament in the eighth year – I could not as Prime Minister be responsible at this stage for binding my successor.' Labour were not impressed; they voted – all except two of those not in office – for firm Government approval of the report by 338 to 121. It was a clear portent, for those who could look ahead to the end of the war. Churchill believed the country had enough on its plate. He was impatient. At Cabinet request he made a long broadcast on post-war aims, but ended it: 'Let us get back to our job . . . [there is a] danger of its appearing to the world that we here in Britain are diverting our attention to peace, which is still remote, and to the fruits of victory, which have yet to be won.'

Brooke, 26 March 1943:

The P.M. sent for me. By the time I . . . reached him in the Annexe he was in his bath. However, he received me as soon as he came out, looking like a Roman Centurion with nothing on except a large bath-towel draped round him. He shook me warmly by the hand in this get-up and told me to sit down while he dressed. A most interesting procedure. First he stepped into a white silk vest, then white silk drawers. Then a white shirt which refused to join comfortably round his neck and so was left open with a bow-tie to keep it together. Then the hair (what there was of it) took much attention, a handkerchief was sprayed with scent and then rubbed on his head. The few hairs were then brushed and finally sprayed direct. Finally trousers, waistcoat and coat, and meanwhile he rippled on the whole time about Monty's battle and our proposed visit to North Africa. However, the main thing he wanted to say was that he thought I looked tired last night at the meeting we had, and that I was to take a long week-end.

(Churchill contrived to meet nearly all the wartime leaders while bathing himself, not excluding the President; his major failure in this respect was Stalin.)

Goebbels, 12 April 1943:

It is a curious fact that we shun the phrase 'European co-operation' just as the devil shuns Holy Water. I can't quite understand why. Such an obvious political and propaganda slogan ought really to become a general theme for public discussion in Europe.

During the first five months of 1943 British and American

troops slowly pushed back the German defenders in Tunisia. In Russia, also, Hitler's forces were withdrawing.

In April 1943, Churchill, after pressure from backbenchers for some years, announced that church bells would no longer be reserved for use as a warning of invasion. He was asked what alternative arrangements had been made. He was able to reply, drily: 'Replacement does not arise. For myself, I cannot help thinking that anything like a serious invasion would be bound to leak out.'

The second conference of the year took place in Washington during May. Churchill again had to fight hard against Marshall for the invasion of Italy, but the logistics of the great Anglo-American army now in North Africa were making Brooke's, and Churchill's, strategy of attacking Europe through 'the soft under-belly' increasingly inevitable. Marshall still didn't like it. Roosevelt pondered on it all like a great baseball umpire who found himself refereeing a football match by mistake.

Admiral Leahy,[1] 12 May 1942:

The Combined Chiefs of Staff conferred with Churchill and Roosevelt in the President's study. The Prime Minister spoke first and addressed us as 'the most powerful group of war authorities that could be assembled in any part of the world'. He made a convincing argument for a strong effort during 1943 to force Italy out of the war, citing three positive advantages – namely, (1) the psychological effect of a definite break in the Axis conspiracy; (2) the effect of withdrawal of Italian troops from countries in the Near East; and (3) the influence it would have on the future alignment of Turkey. Churchill made no mention of any British desire to control the Mediterranean regardless of how the war might end, which many persons believed to be a cardinal principle of British national policy of long standing. As to a cross-Channel invasion in the near future, the Prime Minister said that adequate preparations could not be made for such an effort in the spring of 1944, but that an invasion of Europe must be made at some time in the future. There was no intimation that he favoured the attempt in 1944 unless Germany should collapse as a result of the Russian campaign, assisted by the intensified allied bombing attacks. Regarding Japan, the Prime Minister said the British intended to make every practicable effort to

---

[1] Admiral William D. Leahy; U.S. Navy from 1899; Ambassador to France, 1940; personal Chief of Staff to the President, 1942–9; died 1959.

keep China in the war, and he made a categorical promise to direct the full military and naval power of the Empire toward a complete defeat of Japan as soon as Germany should surrender. For immediate operations, Churchill recommended for consideration a campaign against Sumatra, which he believed to be lightly garrisoned by Japanese troops.[1] In a brief talk following the Prime Minister, President Roosevelt advocated the Channel operation at the earliest possible date and not later than 1944. He expressed disagreement with any Italian venture beyond the seizure of Sicily and Sardinia, and reiterated his frequently expressed determination to concentrate our military effort first on destruction of Nazi military power before engaging in any collateral campaigns and before exercising our full effort against Japan.

On that day Axis resistance in North Africa collapsed, five months later than expected.

The Americans had prepared a plan for an offensive later in the year in Burma.

Stilwell, Washington, May 1943:

With Wavell in command, failure was inevitable; he had nothing to offer at any meeting except protestations that the thing was impossible, hopeless, impractical. Churchill even spoke of it as silly. The Limeys all wanted to wait another year . . . the four Jap divisions in Burma have them scared to death. The inevitable conclusion was that Churchill has Roosevelt in his pocket. That they are looking for an easy way, a short cut for England, and no attention must be diverted from the Continent at any cost. The Limeys are not interested in the war in the Pacific, and with the President hypnotized they are sitting pretty. Roosevelt wouldn't let me speak my piece. I interrupted twice, but Churchill kept pulling away from the subject, and it was impossible . . . Farewell lunch. Mr Churchill: 'Mr President, I cannot but believe that an all-wise Providence has draped these great events, at this critical period of the world's history, about your personality and your high office.' And Frank [Roosevelt] lapped it up. Henry Stimson and George Marshall were understanding. The War Department was O.K. . . . But what's the use when the World's Greatest Strategist is against you.

As usual in military matters, Roosevelt gave way in the end to Churchill. It was agreed that plans would be made for invading Italy. Churchill agreed that the cross-Channel invasion would definitely take place after that, and was even pinned down to a

---

[1] This was one of Churchill's favourite ideas; for two years he urged it on the British Chiefs of Staff.

date, 1 May 1944. Churchill, irritated that he had not been able to get Marshall to share his enthusiasm for Italy, persuaded the American Chief of Staff to go with him to Algiers. There Marshall found that the local commanders were mostly in favour of the invasion of Italy. The phlegmatic general was, as it was said, 'overwhelmed by the flow of Churchill's argument'.

Butcher, Algiers, 29 May 1943:

The P.M., General Marshall, Sir Alan Brooke, General Ismay, and entourage arrived at Maison Blanche Friday afternoon, May 28, about 4.30. They had flown from Botwood, New Brunswick, direct to Gibraltar in a C–54 – the first time it has been done – distance, 2700 miles ... General Marshall is accompanying the Prime Minister this far, at the P.M.'s request to the President, because the P.M. openly and avowedly is seeking to influence Ike to pursue the campaign in the Mediterranean area until the Italians are out of the war. Presumably, he then wants the allied effort to continue in the Mediterranean area rather than across the Channel as already agreed by the Combined Chiefs at their Washington meeting. He makes no bones of his point of view and apparently regards the decision already taken as quite open to review and change. The Prime Minister had told the President he felt it only fair for General Marshall, as the representative of the American point of view to the contrary, to be present. During the trip, especially at Gibraltar, the P.M. has shown every courtesy to General Marshall, making certain that he was accorded all honours meant for the P.M., and, in general, looking after the little details of courtesy. The P.M. recited his story three different times in three different ways last night. He talks persistently until he has worn down the last shred of opposition. Ike is glad to have General Marshall on hand.

Butcher, 30 May 1943:

Before dinner, I received a call from Commander Thompson, the P.M.'s aide, inquiring if the General could see the Prime Minister at our house at 10.45 that night. Of course, Ike could, although the date jolted the free and easy lounging he needed so badly. We returned to the villa in town in time for the P.M.'s late visit. Ike and I sat reminiscing while waiting for the Prime Minister. Ike was growling because of the necessity of spending another night, probably until 1.30, going over the same ground, i.e. 'Keep on until you get Italy', which the P.M. had already covered, recovered, and uncovered – and there were really no serious questions of difference between the two ... The Prime Minister arrived at the house alone and soon was engaged in a 'repeat' of various factors relating to the prospective collapse of Italy and the necessity, in his view, of vigorous prosecution of our campaign after we have taken Sicily.

The P.M. said that he had 'sensed' at home a strong feeling by the Americans that he and the British generally were more desirous of prosecuting the war in the Mediterranean, possibly because of its strategic value for Britain's commerce, than in making a cross-Channel attack. This was incorrect, he felt, as the only difference between them was the matter of 'emphasis'. The Prime Minister felt we should exploit our advantage in the Mediterranean to knock Italy out of the war while we have the chance ... The P.M. is so persistent in his desire to knock out Italy that he said that the British people would be proud to halve their already short rations for a month if the shipping thus released would contribute to cure the supply difficulty inherent in the conquest of Italy[1] ... I have used a variety of schemes to hustle visitors away at night. On occasions, I have yawned openly and loudly. On others, I have paraded in my bathrobe before the lingering guest or guests. Neither of these seemed appropriate for this occasion, so I found my flash-light and walked in front of the door. This was at 1 o'clock. The P.M. left at 1.10, trudging up the driveway to the Admiral's house with a Scotland Yard man who, I found, had waited outside our front door.

Butcher, 31 May 1943:

Some time during the dinner-table conversation, the question of diaries came up. The Prime Minister said that it was foolish to keep a day-by-day dairy because it would simply reflect the change of opinion or decision of the writer, which, when and if published, makes one appear indecisive and foolish. He cited the diary of a British general who had written in his diary one day, 'There will be no war.' On the next day war was declared. The diary was published posthumously and, consequently the general was made to appear foolish. For his part, the Prime Minister said, he would much prefer to wait until the war is over and then write impressions, so that, if necessary, he could correct or bury his mistakes.

During the Algiers conference Churchill made great efforts to improve the relationship between de Gaulle, his rival General Henri Giraud, and the French authorities in North Africa. Churchill said: 'Sharp and sulky negotiations were begun.' Churchill was already finding that the proud de Gaulle, whom he had first set up in London, was a man of extreme difficulty as well as ability: the French humiliation had left a psychological scar on one so

---

[1] In order to find the necessary shipping for the Mediterranean campaign, British sailings to the Indian Ocean were cut by more than half; there was famine in Bengal, and the foodstuffs urgently needed could not be got through; a million and a half Indians died of starvation.

patriotic, and the resulting prickliness was complicated by what appeared to be signs of paranoia. Churchill had the greatest difficulty in championing him with Roosevelt, who detested the Frenchman and saw little practical reason in building up a French political presence. During 1943 de Gaulle ruthlessly gained for himself power over all Free French authorities. Churchill admitted to Roosevelt that he was 'not at all content about the changes in the French National Committee which leave de Gaulle sole President'.

In July Churchill was asked in the House of Commons about the existence of a dossier on de Gaulle which was said to show that the Frenchman was not 'a democrat according to our definition of the term'. This was believed to have been prepared at the behest of, or at least with the agreement of, Roosevelt. Churchill admitted the existence of such a dossier, but nothing more was heard of it. Meanwhile de Gaulle directed his growing empire from London, and became increasingly independent, audacious, and officious, much to the despondency of the man who had made him.

The Australian Casey, not without his diary, was in London during the summer.

27 June 1943:

Tonight at Chequers, in the course of a film showing the bombing of German towns from the air (made up from films taken during actual bombing raids) very well and dramatically done, W.S.C. suddenly sat bolt upright and said to me, 'Are we beasts? Are we taking this too far?' It was a momentary reaction from the very graphic presentation. I said that we hadn't started it, and that it was them or us.

Harris's bomber offensive was now in full operation. The R.A.F. had started what was known as 'round-the-clock' bombing. The U.S.A.F. had begun its heavy-bomber raids on Germany, often in daylight. The first 'saturation raid' on Berlin had taken place on 1 March.

Secret German report of saturation raid on Hamburg, 24-25 July 1943:

Trees three feet thick were broken off or uprooted, human beings were thrown to the ground or flung alive into the flames by winds which exceeded 150 miles an hour. The panic-stricken citizens knew not where to turn. Flames drove them from the shelters, but high-explosive bombs sent them scurrying back again. Once inside, they were suffocated by carbon-monoxide poisoning and their bodies reduced to ashes as though they had been placed in a crematorium, which was indeed what each shelter proved to be. The fortunate were those who jumped into the canals and waterways and remained swimming or standing up to their necks in water for hours.

The overheated air stormed through the street with immense force taking along not only sparks but burning timber and roof beams, so spreading the fire farther and farther, developing in a short time into a fire typhoon such as was never before witnessed, against which every human resistance was quite useless.

Harris tended to back area bombing against all other targets; on 6 March 1943, he stated that it was 'aimed at undermining the morale' of the German people – a strategy similar to that employed on the Western Front in the First World War, when offensives failed to take their original military objectives.

The most consistent campaigner against the policy was Richard Stokes. But his questions in the House were invariably answered – by Sinclair or one of his Under-Secretaries – ambiguously or with outright denials. Harris himself saw no reason to be ashamed of his task; he objected to parliamentary hypocrisy on the subject.

There is evidence to suggest that Stafford Cripps, when he became Minister for Aircraft Production, was also critical of the strategy.

Richard Stokes, House of Commons, 1 December 1943, on being informed that it was impossible to answer his questions without giving information to the enemy:

Would not the proper answer be that the Government dare not give it?

Sir A. Sinclair:

No, sir. Berlin is the centre of twelve strategic railways; it is the second largest port in Europe; it is connected with the whole canal system of Germany; and in that city are the A.E.G., Siemens, Daimler-Benz, Focke-Wulf, Heinkel and Dornier establishments; and if I were allowed to choose only one target in Germany, the target I should choose would be Berlin.

Stokes:

Does not my right hon. Friend admit by his answer that the government are now resorting to indiscriminate bombing, including residential areas?

One of the best critiques of area bombing was written at the time by that blunt but effective military propagandist, J. F. C. Fuller:

The key to common sense is simple thinking, and surely the simplest and most obvious fact in our lives is that we cannot live without food. As food is the basis of life, it is also the basis of war ... Food is, consequently, the foundation of strategy, as supply in all its many forms is of tactics ... 'Once we have demolished every city in Germany,' says Bomber Command, 'all that you soldiers need do is to catch the Golden Arrow and the Orient Express.' Fortunate P.B.I. [Poor Bloody Infantry] – yes! Nevertheless, unfortunate P.B.P.; for this time it is the poor bloody public who take it in the neck ... Air power must be linked to sea power and land power, if within any reasonable time we are to win through ... Cease to be air-minded and become war-minded; for air-mindedness simply means bomb-mindedness, and bomb-mindedness is Somme-mindedness.

In an official report to the United States Senate immediately after the war, it was stated that allied bombing attacks had 'left threequarters or more of German industrial capacity untouched ... Air warfare had been helpful by interrupting production, but the total damage inflicted on German industry was only estimated at about 20 per cent.'[1]

Casey, in London, had a rare glimpse of the War Cabinet at work:

2 July 1943:

W.S.C. in Cabinet, always somewhat impatient on non-war matters, in discussion of post-war agriculture and what to say about it in the House – 'Can't we confine ourselves to saying that agriculture is a very good thing and that there should be more of it?' Again – 'The business of Generals is to lead their troops to victory – under the direction of the civil power.' Again – 'I should feel very worried if I thought that you wanted me to agree to such-and-such – and I am sure you would not consciously add to my burdens.'

13 July 1943:

Interesting Cabinet at which R. A. Butler's White Paper on education was discussed. W.S.C. in very good form, and everyone in agreement with Rab's paper. Quite remarkable how practically all the Labour

---

[1] Kilgore Committee of the United States Senate, 1945.

Ministers integrate loyally and helpfully with the Tories, particularly Bevin. Herbert Morrison shows signs at times of thinking how the party machine will look on something, but I can't detect this in Attlee, Bevin or Cripps.[1]

On 10 July allied forces invaded Sicily. Planning, under Eisenhower, had been continuing since February; 'Ike' was proving himself a brilliant committee and military chairman; in the tremendous work involved in the preparation of such an undertaking, both in the broad view and the detailed decision, he was outstanding.

Butcher, Algiers, 27 July 1943:

We sat on the veranda, Ike answering questions of the Secretary[2] and expounding at length on the current Italian situation . . . [Stimson] had just arrived from London, where he had conferred off and on for a week with the Prime Minister. He felt that the Prime Minister was obsessed with the idea of proving to history that invasion of the Continent by way of the Balkans was wise strategy and would repair whatever damage history now records for Churchill's misfortune at the Dardanelles in the last war. The Secretary seemed apprehensive lest the P.M. would seek to avoid the commitment of the British and American governments to invade France next spring. The P.M. had repeatedly referred to corpses floating in the Channel. What the Secretary wanted from Ike was his opinion because he had to hurry home to express not only Ike's but his own views to General Marshall and the President before the next meeting of the Combined Chiefs at Quebec.

But Churchill had not forgotten his promise to Roosevelt and Stalin.

Major-General Kennedy, 1 August 1943:

He has had some late sittings with the Chiefs of Staff, the usual hour for meetings to assemble now being 10.30 p.m. Last week, he held a meeting, a sort of indignation meeting, to discuss telegrams from India which pointed out, quite rightly, the impossibility of extensive operations in Burma till after the monsoon. The fact of the matter is that nothing big

---

[1] Butler's Education Act, of 1944, established free secondary education for all and raised the school-leaving age to fifteen; it brought great credit to the Coalition Government.

[2] H. L. Stimson, United States, Secretary of State for War, 1940–5; died 1950. Churchill does not mention Stimson's visit in *The Second World War*.

can be done from India till Germany is finished. But he urged that we should try an operation against Sumatra and Malaya.

The conquest of Sicily was completed on 17 August: a campaign of thirty-eight days, in which over 30,000 allied troops were killed, wounded, or missing.

Lionel Shapiro, Canadian war correspondent, August 1943:

American troops steamed into Messina from the west, followed closely by British troops pushing up from the south. The conquest of the island was complete. In the sleepy upper town of Taormina, an aged native trudged into the main square, carefully selected two sheets from a roll of paper under his arm, and slapped these on the town's official notice board. One was a picture of President Roosevelt, the other of Prime Minister Churchill.

It was time for more argument. The fourth conference of the year was held at Quebec.

At the Quebec conference the Americans were relieved to find that the British had no desire to put off the invasion of France, planned for 1944, as they had done twice before. The main argument was over Italy, in which the Americans did not seem to the British to show sufficient interest; and Burma, in which the British did not seem to the Americans to show sufficient interest. The British also had the problem of their leader, and a number of his pet schemes.

Brooke, 30 August 1943:

The Quebec conference has left me absolutely cooked. Winston has an unfortunate trick of picking up some isolated operation, and, without ever really having it looked into, setting his heart on it. When he once gets into one of those moods he feels everybody is trying to thwart him and to produce difficulties. I wonder whether any historian of the future will ever be able to paint Winston in his true colours. It is a wonderful character, the most marvellous qualities and superhuman genius mixed with an astonishing lack of vision at times, and an impetuosity which, if not guided, must inevitably bring him into trouble again and again. He is quite the most difficult man to work with that I have ever struck, but I would not have missed the chance of working with him for anything on earth.

It was at this conference that Churchill told Brooke that, despite explicit previous promises, he could no longer support Brooke for the role of Supreme Commander of the Channel invasion forces. It was 'a crushing blow' to Brooke. The Chiefs of Staff had told the President in a memorandum that the only British officer they were 'willing to accept' for overall European command was Sir John Dill. The President wanted Marshall to have the job; he wanted him to be 'the Pershing of the Second World War', an unconsciously mixed compliment. Churchill agreed. But Eisenhower was appointed to the command of 'Overlord' on 6 December.

At Quebec the Americans agreed to invade Italy only on the condition that it was to be secondary to 'Overlord' [the cross-Channel operation]. With a vast army and air force in Europe, the American Chiefs of Staff felt stronger in relation to the British Prime Minister. And they did not trust him. Quebec was a watermark, for at it, the United States took over control of the Second World War from Britain.

Meanwhile, British and American troops braced themselves for the next jump: Sicily to Italy.

Alan Moorehead:

The truth was that we were very tired. We were suspended in the very middle of the war at a point where we could neither remember the beginning nor see the end. Only lately, in the past year, had we grown used to advancing. Alamein, Tripoli, Tunis, Sicily. All victories. But the way seemed endless. No matter how far you advanced – a thousand, two thousand miles – there was always the enemy in front of you, always another thousand miles to go.

On 3 September British and Canadian troops landed in Italy. The Italians did not delay. Four days later they signed an armistice (Mussolini had resigned, been arrested, and had escaped to the Germans). But Hitler's men were descending into Italy like a hardy old foot into a flabby boot. The 'rake of war', in Churchill's phrase, would have to tear over Italy after all: the foreign foot would have to be withdrawn from the boot, and it would be a slow and painful affair. Allied troops landed at Salerno on 9 September. Salerno was not far above the ankle of the boot, and not far enough – as Smuts predicted – to jab the foot into a rapid withdrawal.

Goebbels, 10 September 1943:

The Duce will enter history as the last Roman, but behind his massive figure a gypsy people has gone to rot.

From Quebec Churchill went on to Washington. There, in asking for a more flexible policy, he seemed to be trying to escape from the Quebec agreements. Roosevelt rebuffed him and left the capital.

Two days after landing in England Churchill suffered another blow in the unexpected death of the Chancellor of the Exchequer, Kingsley Wood, who had been responsible for the introduction of 'Pay As You Earn' tax. His place was taken by the redoubtable John Anderson (now also in charge of Britain's secret atomic research, under its cover of 'Tube Alloys'). At this time Beaverbrook also quietly returned to the Government, although without much to do. After his agitation of the previous year, Churchill and Beaverbrook had barely been on talking terms during the first part of 1943, when Beaverbrook was still speaking out strongly, often in the House of Lords, on ministerial incompetence and supplies for Russia. But the Second Front campaign began to peter out after the matter became apparently settled at Quebec, and Beaverbrook suddenly took up a new campaign – milk distribution. In this Churchill was not interested at all. Churchill was glad to renew the friendship, which, like that with Smuts, was so important to him because of its links with a distant past. Beaverbrook, meanwhile, extended his interests to the first of a number of agricultural estates. His reappointment to the Government was seen as an encouragement to the Russians and Americans about British intentions for a Second Front in 1944; no doubt the message was also received in Berlin. Churchill had always intended to bring his old friend back when he was 'restored to health and poise'.

John Steinbeck, author and war correspondent, Salerno, 8 October 1943:

The invasion and taking of the beachhead at Salerno has been very rough. The German was waiting for us. His .88s were on the surrounding hills and his machine guns in the sand dunes. His mines were in the surf and he sat there and waited for us ... for a time, it looked as though we might be pushed out. The litter spreads out to sea on little currents. The endless line of landing craft go ashore, carrying the supplies for men who are lying off in the bushes on the forward lines. And the battle line has moved up. The beach is taken now and the invasion moves ahead. The white hospital ships move inshore to take on their cargoes.

George VI, after an interview with Smuts, 13 October 1943:

Smuts is not happy about 'Overlord' and is doing his best to convince Winston that we must go on with W's own strategy of attacking the 'underbelly of the Axis'.[1] We are now in Italy, Italy has surrendered to us, and has declared war on Germany today as a co-belligerent, not as an ally, which means the Italian people will help us in Italy. We are masters of the Mediterranean and the Italian Fleet is ours. S. feels we must capture the Dodecanese and Aegean Islands and from there land in Greece and in Yugoslavia across the Adriatic, thus liberating those 2 countries, which in turn may make Roumania and even Hungary give in. Turkey may come in on our side as well. As arrangements are we are committed to 'Overlord' next May which may mean a stalemate in France. I agree with S. about all this. If you have a good thing stick to it. Why start another front across the Channel. F.D.R. wants to give Marshall a good job here as C.-in-C. The Russians do not want us in the Balkans. They would like to see us fighting in France, so as to have a free hand in the east of Europe.

Major-General Kennedy, 13 October 1943:

Returned from leave October 8. All the week I was away Winston was agitating for an attack on Rhodes. C.I.G.S. argued in vain that we had resources sufficient only for Italy, and that we must not divert forces to the Aegean. The Germans have 19 divisions in Italy, and show signs of fighting harder than we expected in Central Italy. On Saturday October 9 the P.M. had actually decided to go to Tunis with C.I.G.S. to discuss with Commanders-in-Chief ways and means of mounting an attack on Rhodes, provided Marshall could come across from the United States. Luckily, Eisenhower . . . cabled to say that it would be impossible to find the forces, and the project has now fallen through. It does seem amazing that the P.M. should spend practically a whole week on forcing forward his ideas about taking an island in the face of all military advice.

But Churchill went ahead, without Eisenhower's approval. A brigade was sent from Malta to the Aegean, and other troops from the Middle East Command, for island-hopping; there was insufficient air support, and it was forced to withdraw. Roosevelt refused to help. A large percentage of the British military force was lost, and there were also severe naval losses. It was Crete all over again: a wretched affair.

---

[1] Smuts had made a strongly worded protest after Quebec; the plans for 1944, he said, were only 'nibbling'; he wanted a link-up with the Russians in the Balkans.

All these operations in the Mediterranean were puny compared to the gigantic struggle taking place in Russia. On 6 November the Russians retook Kiev. The two Western leaders had arranged to meet Stalin at Teheran. Before doing so, they met at Cairo in an effort to find some agreement – for they were fast drifting apart. The basic reason for their differences was the distrust, now affecting Roosevelt, which the American Chiefs of Staff felt towards Churchill's ambitions in the Mediterranean and the Balkans. These suspicions were becoming obsessive. They were quite without foundation.

At the Cairo conference, Eisenhower felt Churchill's favour for the 'soft underbelly' lay 'outside the scope of the immediate military problem'. Typifying the American military attitude, he noted Churchill's 'concern as a political leader for the future of the Balkans. For this concern I had great sympathy, but as a soldier I was particularly careful to exclude such considerations from my own recommendations.' This was the same narrow view which was to be the cause of so much dissension and misunderstanding in the final stages of the war. He shared the view, put about by Stimson, that Churchill's policy was concerned to 'vindicate his strategical concepts of World War I, in which he had been the principal exponent of the Gallipoli campaign. Many professionals agreed that the Gallipoli affair had failed because of bungling in execution rather than through mistaken calculations of its possibilities. It sometimes seemed that the Prime Minister was determined in the second war to gain public acceptance of this point of view.'

Chiang Kai-shek attended the deliberations, at Roosevelt's invitation.

Lord Moran,[1] Cairo, 24 November 1943:

Madame brought Chiang Kai-shek to dine with the P.M. She acted as an interpreter; without her, things would have dragged. The P.M. is always attracted to a soldier who has done something in the field, but he is sceptical of China as a great power and grudges all the time that Roosevelt has given to her affairs. To the President, China means four hundred million people who are going to count in the world of tomorrow, but Winston thinks only of the colour of their skin; it is when he talks of India or China that you remember he is a Victorian.

---

[1] Sir Charles Wilson, Churchill's doctor, had been made a peer.

A Victorian ... Almost incredibly, it was true. Churchill had fought his first election in the nineteenth century. Before the old Queen had died, he had become the most highly-paid newspaper reporter in the world.

The Teheran conference began three days later.

Moran, 29 November 1943:

When I saw the P.M. this morning he was plainly put out. It seems that he had sent a note to the President suggesting they should lunch together, but the President's answer was a polite 'No'. 'It is not like him,' the P.M. murmured. He does not, Harry explained, want an impression to get abroad that he and Winston are putting their heads together in order to plan Stalin's discomfiture. This, however, did not prevent the President seeing Stalin alone after lunch.

The increasing but needless sensitivity of the British to American excesses of tact towards the Russians were to bedevil more and more the 'Big Three' conferences.

Admiral Leahy:

Churchill was sixty-nine years old on this November 30, 1943, so the day ended with the Prime Minister being host at a large dinner in the British Legation. Russian custom was followed, which meant that toasts were proposed and drunk to nearly all of the thirty-four persons at the banquet table, an exceedingly tiresome procedure. The President, Stalin, and Churchill made speeches. Our abiding friendship with the Bolsheviks and our common hopes for a new order in the world were stressed. As the party went on, the monotonous exchange of international compliments was enlivened now and then with some acid humour. Stalin particularly was quick in repartee, sometimes delivered with a sinister expression on his face. The Prime Minister remarked that the political complexion of the British people was undergoing an orderly change, and it might now be said to have gone almost so far as to be termed 'pink'. Whereupon Stalin interjected: 'That is an indication of improved health.' At this memorable dinner, it appeared that the grand coalition had achieved a degree of harmony that should insure a speedy defeat of Nazism, and a peaceful solution of the difficult problems of a post-war world. Unfortunately, the next morning after such affairs usually brings a return to realism.

During the conference Roosevelt received avid support from Stalin in the matter of speeding up the invasion of France; this was hardly surprising to Churchill. The President was also gratified to discover that Stalin strongly supported the American view that any secondary operation should be confined to the south of France, and most definitely not in the Balkans. Satisfied that he had broken for the time being Churchill's 'imperialist intentions' in the Balkans, the President returned to Washington, after a briefly reassuring meeting with the Prime Minister at Cairo.

Moran, Cairo, 5 December 1943:

The P.M. has become very irritable and impatient; at times he seems almost played out. I went to his bedroom tonight and found him sitting with his head in his hands. 'I have never felt like this before,' he said. 'Can't you give me something so that I won't feel so exhausted?' Nevertheless, he still talks of going to Italy to see Alex. I feel so certain that he will get harm if we go to Italy when he is like this that I've written to Smuts in the strongest terms. He is the only man who has any influence with the P.M.; indeed, he is the only ally I have in pressing counsels of common sense on the P.M. Smuts sees so clearly that Winston is irreplaceable that he may make an effort to persuade him to be sensible. But I doubt whether even Smuts can make him alter his plans. Whatever the strain, it is still broken by convivial nights, when for a few hours the P.M. seems to recover his old good spirits as if there has been a new gush of vitality pumped into his veins. Last night at the Embassy in Cairo we sat at the dinner table from 8 p.m. till 11.50 p.m. Mountbatten's eyes closed and opened spasmodically. I looked down the long table at the faces of the soldiers and sailors. They seemed only half awake. I was sorry for Winston: surely someone ought to show some interest in the drawn-out monologue.

Moran, Eisenhower's villa, Carthage, 11 December 1943:

Our luck is out. Soon after daybreak we came down near Tunis. A cold wind blew across the deserted aerodrome, there was no one about, no car, nothing. The P.M. got wearily out of the hot aircraft, looked around blankly and then, in spite of our protests, he sat down on a box, took off his hat and gloomily surveyed the sandy ground. The wind blew a wisp of hair this way and that, his face shone with perspiration. I pressed him to get back into the Skymaster; he only scowled. I went off to find out what had gone wrong, and learned that the airfield where we were expected was fifteen miles from this spot. There was nothing for it but to re-embark. As the P.M. walked very slowly to the aircraft there was a grey look on his face that I did not like, and when he came at last to this house he collapsed wearily into the first chair. All day he has done nothing; he does not seem to have the energy even to read the usual telegrams. I feel much disturbed. I went to bed early and woke to find the P.M. in his dressing-gown standing at the foot of my bed. 'I've got a pain in my throat, here.' He put his finger just above his collar bone. I rubbed my eyes and got up. 'It's pretty bad. Do you think it's anything? What can it be due to?' he demanded in one breath. I reassured him, and indeed I am not unduly perturbed. For a man with his strong constitution he never seems to be long without some minor ailment. Probably in the morning I shall hear no more of this pain.

Even the best doctors can see little to worry about in an exhausted old man with a grey face and a bad pain in the throat.

12 December 1943:

I went, on waking, to the P.M.'s room. The pain had gone, he complained of nothing, but his skin was hot, and on taking his temperature I found it was 101. I could find no signs on examining his chest. We have had alarms like this before that have come to nothing, and in his position you cannot prepare for an illness without letting it be known everywhere. On the other hand, if he is going to be ill we have nothing here in this God-forsaken spot – no nurses, no milk, not even a chemist.

Fortunately, there was a doctor.

14 December 1943:

It was left to me to compose a bulletin, which I gave to Martin when Bedford and Pulvertaft had signed it.[1] 'The Prime Minister has been in bed for some days with a cold. A patch of pneumonia has now developed in the left lung. His general condition is as satisfactory as can be expected.' Mrs Churchill arrived by air today. The P.M. received the news of her arrival with considerable emotion.

16 December 1943:

I think we have turned the corner. The temperature is still 101, but the signs in the chest are clearing up. Though this is the fifth day, Martin told me this morning that the public still do not know the P.M. is ill. Mr Attlee will tell the House at the end of Questions, and the news will be broadcast at one o'clock, just when we are no longer anxious about him. We gave Martin another bulletin, which will appear in tomorrow's papers.

Admiral James, 29 December 1943:

The news that Winston was ill sent a wave of apprehension through the country. We just cannot afford to lose him as our leader. Thank goodness he is on the way to complete recovery. I hear the wires are sizzling with telegrams already!

Despite the seriousness of Churchill's condition, no one around

---

[1] John Martin, Churchill's principal private secretary; Dr Bedford, a leading consultant for heart diseases; Dr Pulvertaft, leading pathologist. The doctors had been flown out from London.

him really seems to have faced the fact that he might very well have died. This confidence reflected, also, the mood of the public.

Spectator, 31 December 1943:

That a man of sixty-nine, who had been working as Mr Churchill has been working, should go down with pneumonia for the second time in twelve months was enough to create universal alarm. But the fact is we can no longer believe anything can happen to the Prime Minister. A blind fatalism it may be, but at the same time rather more than that. It is not simply that because the mind cannot conceive the scheme of things without Mr Churchill, the mind determines that the scheme of things will not be without Mr Churchill, but rather that we have acquired a deep conviction that there is something in the man himself that will keep him at his post, fit and able, till (in his own words) he has finished the job.

It was not a sensible attitude; but it did show how Churchill had re-established himself at home during 1943, after the vicissitudes of 1942. It was ironic, for probably only he knew how his precious Anglo-American alliance was beginning already to break up.

CHAPTER EIGHT

1944 Struggling Statesman

To restore his health Churchill went to Marrakesh in Morocco. There he was surrounded by those whom it was thought would amuse him – Beaverbrook and the Coopers.

Duff Cooper, 10 January 1944:

Clemmie and Sarah met us and took us straight to the villa where they are all living – a beautiful place belonging to a rich American lady. There we found Winston in his siren suit and his enormous Californian hat. When it got cooler he completed this get-up with a silk dressing-gown embroidered with gold dragons ... He was much annoyed at having lost the Skipton by-election to a Commonwealth candidate.[1] He has a huge staff, including half-a-dozen cypher girls and a map-room with a naval officer permanently on duty.

The same, 11 January:

Diana went out shopping early with the Consul's wife. I took it easy. We both went round about twelve to the villa, where we were due to pick up others of the party for a picnic. There were large supplies of food and drink – two servants to wait as well as the staff, and a host of American military police standing round to protect. He sat there for more than an hour after lunch, reading the memoirs of Captain Gronow. This was the seventh picnic they had had during the fourteen days they have been there. It seemed to me a curious form of entertainment. I drove back with Clemmie, Diana going with Winston. Clemmie said she had given Winston a Caudle curtain lecture this morning on the importance of not quarrelling with de Gaulle. He had grumbled at the time, but she thought it would bear fruit. I sat between Winston and Colville at dinner, and all went well until just as we were leaving, when a message came from Algiers to say that General de Lattre de Tassigny,

---

[1] A number of by-election successes by the new left-wing Commonwealth Party, were said to emanate from public dissatisfaction with the Coalition's cautious reaction to the Beveridge social security plan. The party was led by Sir Richard Acland, M.P., 1939–45; Labour M.P., 1947–55.

whom Winston had invited for later in the week, had reported that de Gaulle, whose permission to come he had asked, had answered that it would be most inopportune for him to do so at the present time. This produced an explosion. Winston wanted to send a message at once to tell de Gaulle not to come. I did my best to calm him, and he decided to do nothing.

The same, 12 January 1944:

I was woken by the telephone ringing at 8.15. Colonel Warden [the code name under which the Prime Minister was travelling] wished to speak to me. He said he had been thinking things over. The matter was not so simple, would I go over and see him? I got over to him in half an hour. He was in bed, and had apparently worked himself up again about de Gaulle. He suggested sending him a note to the airfield to say he was sorry he had been troubled to come so far but that he would not be able to see him after all. I strongly dissuaded him from this course, pointing out that we knew nothing of the reasons which had caused de Gaulle to prevent de Lattre from coming here ... This worked, but Winston then said he would receive de Gaulle on a purely social basis, would talk about the weather and the beauty of the place and then say good-bye. This was better, but I suggested that Palewski [de Gaulle's Private Secretary] would probably ask me whether there were going to be serious conversations after lunch – what was I to say? He said he didn't mind having a talk if de Gaulle asked for it, but that he would not take the initiative. Nor would he see him alone. If he did, de Gaulle would misrepresent what he had said. I must be present and Max [Beaverbrook] too, and de Gaulle could bring whom he liked. All passed off well. Winston was in a bad mood when de Gaulle arrived and was not very welcoming. He had just read of the shooting of Ciano,[1] which had rather shocked him. As lunch proceeded, however, Winston thawed. He had Diana on one side, and Palewski on the other. I sat the other side of Palewski and was able to inform him quietly of the delicacy of the situation and of the P.M.'s irritation over the de Lattre episode. De Gaulle sat opposite, next to Clemmie. When the ladies left, Winston invited de Gaulle to sit next to him, but things were still sticky. We then moved out into the garden – Winston, Max, the British Consul and I on the one side – de Gaulle and Palewski on the other. The conversation lasted about two hours. Winston was admirable, I thought, and de Gaulle very difficult and unhelpful. He talked as though he were Stalin and Roosevelt combined. Winston dealt first with the prisoners questions – about Syria – always on the line 'Why should we quarrel?

---

[1] Mussolini, under pressure from the Nazi masters of his puppet 'republic' in North Italy, had agreed to Ciano's execution as a traitor.

Why can't we be friends?' De Gaulle did very little towards meeting him half-way, but they parted friends and the Prime Minister agreed to attend the review on the following day.

To whatever extent Cooper imagined himself invaluable, the fact remained that his efforts to bring about an understanding and easy relationship between de Gaulle and Churchill were without any success at all.

Diana Cooper, 13 January 1944:

Later, after the review, which seemed gruelling enough on Winston in one day, we had our eighth and last picnic. The picnic consists of eight cars with white stars and U.S. drivers (the whole town is run by the U.S. exclusively) with two or three guests in each, some 'tecs distributed around, and a van laden with viands, drinks, cushions, tables, chairs and pouffes ... we laid out our delicatessen, the cocktail was shaken up, rugs and cushions distributed, tables and buffets appeared as by a genie's order, and as we finished our preparations the main party arrived. The Colonel ['Warden'] is immediately sat on a comfortable chair, rugs are swathed round his legs and a pillow put on his lap to act as table, book-rest etc. A rather alarming succession of whiskies and brandies go down, with every time a facetious preliminary joke with Edward, an American ex-barman, or with Lord Moran in the shape of professional adviser. I have not heard the lord doctor answer; perhaps he knows it would make no difference. I had just time to run down the dangerous steep mule-track to the cyclopean boulders, sprayed by gushing cascades that divided them. The pull up was a feat, and the sun turned the cold weather into a June day. All spirits rose to the beauty and the occasion – all, that is, except old Max Calvin [Beaverbrook], whose creased livid face is buried between a stuffy black hat and a book. A lot of whisky and brandy, good meat and salad, and 'little white-faced tarts' (to use Winston's expression) are consumed and then, of course, as I feared, nothing will quiet the Colonel (no assurance of the difficulties and the steepness) but he must himself venture down the gorge. Old Moran once mumbled a bit about it being unwise. It carried as much weight as if it had been said by an Arab child in vulgar, rustic tongue. So down he goes and, once down, he next must get on top of the biggest boulder. There were a lot of tough 'tecs along, including the faithful Inspector Thompson, but even with people to drag you and heave you up, it is a terrific strain and effort in a boiling sun when you have just had a heart-attack. Clemmie said nothing, but watched him with me like a lenient mother who does not wish to spoil her child's fun nor yet his daring – watched him levered up on to the biggest boulder, watched him spatchcocked out on top of it. Shots were snapped, a little Arab boy was bribed to jump into the pool, and then this steep, heart-straining ascent began. I tore up for the second time, puffing like a grampus. It seemed to me that if a rope or strap could be found to pass behind his back, while two men walked in front pulling the ends, it would be better than dragging him by his arms. I could find nothing but a long tablecloth, but I wound that into a coil and stumbled down with it. Big success! He had no thought of being ridiculous (one of his qualities) so he leaned back upon the linen rope and the boys heaved our saviour up, while old man Moran tried his pulse at intervals. This was only permitted so as to prove that his heart was unaffected by the climb. The picnic was over.

Such is war.

During Churchill's convalescence first preparations were beginning for the invasion of France. Eisenhower took up Supreme Command of the projected allied expeditionary force on 16 January. He returned to London and the same planning H.Q. in St James's Square that he had used in 1942 for the invasion of West Africa. Montgomery, who was to have command of the land forces, also returned to England, visiting Churchill first at Marrakesh. He had been with the Eighth Army for just over eighteen months, one of the most successful commands in British military history, from Egypt to half-way up Italy. Despite his success, he had become the subject of controversy. Churchill's position as British supremo in the war was now unassailable. Once there had been only defeats. Now there were only victories. That this was so had much to do with one man, Montgomery.

As a general, Montgomery was almost the exact opposite of what the public imagined. Not in the least dashing, he was slow, careful, meticulous. Unlike Wavell and Rommel, he never gambled until he held all the cards. He had a very good understanding of ordinary soldiers. And, in that he got the necessary materials of war, he was lucky.

At Marrakesh, Montgomery saw for the first time the plan for 'Overlord'. He read it, and said immediately: 'This won't do. I must have more in the initial punch.'

Harold Nicolson, letter, 18 January 1944:

This was an exciting day. The House met again after the Christmas Recess and I went down there early. I happened to have been told that Winston had arrived home that morning, but the rest of the House were wholly unaware of that fact. We were dawdling through Questions and I was idly glancing at my Order Paper when I saw (*saw* is the word) a gasp of astonishment pass over the faces of the Labour Party opposite. Suddenly they jumped to their feet and started shouting, waving their papers in the air. We also jumped up and the whole House broke into cheer after cheer while Winston, very pink, rather shy, beaming with mischief, crept along the front bench and flung himself into his accustomed seat. He was flushed with pleasure and emotion, and hardly had he sat down when two large tears began to trickle down his cheeks. He mopped at them clumsily with a huge white handkerchief. A few minutes later he got up to answer questions. Most men would have been unable, on such an occasion, not to throw a flash of drama into their replies. But Winston answered them as if he were the youngest Under-Secretary, putting on his glasses, turning over his papers, responding tactfully to supplementaries, and taking the whole thing as conscientiously as could be. I should like to say that he seemed completely restored to health. But he looked pale when the first flush of pleasure had subsided, and his voice was not quite so vigorous as it had been.

On 22 January allied troops landed at Anzio behind the German lines in Italy. It was a somewhat obvious tactic and it did not go well. Churchill was criticized for his interference, which was compared to his action over the landings at Suvla Bay in the Gallipoli campaign. Churchill had only to mention the word 'landing' or 'beach' in the Second World War for the name 'Gallipoli' to come echoing back. He told Moran: 'Anzio was my worst moment in the war. I had most to do with it. I didn't want two Suvla Bays in one lifetime.' Anzio was tragedy and farce.

Harold Nicolson, diary, 7 February 1944:

I fear that Winston has become an electoral liability now rather than an asset. This makes me sick with human nature. Once the open sea is reached, we forget how we clung to the pilot in the storm. Poor Winston, who is so sensitive although so pugnacious, will feel all this. In the station lavatory at Blackheath last week I found scrawled up, 'Winston Churchill is a bastard.' I pointed it out to the Wing Commander who was with me. 'Yes,' he said, 'the tide has turned. We find it everywhere.' 'But how foul,' I said. 'How bloody foul!'

House of Lords, *The Times* report for 9 February 1944:

The Bishop of Chichester[1] said . . . It was not sufficiently realized that it was no longer definite military and industrial objectives which were

---

[1] G. K. A. Bell, widely predicted at one time as a future Archbishop of Canterbury; Dean of Canterbury, 1924–9; Bishop of Chichester, 1929–58; author of *The Church and Humanity*, 1946; died 1958.

the aim of the bombers, but the whole town ... It would be the sort of crime which even in the political field would turn against the perpetrator. It had been said that area bombing was definitely designed to diminish the sacrifice of British lives and to shorten the war ... To justify methods inhumane in this way smacked of the Nazi philosophy of 'might is right'.

This outspoken attack was half-heartedly supported by Archbishop Lord Lang. The Government defended its policy – vaguely defined – in the person of Viscount Cranborne, Secretary of State for Dominion affairs. He promised that the offensive would be continued 'with increasing power and more crushing effect (Cheers)'.

And so it was.

The most unexpected parliamentary event of 1944 was the defeat of the Government on an amendment of Butler's Education Bill, in favour of equal pay for women teachers. A number of progressive Tories joined with Labour for the vote. On the following day, Churchill asked for a vote of confidence on the question, and he got it without trouble. Although few people were prepared to lose the Prime Minister in the middle of the war on behalf of the schoolteachers, the defeat had shown an increasing awareness of social problems already discernible in 1943 and that became marked in 1944.

English correspondent[1] in America, June 1944:

Within the past few weeks United States newspapers have widely commented on and widely censured Mr Churchill for seeking a vote of confidence after being defeated on whether or not women should have equal pay with men. This, I suggest, was a purely domestic British issue. New Orleans said the Prime Minister should not have forced that choice on the Commons; 'Churchill cracks his whip,' said the *Herald-Tribune*; 'He was fundamentally wrong,' said Oklahoma; Cleveland spoke of 'this arrogance in home affairs'; Atlanta said Mr Churchill had done himself and his party great harm, and Savannah had an article on Mr Eden as the next Prime Minister. Louisville said the British political truce wears thin, and that Mr Churchill's attitude was that of a 'weary and somewhat disheartened man'. The *St. Louis Star-Times* said it was too bad that because of stupid censorship most Americans were unaware of this drift in British politics ... American

---

[1] J. L. Hodson, author and journalist.

sniping at Lord Louis Mountbatten and our army in Burma is pretty widespread. The *Boston Globe* on March 14, when extolling in its leading article the work of your General Stilwell in Burma, ended: 'To compare this military feat with the slow advance of the British–Indian forces towards Akyab may seem unfair. Yet the comparison is inescapable. Stilwell's handful of soldiers and road builders seek to save China by re-opening her supply line. Lord Louis Mountbatten's gigantic army is concerned with the reconquest of imperial preserves. Does this explain the difference?' On April 11, in the same journal, Mr Fletcher Pratt, a columnist, returned to the attack, ending his article: 'In other words, the British India Government is still fighting to restore the Empire as it was, not to beat the enemy.' I was with our army in Burma for a brief time, and I should say Mr Pratt's statement is great nonsense, but my point is this: Suppose English journalists were to animadvert on an American army in this critical fashion? Can anybody imagine Americans enduring it with equanimity? The *Journal–American*, on April 7, 1944, published a feature article by Krishnalal Shridharani, illustrated by a large picture of a child and mother said to be dying of starvation in a Calcutta street. The writer said, among other things 'the unprecedented appointment of an Australian, R. G. Casey, as the Governor of Bengal has heightened the suspicion in India that the British Tories are lining up even the Dominions in order to maintain India as a colony'; and again: 'The war in Asia deserves the highest priority, and it should be conducted under American leadership in order to offset the unpopularity of other partners.' To do justice to the *Chicago Tribune* would require a good deal of space. On March 29 this journal said: 'Our soldiers [in England] may be unhappy, but they may console themselves with the thought that they are doing more for the British than merely winning the war for them. Our men overseas are going to vote . . . [in] England, where there is no written constitution to safeguard the people's rights; where parliament is unchecked; where men can be held in jail indefinitely without trial, and where elections can be dispensed with.' On the same day: 'Americans refuse to accept the British view that the military are a superior class entitled to rule and instruct the common people.' On March 30, under the heading, 'Overtaxed Executives', they said: 'Perhaps Mr Churchill can lighten his load . . . [the meaning was by leaving military decisions to military men] and also by strengthening his war cabinet by getting an abler man as Foreign Secretary.'

The planning of 'Overlord' proceeded with the strategical background still unsettled between Americans and British.

Major-General Kennedy, Memo. on strategy, 5 April 1944:

Vast energy has been expended fruitlessly here, and tempers frayed without any result which helps the war. The Chiefs of Staff have been in a state of desperation time after time. If we could only get on in a rational manner here, we could at least arrive at some basis of discussion with the Americans. As regards the question whether to land in the South of France, we hold the view here that the overriding consideration in the Mediterranean at the moment is to contain the maximum number of German forces there during 'Overlord'. The British Chiefs of Staff feel that to mount an expedition against Southern France will inevitably mean going over to the defensive in Italy and a long period of quiet in the Mediterranean (six to eight weeks) at the very time 'Overlord' is being prepared and launched. We have not enough infantry for both an Italian offensive and a large-scale operation against Southern France. Despite all possible efforts, we have failed to convince the Americans of this, and they are obsessed with the idea of the French landing.

Major-General Kennedy, at Montgomery's H.Q., 7 April (Good Friday) 1944:

When the conference started in the morning, Montgomery had asked us not to smoke on account of the bad ventilation of the room. Later on he announced that he had had a message from Winston to say that he would join us after tea. Monty added that, as the Prime Minister would undoubtedly arrive with a large cigar, smoking would be allowed after tea. He made the announcement in such a puckish way that there was a great roar of laughter. Winston duly arrived. He looked puffy and dejected and his eyes were red. When he had taken his seat, Montgomery spoke again for ten minutes, as he said, to emphasize three main points ... Monty did it extremely well. He is a highly skilled speaker, and he shows great sense in selecting and emphasizing points, and not too many of them. Winston then mounted the platform. He was in a short black jacket and had a big cigar as usual. He said he had not been convinced in 1942, or in 1943, that this operation was feasible. He was not expressing an opinion on its feasibility now. But, if he were qualified to do so, and if he were one of us, he would have the greatest confidence from all he had heard of the plans. But he had hardened very much on *this*: that the time was now *ripe*. We had experienced commanders, a great allied army, a great air force. Our equipment had improved. All the preparations, strategical and tactical, had been made with the greatest skill and care. We were now going to write a glorious page in the history, not of one country or of two, but of the world. He felt very strongly that this should not be an operation designed to dig in on a bridgehead. At Anzio we had lost a great opportunity – *there* was a lesson for all to study. The object must be to fight a battle.

Richard Dimbleby,[1] war correspondent:

Within the country two questions were on everybody's lips – When ? Where? Many theories were advanced. Some said the Channel Ports, others declared for Brittany. There were those who supported Holland and those who, with an air of great secrecy, whispered that it was Belgium, Holland, Denmark, Finland, the Channel Islands, the South of France ... Meanwhile, the months of 1944 went by. False alarms came and passed. There were exercises galore, some of them amphibious and wet, others involving hundreds of tanks and self-propelled guns and watched by the leaders of Supreme Command. As the weeks passed, the strength of the allied army waiting in Britain was growing, and day by day the united air forces of Britain and America struck harder and deeper at the enemy ... In the south of England the leaders, Eisenhower, Tedder, Montgomery, Bradley, Leigh-Mallory and Spaatz travelled, inspected, approved, and talked to their men as generals have always talked on the eve of battle. Around the coast the landing craft fussed and jockeyed, rehearsing endlessly, formating, embarking, disgorging. Over them as they exercised flew the battle squadrons, roundel and star together, striking simultaneously at the enemy's centres of industry and his emplacements on the Atlantic coast.

In Europe, they waited. And suffered.

Anne Frank, in hiding, Holland, 11 April 1944:

Be brave! Let us remain aware of our task and not grumble, a solution will come; God has never deserted our people. Right through the ages there have been Jews, through all the ages they have had to suffer, but it has made them strong too; the weak fall, but the strong will remain and never go under!

Butcher, S.H.A.E.F. H.Q., 14 April 1944:

Ed Stettinius [Secretary of State] told me the President was far from well and that he is becoming increasingly difficult to deal with because he changed his mind so often. There have been discussions with him as to the meaning of 'unconditional surrender' as applied to Germany. Any military person knows that there are conditions to every surrender. There is a feeling that, at Casablanca, the President and the Prime Minister, more likely the former, seized on Grant's famous term without realizing the full implications to the enemy. Goebbels has made great capital with it to strengthen the morale of the German Army and people. Our psychological experts believe we would be wiser if we

---

[1] First B.B.C. news-reporter, 1936–9; first B.B.C. war correspondent, 1939–45; covered all great post-war State occasions for B.B.C.; died 1965.

created a mood of acceptance of surrender in the German Army which would make possible a collapse of resistance similar to that which took place in Tunisia.

A woman broadcasting on the B.B.C., 5 May 1944:

If you live in Sussex or Kent nowadays (or I suppose in a good many other counties besides), you know before getting out of bed and pulling aside the black-out if it's a nice day. A clear dawn has a new clarion – the deep and throbbing roar of hundreds of planes outward bound ... the impressive thing – the thing that makes land-girls pause in their stringing of the hopfields and makes conductors of country buses lean out and look up from their platforms – the impressive thing is the numbers. Never in the Battle of Britain, in the days when the Luftwaffe was beaten over these fields and woods, did the Germans send out such vast fleets ... As the roar fades with them, another rises until things on the kitchen mantelshelf tinkle and rattle as they catch the vibration. Some days it will go on like this pretty well all day.

Bomber Command was now going over to the use of 'heavy-case' bombs. Ordinary bombs were becoming of little use 'against already ruined cities in which life was mostly going on in cellars and only the essential factory buildings had been partly restored', as Harris said.

In Greece, guerrilla bands, mostly Communist, were harassing the German occupation, which was barely in control of the country. The Greek king, fretting about his traditionally insecure throne, was not with his forces in exile, which were languishing in Egypt and rent with political discontent. On 24 April there had been firing between British and Greek forces near Alexandria. It was evident that many Greeks would not welcome the return of the old régime after the Germans went.

New Statesman & Nation, 6 May 1944, wrote of:

... a fact which Mr Churchill seems unwilling to recognise. The vast majority of Greeks are republican, and have no wish to see their king return ... [Churchill's] blood is up and he knows that he holds the trumps. Will he now have the magnanimity to make King George [of Greece] grant an amnesty to men whose crime is their desire to liberate their country? We doubt it ... Will supplies continue to be sent to E.L.A.S.? [the Communist guerrillas] ... Not if Mr Churchill proposes to continue this truculent and foolish policy which is crippling and frustrating the anti-Fascist energy of one of the most politically conscious allied peoples. We all know that he wishes to uphold the principle of legitimacy and the right of Britain to preserve a 'friendly' government for the coast and islands that control the Western Mediterranean. But the present policy will leave us without friends in Greece, will discredit our declared war aims, and will sow seeds of suspicion in every country in which our 'liberating' armies hope to find, among the 'resistance' elements, essential helpers.

The parentheses around 'liberating' typified the kind of stance which Churchill's critics took on this question. There were genuine, and understandable fears, that British troops were being outrageously misused. The old suspicions about Churchill 'the fanatical right-wing imperialist' were by no means dead. Thus began the Greek problem, which was to bedevil the last months of 1944, and to test Churchill's diplomatic skills – of which his critics believed him to have little or none – to the limit.

On 25 May 1944, Churchill gave a long review of foreign affairs to the House of Commons. The occasion was on the ending of a conference of Commonwealth Prime Ministers. He spoke of a successor to the League of Nations, and the re-establishment of governments in Italy, France, Greece, Yugoslavia, and Roumania. It did not, perhaps could not, convey what his real fears were. 'The terms offered by Russia to Roumania made no suggestion of altering the standards of society in that country and were in many respects, if not in all, remarkably generous . . . The victories of the Russian Armies have been attended by a great rise in the strength of the Russian state and a remarkable broadening of its values. The religious side of Russian life has had a wonderful rebirth . . . ' This did not escape without some criticisms. Harold Nicolson regretted that the Prime Minister had not reaffirmed the traditional principles of British foreign policy:

We are not taking sufficient account of the rights, interests, and independence of the smaller powers of western Europe.

Lord Dunglass[1] said that Europe after the defeat of Hitler would be a cauldron of suspicion and civil war. There was no security there:

The government should tell the people of this country, if they can, that

---

[1] Conservative M.P., 1931–45; House of Lords, 1951–63; Foreign Secretary, 1960–3; Conservative M.P., as Sir Alec Douglas-Home, since 1963; Prime Minister, 1963–4.

for many years ahead we shall be unable to shift the burden of our defence on to somebody's else's shoulders.

Predictably, Driberg, Hore-Belisha, and Shinwell, were among those who condemned the Prime Minister's speech.

There was also discomfort in America at this speech of Churchill's, in which he had seemed to be too blandly contemplating the carving-up of Europe. The Scripps–Howard newspapers noted that a 'big disappointment' of the speech was that:

> Mr Churchill made the Atlantic Charter appear only a noble set of words rather than a commitment ... [he had hinted at] a future League of Nations in which the big powers apparently would dictate ... but Americans share the fear of the smaller nations that the trend is toward another balance of power system with British and Russian spheres of influence.

New Statesman & Nation, 27 May 1944:

> The bulk of Mr Churchill's speech was devoted to a survey of Europe. Ideology played a very important part, and Mr Churchill's ideology is to maintain, as far as possible, British interests and the political and economic *status quo*. Like Metternich after the Napoleonic Wars, he fears the upheaval of popular forces; he is willing to modify his insistency on the 'principle of legitimacy' (which after 1815 bedevilled Europe for thirty years until it was swept away by revolution) only when he is absolutely compelled to do so by military necessity.

The Prime Minister was finding it increasingly difficult to arrange military matters as had been his custom. He was, understandably perhaps, always more inclined to give way to Americans than to his own countrymen. Moreover, the C.-in-C. of the invasion land forces, was, as he had already experienced, a different man from Wavell, for instance. Churchill was not satisfied with the balance of fighting men to vehicles planned for the initial assault. He said he intended to visit Montgomery's H.Q., in order to discuss the matter with the staff. On arrival, Montgomery firmly invited the Prime Minister to his office.

Montgomery, 19 May 1944:

> I understand, sir, that you want to discuss with my staff the proportion of soldiers to vehicles landing on the beaches in the first flights. I cannot allow you to do so. My staff advise me and I give the final decision. They then do what I tell them. That final decision has been given. In any case I could never allow you to harass my staff at this time and

possibly shake their confidence in me. They have had a terrific job preparing the invasion. That work is now almost completed, and all over England the troops are beginning to move towards the assembly areas, prior to embarkation. You can argue with me but not with my staff. In any case, it is too late to change anything.

Churchill, aware he was badly placed, left the room without a word. No more was heard of the matter. He took the point; on leaving, he recorded his confidence in Montgomery and his plans in the general's visiting-book.

Remembering the failure of the generals in the First World War to make personal contact with the troops, Montgomery determined to talk to every soldier who would take part in the invasion – a vast undertaking. Alan Moorehead, reporter, recorded it well:

At the end of the inspection Montgomery would get on to a jeep in front of a loudspeaker and tell the soldiers to break ranks and gather round him. This was always an astonishing moment. Five thousand men in heavy boots would charge together towards the jeep like stampeding buffaloes. It caused a heavy rumbling in the earth, and often the jeep would be nearly overwhelmed. And then Montgomery's speech would go like this: 'I wanted to come here to-day so that we could get to know one another: so that I could have a look at you and you could have a look at me – if you think that's worth doing. We have got to go off and do a job together very soon now, you and I, and we must have confidence in one another. And now that I have seen you I have complete confidence . . . complete confidence . . . absolutely complete confidence. And you must have confidence in me.' That was the beginning. They sat on the grass keeping utterly still lest they should lose a word. They were committed to the assault. Everything in their lives, for month after month, had been shaped to that end: the assault landing on the beaches. Even the most intelligent showed no glimmer of irony or sarcasm or criticism in their faces. The atmosphere was completely subjective and unselfconscious. They were to run and shoot and kill, and here was the expert, the man who knew all about it. It was vital not to miss a word he said, vital not to miss a clue. 'We have been fighting the Germans a long time now,' Montgomery went on. 'A very long time . . . a good deal too long. I expect like me you are beginning to get a bit tired of it . . . beginning to feel it's about time we finished the thing off. And we can do it. We can do it. No doubt about that. No doubt about that whatsoever. The well-trained British soldier will beat the German every time. We saw it in Africa.' Monty was all right. He didn't talk a lot of cock about courage and liberty. He knew what it was like. And perhaps one had been taking the whole thing a bit too seriously. It wouldn't be so bad. Then – 'We don't want to forget the German is a good soldier . . . a very good soldier indeed. But when I look around this morning and see the magnificent soldiers here . . . some of the finest soldiers I have seen in my lifetime . . . I have no doubt in my mind about the outcome . . . no doubt whatever. No doubt at all that you and I will see this thing through, together.' Finally – 'Now I can't stay any longer. I expect some of you have come a long way to get here this morning and you want to get back.' (Some of them had been travelling since 4 a.m.) 'I just want to say goodbye and very good luck to each one of you.' That was the speech, followed by three cheers for the general. I listened to it four and sometimes five times a day for nearly a week. We went from camp to camp over southern England . . . I suppose I have heard fifty generals addressing their soldiers, most of them with much better speeches than this. Indeed I suppose this speech in print is just about as bad as one could hope to read, outside the hearty *naïveté* of the kindergarten. Spoken by Montgomery to the soldiers who were about to run into the Atlantic Wall it had magic. No mention of God, of Divine assistance. No mention of England . . . In the end Montgomery had made that speech to every British, American and Allied soldier who was to go on the landing; he must have talked to at least a million men . . . He had no fear of the future, no doubts about the success of the landing. He would say slowly: 'It will succeed. It will certainly succeed provided we make no mistakes. We must make no mistakes.' . . . In England there was no such certainty. The waiting had gone on so long . . . A dead, heavy mood settled over the country . . . There had again been heavy raids on London. May turned into June. Surely it could not be much longer now. Standing on the South Downs one could see the Channel, bright and clear and calm. It was a hot midsummer sun. The country never looked more calm and beautiful.

There is no doubt that it was only the insistence of the King which prevented Churchill sailing with the fleet on D-Day. Apart from the palace, and Ismay, hardly anyone knew of Churchill's intention. Brooke, for instance, knew nothing about it.

On 4 June allied troops entered Rome.

Then – the fuse of that hot summer having simmered for so many unbearable weeks and with such wearying suspense – the explosion of D-Day itself.

War correspondent:

Some of the men were talking, some smoking, some vomiting quietly into brown bags of greaseproof paper. The wind was bringing to them now the sound of shells bursting ashore. The talking stopped. Men took up their rifles and machine carbines; there was the clack of bolts being drawn and rammed home. The slow, wallowing motion of the craft eased; they were coming into shallower water. Orders were being shouted in the stern and a marine heaved himself up and began taking soundings. There was smoke sprawling across the black ahead, and the black plumes of explosives, each with a cherry-red flicker of flame at its heart, were leaping up in front of the high bows. The landing craft nosed inshore through a mass of floating rubbish. A dead sailor came floating out to sea, face and legs under water, rump poking upwards; then a dead soldier, his waxen face turned up to the sky, his hands floating palm upwards on the water; he was kept afloat by his inflated lifebelt. Ahead of them lay beached landing craft, some wrecked, scattered untidily along the waterline. Men ran splashing down into the water ... wading with weapons held above their heads towards the wet sand ahead.

The moment for which so many critics had been calling for for so long had at last arrived. Churchill was nothing if not unruffled.

William Barkley, *Daily Express*, 7 June 1944:

The Speaker took the chair. The chaplain read the prayer. The announcement of the death of an M.P. during the recess was made, in accordance with form. The Speaker then announced: 'I have received a telegram from the Chilean Chamber of Deputies containing a copy of a resolution of friendship towards the British House of Commons. (Cheers.) It will be your desire that I should send a suitable reply.' (More cheers.) Warm reply accordingly sent to Chile. Then came the hour of questions, one M.P. after another agitating Minister after Minister on topic after topic concerning the people. Are soldiers securing their voting rights? Could not cheaper homes be built if interest did not have to be paid on the loans? Why has a disabled soldier been refused a permit to open a shop in Wimbledon?... It was, you might think, a normal day, with Lady Apsley (Cons. Central Bristol) asking Sir James Grigg, the War Minister, to issue berets to the A.T.S., Sir James replying that this is no time for new hats for A.T.S., and Sir Archibald Southby (Cons. Epsom) gallantly championing the rights of women to new headgear in the springtime... Mrs Churchill came in above. It was now ten to twelve, but Mr Churchill had not yet entered below. An unusual pause occurred. Questions were ended. For once the flood of curiosity had abated with ten minutes still to go. Mr Attlee and Mr Eden studied the clock. A message was hurriedly sent to the Prime Minister's room. Still no Prime Minister. The Speaker remarked: 'I think the House would like to hear the Prime Minister.' The House instantly showed its agreement with that view in a loud 'Hear, hear!' So the unusual scene occurred of the House sitting in full session with no business except chat and small talk for ten minutes, until, on the accustomed stroke of midday, Mr Churchill entered. He strode with a firm, unhurried pace to the despatch. Members gave him a great cheer, one or two standing up the better to expand their lungs. He was in a mood neither solemn nor smiling. A trace of distress might have been noted in his features. It was explained at once when he said: 'I must apologize to the House for having delayed them, but questions went through more rapidly than I anticipated.' On this day of days M.P.s answered back to him. 'No need to apologize.' Brisk and business-like, Mr Churchill took things in their order. He spoke of the fall of Rome before he came to the landing in France. The fall of Rome! – let us see, that was forty-eight hours ago; we move fast these days. There was actually some impatience as the Prime Minister, saying: 'The House should, I think, take formal cognizance of the liberation of Rome', gave nearly ten minutes to this memorable and glorious event, as he called it. Loud were the cheers at the mention of General Alexander, at the way he 'broke the teeth' of the German attacks at Anzio before launching a frontal attack all along the front in which, counting from right to left, Polish, British Empire, French and United States forces all broke through the German line. Then, a sigh of anticipation wafted through the audience as Mr Churchill, without variation of voice or manner, proceeded: 'I have also to announce to the House that during the night and the early hours of this morning the first of a series of landings in force on the European Continent has taken place.'

There was a burst of cheering. But, as Barkley said: 'Anybody who thinks the House of Commons tore up its business in a rush of excitement to hear the great news yesterday does not know the first thing about this venerable institution.' Among those who offered their congratulations to the Prime Minister was Lloyd George; it was the last time the two men met.[1]

Fighting at the beachheads was severe. The enemy was resisting stubbornly. And they were not unprepared. Their commander was Erwin Rommel. Superior to Rommel as C.-in-C. of all the West was von Rundstedt; he was utterly pessimistic, and hampered by Hitler's directions: 'My only authority was to change the guard in front of my gate.' Hitler's policy, as usual, was to try to hold every inch of territory.

Seven days later the first 'flying-bombs' landed in southern England – a new and gruelling test for the civilian population, already nerve-stretched after a long war; a weapon which had an

---

[1] Lloyd George died in 1945.

added sinister, eerie quality in that, unlike a bomb or shell, death could be heard approaching with apparently remorseless inevitability. 92 per cent of fatal casualties from flying-bombs occurred in the London area. Every 'V1' which got through the air defences – about 2,400 – killed or injured on average ten persons.

With the intention of his Anglo-American allies to free his country now beyond all doubt, de Gaulle was still sulky, proud, and reserved.

Harold Nicolson, diary, 5 July 1944:

Anthony [Eden] begins by telling me about his bitter battles on behalf of de Gaulle. The Prime Minister had invited de Gaulle to come over here for the big battle of France. On June 4, Winston and he had gone down in a special train to near Portsmouth. De Gaulle and his own party came there by car and Anthony went to meet them. Then they lunched in the train and Winston produced champagne and drank to the health of France. Roosevelt had said that de Gaulle was not to be told the plan of operations, but Winston ignored that, told him everything, took him across to see Eisenhower and forced the latter to show him the maps. Not one word of thanks from de Gaulle. Winston, feeling rather hurt, said, 'I thought it only fitting that you should be present with us today.' 'I see,' said de Gaulle glumly; 'I was invited as a symbol.' Anthony was almost beside himself, feeling that Winston was deeply moved emotionally by the thought of the occasion, and that de Gaulle's ungraciousness would make him dislike the man all the more. Finally Winston asked de Gaulle to dine with him. 'Thank you, I should prefer to dine alone with my staff.' 'I feel chilled,' said Winston to Anthony. Anthony went on to say that his great difficulty throughout has been that Winston is half an American and that he regards Roosevelt almost with religious awe. Anthony does not share these feelings. He regards Roosevelt as an astute politician and a man of great personal vanity and obstinacy. Thus, over this de Gaulle business, Winston and Anthony have had terrible rows.

On 17 July Rommel was seriously wounded. (He made a splendid recovery, in time to commit suicide at Hitler's orders for his suspected part in the attempt on Hitler's life.) On 20 July Churchill visited France. He spent three days on board a British cruiser, studying 'the whole process of the landing of supplies and troops, both at the piers, in which I had so long been interested, and on the beaches'. The artificial 'Mulberry' harbour, which had played an important part in the operation, was largely due to Churchill's inventiveness and vigorous support. On 27 July

American forces began their break-out. Anglo-American military relations were not good. Montgomery was in command of the American land forces, and the American commanders did not care for, or more probably did not understand (and evidently still don't), his tactic of trying to unbalance the enemy while remaining balanced himself. It was thought that he was trying to save British lives at the expense of American (it was true that no American commander was more careful than Montgomery in considering tactics in terms of loss of life). There was much bitter comment in the American Press. Fortunately, the enemy did not fully understand Montgomery's plan either, and it was a success.

But Churchill's eyes were on the East more than the West.

Lord Moran, London, 4 August 1944:

He is less certain of things now than he was in 1940, when the world was tumbling around his ears . . . 'Good God, can't you see that the Russians are spreading across Europe like a tide?' . . . The American landings in the south of France are the last straw. He can see 'no earthly purpose' in them: 'Sheer folly,' he calls them. He had fought tooth and nail, he said, to prevent them. If only those ten divisions could have been landed in the Balkans . . . so we're off to Italy next week. I dread the way he's banking everything on Alex. The Prime Minister is distraught, but you cannot get him down for long. He has got it into his head that Alex might be able to solve this problem by breaking into the Balkans . . . for the first time since he became Prime Minister, I believe that he feels a sense of isolation.

Eisenhower, Memo., 8 August 1944:

Experience of the past proved that we were likely to be vastly disappointed in the usefulness of the Brittany ports. Not only did we expect them to be stubbornly defended but we were certain they would be effectively destroyed once we had captured them. We did not expect this destruction to be so marked at Marseilles because we knew that a large portion of the defending forces had already been drawn northward to meet our attacks. Capture should be so swift as to allow little time for demolition. Unless Marseilles were captured, we would be unable to speed up the arrival of American divisions from the homeland. The entry of a sizeable force into southern France provided definite tactical and strategic support to our own operation . . . Another factor was that the American Government had gone to great expense to equip and supply a number of French divisions. These troops naturally wanted to fight in the battle for the liberation of France. At no other point would they fight with the same ardour and devotion, and nowhere else could they obtain needed replacements for battle losses. These troops were located in Italy and North Africa, and the only way they could be brought quickly into the battle was through the opening in the south of France.

After the war, Eisenhower wrote: 'I told him that if [politics] were his reason for advocating the campaign into the Balkans he should go instantly to the President and lay the facts, as well as his own conclusions, on the table. I well understood that strategy can be affected by political considerations, and if the President and the Prime Minister should decide that it was worth while to prolong the war, thereby increasing its cost in men and money, in order to secure the political objectives they deemed necessary, then I would instantly and loyally adjust my plans accordingly. But I did insist that as long as he argued the matter on military grounds alone I could not concede validity to his arguments.'

Butcher, Normandy, 10 August 1944:

Ike is in England to-day, reviewing the 82nd and 101st Airborne Divisions. He left the camp yesterday and flew to Heston to reach SHAEF Main. The P.M. was still a bit pouty over ANVIL [the South of France operation] favouring diversion into Brittany, despite our absence of satisfactory ports. So Ike went to 10 Downing Street to have a further talk with him. The Combined Chiefs of Staff have supported Ike completely. But now the P.M. was bemoaning the future of Alexander's campaign in Italy. He saw the Italian front drying up just when such fine opportunity presented itself to enter Yugoslavia.

Butcher, Normandy, 11 August 1944:

Ike has been increasingly concerned about the P.M.'s attitude regarding ANVIL and, above all, the feeling that the questioning and apparent dissension might cause a rift in the unity of the Allies at a time when success is almost in our grasp. The P.M. is upset over Ike's insistence for the landings in southern France, still set for August 15. Mr Churchill knows that the American chiefs – Marshall, King, and Arnold – defer all questions in the European Theatre to General Ike. Consequently, the Prime Minister unlooses on Ike all his art of persuasion. The other day he went so far as to say, with considerable emotion, that he might have to go to the Monarch and 'lay down the mantle of my high office'.

Allied forces duly landed in the south of France on 15 August. Differences were inevitable in any such vast undertaking, in peace or war, whether it was conducted by allies or otherwise.

Lord Moran, Naples, 20 August 1944:

I think I am beginning to get the hang of things here in Naples. If Winston came to Italy eager to see Alex, Alex is even more eager to see Winston. He has found that the preoccupation of the Americans with the invasion of France and their indifference towards the Italian campaign is wrecking his command. He knows that only Winston can stop the rot. While I have been busy exploring the side streets of Siena, Winston has spent the sunny days working in bed. But at night Alex comes into the picture. Tonight he turned to me and said: 'The Prime Minister knows so much about our job that he was the first to see that we should soon be well on our way to Vienna if only the Americans would be sensible.' *P.M.*: 'Glittering possibilities are opening up.' *Alex*: 'There is still time to set things right. I am not at all pessimistic.' A clock struck two, but the P.M. had no intention of going to bed. It is not what Alex says that wins the day. He is not so foolish as to suppose that anyone has ever got his way with Winston by argument. Winston likes a good listener; he is always ready to do the talking. And Alex seems to wait on his words. He will listen attentively until half the night is over. Like a woman, he knows intuitively that listening is not just a question of keeping silent, it can be a means of communication of a more subtle kind. Besides, when Alex does open his mouth he is always so reassuring, always so sure that the P.M.'s plans are right, and that there will be no difficulty at all in carrying them out. That is what Winston wants; he dislikes people who are forever making trouble. 'Anyone can do that,' he snorts impatiently. Soon he found himself confiding to Alex his most intimate thoughts. 'I envy you', he said, 'the command of armies in the field. That is what I should have liked.'

On 21 August American forces crossed the Seine.

General Stilwell, letter to Mrs Stilwell, 24 August 1944:

The situation in Europe looks good. I begin to believe the crack-up can come almost any time. Then with one war on our hands, maybe Mr Churchill will allow Mr Roosevelt to give me some help.

Private First Class, U.S. Army:

We didn't have a damn thing to do with the taking of Paris. We just came in a couple of days later when somebody got the bright idea of having the parade and we just happened to be there and that's all there is to it. What can you do, though – that's just the way it goes. And after all, we did a helluva lot of things that we didn't get credit for . . . It was a good place to be, too, because every guy marching on the outside had at least one girl on his arm kissing him and hugging him. We were marching twenty-four abreast down the Champs Elysées and we had a helluva time trying to march, because the whole street was jammed with people laughing and yelling and crying and singing. They were throwing flowers at us and bringing us big bottles of wine. The first regiment never did get through.

Six days later, the Russian Army entered Bucharest. The race was on.

On 1 September Eisenhower took over command from Montgomery of the land forces in France, as previously arranged. Eisenhower, to the increasing chagrin of Churchill, did not recognize that the race existed. It was time for more talks.

Churchill left for the Second Quebec Conference on 5 September. Two days previously, Brussels had been liberated by British troops, with a vast concourse of delirious Belgians singing 'Tipperary' and other First World War songs to the much-loved 'Tommies'. On the 8th, German V2 rockets began falling on southeast England, the Canadians reached Ostend, and the Russians were outside Warsaw, where the Polish resistance had risen and was being annihilated by the German defenders. The long-promised death-struggle between Communism and Fascism in east and central Europe had begun, and before it was over it was to rip the guts for ever from nineteenth-century Europe.

At Quebec Churchill pleaded for reinforcements for Alexander, to enable a thrust into central Europe: 'to give Germany a stab in the Adriatic armpit', as he put it. He was refused. But the Americans agreed to draw Eisenhower's 'attention to the advantages of the northern line of approach [i.e. that under British command] into Germany'. Ike was not impressed. The Americans agreed to extend Lend–Lease until the defeat of Japan, which now took up the major part of Anglo-American discussions. Churchill justly pointed out that the Burma campaign, which had saved India and kept open the link with China, had been the largest land engagement of Japanese forces; the British Army had so far suffered 40,000 battle casualties there. He offered the British fleet to be placed under American command. This Roosevelt accepted, overruling Admiral King. Churchill had to assure the Americans, still obsessively suspicious, that this would not mean 'interfering in any way with MacArthur's command'.

Brooke, diary, 15 September 1944:

[Churchill] did his best to pull the whole of our final report to pieces, found a lot of petty criticisms and wanted to alter many points which we had secured agreement on with some difficulty. Anthony Eden was there and did his best to help us, but unfortunately Winston was in one of his worst tempers ... The tragedy is that the Americans, whilst admiring him as a man, have little opinion of him as a strategist. They are intensely suspicious of him. All his alterations or amendments are likely to make them more suspicious than ever.

Roosevelt and his Chiefs of Staff were now in full control of the war. Churchill and Brooke, although they had much to say, had little real influence over major strategy – in contrast to the position two years previously. Britain was heavily in debt to the United States.

After the Conference Churchill went to Washington, where he had secret talks with Roosevelt about the progress made with the atom bomb. This had very largely sprung from British scientific knowledge, which had been taken to America at the beginning of the war in the common cause (and not least because Britain could not afford to develop it). Churchill's scientific advisers were now alarmed. They believed that the Americans were cornering the knowledge for themselves; Britain was being kept out of the development of nuclear weapons. On 18 September Roosevelt and Churchill initialled a memorandum guaranteeing post-war interchange of atomic information between the two nations. The American authorities later lost the document, which was convenient for those agencies which wished to keep nuclear weapons from a suspect Britain.

Lord Moran, at sea, 22 September 1944:

After breakfasting today on an omelette, grouse, melon, toast and marmalade, he ought to have been at peace with the world. But I found him militant. 'I'm distressed about France. I must not let de Gaulle come between me and the French nation. He is an enemy of the English people. I must not let him have the revenge of putting me wrong with France.'

De Gaulle had taken up residence in Paris, amid scenes of wild jubilation. Churchill made the error of deciding to go and see him there; he should have realized by now that the general would see this as a psychological defeat for the Prime Minister rather than as a generous gesture.

As a result of the Quebec Conference, Britain began to enter the second stage of the war, the defeat of Japan. This, in fact, meant a running-down of the war effort. On 23 September the American public were surprised to read in their newspapers details of Britain's demobilization plans.

Lord Moran, at sea, 23 September 1944:

When he stands in the Map Room, gazing at the enemy submarines on the vast chart, I'm sure he sees the great ship torpedoed. He has too much imagination for these times. But the only thing he seems to dread is being taken prisoner. He'd much rather die, and he says so. On the last voyage he arranged that a machine-gun should be kept in the boat detailed to take him off if anything happened. This voyage the same arrangement has been made. 'How long', he asked the First Sea Lord, 'would the Queen Mary take to sink after she was torpedoed: would it be a few minutes?' First Sea Lord (Cunningham): 'More likely a few hours; she is well divided into watertight compartments.'

After the Quebec Conference, some ill-considered remarks to the Press gave his critics an unusually good opportunity.

New Statesman & Nation, 23 September 1944:

Temperamental buoyancy and personal enjoyment in the art of war have sustained both Mr Churchill and Mr Roosevelt through difficult years. Viewed from the heights of Quebec the military prospect is splendid ... But as soon as we turn to the actualities we are impressed by the adolescent irresponsibility of some of Mr Churchill's phrases. What are soldiers in the forgotten outposts in Burma and New Guinea, fighting a remorseless enemy in a cruel climate, to think when they are told by the Prime Minister that we do not wish to miss any of the 'fun' (as the B.B.C. reported it) or of 'the good things' (as the press accounts prefer to translate it)? Strange words for a process whereby human beings are being disembowelled, roasted to death, drowned, blown into fragments, or are dying slowly of agonizing wounds.

When the *New Statesman* got its teeth into Winston Churchill, it liked to bite deep.

On 26 September the Government's social security plan was announced. The *New Statesman* found something to please it here: 'it goes further than most people expected it to go towards accepting Beveridge ... better than most people expected.' The Government had asked Beveridge to take charge of a review of the social services in June 1941; Beveridge had published his report on 1 December 1942; it had been debated in February 1943 – a rate of progress that none could describe as hasty, but which was not without credit in the context of the war. For most of the time it had been under the loving care of Arthur Greenwood; when asked about the cost, he reassured Labour M.P.s with the words: '£.s.d. have become meaningless symbols'.

On 25 September the 1st British Airborne Division began its withdrawal from Arnhem, after the biggest airborne operation by any country in the war. The operation had been a disaster; three-quarters of the Division were lost.

B.B.C. war correspondent:

At two minutes past ten we clambered out of our slit trenches in an absolute din of bombardment – a great deal of it our own – and formed up in a single line. Our boots were wrapped in blanket so that no noise would be made. We held the tail of the coat of the man in front. We set off like a file of nebulous ghosts from our pock-marked and tree-strewn piece of ground. Obviously, since the enemy was all round us, we had to go through him to get to the River Rhine. After about two hundred yards of silent trekking we knew we were among the enemy. It was difficult not to throw yourself flat when machine-gun tracers skimmed your head or the scream of a shell or mortar bomb sounded very close – but the orders were to 'keep going'. Anybody hit was to be picked up by the man behind him ... In a barn there was a blessed hot mug of tea with hot rum in it and a blanket over our shoulders. Then we walked again – all night. Then we were put in trucks and that's how we reached Nijmegen. That's how the last of the few got out to go and fight in some future battle.

On 29 September Churchill gave another of his long and meticulous surveys of the war to the House of Commons. 'I may say that everything depends on the agreement of the three leading European world powers ... I have sedulously avoided the appearance of any one country trying to lay down the law to its powerful allies or to any other states involved.'

Apart from a short and predictable stab from Richard Stokes, the only notable critique of the speech came from the member for Lanark, who was not often heard from in the House and was not well known to the public. He had held a junior post under Chamberlain in the days of Munich, which now seemed so far off. His name was Lord Dunglass, later better known as Sir Alec Douglas-Home.

The Times, 29 September 1944:

Lord Dunglass said that the question of the political relationship between Russia and Poland could not be left to be settled between those two countries without any intervention by us. We had accepted definite legal and moral commitments to Poland, and it was our habit to honour our commitments. (Cheers.) The situation had changed since 1939 in a way which no one could then have foreseen. For us, the question was whether we could, in the new circumstances, fulfil our guarantee to Poland. We should be absolutely frank and state the position as we saw it today. If so, we should have to say that we could not hope to restore the old Poland, but our aim must be to restore a Poland independent and free, a Poland as nearly equivalent as possible in territory, economic resources, and international status as in the Poland of 1939. The question inevitably followed whether, in view of Russia's attitude, we could make that independence and freedom a reality. He believed we could succeed, but success would be useless unless we recognised two things. The first was that Russia operated under a code of ethics by no means the same as our own – he did not blame the Russians for that; they were at a different point on the historical road – but unless we faced that fact we should look down a long vista of political misunderstanding. The second point was that we must not shirk plain speaking, for to that alone would the Russians respond.

The speech did not make much of a stir. The House went on to discuss other affairs. It was, however, one of the most important speeches in the House of Commons of the Second World War; and it was the first true expression of the post-war era. But if there was a subject which people did not want to consider in 1944 it was Poland – it seemed a sigh from an age long ago. Had not Britain done enough for Poland? Had not Britain gone to war over Poland in the first place . . . ?

If there was one person who doubtless appreciated the full import, the irony, of that speech it was the Prime Minister himself.

Churchill's speeches were becoming repetitive in certain phrases, and in their inevitable exhortations. They lacked the inspired quality of 1940.

Some people found them stimulating and encouraging, but lacking in 'spiritual leadership'. The author Laurence Whistler wrote: 'It seemed that the only objective of the free world was a negative one: not to be beaten.' His wife, the actress Jill Furse, said of Churchill:

when he gets through his speeches I always feel something is missing.

But many people listened to Churchill's radio speeches with a genuine pleasure drawn from a nostalgia for the comradeship and certainties of 1940, no matter what he now said.

With the liberation of Belgium, the hideous flying-bomb offensive was eased from London.

New York Times, September 1944:

London has been under fire since 1940. Her people know the terror of bombs dropped night after night and week after week. Recently they have endured the even greater terror of the robot bomb which, arriving at any moment, hurtled its victims into eternity as they slept, or walked the streets, or chatted with their neighbours. In these risks there seems to have been for many temperaments a kind of exhilaration. Very ordinary persons, not considering themselves heroic, doing humdrum kinds of work and rarely finding words for lofty thoughts, discovered that they could conquer fear.

Increasingly depressed about Poland and Greece (from which Hitler was at last withdrawing), Churchill went to talk to Stalin – with little hope but much determination – on 9 October. At the same time he literally pleaded with Roosevelt to support Alexander.

Lord Moran, Moscow, 9 October 1944:

This morning the first thing I heard was Winston's voice above the noise of the plane. 'What do you take, Anthony?' *Eden*: 'I always take a red. I think it's good stuff if you want to sleep on these trips.' *P.M.*: 'I took two. I'm a hardened case.'

In Moscow, Churchill was surprised to discover 'an extraordinary atmosphere of goodwill here'. There was not much more that the West could do for the U.S.S.R. in the way of second fronts or other matters, but Stalin was quite prepared to listen with a smile while he prepared for his conquest of eastern Europe.

On 22 October Roosevelt wired Churchill:

I am delighted to learn of your success at Moscow in making progress toward a compromise solution of the Polish problem. When and if a solution is arrived at I should like to be consulted . . . most interesting. We should discuss these matters, together with our Pacific war effort, at the forthcoming three-party meeting.

Two days previously, MacArthur's troops had landed in the Philippines.

At the end of 1944, efforts were made to involve Churchill in another military controversy: the suitability of Eisenhower as land commander. On 7 November Montgomery had complained to Brooke that he had not seen or spoken on the telephone to his commander for a month. He had seen him only four times since the end of the Normandy campaign.

> He is at a Forward Headquarters at Rheims; the directives he issues from there have no relation to the practical necessities of the battle. It is quite impossible for me to carry out my present orders ... Eisenhower should himself take a proper control of operations or he should appoint someone else to do this. If we go drifting along as at present we are merely playing into the enemy's hands and the war will go on indefinitely ... He has never commanded anything before in his whole career; now, for the first time, he has elected to take direct command of a very large-scale operation and he does not know how to do it.

Brooke promised to see what he could do; but he was not hopeful. He wrote in his diary on 24 November about:

> the very unsatisfactory state of affairs in France, with no one running the land battle. Eisenhower, though supposed to be doing so, is on the golf links at Rheims, entirely detached and taking practically no part in the running of the war.[1] Matters got so bad lately that a deputation of Whiteley [a senior British officer of the SHAEF Staff], Bedell Smith [Eisenhower's Chief of Staff] and a few others went up to tell him that he must get down to it and RUN the war, which he said he would.

Montgomery and Brooke planned to get Bradley promoted; Tedder remained loyal to Eisenhower. Two years before, Churchill would not have been backward in making his contribution to this affair. But now he was pondering more on the political implications and outcome of the war, than on military personalities. Two years before, victory was not certain: now it was. As usual, Churchill was thinking of one move ahead of most of the other players.

Brooke, 28 November 1944:

> At 12.30 I went to see the P.M., having asked for an interview with him. I told him I was very worried with the course operations were taking on the Western Front. I said that when we looked facts in the face this last offensive could only be classified as the first strategic reverse that we had suffered since landing in France. I said that in my mind two main factors were at fault, i.e. (a) American strategy; (b) American organisation. As regards the strategy, the American conception of always attacking all along the front, irrespective of strength

---

[1] Alas for Eisenhower, the links were not in use.

available, was sheer madness. In the present offensive we had attacked on six Army fronts without any reserves anywhere. As regards organisation, I said that I did not consider that Eisenhower could command both as Supreme Commander and as Commander of the Land Forces at the same time. I said that I considered Bradley should be made the Commander of the Land Forces ... Winston said that he also was worried about the Western Front. He agreed with most of what I had said, but was doubtful as to the necessity for a Land Forces Commander. I think I succeeded in pointing out that we must take the control out of Eisenhower's hands, and the best plan was to repeat what we did in Tunisia when we brought in Alex as a Deputy to Eisenhower to command the Land Forces for him.

But Churchill did little or nothing about the matter. Montgomery, with Brooke's approval, began writing a series of letters to Eisenhower pointing out the need for a plan, clear objectives, and above all one strong thrust instead of an advance in line. Predictably, this latter idea was dismissed by Americans around Eisenhower, as a British ploy to gain all the glory for themselves of ending the war. Apart from the purely military consideration of the American reluctance to concentrate – anyway hotly denied by Eisenhower – there was a situation in which the British forces were motivated by political factors, being run as they were by a politician and statesman, whereas the American forces had considerable freedom from Roosevelt and did not take political factors into account. Matters were complicated by two factors: American dislike of the prickly Montgomery, the best active commander still in the war, and Churchill's reluctance to do anything to irritate the crumbling Anglo-American alliance still further. Some British military men even believed that the war could have been won in 1944, if Montgomery's advice had been followed, and if Eisenhower had been a little reckless, more forceful, and less studious over problems of supply.

Brooke, 1 December 1944:

Went to see Winston at 10 a.m. to tell him about Monty's wires. Found him in bed finishing his breakfast surrounded by birthday presents. 'This is delicious butter sent to me by my doctor, his wife makes it with her cow, she milks it and beats it up! etc.' He was in good mood and approved the steps that Monty had taken, including the latter's letter to Ike laying down in black and white, the results of their talk together. If only all Monty thinks he has settled materialises we shall be all right, but I have fears of Ike going back when he has discussed with Bedell Smith, Tedder, etc.

Churchill hesitated.

Brooke, 4 December 1944:

During our discussion, he said he did not want anybody between Ike and the Army Groups, as Ike was a good fellow who was amenable and whom he could influence. Bradley, on the other hand, might not listen to what he said! I replied that I could see little use in having an 'amenable' commander if he was unfit to win the war for him.

Churchill agreed to try to arrange a meeting between Brooke and Marshall. He wrote to Roosevelt about it that day. But Marshall and Roosevelt were content to trust Eisenhower; they declined. Instead, the amenable Eisenhower, wonderfully patient throughout, but not without his pride, came over to London. Churchill seemed now to be supporting him.

Brooke, 12 December 1944:

I have just finished one of those days which should have been one of the keystones of the final days of the war. I feel I have utterly failed to do what is required, and yet God knows how I could have done anything else. At 6 p.m. met Ike and Tedder with P.M. in the latter's Map Room, with the whole Chiefs of Staff. Ike explained his plan which contemplates a double advance into Germany, north of Rhine and by Frankfurt. I disagreed flatly with it, accused Ike of violating principles of concentration of force, which had resulted in his present failures. I criticised his future plans and pointed out impossibility of double invasion with the limited forces he has got. I stressed the importance of concentrating on one thrust. I drew attention to the fact that with his limited forces any thought of attack on both fronts could only lead to dispersal of effort. Quite impossible to get the P.M. to understand the importance of the principles involved. Half the time his attention was concentrated on the possibility of floating mines down the Rhine! He must get down to detail... Finally dined at 10 Downing Street with P.M., Ike, Tedder, Cunningham, Portal and Ismay. Conversation again to the same topic of the strategy, but I got no further in getting either Winston or Ike to see that their strategy is fundamentally wrong.

Brooke, 13 December 1944:

I was very depressed last night and seriously thought of resigning, as Winston did not seem to attach any importance to my views ... I found, however, today that the situation was far better than I thought. After the C.O.S. meeting I went to see Winston at 1 p.m. He told me that he had to support Ike last night as he was one American against five of us with only Tedder to support him. And also he was his guest. I think he felt that I had been rather rough on Ike, but on the other hand I found that I had convinced him of the seriousness of the situation. What I had said last night had had far more effect on him than I had thought.

Churchill, in fact, had been deeply preoccupied with other affairs during this tiff with Eisenhower.

On 8 December 1944, the House of Commons debated the worrying situation in Greece. The Prime Minister insisted that the Communists were illegally attempting to seize power: his critics insisted that Britain was illegally interfering in Greek sovereignty by sending her troops to support one faction in that country.

Seymour Cocks:[1]

Much as I prefer the ballot box, I do assert that it is none of our business to intervene in a friendly and foreign country to prevent the overthrow of a dictatorship ... British forces who won the battle of Bunkers Hill in 1775 lost America. In the scroll of history Athens might rank in the same category as Bunkers Hill and we might lose the friendship of Greece to gain the favour of a Hohenzollern prince. Throughout this war the Prime Minister has acted like Lord Chatham, and he has spoken with the accents of Lord Chatham on many occasions. Let him not sink now to the level of a Lord North ... I am only a humble backbencher, and I do not aspire to be anything else; but I would rather this right hand of mine were burnt off at the wrist, leaving a blackened and twisted stump, than sign an order to the British Army to fire on the workers of Greece.

Churchill's eighty-minute speech, defending his policy, was longer and more confused than the basic and straightforward issue at stake warranted. He was interrupted on several occasions by Willie Gallacher, Bevan, and Shinwell.[2] Tempers were short. He did not succeed in dispersing the suspicions and indignation of left-wingers.

---

[1] Labour M.P., 1929–53; Leader of All-Party Parliamentary Delegation to Greece, 1946; died 1953.

[2] Another interruption was from Dr Edith Summerskill. When Churchill was speaking of 'man' in the general sense of mankind, she called out: 'And woman.' Churchill, hardly pausing in his speech, rejoined: 'It is always the stock answer that man embraces woman – (Laughter) – Unless the contrary appears in the text.' Despite such speed of wit, some historians continue to convince themselves that Churchill was at a loss as a parliamentarian outside a text.

Daily Telegraph, 9 December, 1944:

[Tom] Driberg thought the blame for the situation should be placed on the British Government. The Prime Minister had been very ingenious, very evasive, and in some respects very unsound. He did not think that what was happening was Civil War. It was a war between the bulk of the Greek population on one side and a few quislings and royalists backed up by British bayonets.

After some more forceful contributions from Labour and Independent members, the Foreign Secretary declared:

Our purpose is to enable the Greek people to express their own will and decision, but we must insist that that expression shall be through the ballot box and not by the bomb . . . As soon as arms are laid down and peace is restored, then it is our hope that at the earliest possible moment a free election may be held.

No parliamentary debate during the war was watched with such close interest in the United States. In December 1944, Churchill–Washington relations were at their worst. The British had objected to the inclusion of the anti-monarchist Count Carlo Sforza in any new Italian government. Sforza had spent the war in America, and he was personally known in Washington. British moves were seen as anti-democratic and even 'imperialist'. The United States Government was embarrassed, and found it difficult to support Britain. In Greece, meanwhile, American ships were being used to transport supplies to British troops who were fighting men who had recently been engaged in killing Nazis. The situation was explosive. During the debate Churchill made several references directly and indirectly to American opinion. He said: 'Poor old England! (Perhaps I ought to say, "Poor old Britain!") We have to assume the burden of the most thankless tasks, and in undertaking them to be scoffed at, criticized and opposed from every quarter; but at least we know where we are making for, know the end of the road, know what is our objective . . . We have not attempted to put our veto on the appointment of Count Sforza. If tomorrow the Italians were to make him Prime Minister or Foreign Secretary, we have no power to stop it, except with the agreement of the Allies. All that we should have to say about it is that we do not trust the man, we do not think he is a true and trustworthy man, nor do we put the slightest confidence in any Government of which he is a dominating member. I think we should have to put a great deal of responsibility for what might happen on those who called him to power.'[1]

Churchill was supported by 281 votes to 32 with many abstentions.

After this, relations between Churchill and Roosevelt were distinctly strained.

Harold Nicolson, letter, 8 December 1944:

This was the day of the Greek debate. Winston was in one of his boyish moods, and allowed himself to be interrupted all the time. In fact, he seemed to me to be in rather higher spirits than the occasion warranted. I don't think he quite caught the mood of the House, which at its best was one of distressed perplexity, and at its worst one of sheer red fury. The debate became heated, and when I was at last called, I tried, not without success, to throw oil upon the waters. But everything in the end was redeemed by Anthony making by far the best speech that I have ever heard him make. He just narrated the facts ... In the smoking-room afterwards Winston came across to congratulate me on my speech. 'I was not in the House at the time,' he said, 'but I am assured on all sides that it was most helpful. I am most obliged to you.' 'At one point,' I said, 'I went rather far, I fear. I called Sforza "an elderly peacock".' 'You did not go too far,' he answered. 'That is exactly what he is. When he came to see me on his way through London, he wasted ten minutes in explaining to me how far older the Sforza family was than the House of Savoy. I was obliged to interrupt the man. I was obliged to say to him, "Count Sforza, these dynastic personalities have little to do with the prosecution of the war." ' 'Since then,' continued Winston, 'he has behaved with the utmost lack of faith. When I saw him the other day at Naples, I was rude to him. I was very rude. I will show you exactly how rude. Now you be Sforza queuing up with the other Ministers and I shall be me.' Then followed a dumb-crambo in which Winston, all genial and smiles, bowed and grinned and grasped the hand of the man who came in front of Sforza. Then it came to my turn, in my unwanted role as Sforza's impersonator. Winston drew himself up with an expression of extreme disgust and gave me a hand like the fin of a dead penguin. I do not know how my colleagues in the smoking-room interpreted this strange scene.

The Manchester Guardian, December 1944, after the debate on Europe:

Must we be schoolmasters and policemen to countries in incipient revolution? ... the Prime Minister has the defects of his great qualities.

---

[1] Sforza became Minister of State, 1944–6, and of Foreign Affairs, 1947–51.

Reluctantly we shall have to assume that he may be an uncertain, even a dangerous, guide in our passage through the European maelstrom. Let us hope he does not wreck us.

British troops were engaged in heavy street fighting in Athens, and they were not fighting Germans or Japanese. It was not only the left-wing Press which was so angered at what it considered an abuse of British servicemen, *The Times* also (always seeming more than glad to attack Churchill when the opportunity arose) was apparently roused:

The British government and the British army [have] associated Britain with what is everywhere condemned as Fascist action.

Ambassador Winant to Hopkins:

The parliament is definitely to the right of the country, and did not reflect, in my opinion, the extent of a troubled public opinion ... Protest resolutions passed by big trade-union groups were an indication of this fact. The Conservatives in parliament are also going to make the Polish–Russian debate scheduled for this week difficult. This is the first time that I have felt the government weakened following a Vote of Confidence by parliament. The man most hurt, in my judgment, was the Prime Minister. It is a time here when many people are discouraged by the prolongation of the war and I hope that, without surrender of principle, we can so work out our difficulties as to encourage the continuation of a coalition government here.

Hopkins, personal note:

On Saturday night, December 9, 1944, at about 7 p.m. the White House operator told me that 'John Martin' was calling me on the overseas phone. This is the name the Prime Minister uses in his telephone calls.[1] The connection was bad and I could not, therefore, know what the Prime Minister was talking about. He sounded as though he was very angry and stirred up about something and wanted me to do something about it. I got the words 'Greece' and 'Halifax'. Inasmuch as it was impossible to make him understand what I was saying, I told him I would find out about it in the morning. I then tried to get Halifax on the phone to see if he knew what it was all about, but could not reach him. On Sunday morning I went to the Map Room and saw in the morning news summary a sentence that Admiral King had ordered Admiral Hewitt, our American Commander of the Mediterranean

---

[1] It was in fact the name of Churchill's private secretary, who made the connections.

Fleet, not to permit any American L.S.T.s to be used to transfer supplies to Greece. I went to see Admiral Leahy about this.

Hopkins and Leahy succeeded in getting the order countermanded.

I met Halifax at my house at 12.30 and he had a full-blown protest which he was going to make to Stettinius [Secretary of State] but Stettinius was out of town and his instructions were to tell it to me, which he did in no uncertain terms. Halifax said he was sure Churchill was planning to send a very strong protest to the President ... I told Halifax I hoped Churchill would not send the message; that I was sure the President knew nothing about it; that the matter was all cleared up anyway, and that I knew instructions had gone to Admiral Hewitt countermanding the previous order and that I thought it would just make trouble if Churchill submitted a protest. I asked Halifax, in the light of the fact that the matter was now settled, if he would not cable Churchill and tell him I thought that any cable from him on this matter would serve no useful purpose, but merely complicate the Greek situation further. I told him that public opinion about the whole Greek business in this country was very bad and that we felt the British Government had messed the whole thing up pretty thoroughly.

Churchill was, indeed, incensed at the suggestion that he was acting in a dictatorial way in Greece. To him, Communist takeovers at the point of the gun were the antithesis of what Britain had been fighting the Second World War about. The fact that America did not, apparently, wish to be seen in Britain's company in this – to him – honourable, if disagreeable, duty, filled him with dismay. He decided on a characteristic and dramatic action. The problem of Greece would have to be solved immediately, or it would get worse, and poison still further the Anglo-American relationship which Churchill still saw as so vital to British interests. He would have to solve it himself. He would go to Greece.

H. G. Wells, who for many years had considered Churchill a dangerous imperialist, was outraged at what was happening in Greece – or what he thought was happening. He wrote in *Tribune*, 15 December 1944:

Either this war is an insane convulsion of mankind or else it is a war of democracy – the rule of the sovereign people – against the Fuehrer principle. From our side it means that or nothing at all ... Winston

Churchill, the present would-be British Fuehrer, is a person with a range of ideas limited to the adventures and opportunities of British political life. He has never given evidence of thinking extensively, or of any scientific or literary capacity ... Now he seems to have lost his head completely ... Winston seems to have overlooked everything that has happened since his pampered political infancy ... His ideology, picked up in the garrison life of India, on the reefs of South Africa, the maternal home and the conversation of wealthy Conservative households, is a pitiful jumble of incoherent nonsense. A boy scout is better equipped. He has served his purpose and it is high time he retired upon his laurels before we forget the debt we owe him. His last associations with the various European Royalties who share his belief in the invincible snobbishness of mankind and are now sneaking back to claim the credit and express their condescending approval of the underground resistance movements that have sustained human freedom through its days of supreme danger, are his final farewell to human confidence. We want him to go – *now* – before he discredits us further.

On the same day, Churchill announced in the House that Britain supported the Russian intention of taking a large slice of eastern Poland and giving her German territory instead. He called for an immediate Big Three meeting, 'a meeting in this island, a meeting in Great Britain, which has waged war from the very outset'.

Roosevelt was particularly prone to accept any suggestion that Britain was going to forgo the obligations of the Atlantic Charter by 'secret agreements' and 'the carving up of Europe'.

On 16 December, the day after Churchill's speech to the Commons, Hopkins cabled to Churchill:

Due to the Greek situation and your statement in parliament about Poland public opinion has rapidly deteriorated here. I must confess I am greatly disturbed by this turn of diplomatic events which gives publicity to our various difficulties at a time when the battle is joined in Europe and in Asia and all of our energy is required for the defeat of the enemy. Although I do not know what the President or Stettinius may be compelled to say publicly, it is quite possible that one or both of them will have to proclaim their determination in unequivocal terms to do everything we can to seek a free world and a secure one.[1]

---

[1] Two and a half years later, Dean Acheson, United States Acting Secretary of State, said: 'A Communist-dominated government in Greece would be considered dangerous to U.S. security.'

This was from the man who had so often been Churchill's advocate in the past. Americans' suspicions of Churchill had now risen to a pitch that can only be described as idiotic; if there was legitimate reason or excuse for genuine fears, there was no call for such lunatic exaggeration. There were those in the State Department, for instance, who had convinced themselves that Churchill had territorial ambitions in the eastern Mediterranean and Asia and desired to set up British puppet states in the Balkans (despite the undoubted fact that Britain was virtually bankrupt). Such residues of distrust and antipathy were the natural lot of a decaying power which once had ruled the waves and much of the continents as well.

On the same day, the Germans gave some indication that arguments about the future of Europe might be premature. And the clash of military personalities and views were temporarily solved, not by Churchill but by Hitler. The Ardennes offensive was a considerable shock. The British Government called up an additional quota of a million men. American troops were cut off, and a ferocious battle was fought in snow, frost, and fog. This gave the American Press an excuse to return to the theme of British troops not doing their 'share of the fighting'. Eisenhower kept his head, and acted with a speed and intelligence which confounded his critics. The situation was sufficiently serious for American troops to come under the command once more of Montgomery. By the end of the year this final kick of Hitler's, like a spasm from a dying body, had been contained and sent back.

Churchill flew to Athens on 24 December. Hopkins relented. He cabled:

No one knows better than I what a gallant role you are playing in the greatest drama in the history of the world. On this fateful Christmas, I want you to know that I am well aware of the heavy burdens that you carry. I am proud to be known and even to be attacked by some of my countrymen as your good friend.

And at the Trades Union Congress, Churchill's policy had been brilliantly vindicated by Ernest Bevin; he carried the whole Congress with him.

The Foreign Secretary had, of course, accompanied the Prime Minister.

Lord Moran, Piraeus, 27 December 1944:

As I was waiting for breakfast Eden passed through the cabin on his way to see the P.M., who had apparently sent him a message that he was going ashore forthwith to see the Archbishop. Eden, a little wearily: 'I do wish he'd let me do my own job.'

Macmillan, still Churchill's political representative in the Mediterranean theatre, had considerable admiration for Archbishop Damaskinos, the prospective Regent. But Churchill described him as this 'pestilent priest from the Middle Ages'. The Archbishop and Papandreou, provisional Premier, were brought together with Churchill on a British warship on Christmas Day – after an awkward moment when Damaskinos unaccountably became mixed up with sailors in fancy dress who thought he was one of them.

Churchill, naturally, took at least as much interest in the military operations as in the political scrabbling.

Harold Macmillan, diary, December 1944:

He was ... taken in by Alex to an 'observation post' from which he could see the whole city and get an idea of the fighting. Of course this affair is a sort of 'super Sidney Street', and he quite enjoyed having the whole problem explained to him by a master of the military art.[1]

In a series of meetings Churchill arranged a compromise acceptable to most of the Greeks, the Regency and to the King, but not to the Communist guerrillas (who did however sign a truce on 11 January). While the war was still festering in Europe and the Pacific, Greece seemed almost an irrelevance to some at the time: to others it seemed a sinister foretaste of British 'nation-making' ambitions for the peace. At best, Churchill and the Cabinet had used British soldiers on a somewhat dubious mandate – if any. But Churchill saw it as his first victory over the forces which he already saw collecting in the East against the Western allies and their war aims. Would he be able to do as well in 1945, when – as he then knew – the real battles would begin? Or would it be his final as well as his first victory over those forces? All would depend on whether he could gain the support of the Americans.

---

[1] This somewhat supercilious comment refers to when Churchill had been Home Secretary, in 1911; he had gone in person to conduct police operations against anarchists in Sidney Street, London.

CHAPTER NINE

1945 Prophet, Part II

On 11 January 1945, the Russians captured Warsaw. On 16 January two allied pincer movements met and cut off the remaining German forces in the Ardennes bulge.

The House of Commons again debated Greece on 18 and 19 January. Churchill's speech got off to an unusually bad start. He had a troublesome time with interruptions. He also spoke of the policy of unconditional surrender, laying the prime responsibility with the President – 'I endorsed it'.[1] He made an appeal to national unity – in anticipation of the wish for a general election as soon as the war in Europe was over. He gave a sharp and unmistakable retort to the American Chiefs of Staff, the President, and all those across the Atlantic who feared British imperialism, and involvement in 'the European power game' on any side. 'I am greatly indebted to my friend, the illustrious President of the United States, four times summoned by the popular vote to the headship of the most powerful community in the world, for his definition of "power politics". With that marvellous gift which he has of bringing troublesome issues down to earth ... the President declared in his recent Message to Congress, that power politics were "the misuse of power". I am sure I can say, on behalf of all parties in the House, that we are absolutely in agreement with the President. We go further; we define our position with even more precision. We have sacrificed everything in this war. We shall emerge from

---

[1] On 16 January 1945, the Prime Minister had been pressed in the House to reverse this policy and open negotiations. In the House of Commons, 21 July 1949, Churchill again tried to disassociate himself from the policy: 'The first time I heard that phrase used was from the lips of President Roosevelt. ... I had rapidly to consider whether our condition in the world would justify me in not giving support to him.'

it, for the time being, more stricken and impoverished than any other victorious country. The United Kingdom and the British Commonwealth are the only unbroken force which declared war on Germany of its own free will. We declared war not for any ambition or material advantage, but for the sake of our obligation to do our best for Poland against German aggression, in which aggression, it must also in fairness be stated our own self-preservation was involved. After the defeat of France in June 1940, for more than a year we were alone. We stood alone; we kept nothing back in blood, effort or treasure from what has now become the common cause of more than 30 nations. We seek no territory; we covet no oilfields; we demand no bases for the forces of the air or of the seas. We are an ancient commonwealth dwelling, and wishing to dwell, at peace within our own habitations. We do not set ourselves up in rivalry or bigness or might with any other community in the world. We stand on our own rights. We are prepared to defend them, but we do not intrude for our own advantage upon the rights of any friendly country in the world, great or small. We have given, and shall continue to give, everything we have. We ask nothing in return except that consideration and respect which is our due, and if that were denied us we should still have a good conscience. Let no one therefore, in our own country and Commonwealth or in the outside world misname us or traduce our motives. Our actions are no doubt subject to human error, but our motives in small things as in great are disinterested, lofty and true. I repulse those calumnies, wherever they come from, that Britain and the British Empire is a selfish, power-greedy, land-greedy, designing nation obsessed by dark schemes of European intrigue or Colonial expansion. I repulse these aspersions whether they come from our best friends or worst foes.'

Nothing could be plainer than that – as far as those for whom it was intended were concerned. But many ordinary people in Britain had no idea of the rift in Anglo-American relations, and were bemused at the reference, for instance, to 'our best friends'. What effect this proclamation would have on the Americans at the forthcoming conference remained to be seen.

The Times report, 20 January 1945:
Mr A. Bevan said he was shocked and surprised by the Prime Minister's

speech. He thought that the right hon. Gentleman was going to make a conciliatory speech, a statesmanlike speech, and not the speech of a swashbuckler . . . Only the other day a British soldier said to him [Mr Bevan]: 'I was misled by Churchill in 1920. I went to Archangel. I am not going to Greece. I have heard this story before.' There was no politician who was more capable of distorting facts than the Prime Minister.

Sir Richard Acland also spoke strongly against the Prime Minister. Richard Stokes described the policy of unconditional surrender as 'sheer lunacy'. The House supported Churchill by 340 votes to 7.

Butcher, S.H.A.E.F., 27 January 1945:

Hopkins arrived. After pleasant greetings he told of his visit in London, where he had spent three nights with the Prime Minister. The night before, the Prime Minister had given a fatherly lecture to Mr Eden on the art and science of making a speech to the House of Commons. Mr Eden had accepted the lecture as son from father. In the course of the admonition the Prime Minister, according to Harry, had told Eden never slyly to peek at his notes. They should be flagrantly waved in the face of the M.P.s each time he made a point. Then he should proceed to the next. He should obviously study his notes, taking as much time as necessary – 'two or three minutes, if you feel like it'. He added that the speaker should not lounge or lean against 'the box', which is the rostrum, but rather should stand well behind it and pace his remarks with forward and backward steps. The Prime Minister said that he had had special glasses made which permitted him to see his notes five feet away. He advised Eden to patronize the same oculist. Neither should the box be tapped lightly with the hand, as this distracts the attention of the audience. If the box is to be touched at all it should be vigorously pounded with the fist at an appropriate moment. Added theatrical effect could be obtained if Mr Eden then would scowl at the audience.

Adolf Hitler, 4 February 1945:

Churchill seems to regard himself as a second Pitt! What a hope! In 1793, Pitt was 34 years old. Churchill unfortunately is an old man, capable, and only just capable at that, of carrying out the orders of that madman, Roosevelt. In any case, the situations are in no way comparable . . . The crucial new factor is the existence of these two giants, the United States and Russia. Pitt's England ensured the balance of world power by preventing the hegemony of Europe – by preventing Napoleon, that is, from attaining his goal. Churchill's England, on the other hand, should have allowed the unification of Europe, if it wished to preserve that same balance of power... My object in trying to come to terms with England was to avoid creating an irreparable situation in the West. Later, when I attacked eastwards and lanced the Communist abscess, I hoped thereby to rekindle a spark of common sense in the minds of the Western Powers... Had she so wished Britain could have put an end to the war at the beginning of 1941. In the skies over London she had demonstrated to all the world her will to resist, and on her credit side she had the humiliating defeats which she had inflicted on the Italians in North Africa.

The Big Three Conference took place, not in London as Churchill had hoped, but at the bleak Crimean resort of Yalta. It took place to a background of immense Russian power in half of Europe, about which the Western leaders could no nothing, and to a widespread feeling of goodwill towards Russia and Stalin, which the Western leaders could not ignore even had they felt strongly otherwise. Moreover, because of the Ardennes offensive, revealing unexpected tenacity in the German forces, it was expected that the war in Europe could not be won until December unless the Russians could keep up the momentum of their advance. Roosevelt's main object was to get Russia into the war against Japan; this he achieved. Stalin also accepted Roosevelt's plans for a United Nations Organization. Britain was no longer of much use to the United States; her power in the East was broken forever, because she was too poor to restore it; in Europe her forces were not the equal in importance to those of Russia or America. Nevertheless, Churchill fought hard. He fought over German reparations. And he fought over Poland. Roosevelt did not support him. Churchill did not get what he wanted in Poland, free multi-party elections, but Stalin did not reveal this at Yalta. Roosevelt's aid might not have made much difference, but Churchill certainly had a much better appreciation of Russian motives and a deeper sense of the historical process taking place. As for Stalin, his sense of history did not even go back as far as 1921, and the lesson of German reparations after the First World War. Stalin was tough, anxious to do deals, a believer in a particularly ruthless interpretation of Communism, and concerned to realize the centuries-old Russian desire to gain lasting security in the West. Roosevelt was sick, opportunist, and desirous of getting the war over as quickly as possible. Churchill was suspicious, at least half disillusioned, indignant, and handicapped by putting the Anglo-American relationship before all other considerations.

Lord Moran, Yalta, 4 February 1945:

Dined next to Portal. He began: 'Someone maliciously said that the P.M. will fight to the last ditch but not in it. He does not like making decisions.' Alex broke in: 'And he will not listen to evidence.' This remark, coming from Alex, surprised me. It was not in character. Alex went on: 'Winston is not really interested in those around him.'

Perhaps it was that at this time he was interested in more momentous affairs.

Lord Moran, 5 February 1945;

All morning the P.M. has been losing things. 'Sawyers, Sawyers, where are my glasses?' 'There, sir,' said Sawyers, leaning over his shoulder as he sat, and tapping the P.M.'s pocket. At last, when the P.M. was getting ready for his afternoon sleep, he cried out irritably: 'Sawyers, where is my hot-water bottle?' 'You are sitting on it, sir,' replied the faithful Sawyers. 'Not a very good idea,' he added. 'It's not an idea, it's a coincidence,' said the P.M. enjoying his own choice of words, and without a trace of resentment ... The P.M. said: 'Do you suppose Stalin reads books? He talks of France as a country without a past. Does he not know her history?' The P.M. did not expect an answer. He loves France like a woman. When Stalin said that he did not know what France had done for civilisation he felt bewildered. In Winston's eyes France is civilisation.

One of Roosevelt's senior advisers at Yalta was James F. Byrnes, Director of War Mobilization. He said: 'So far as I could see the President had made little preparation for the conference.' Byrnes had the useful skill of a high speed in shorthand, which he put to good use.[1] He recorded Maisky, Deputy Foreign Minister, and Churchill, on the subject of reparations:

Maisky stated that reparations should be fixed at twenty billions of dollars and that the share of the Soviet Union in the reparations fund should not be less than ten billion dollars. Mr Churchill responded first to Mr Maisky's statement. He recalled the experience of the United Kingdom after World War I. 'The process was a very disappointing one,' he said. 'With great difficulty about 1,000 million pounds was

---

[1] Byrnes had learnt his shorthand as a reporter; Secretary of State, 1945–7. The United States documents on Yalta were published in Washington in 1955.

extracted from Germany, and that would never have been extracted if the United States, at the same time, had not loaned Germany a larger sum' ... 'Secondly,' Mr Churchill continued, 'there arises in my mind the specter of an absolutely starving Germany. If our treatment of Germany's internal economy is such as to leave eighty million people virtually starving, are we to sit still and say, "It serves you right," or will we be required to keep them alive? If so, who is going to pay for that? ... If you have a horse and you want him to pull the wagon you have to provide him with a certain amount of corn – or at least hay.' 'But the horse must not kick you,' Mr Maisky objected. Mr Churchill switched to a nonkicking illustration by saying: 'If you have a motorcar you must give it a certain amount of petrol to make it go. I am in favour of having a reparations inquiry committee set up to explore this subject with the object of getting the most we can in a sensible way.'

Another major problem was that of the veto in the Security Council of the United Nations, designed to protect the great powers at the expense of the weak powers. Roosevelt considered this a point more likely to trouble imperialists and potential imperialists like the British and Russians than the United States. Byrnes took a meticulous note:

Prime Minister:

The peace of the world depends upon the lasting friendship of the three great powers ... We should make a broad submission to the opinion of the world within the limits stated. We should have the right to state our case against any case stated by the Chinese, for instance, in the case of Hongkong. There is no question that we could not be required to give back Hongkong to the Chinese if we did not feel that was the right thing to do. On the other hand, I feel it would be wrong if China did not have an opportunity to state its case fully. In the same way, if Egypt raises a question against the British affecting the Suez Canal, as has been suggested, I would submit to all the procedure outlined in this statement. I would do this without fear because British rights would be preserved under paragraph 3 when our veto would kill action if we chose to use it.

Stalin:

I am sure none of those present would dispute the right of every member of the assembly to express his opinion. Mr Churchill thinks that China, if it raised the question of Hongkong, would be content only with expressing opinion here. He may be mistaken. China will demand a decision in the matter and so would Egypt. Egypt will not have much pleasure in expressing an opinion that the Suez Canal should be returned to Egypt, but would demand a decision on the matter.

Prime Minister:

I know that under the leaders of the three powers as represented here we may feel safe. But these leaders may not live forever. In ten years' time we may disappear. A new generation will come which did not experience the horrors of war and may probably forget what we have gone through. We would like to secure the peace for at least fifty years. We have now to build up such a status, such a plan, that we can put as many obstacles as possible to the coming generation quarrelling among themselves.

Lord Moran, 7 February 1945:

Winston is puzzled and distressed. The President no longer seems to the P.M. to take an intelligent interest in the war. To a doctor's eye, the President appears a very sick man. He has all the symptoms of hardening of the arteries of the brain in an advanced stage, so that I give him only a few months to live. But men shut their eyes when they do not want to see, and the Americans here cannot bring themselves to believe that he is finished. His daughter thinks he is not really ill, and his doctor backs her up.

Lord Moran:

Found the P.M. moody when I went to him after breakfast. He gave me a sour look. 'The President is behaving very badly,' he said. 'He won't take any interest in what we are trying to do.'

It was Poland which proved the most intractable point: the post-war boundaries of that unfortunate nation, and its official government – the Russian backed 'Lublin Government' or the pre-war 'Government-in-exile' in London. Was there a fear, behind Churchill's words, that perhaps it had all been wasted; that Poland had been saved from one ogre only to be fed to another? Although the real reason for war had been based on other factors apart from the integrity of Poland, Churchill was doubtless among the first to become aware of the awful irony of the situation, although, having himself been so closely associated with the start of the war, he seldom expressed it as such.

Byrnes:

At this point, Stalin stood at the conference table as he spoke. It was the only time during the entire conference that he exhibited his strong feelings in such a manner. 'I prefer the war should continue a little longer although it costs us blood and to give Poland compensation in the west at the expense of the Germans,' he continued. 'I will maintain and I will ask all friends to support me in this . . . I am in favor of extending the Polish western frontier to the Neisse River.' Mr Churchill doubted the wisdom of extending the western boundary of Poland to the Neisse River. He agreed that Poland's western boundary should be moved into what had been German territory but asserted 'it would be a pity to stuff the Polish goose so full of German food that he will die of indigestion.' He estimated that the taking of territory in East Prussia as far west as the Oder would necessitate the moving of six million Germans ... The discussion was long and earnest but Stalin finally accepted the Curzon Line in principle. Not only Poland's boundaries but Poland itself was one of the most serious issues of the entire conference. More time was spent on this subject than on any other. Because of the intensity of the argument, Mr Roosevelt would assume a role more of arbiter than of advocate although he, as well as Prime Minister Churchill, urged the establishment of a new Polish government in Warsaw. The Soviet Union, on the other hand, wanted to continue the Lublin government. Stalin was willing to add a few persons but he wanted to make certain that those who were added did not affect the Soviet Union's control of the government ... 'Britain,' the Prime Minister said, 'declared war on Germany in order that Poland should be free and sovereign. Everyone knows what a terrible risk we took and how nearly it cost us our life in the world, not only as an Empire but as a Nation. Our interest in Poland is one of honor. Having drawn the sword in behalf of Poland against Hitler's brutal attack, we could never be content with any solution that did not leave Poland a free and independent sovereign state.' ... Stalin displayed great earnestness in replying. 'For the Russian people, the question of Poland is not only a question of honor but also a question of security...'

At length, an agreement was formulated, to be signed by the three war leaders.

The discussion of the proposal was brief. Stalin opened it by saying, 'On the whole, I approve of the declaration.' The President called attention to the paragraph containing the agreement to 'facilitate if necessary the holding of elections', and Stalin quickly replied: 'I accept that.' 'Poland will be the first example of operating under this declaration,' the President said ... 'I want the election in Poland to be beyond question, like Caesar's wife. I did not know Caesar's wife, but she was believed to have been pure.' Stalin smilingly replied: 'It was said so about Caesar's wife, but, in fact, she had certain sins.'

Roosevelt was no doubt aware that elections in Communist countries are not party elections.

Leahy, 11 February 1945:

Churchill, I thought, was at his best at Yalta. He was completely and wholeheartedly devoted to the interests of the British Empire ... He made a truly prophetic comment at one point, although I do not remember exactly which day it occurred. He observed to Roosevelt and Stalin that he was the only chief of Government at the table 'who could be thrown out of office on any given day' by his own Government.

Lord Moran, 11 February 1945:

The P.M., who has been in a vile mood throughout the conference, irritable and bad-tempered, is now in tearing spirits. 'I'm so relieved to get this bloody thing off.' The bloody thing was the agreed communiqué. 'Anyway,' he growled, 'that's done with and out of the way.' He is trying to forget that he has achieved little ... Twice he sang (very flat) snatches of old songs, 'The Soldiers of the Queen' ...

From Yalta, Churchill went to Athens and Egypt. At Alexandria, he had his last meeting with Roosevelt, whom he found 'placid and frail'. He also met Ibn Saud of Arabia. In Egypt, a British Prime Minister was still the equal of any potentate. The guests at one of the best hotels were 'temporarily removed' for the reception for Ibn Saud. Having been informed that neither smoking nor alcoholic drinks were customary before a Moslem king, Churchill announced to him through the interpreter, 'That my rule of life prescribed as an absolute sacred rite smoking cigars and also the drinking of alcohol before, after, and if need be during all meals and in the intervals between them.' It was a declaration of which Palmerston himself would have approved.

Roosevelt had hoped to meet de Gaulle at Algiers, but de Gaulle had refused; he was annoyed because France had not been invited to Yalta. Roosevelt was infuriated.

On 27 February Churchill asked the House of Commons to approve the joint declaration of the Yalta Conference. When he reached the question of Poland and the elections there, Lord Dunglass jumped to his feet:

I am sorry to interrupt the Prime Minister, but this point is highly important ... is there going to be some kind of international supervision?

The Prime Minister:

I should certainly like that, but we have to wait until the new Polish government is set up and to see what are the proposals they make ...

No arrangements, in fact, had been guaranteed for supervision of the elections.

Churchill's speech on the Yalta Conference lasted two hours. It was not exactly what some people had hoped for. It did not seem that Britain was resisting brute force and national ambitions quite as she had done in 1940. But it ended with the customary appeal ('Let us walk forward together'). Who could doubt that the genial, pipe-sucking 'Uncle Joe', Britain's ally, was not a reasonable man, a responsible statesman, unlike the 'blood-thirsty guttersnipe' now cowering in his Berlin bunker? Churchill, of course, had every reason to doubt it. But it was Lord Dunglass, frail-looking and bespectacled, branded as 'a man of Munich' who was more free to express it. First, Arthur Greenwood made some mild protestations about Poland ('I hope I am not hurting my right hon. Friend's feelings'). Then Dunglass spoke:

... In 1939, when the people of this country had to make a choice between peace and war, they chose war because they were convinced, to the point of certainty, that so long as appeals to force were the rule in international affairs, there could be no peace nor progress. Since then, whenever we have had time to lift our eyes for a moment from our own self-preservation, we have re-affirmed our intention to rebuild and to restore at least the elementary standards in international behaviour. A first British interest in peace, a first British desire, is to provide, over the widest area possible, a setting in which the individual may live out his life in liberty and under justice. That is a British conception, but we believe it to be a world interest. It is true we must face facts. It would be comfortable to believe that relationships between different communities of men were always governed by reason, but the reality, as history reveals it, is that the governing principle is that of power. Power has not been destroyed in this war; it has been redistributed. It is still there. It is still used ... [This] is the first case, a test case, in the relationship between a great power wielding great military might, and her smaller and weaker neighbour ... What about the free elections about which I asked the Prime Minister? ... Do they give a real hope that that section [of the Atlantic Charter] will be fulfilled which reads: 'that they wish to respect the rights of all people to those forms of government under which they wish to live'? ... It is imperative that these elections should be really and truly free, and a good deal depends on what is our government's intention with regard to the machinery to achieve it ... There are much wider issues here as I have tried to suggest – much wider than the freedom of Poland. Can we go forward with confidence into a world organisation by which peace may be built up?

My answer is that we can – but only if the three nations have certain common principles, and three of them at least must be these: integrity of dealing, respect for the rights and interests of others, and responsibility in the use of power.

Lord Dunglass's speech caused little comment at the time. But his protest was supported, 'on the whole', by Sir William Beveridge. The debate continued on the next day, when Maurice Petherick[1] moved the following amendment, at the end of the motion in which Churchill asked for approval:

but, remembering that Great Britain took up arms in a war of which the immediate cause was the defence of Poland against German aggression and in which the overriding motive was the prevention of the domination by a strong nation of its weaker neighbours . . . regrets the failure to ensure to those nations which have been liberated from German oppression the full right to choose their own government free from the influence of any other power.

Where were the noble warriors of 1939, to support this amendment? The debate became enmeshed in territorial argument, but the question of free elections bobbed up from time to time like some irresistible but discomforting probe. Right-wingers saw in it an opportunity of supporting the 'Government-in-exile' in London, at the expense of the Communist-backed Lublin Government in Poland. Among those who spoke against the amendment were such impeccable anti-Munich men as Harold Nicolson, Emanuel Shinwell, and Anthony Eden (who, as Foreign Secretary, wound up on behalf of the Government).

W. J. Brown:[2]

The Prime Minister has brought back in that document a great deal more than I expected him to bring – a great deal more. We do not make agreement in a political vacuum . . . It was not the British Army that liberated Warsaw. It was not the American Army that liberated Poland. It was the Russian Army. Suppose that the Prime Minister, because he feared that Stalin had too many cards, had come away with

---

[1] Conservative M.P., 1931–45. It is significant that Churchill gave Petherick and Dunglass posts in the 'Caretaker Government', May–July 1945.
[2] Trade unionist, writer, and M.P.; Labour M.P., 1929–31; Independent M.P., 1942–50; died 1960.

no agreement at all? I wonder what the effect of that would have been in Poland...

It was such appeals to realism, particularly from an Independent as respected as Brown, that salved many a twinge of guilt. The amendment was defeated by 396 votes to 25. Churchill's motion was carried by 413 votes. No one voted against, but a junior minister, Henry Strauss, resigned.

Churchill now returned to the struggle over military matters with the Americans. The Ardennes offensive had given him the opportunity and time to try to persuade Eisenhower again to mount a single thrust in the North, in order to pluck Berlin from Stalin's grasp. Eisenhower did not think plans to get to Berlin first could be feasible; he was probably right. He had his orders, and they were to destroy the forces of Hitler. Germany had already been carved into occupation zones, and Berlin was well beyond the sectors of the Western allies. At first, Churchill did not mention Berlin as an objective, when advocating the single thrust.

Butcher, Paris, 3 March 1945:

We spent Monday night with General Ike at his new quarters in Rheims. This is a handsome château in the heart of the town and is owned by one of the champagne kings. I found that the Prime Minister had advanced the idea of making Air-Marshal Tedder second in command in the Air Ministry, and, as the Deputy Supreme Commander was a British spot in the SHAEF organization, hoped to move Field-Marshal Alexander into it. It was obvious to me that this move, if consummated after the campaign in some of the British press for a ground commander-in-chief, immediately would be misinterpreted. The idea had been discussed and General Ike was perfectly willing to accept Alexander, not as Ground Commander, but as a true deputy to the Supreme Commander, in which position he would take part in all SHAEF operations – land, sea, and air. I feel strongly that if this appointment were made now, the interpretation placed on it in the press would be very bad, indeed, for Allied relations. Some of the British press would say, 'I told you so', and inevitably there would be inference that Ike had failed. Some inferences would be counter-attacked in the American press, and a merry war of words would ensue. General Ike had not thought of the reaction in quite that way. His admiration and respect for Alexander are such that he would not want him placed in a position which would make him unhappy or create any bad feelings whatsoever. If Alexander were appointed, General Ike would simply make clear to the press the nature of his duties.

Thus failed Brooke's ploy to remove from Eisenhower one of his most convinced supporters – Tedder.

On 3 March Churchill visited the Front, or as near it as he could get. On that day he enjoyed his celebrated urination on the Siegfried Line, having first warned the photographers: 'This is one of the operations connected with this great war which must not be reproduced graphically.'

Brooke, 4 March 1945:

Tonight we dined in the train and Monty and de Guingand came to dinner. Winston fretting because he was not allowed nearer the front, and trying to make plans to come back for the operations connected with the crossing of the Rhine! De Guingand, not knowing the P.M., unfortunately adopted quite the wrong attitude with him and I at one time was afraid that we might have trouble. Winston was in deadly earnest in his desire to come out for the crossing of the Rhine and to be well forward in this operation. I knew we should have difficulties in providing for his security, but I was even more certain that de Guingand's rather grandmotherly arguments against Winston's wishes would ultimately lead to an explosion.

A soldier, somewhere in Germany, 4 March 1945:[1]

We had a visit from Winston, and were very proud that we were the only Division he spoke to. He looked very well and as pugnacious as usual. Monty (in a green sniper's jacket) accompanied him, and all the big shots. He came to a Divisional Retreat, the massed Pipes and Drums. It started with the Last Post and 'Flowers of the Forest', that haunting piper's lament, in memory of those who have fallen since the start of the campaign. I thought of some of the Gordon officers: David Martin, Albert Brown, Murray Reekie, Johnnie Grant, Arthur Thomson, George Stewart, magnificent chaps every one of them and what a loss to the nation! I remember officers in England saying how quickly in war you recover from the death of a comrade. I suppose this is true in a way, since though you may lose half the officers of a battalion in one day, others take their place and the machinery still goes on. But I for one could never forget these good fellows. All my closest friends seem

---

[1] Lieut.-Colonel M. Lindsay, D.S.O., 1st Gordon Highlanders; explorer, author, and Conservative M.P., 1945–64; knighted, 1962. From D-Day to the end of the war 106 officers served with the 1st Gordon Highlanders: of these 21 were killed, 60 wounded.

to have been killed in this beastly war: Dan Godfrey, one of my two companions for seven months over the Greenland ice-cap, killed in action in 1942; Roger Pettiward (we were mutual godfathers to each other's children), killed with No. 4 Commando at Dieppe: John Rock, killed in an experimental glider flight – we shared an office and a cottage for fourteen months; and Sandy Cuninghame, my greatest friend at Sandhurst and in the regiment – killed commanding a Scots Fusilier battalion in Normandy last July, the day before his D.S.O. came through. Unfortunately Winston arrived one and a half hours late and we were standing in a drizzle until then. We had been told to cheer when he left but there was not a murmur from the Jocks. They think the world of Winnie but they are independent and undemonstrative at the best of times, and they just weren't feeling like cheering.

On 6 and 7 March questions were asked in the House of Commons about air strategy. Sinclair, Air Minister, said that the Cabinet 'had determined to launch this tremendous offensive' in 1941. He explained that bombing was continuing in order to aid the Red armies in the East, to have an effect 'on every front', and to create a shortage of tanks, equipment, and oil. Richard Stokes, who had long been critical and suspicious of Bomber Command, asked what was the need to bomb large areas of population when the war was nearly over? On 13 and 14 February, as Stokes knew, Dresden had been bombed by the R.A.F. and U.S.A.F. in the most destructive attack of the war. About 135,000 Germans had been killed.[1] Stokes said –

When I heard the Minister speak of the 'crescendo of destruction', I thought: What a magnificent expression for a Cabinet Minister of Great Britain at this stage of the war.
The terror bombing raids on the German population will stand for all times as a blot on our escutcheon.

Sinclair had left the chamber before Stokes had begun to speak.
On 13 March Stokes returned to the attack, but this time he accused Churchill of lying about tank production. The Speaker declared he was glad to hear the end of his speech, which remark Aneurin Bevan indignantly declared was 'a perfectly improper

---

[1] On 9 and 10 March, the U.S.A.F. bombed Tokyo, inflicting 83,793 deaths. The bombing of Coventry, on 14 and 15 November 1940, had resulted in 380 deaths. Civilian casualties in the United Kingdom during the war were 146,760, more than half in London.

statement' – there should, he said, be an inquiry as to whether the Prime Minister had lied. Churchill complained in the House next day. Stokes withdrew his charge – to the extent that he now said the Prime Minister had been guilty of 'a terminological inexactitude'. Churchill and the Speaker declared that this was not a withdrawal. Bevan said that it was. Argument continued for some time about the nature of a withdrawal. Churchill went on insisting. Stokes retorted that 'This is not the Reichstag yet.' A little later, he said, 'I quite unequivocally withdraw the word lie.' The Prime Minister accepted that.

As reports of the Dresden raid from neutral sources began to reach authorities in London, Churchill seems to have become alarmed; whether or not he had wanted the raid, he knew he would have to accept much responsibility for it. It is a responsibility he has not escaped.[1]

On 6 April Bomber Command received notice from the Chiefs of Staff that area bombing was causing more difficulties than help to the allies. On 28 March Churchill wrote a curious minute to the Chiefs of Staff. In this he queried the wisdom of area bombing at that stage in the war: 'The question of bombing of German cities simply for the sake of increasing the terror, though under other pretexts, should be reviewed ... The destruction of Dresden remains a serious query against the conduct of Allied bombing.' It was curious, because the Prime Minister had been party to the air offensive, and of increasing the terror, all along. The Chief of Air Staff refused to accept the note, for it looked as if the Prime Minister was trying to put all responsibility for the area bombing, and for Dresden in particular, on the Chiefs of Staff. In fact, as recently as 26 January, he had confirmed the policy of bombing Berlin and large cities in Eastern Germany – of which Dresden was one – no doubt to impress Stalin or Roosevelt. Harris later wrote: 'The attack on Dresden was at the time considered a military necessity by much more important people than myself.' It

---

[1] In 1964 R. H. S. Crossman went so far as to suggest that Churchill ordered a raid on Milan, 'in bad weather and with heavy R.A.F. casualties', because of sheer pique; he withdrew the imputation and paid 'a substantial donation' to the R.A.F. Benevolent Fund. A more impressive critique was published in 1963 in the *Bombing of Dresden*.

would have been inconsistent for Churchill to have personally demanded this particular and vast raid, for his secret policy to get to Berlin first would not want to help at that stage the Russian armies in the East. Roosevelt, however, was extremely anxious that the war should end quickly; he dreaded it continuing till the end of the year. The raid on Dresden was in Roosevelt's interests.

Churchill was determined to be back with the armies for the crossing of the Rhine.

Brooke to Montgomery, March 1945:

As regards the P.M.'s proposals for his next visit, do not take this matter too lightheartedly; there are the seeds of serious trouble ahead. In his mind you stopped him before the start of *Overlord* visiting troops, you tried to stop him in Normandy, and now you are attempting to do so again! Note that I said 'in his mind'; but that is the important point, as when he gets such ideas nothing on earth gets them out. De Guingand was working on the wrong lines after you left the night you dined; he was treating the whole visit as an impossibility. I can tell you the P.M. is determined to come out for the crossing of the Rhine and is now talking of going up in a tank! I feel the safest way would be to find some reasonably secure view-point (not too far back) to which he can be taken and from which he can see and have explained what is happening.

Montgomery replied:

As regards the P.M., if he is determined to come out for the Battle of the Rhine, I think there is only one course of action: and that is to ask him to stay with me in my camp. I shall then be able to keep an eye on him and see that he goes only where he will bother no one. I have written him a letter; it should please the old boy.

Brooke, diary, 22 March 1945:

Tomorrow I start off with P.M. on this visit to see the Rhine crossing. I am not happy about this trip: he will be difficult to manage and has no business to be going. All he will do is to endanger his life unnecessarily. However, nothing on earth will stop him!

The same, 23 March:

After lunch I drove with Winston to Northolt. The road was up on the way and the driver was going to take the diversion, but this did not suit Winston and we had to go straight through. This meant lifting some of the barriers, driving on the footpath, etc., and on the whole probably took longer than going round. However, Winston was delighted that he was exercising his authority and informed me that the King would not take such action; he was far more law-abiding!... Crossings take place throughout the night, and the guns have already started and can be heard indistinctly in the distance. After dinner Monty went off to bed early and Winston took me off. First of all, we walked up and down in the moonlight; it was a glorious night, and we discussed the situation we were in at the momentous moment of crossing the Rhine.

But other problems were never far from the Prime Minister's mind:

We then went into the caravan and examined his box which had just arrived. It contained a telegram from Molotov which worried him a great deal, connected with the Russian attitude in the peace negotiations... He dictated a reply, let his secretary out of the caravan, called him back, considered it, started writing another and finally very wisely left it till tomorrow to think over carefully.

Alan Moorehead, 24 March 1945:

Churchill stood on Xanten hilltop and looked down across the morning battle mist at the place where the troops were still crossing on boats and rafts. 'I should have liked,' he said, 'to have deployed my men in red coats on the plain down there and ordered them to charge.' And he added with vim: 'But now my armies are too vast.' Suddenly the Prime Minister sprang to his feet, and went coursing wildly for a few steps down the hill. 'They're coming,' he shouted, 'they're coming!' It was the first airborne troops. Indeed it was a wonderful sight. They passed only two or three hundreds of feet above our heads, the tow planes drawing sometimes one and sometimes two gliders and flying in tight formation. Then single planes with the parachutists waiting intensely inside for the moment to plunge out through the open hatches. Here and there among all these hundreds of aircraft one would be hit by ack-ack fire, and it was an agonising thing to see it break formation and start questing vainly back and forth in search of any sort of landing field and then at last plunge headlong to the ground. Within a few minutes nothing would be left but a black pillar of petrol smoke and the unidentifiable scraps of wings and propellors and human beings.

Brooke, diary, 24 March 1945:

Winston then became a little troublesome and wanted to go messing about on the Rhine crossings and we had some difficulty in keeping him back. However, in the end he behaved well and we came back in our armoured cars to where we had left our own car, and from there on back to the H.Q. P.M. went off for a sleep which he wanted badly; he had been sleeping in the car nearly all the way home, gradually sliding on to my knee.

The same, 25 March 1945:

We got into a tank-landing craft which was plying across the Rhine and crossed over. It was a great thrill setting foot on the far bank. We spent a little time examining the German river-defences and then recrossed the river. We got back into the car and motored to the main road bridge over the Rhine at Wesel. The bridge had been broken in several places, but partly boarded over so that one could scramble about on it. Winston at once started scrambling along it for about forty yards ... We decided it was time to remove the P.M., who was thrilled with the situation and very reluctant to leave! However, he came away more obediently than I had expected.

Brooke, in a letter to his mother, March 1945:

He was determined to take every risk he could possibly take and, if possible endanger his life to the maximum. I rather feel that he considers that a sudden and soldierly death at the front would be a suitable ending to his famous life and would free him from the never-ending worries which loom ahead with our Russian friends and others.

After the Rhine, there was nothing left for Churchill in the war with Germany – except the race. He was now more definite about his real views, concerning Berlin. Eisenhower, not unnaturally, insisted on sticking to his brief, which was to beat the Germans. He insisted that he was now going to carry out 'the principle that Field-Marshal Brooke has always shouted to me' – one major thrust. But:

May I point out that Berlin is no longer a particularly important objective. Its usefulness to the German has been largely destroyed and even his government is preparing to move to another area.

American political writer, Ralph Ingersoll:

The British blast was that Bradley had no right to drive due east to the Elbe but should join Montgomery to force the way to Berlin. The British Chiefs accused Marshall and the other American Chiefs of breaking a firm agreement to back Montgomery to take Berlin. The complaint charged the War Department and American Government with a specific act of bad faith. The spirit of the reply which came boiling back from the American Joint Chiefs of Staff was in the idiom of General McAuliffe's famous 'Nuts!' at Bastogne. The chapter and verse, spelled out, was that there had been no agreement, written, oral or implicit – and that there would be no change whatever in Bradley's plans, which promised the surest, quickest, most decisive total victory over the German State. In general, both these papers, while sharp, were still in purely military language. The next blast was neither pure nor military. Winston Churchill's hat sailed into the ring. He let go with a personal cable to Roosevelt in which the Prime Minister pulled out every stop ... Mr Churchill apparently said everything but the truth, which was that the military situation had nothing to do with it – Bradley being militarily one thousand per cent sound. President Roosevelt said NO – and the war and the President's life ended with very bad blood between the two great leaders of the Western powers. Roosevelt never forgave Churchill for his last message – and Churchill never forgave Roosevelt for turning it down.

Harold Nicolson, letter, 13 April 1945:

I woke up to hear on the wireless the awful news about Roosevelt. It is really a disaster. I feel deeply for Winston, and this afternoon it was evident from his manner that it was a real body-blow. Under that bloody American Constitution they must now put up with the Vice-President who was actually chosen because he was a colourless and harmless man.

There was more colour and harm in Harry Truman than anyone, except perhaps himself, realized. He picked up the reins dropped from Roosevelt's by then feeble hands, and soon the United States were being more firmly and decisively directed than they had been for many months. At first, he continued with Roosevelt's policy towards Britain and America, but he was more inclined to make up his own mind about Churchill's warnings than Roosevelt had been, who had leaned so heavily on the State Department and the Chiefs of Staff.

The day after Roosevelt's death, Russian troops occupied Vienna.

Butcher, Paris, 13 April 1945:

Ike returned before midnight. The Prime Minister wants him to take Berlin and Ike sees no military sense in it.

In Italy, Alexander advanced. Mussolini was captured by partisans, and later executed. Stuttgart was entered by French troops.[1]

---

[1] But having got there, they would not move out. This was on de Gaulle's order. Truman, roused, pointed out that 'land-grabbing was out of order'. A French zone had not then been settled. The French troops only left when Truman personally ordered the cutting off of their supplies.

Truman to Churchill, 21 April 1945:

Zones of occupation for Germany were the subject of long and careful study and negotiation. They were formally agreed upon by the American, British, and Soviet governments just prior to the Yalta Conference. Following a difference of opinion lasting many months, the British obtained a north-western zone, which they were so insistent upon having ... The question of tactical deployment of American troops in Germany is a military one. It is my belief that General Eisenhower should be given certain latitude and discretion; and that where time permits he should consult the Combined Chiefs of Staff before any major withdrawal behind our zone frontiers. [U.S. troops at this time were at some points over 100 miles inside the projected Soviet zone.]

Churchill continued to argue against a withdrawal.

As the allied forces advanced in Germany, they uncovered the bestialities of the Nazi régime. The world was horrified, disgusted, and then shamed. They were revealed to a world which purported to be not only shocked, but also surprised. This was strange, for in November 1939, the British Government had produced a White Paper on German concentration camps, including details of Buchenwald and Dachau. The *New Statesman & Nation* had then said, 'none of it is new'. On 17 December 1942, the House of Commons had stood in silence for one minute, in sympathy for Jews who were being 'transported in conditions of appalling horror and brutality ... deliberately massacred in mass executions'.

German forces, during April, tried to mass themselves for a stand. It was hopeless. They were being split down the middle by the advances from East and West. Resistance continued in the North, in the South, around Berlin, and facing the East. Hitler, far below ground, brooded as his empire – the most powerful that Europe had known since the Romans – collapsed around him.

On 25 April Russian and American forces met at the Elbe. Montgomery reached the Baltic, in a dramatic dash, thus saving Denmark for the West. The Third Reich was bisected. For a few moments the dismembered corpse lived on.

CHAPTER TEN

1945 Victor

Word came from Sweden that Himmler was anxious to negotiate a surrender.

Truman and Churchill, their first telephone conversation, 25 April 1945:

Churchill: Is that you, Mr President?
Truman: This is the President, Mr Prime Minister.
Churchill: How glad I am to hear your voice.
Truman: Thank you very much, I am glad to hear yours.
Churchill: I have several times talked to Franklin, but ... have you received the report from Stockholm by your Ambassador?
Truman: Yes, I have.
Churchill: On that proposal?
Truman: Yes. I have just a short message saying that there was such a proposal in existence.
Churchill: Yes, it's of course ... we thought it looked very good.
Truman: Has he anything to surrender?
Churchill: I called the War Cabinet together and they proposed[1] my telegraphing to tell Stalin and also repeating our news through the usual channels to you.
Truman: What has he to surrender: does that mean everything, Norway, Denmark, Italy, and Holland?
Churchill: They mentioned Italy, and Yugoslavia. We mentioned everything and have included that to take in Denmark and Norway. Everything on the Western Front, but he hasn't proposed to surrender on the Eastern Front. So we thought perhaps it would be necessary to report it to Stalin; that is, of course, to say that in our view the surrender must be simultaneous to agree to our terms.
Truman: I think he should be forced to surrender to all three governments, Russia, you and the United States. I don't think we ought to even consider a piecemeal surrender.
Churchill: No, no, no. Not a piecemeal surrender to a man like Himmler. Himmler will be speaking for the German State as much as anybody

---

[1] In Truman's account this is incorrectly given as 'opposed'.

can. And therefore we thought that his negotiations must be carried on with the three governments...
Truman: I hope to see you some day soon.
Churchill: I am planning to. I'll be sending you some telegrams about that quite soon. I entirely agree with all that you've done on the Polish situation. We are walking hand in hand together.
Truman: Well, I want to continue just that.
Churchill: In fact, I am following your lead, backing up whatever you do on the matter.
Truman: Thank you. Good night.

It was a premature conversation. For the Nazi corpse was not yet quite drained of life. It gurgled and twitched in its final convulsions before the massive forces which had squeezed through its rotting flesh from both sides. A savage battle was taking place in Berlin, where Hitler's last line – hysterical youths of sixteen – attempted to beat off the Russian armour.

On 30 April Hitler committed suicide. The Soviet flag was raised over the mutilated Reichstag. The flickering torch was passed to a stubborn, uncomprehending admiral in the north.

Grand-Admiral Karl von Doenitz, broadcast, 1 May 1945:

German men and women, soldiers of the German Armed Forces. Our Fuehrer, Adolf Hitler, is dead. The German people bow in deepest sorrow and respect. Early he had recognized the terrible danger of Bolshevism and had dedicated his life to the fight against it. His fight having ended, he died a hero's death in the capital of the German Reich, after having led an unmistakably straight and steady life.

The death of modern history's most debased and outrageous dictator, who had brought more misery to mankind than any other human had succeeded in doing, was soon confirmed. President de Valera of Ireland conveyed his deep condolences to the German Ambassador in Dublin, calling on him personally.

Berlin, largely demolished, went silent on 2 May. On the 5th Montgomery accepted the surrender of all the German forces in north-west Europe from a tearful admiral. On 7 May the document of unconditional surrender was signed by Doenitz's emissaries at a school table.

General Eisenhower, to Combined Chiefs of Staff, 7 May 1945:

The mission of this Allied Force was fulfilled at 3.0 a.m., local time, 7 May 1945. Eisenhower.

Daily Telegraph, 8 May 1945:

This is VE Day. The war in Europe is over. After five years and eight months 'complete and crushing victory' has, in the words of the King, crowned Britain's unrelenting struggle with Nazi Germany ... After signing General Jodl said: 'With this signature the German people and the German armed forces are, for better or worse, delivered into the victors' hands'... The Prime Minister yesterday gave a special lunch at 10, Downing Street, to the Chiefs of Staff. It was a private party. The principal guests were Admiral of the Fleet Sir Andrew Cunningham, First Sea Lord, Field-Marshal Sir Alan Brooke, Chief of the Imperial General Staff, and Marshal of the R.A.F. Sir Charles Portal, Chief of the Air Staff...

... Our thoughts will go out in this hour to Mr Churchill, Prime Minister and Minister of Defence from the darkest hour to the brightest. No words can express what his country owes to him. At every turn of the war, he has been able to express the feelings in magnificent language and to direct the actions with unflinching resolution of a people whom he loves in a cause worthy of them and of him.

The bitter arguments of strategy were all forgotten and forgiven – for the time being. None was more effusive than *The Times*, which in 1942 had worried and nagged about the Minister of Defence and in 1945 had been so indignant about Greece.

The Times, 8 May 1945:

With a mind steeped in military history, the Prime Minister committed his country to the pursuit of its traditional strategy, to maintain the Empire's lines of communications round the globe, to contain the enemy within the ring of sea-power, and to challenge him on land at the extreme limits of his dominion until his strength should begin to exhaust itself. Thus would time be won to mobilize the reserves of the imperial Commonwealth, and to range in the line for the decisive stroke the forces of all other nations that would rally to the standard of liberty.

How clear it all seemed now.

Churchill broadcast at 3 o'clock that afternoon: 'Our gratitude to our splendid allies goes forth from all our hearts in this island and throughout the British Empire. We may allow ourselves a brief period of rejoicing, but let us not forget for a moment the toil and efforts that lie ahead.' In this broadcast Churchill made an unexpected and savage attack on de Valera (not reproduced in his history). Churchill preached magnanimity in victory, but he could find none for the gaunt, stubborn, self-righteous Irish leader.

Churchill was delayed in arriving at the House, which had to fill in time by the raising and answering of frivolous and trivial questions. Then he came from behind the Speaker's Chair, and was greeted by scenes of fervour and acclaim unsurpassed in that House. He said that the Commons had 'proved itself the strongest foundation for waging war that has ever been seen in the whole of our long history. We have all of us made our mistakes, but the strength of the Parliamentary institution has been shown to enable it at the same moment to preserve the title deeds of democracy while waging war in the most stern and protracted form. I wish to give my hearty thanks to men of all parties, to everyone in every part of the House where they sit, for the way in which the liveliness of Parliamentary institutions has been maintained under the fire of the enemy and for the way in which we have been able to persevere – and we could have persevered much longer if the need had been – till all the objectives which we set before us of the procuring of the unlimited and unconditional surrender of the enemy had been achieved.'

The Times, 9 May 1945:

The Prime Minister was given a great ovation when he entered the House of Commons today to announce, as he had already done in his broadcast, the unconditional German surrender. The members filling every part of the Chamber sprang to their feet when he appeared from behind the Speaker's Chair and, waving order papers, cheered loudly, repeating their cheers when Mr Churchill rose and stood at the Table to deliver his message ... Then, following the precedent at the end of the last war, he moved that the House proceed to St Margaret's Church, Westminster, to 'give humble and reverent thanks to Almighty God for our deliverance from the threat of German domination'. The House unanimously agreed ... One of the most moving and remarkable scenes of all yesterday's national rejoicing was that which took place just before 6.0 o'clock in the evening when Mr Churchill spoke from a balcony in Whitehall to a great crowd ... Mr Churchill said: 'This is your victory! It is the victory of the cause of freedom in every land. In all our long history we have never seen a greater day than this ...'

It was true. Churchill reappeared on the balcony several times during the evening, to clamorous demands from the enormous crowd which stretched from Parliament to Trafalgar Square. As the evening wore on his utterances, booming down Whitehall from a loudspeaker, became more and more high-flown and immoderate, not to say maudlin. He conducted the gathering in

'Land of Hope and Glory'. It was a joyous and unforgettable night – five years less two days since Winston Churchill had accepted the leadership of Britain at war.

German G.H.Q. Radio broadcast, Flensburg, 8 May 1945:

Thus a heroic struggle which lasted almost six years has ended. It brought us great victories, but also heavy defeats. In the end the German *Wehrmacht* honourably succumbed to an enormous material superiority. The homeland has supported the German soldier to the last with all its strength and with very heavy sacrifices. The unique performance of front and homeland will find a final appreciation in a later, just verdict of history.

The country did believe that the Second World War was as good as over. The Pacific, the East, Japan, were far away. Churchill had, perhaps, not done enough to disabuse it of this impression – for many British servicemen were still to die – until his victory broadcast on the night of 13 May. He then made up for the omission, and, no doubt refreshed by the celebrations and righteous joy of the defeat of the Nazis, his exhortation had all the vigour of his speeches of 1940. But in it, there was a warning, too, of a hard peace. 'On the continent of Europe we have yet to make sure that the simple and honourable purposes for which we entered the war are not brushed aside or overlooked in the months following our success ... There would be little use in punishing the Hitlerites for their crimes if law and justice did not rule, and if totalitarian or police governments were to take the place of the German invaders.' Lord Dunglass could certainly not have expressed it better. 'We must never forget that beyond all lurks Japan ... I told you hard things at the beginning of these last five years; you did not shrink, and I should be unworthy of your confidence and generosity if I did not still cry: Forward, unflinching, unswerving, indomitable, till the whole task is done and the whole world is safe and clean.'

The second European war of the century was finished. Britain, exhausted, bankrupt, was almost finished too. To fight the war against German domination of Europe and the Mediterranean with America and Russia, as a great world power, had drained away what had been left of her once vast wealth and resources. More than a quarter of Britain's total overseas capital had been sold.[1] A debt of £2,879 million had been incurred. Nearly two-thirds of the country's merchant shipping had been sunk. As the economist Keynes said, 'We fought this war on the principle of unlimited liability.'

The Listener, 17 May 1945:

Perhaps the best guarantees that things will be better than they were in the 'twenties are, first, that in this war many civilians have shared, at least to some degree, the soldiers' dangers; and, secondly, that neither soldier nor civilian will begin the peace with any of the exaggerated hopes nurtured by the 'war to end war' of 1914–18. We know, without politicians rubbing it in, that we are in for a thin time.

An M.P.,[2] London 1945:

It seems years and years since we heard that challenging voice, 'We will not flag or fail. We will go on to the end. We will defend our island, whatever the cost may be. We will never surrender', and we knew that the greatest crisis in our history had discovered a leader of rare quality. In the history of the world there have been a small number of national leaders whose names have become household words. Churchill joins the select few, but I think his task has been the hardest of them all, because those others were virtually dictators and the influence of the Press and Parliament was unknown in their day. Even at the most critical moments some M.P.s and poor-class journalists have been sniping at the Prime Minister, and though he no doubt treated them with contempt they did have some nuisance value to a man whose every hour was highly charged with responsibilities that these pygmies could never have shouldered. Roosevelt, too, had to impel and compel against much opposition, but his crusade did not last so long. Stalin, of course, has had the advantage that his word is law. How wrong the outside world and many of our own friends were about the quality of our people! That nasty veneer overlaid intentionally by people who are temperamentally incapable of seeing any good in their own country, and unintentionally by the pacifists with their slightly dishonest Peace Ballot, and youngsters at Oxford led by a few exhibitionists, deceived many people, including Hitler and his gangsters. It was soon after we stood alone that the world knew the truth about us. Warburton–Lee's destroyer men at Narvik, the British Army at Dunkirk and Calais, the magnificent pilots of the Battle of Britain, and finally the ordinary man and ordinary woman who came under fierce bombing proved to the world that it was no empty boast that we would never surrender.

---

[1] At the time of writing British investment abroad, at comparable values, was about half what it had been in 1939.

[2] Admiral James.

CHAPTER ELEVEN

Epilogue: Loser

With the end of the war in Europe Churchill struggled to maintain the Coalition. He dreaded the return to party politics with its bitterness and strife. He wanted to attend the next Big Three meeting and to continue his efforts to contain Stalin from a position of as much strength as he could. But neither the politicians nor the public were with him. And he himself had promised an election on the defeat of Hitler. The last general election had been in 1935, in a different age, when Baldwin had become Premier. The country was tired of the old faces. No one under thirty had voted in a general election. The Labour leaders said they were prepared to go on until the autumn. Men like Bevin and Attlee had also enjoyed the atmosphere of mutual respect and common cause engendered by the war. But others, both Labour and Conservative, were against this. Then the Conservatives won a surprising by-election at Newport. On 23 May the Coalition was dissolved. An election was to be held on 5 July. In an effort to ward off the Conservative hierarchy a little longer, and to give the new Government a national air, Churchill brought into it several non-political members. Of the Ministers, thirty were Conservative or allies, one was Liberal, eight were Independents, and one was not in Parliament. Among the new Ministers were several members who hitherto had been critics of Churchill and the Coalition Government.

Hore-Belisha, diary, 24 May 1945:

At 6.50 p.m. a telephone call came through asking me to go and see the Prime Minister. Went to Storey's Gate entrance. The P.M. asked me to come in at once. He was lying in bed, wearing a blue flowered silk dressing-gown with a golden collar and smoking a big cigar. He had a breakfast tray in front of him and a sponge at either side on which to lean his elbows. He apologised for being in bed, but said he worked better there. He then said he was engaged in the task of Cabinet making and invited me to be Minister of National Insurance. He said he attached great importance to this office, particularly from an electoral point of view. The Scheme wanted humanising and purging of its present traces of Socialism. He felt that it was a matter of great urgency that I should go into the scheme forthwith and see him in a fortnight with proposals for its reform, which he might include in his Election programme. He said there was a great field here which wanted popularising, and that is why he had asked me to to do the job. He said that nothing was to be said on any account until Saturday, when he hoped to have all the offices filled, except perhaps two. He wanted me to go into the office on Saturday and take over from Jowitt [Sir William, Minister of National Insurance, later Lord Jowitt], or as soon as I can take the oath. Our talk lasted three-quarters of an hour.

Churchill's 'Caretaker Government', as it was known, was not without its virtues during its two months of office. Churchill was not, as so many believed, against the Welfare State. Why should he have been? He had been in politics so long that few could remember that Churchill had laid the foundations of the Welfare State, as Lloyd George's most unyielding ally, before the First World War. As president of the Budget League of 1909, he had attacked the Tory peers to such effect that in future years he was never to be accepted as a trustworthy Conservative. He had described their delaying tactics as 'something very like an incitement to violence'. The 'Caretaker Government' brought in the Family Allowances Bill. But Churchill was too involved in foreign affairs to pay anything but the most cursory attention to social matters – or indeed to winning the election. He fought the election with about half his mind. He relied much on Bracken and Beaverbrook. His tactics, from beginning to end, were naïve, misplaced, and disastrous. Labour, under the direction of Morrison, fought with skill. At first, their policy was not to attack Churchill personally. That was seen as dangerous.

Stafford Cripps, speech in Lancashire, May 1945:

Parliament is already ten years old and has ceased altogether to be representative of the views of the people ... We have had the good fortune to have a great war leader in Mr Churchill and we have all most willingly served under and with him in the government while the winning of the war was our sole aim ... but now we can no longer justify subordinating our ideas and policies to the necessity of a coalition because the tasks of government have altered ... I shall certainly be no less grateful for what he has done for this country in the last five years because I oppose the policies for which he stands.

Emanuel Shinwell, Labour Party Conference, Blackpool, 25 May 1945:

Mr Churchill is now engaged searching on the hills, the beaches and the seas – (laughter) – for a government of men of good will. There can be no government of men and women of good will outside the ranks of the Labour party (cheers). Mr Churchill has carried heavy burdens in the last 5½ years. He has borne a heavy responsibility, but none greater than the responsibility he now carries of searching for men of good will in the ranks of the Tory party. We have had enough of them.

Harold Nicolson, letter, 27 May 1945:

People feel, in a vague and muddled way, that all the sacrifices to which they have been exposed and their separation... from family life during four or five years, are all the fault of 'them' – namely the authority or the Government. By a totally illogical process of reasoning, they believe that 'they' mean the upper classes, or the Conservatives, and that in some manner all that went well during these five years was due to Bevin and Morrison, and all that went ill was due to Churchill. Class feeling and class resentment are very strong. I should be surprised, therefore, if there were not a marked swing to the left.

The Conservatives fought the election on two fronts: personal loyalty to Churchill, and propaganda about the 'evils' and dangers of socialism.

Manchester Guardian, June 1945:

When Winston Churchill calls up the nation's vast reserves of affection towards him for the benefit of a reactionary party which only lately despised and rejected him, when he divides the candidates at the election into his friends and opponents, when, in short, he asks for a personal plebiscite he is straining loyalty too far.

Churchill opened his campaign with a broadcast. The nation heard it with some embarrassment. 'I declare to you, from the bottom of my heart, that no Socialist system can be established without a political police. Many of those who are advocating Socialism or voting Socialist today will be horrified at this idea. That is because they are short-sighted. No Socialist Government conducting the entire life and industry of the country could afford to allow free, sharp, or violently worded expressions of public discontent. They would have to fall back on some form of *Gestapo*.'

Some Labour politicians took the opportunity of spreading it about that this speech had been composed by the old enemy, Beaverbrook. The accusation remained with Beaverbrook, much to his displeasure for – oddly enough – he had had nothing to do with it. After the 1945 election Beaverbrook lost for ever such influence as he had ever enjoyed in the Conservative Party. The broadcast changed the Labour attitude. Criticism of the Prime Minister became more open and outspoken. On 7 June the *Daily Mirror* published a bitter letter, which claimed that Churchill 'hasn't changed' – a reference apparently to pre-war days, when he was supposed to be a reactionary High Tory. He was also, the letter claimed, 'a worn-out, tired man'. He was urged to retire, while he still had the respect of the public.

Vita Sackville-West,[1] letter, 22 June 1945:

You know I have an admiration for Winston amounting to idolatry, so I am dreadfully distressed by the badness of his broadcast election speeches. What has gone wrong with him? They are confused, woolly, unconstructive and so wordy that it is impossible to pick out any concrete impression from them. If I were a wobbler, they would tip me over to the other side.

The *Daily Mirror* had a great influence on the election, particularly on the Service wives, who had, according to the *Mirror*, the responsibility of voting for their husbands serving overseas. On 25 June it published on the front page a letter from Mrs C. Gardiner, 'Ilford, Essex':

My husband won't be here to vote . . . He has fought against the Fascist enemy in Italy and North Africa for a better Britain – now he is denied the chance of hearing candidates give their views for a better Britain. I shall vote for him. I know what he wants. He has told me in many letters from the battle fronts. I shall vote to ensure that he gets what he wants. He wants a good house with a bit of a garden. He wants a job at a fair wage, however hard the work may be. He wants a good education for the children . . . If he and his pals had not had the courage to laugh and have faith in each other after Dunkirk where would we be now? My husband would say, 'Vote for Courage'. I shall. I shall vote for him.

Nowhere did the lady say she would vote for Labour; if she was to vote for husband, then that, it seemed, went without saying.

---

[1] Writer; wife of Harold Nicolson.

It was not a bad letter from an Ilford housewife – written as it was with all the succinct power and brimming emotion of the best *Mirror* writers. Two days later, the *Mirror* opened its brilliant and insistent 'I'll Vote For Him' campaign. Against this the Conservatives had to rely mostly on the *Daily Express*, also widely read. But whereas the *Daily Mirror* understood the British people to an almost uncanny degree – had indeed established over the war years a rapport with its readers never equalled in Britain by a newspaper before or since – the *Express* was clumsy, and directed by a proprietor who, though determined at this time to give the utmost loyalty and support to Churchill, had never really understood the British at all. His papers were technically good and much enjoyed, but had little political weight owing to the all too obvious way in which Beaverbrook used them for his personal views – a circumstance particularly galling to one who owned newspapers purely for the purposes of propaganda. Before the campaign, the editor of the *Evening Standard*, another Beaverbrook newspaper, was obliged to resign because of his left-wing sympathies. Beaverbrook was not as subtle a propagandist as he was an intriguer.

In the last few days before polling, the *Mirror* added 'I'll Vote For Them' to its call: parents were asked to vote for their sons under twenty-one, who did not have the vote but were 'old enough to die for their country'. Once more, it was not suggested that this meant voting Labour: it was just 'Voting For Them'.

Daily Mirror, 4 July 1945:

Tomorrow the future of Britain and of yourselves is at stake, your hearths and homes, your families, your jobs, your dreams. Vote for Them! For five long years the lusty youth of this great land has bled and died. From Berlin to Burma, through desert and jungle, on the seas and in the air, they have fought and are still fighting for YOU. Vote for Them! You women must think of them. For five years you have depended on them. Tomorrow they depend on you. The choice is plain: to march forward to a better and happier Britain or turn back to the dangers that led us to the brink of disaster. You know which way your men would march. Vote for Them!

Any woman who saw it would have hardly been able to resist it. And as it took up the whole front page, apart from headline and title, of the world's most widely read newspaper, most of them did not miss it. In the past, women in Britain had been suspected of being traditionally Conservative voters, often in secret even from their husbands. The *Mirror* had rightly seen that the key to the 1945 election was not the servicemen's vote at all: it was the women's vote. They brilliantly exploited this, and Labour had the added windfall of much of the servicemen's vote as well. The combination was overwhelming.

Labour, oddly, did not contest Churchill's own constituency. But the Prime Minister was not to have a 'walk-over'. He was opposed by a local Independent candidate, who believed that every constituency ought to have the benefit of a choice.

The Times, 4 July 1945:

The greatest task confronting the organizers of Mr Churchill's election campaign at Woodford is that of making his adherents realize the importance of recording their votes. The result is such a foregone conclusion that when his Independent opponent, Mr Alexander Hancock, is asked whether he thinks he has a chance of defeating Mr Churchill he shrugs his shoulders and says: 'Could anyone?'

Stephen King-Hall, 5 July 1945:

There can be no doubt that the men responsible for this campaign have not done their duty by the electorate. It is not possible in an election speech to go into all the complexities of a great social or industrial problem, but it is possible to speak in a clear, sensible and unprovocative manner about issues that really interest the people. Surely, the very least that democratic good manners and a respect for the people they wish to serve require of the party leaders is that they should not make misleading insinuations about each other or merely repeat catchphrases and slogans.

Raymond Mortimer, literary critic, letter, 10 July 1945:

I think that Churchill more than anyone else was responsible for the squalid lies in these elections. He started the rot with his talk of Mr Attlee's Gestapo. But I dare say that these Hogarthian spatterings are inseparable from our parliamentary system. The gloomy result is to make sensitive people keep out of politics.

Stephen King-Hall, 19 July 1945:

[The election] might have been a dignified and serious exercise in the arts of citizenship and an example to the world. It was a tawdry affair; a cheap-jack business; a stunt redolent with the odour of the *Daily Express*. For this deplorable state of affairs the Prime Minister must shoulder the chief blame. He set the tone ... [there] were episodes which Mr Churchill will live to regret. The historians will have difficulty in reconciling them with his utterances and behaviour as a war leader.

In the last days of the campaign Churchill grudgingly embarked on a whirlwind, almost presidential, railroad tour of the country. He was received nearly everywhere with multitudinous enthusiasm. The man the crowds cheered was the great war leader – not the leader of a party. Attlee, meanwhile, had been touring the country in a small saloon car driven by his wife.

General Slim, back from Burma, lunched with Churchill at Downing Street. Churchill asked: 'How are your soldiers going to vote?' Slim replied: 'Ninety per cent Labour.' Churchill grunted. 'What about the other ten per cent?' Slim said: 'They won't vote at all.'

Slim knew his men, better than most generals.

While waiting for the people's verdict, Churchill continued to sweat and strain through his three-cornered wrestling match with the Americans and the Russians. All this, of course, was still unknown to the public.

Churchill wrote to Stalin, on the Polish question, on 29 April. 'There is not much comfort in looking into a future where you and the countries you dominate, plus the Communist parties in many other states, are all drawn up on one side, and those who rally to the English-speaking nations and their associates or dominions are on the other,' he said. 'It is quite obvious that their quarrel would tear the world to pieces and that all of us leading men on either side who had anything to do with that would be shamed before history. Even embarking on a long period of suspicions, of abuse and counter-abuse and of opposing policies would be a disaster hampering the great developments of world prosperity for the masses which are attainable only by our trinity.'

Churchill wrote to Truman on 12 May: 'An iron curtain is drawn down upon the front.' He was now almost in despair.

On 27 May he wrote to the Chiefs of Staff: 'You cannot at this moment throw yourselves heartily into the business of demobilization. I had hoped that this would be so, but I am sure that we had better get some solution in the main field of international relations.'

Truman, feeling – with some justification – that much of the trouble was Russian fear of the capitalist and supposedly imperialist West, was anxious to try his luck with Stalin. To placate Churchill, he sent Joseph E. Davies, a former United States Ambassador to Moscow, to London. It was an unfortunate choice; Davies took a confident, strong attitude with Churchill.

On Davies's return to Washington, the President had him to dinner. Davies repeated his conversation with Churchill:

I said that frankly, as I had listened to him inveigh so violently against the threat of Soviet domination and the spread of Communism in Europe, and disclose such a lack of confidence in the professions of good faith in Soviet leadership, I had wondered whether he, the Prime Minister, was now willing to declare to the world that he and Britain had made a mistake in not supporting Hitler, for as I understood him, he was now expressing the doctrine which Hitler and Goebbels had been proclaiming and reiterating for the past four years in an effort to break up allied unity and 'divide and conquer'. Exactly the same conditions which he described and the same deductions were drawn from them as he now appeared to assert. I simply could not bring myself to believe that his considered judgment or expressions would ultimately confirm such an interpretation. He heard me through, and with intentness. He said that he had been under very great pressure, that he had been just thinking out loud, and that the expressions might have been stronger than he had intended to convey.

Leahy, 5 June 1945:

One conclusion that Davies drew was that the Prime Minister, being 'first, last and all the time' a great Englishman, was basically more concerned over preserving England's position in Europe than in preserving peace. This was consistent with our Staff estimate of Churchill's attittude throughout the war.

This impression of Churchill as a greedy, imperialist ogre, straight out of a Chicago *Tribune* cartoon, munching up praiseworthy little Balkan states, was still firmly lodged in the minds of American statesmen and service chiefs.

Truman informed Churchill of his final decision to withdraw American troops from the Russian zone, 12 June 1945:

In consideration of the tripartite agreement as to zones of occupation in Germany, approved by President Roosevelt after long consideration and detailed discussion with you, I am unable to delay the withdrawal of American troops from the Soviet zone in order to use pressure in the settlement of other problems. Advice of the highest reliability is received that the Allied Control Council cannot begin to function until Allied troops withdraw from the Russian Zone. I am also convinced that the Military Government now exercised by the Allied Supreme Commander should, without delay, be terminated and divided between Eisenhower and Montgomery, each to function in the zone occupied by his own troops. I am advised that it would be highly disadvantageous to our relations with the Soviet to postpone action in this matter until our meeting in July.

Two days later, Churchill replied with reluctance and resignation: 'Obviously we are obliged to conform to your decision.' By suggesting one firm line on the Austrian zone, requiring a simultaneous withdrawal of Russian troops, he endeavoured to salvage something from what he regarded as the giving-away of vital bargaining-counters. In the confusion, bewilderment, and disillusion of the early days of peace, there was much confused thinking.

An American commentator, Ralph Ingersoll:

Now, in British eyes, the question of whether we will, if called upon, fight a war against Russia with them is crucial. There are not strong enough adjectives to describe its importance. The British are patently not strong enough to stand up to Russia by themselves and there is no one else but us, now, to win a war for their side. On the whole continent of Europe there are only the remnants of the beaten Fascists and Nazis, exiled Poles and starving Spaniards, for the British to recruit for war on Russia. During the war, the British attempted to manipulate our military policy so that we would fight the war the way they wanted it fought – which was an anti-Russian way. They did not succeed. Now with equal determination, they are attempting to manipulate American foreign policy to link our future irretrievably with theirs. If they succeed, and if there is a third world war, we will surely fight it for them – against the Russians. The British have already made a start. They caused us to break our word to the Russians even before the war was over. We had agreed at Yalta to turn over the Russian sphere in Germany as soon as hostilities were over. Instead, on Churchill's personal persuasion, we rattled a sabre at the Russians across the Elbe for months before we went back to our territory with all the grace of a grudging giver.

Before attending the next conference, at Potsdam, Churchill went to the Basque coast of France near St Jean de Luz for a short holiday. It was the first full holiday, without paperwork and telephones, that he had had since 1940. 'I did not prepare myself for the conference, for I carried so much of it in my head.'

Lord Moran, 8 July 1945:

'I'm very depressed,' said the P.M., walking into the room before luncheon and flopping into an armchair. 'I don't want to do anything. I have no energy. I wonder if it will come back.' The election festers in his mind. 'Nothing,' he says, 'will be decided at the conference at Potsdam. I shall be only half a man until the result of the poll. I shall keep in the background of the conference.'

The Prime Minister was accompanied on holiday by an unfriendly ghost. 'The mystery of the ballot-boxes and their contents had an ugly trick of knocking on the door and peering in at the windows.' Only with brush and palette were all worries dissolved.

Lord Moran, 11 July 1945:

The P.M. disclosed during luncheon that he had reassuring reports from both Ralph Assheton [Chairman of the Conservative Party] and from Max, which confirmed Margesson's earlier estimate of a hundred. I said Max had set his heart on winning this election. The P.M. turned to me and said: 'Do you think his support is a liability or an asset? ... The *Express* has a circulation of between three and four millions.'

Duff Cooper, July 1945:

There is some indignation among the French that de Gaulle should have made no gesture of recognition of the Prime Minister's presence in France. Winston said to me himself 'If he had taken a holiday in Scotland I think I should have sent him a message to say I hoped he was having a good time.' The local General, the same who was at Marrakesh, had wanted to go to Paris and tell de Gaulle, who is of the same promotion as himself, that he ought to come down and pay the P.M. a visit. He had been restrained from doing so.

French and British forces had been fighting in Syria. France, with an unusually frank exhibition of colonialism, had taken over the country with the help of an artillery bombardment on Damascus. French troops had been escorted to the coast by British soldiers. As Churchill said of this sordid episode: 'The less said the better.' Meanwhile, American leaders and writers continued to writhe under the thought of the colonialist Churchill dominating and bullying the small nations, and perhaps even contaminating with his wiles the United States themselves.

EPILOGUE: LOSER   305

Duff Cooper, 16 July 1945:

The Prime Minister had sent a charming message to de Gaulle on leaving French territory, thanking the French Government for having allowed him to come and expressing the hope of seeing de Gaulle before long. These are coals of fire, because during the whole time he was here de Gaulle made no sign of civility whatever.

James F. Byrnes, with shorthand-pad, at Potsdam, July 1945:

On the opening day of the conference, Stalin announced his desire to discuss the question of trusteeship, stating that the Soviet Union 'would like some territory of the defeated states'. His delegation accordingly submitted a paper proposing that the Soviet Union be named trustee of one of the Italian colonies. The Atlantic Charter was a forgotten pledge. When the item was reached on the agenda. Mr Churchill was reluctant even to discuss it. The President immediately made clear our belief that it was a matter for the peace conference and the United Nations but that no bars should be raised against discussion. Thereupon, Mr Churchill delivered an impassioned statement. 'Britain,' he said, 'expects no gain out of this war. We have suffered terrible losses. Our losses have not been so heavy in human life as those of our gallant Soviet Ally. We have come out of the war, however, a great debtor in the world. There is no possibility of our regaining naval equality with the United States. We built only one capital ship during the war and lost ten or twelve. But in spite of the heavy losses we have suffered, we have made no territorial claims – no Königsberg, no Baltic states, nothing. We therefore approach the question of the colonies with complete rectitude...'

Leahy, 18 July 1945:

Stalin opened the first of many discussions on Poland by demanding a transfer to the present Warsaw Government of all property, Army and Navy forces, merchant ships, etc., then under the control of the former Polish Government-in-exile. Churchill replied that there was then no property of any kind in England in the possession of the former Government. The Prime Minister then made a long, valiant defence of the Polish military force which had fought shoulder to shoulder with his troops against Germans and Italians throughout the war. Churchill said British honour was involved, and that he hoped to enable Polish soldiers to return to their homeland, but that any who did not wish to do so could become British citizens and remain under the protection of the British Government. Britain had gone to war because of its promise to Poland, and that was the Poland represented by the exiles in London.

At Potsdam, the decision to use the new atom bomb was made by Truman: Churchill agreed. Neither man, at the time, seems

x

to have been clear as to the nature of the decision. Churchill's agreement was purely formal. There is every likelihood that the United States intended using the bomb, irrespective of Churchill's views. Practice runs had already been made. Development of the two existing bombs had cost billions of dollars. Leahy and Arnold were against immediate use of the bomb. Marshall, Byrnes, and eventually Stimson, were for it. The British were excluded from this debate, which had been in progress for some months.

Brooke, diary, Berlin, 23 July 1945:

He had absorbed all the minor American exaggerations, and, as a result was completely carried away ... It was now no longer necessary for the Russians to come into the Japanese war; the new explosive alone was sufficient to settle the matter. Furthermore we now had something in our hands which would redress the balance with the Russians. The secret of this explosive and the power to use it would completely alter the diplomatic equilibrium ... I tried to crush his over-optimism ... I was trying to dispel his dreams and as usual he did not like it.

The conference was interrupted, to enable Churchill to go to London for the result of the election.

Leahy, 25 to 26 July 1945:

I flew to London on Wednesday afternoon to confer with Ambassador Winant and to visit some friends. The military work at Potsdam had been practically completed with the approval of the final report of the Combined Chiefs of Staff. I spent the evening with some old friends, and the conversation centred on the election, the results of which had been announced that day. I had not discussed this political campaign with Churchill at Potsdam, but members of the British delegation had talked about it very freely. I recalled Churchill saying – I think it was to the President – that he expected the majority of his Conservative Party to be reduced, but that his group would remain in control. However, some members of his staff had told me that there was a very likely prospect that Churchill's party would lose. It was apparent on Thursday that there had been a landslide – against Churchill ... Ambassador Winant was surprised that Churchill's party had been so badly defeated.

Churchill awoke on 26 July, the day the results were to be declared, with misgivings; misgivings which had evidently been latent for many weeks in a politician of such long and intimate experience. He rose earlier than usual. At the old underground war-room at

Storey's Gate, the wall maps had been replaced by constituency charts. Here Churchill, despondent but not shocked, watched progress in the seat from which he had once surveyed strategy and battles. He wore, as if in defiance, the 'siren-suit' in which he had faced the war's worst moments. He had hardly had time to light a cigar before the news came in of the defeats of Harold Macmillan and Brendan Bracken. He received the results without comment. He was joined by Beaverbrook, and a little later by Mrs Churchill, who dashed from Woodford to be with him when a telephone call to Storey's Gate revealed to her the extent of the débâcle. The only cheerful moment of the day was the announcement of the defeat of Beveridge by a Conservative.

Lord Moran, 26 July 1945:

I walked down to the Annexe. The P.M. was with Alan Lascelles; I wrote him a note. He sent out a message that he would like to see me. He was sitting in the small room next to the secretaries', where I had never seen him before, doing nothing. He was lost in a brown study. He looked up. 'Well, you know what has happened?' I spoke of the ingratitude of the people. 'Oh, no,' he answered at once. 'I wouldn't call it that. They have had a very bad time ... I do not feel down at all. I'm not certain that the Conservative Party could have dealt with the labour troubles that are coming. It will be said Max brought me down,' he mused, 'but I shall never say that. He is far harder hit by this result than any of us.' ... He blamed no one. He was very sad as he talked quietly about what had happened. I left him, for I did not want to add to his discomfort by showing my own feelings. For some time I have had a growing disquiet that he has lost touch with the way people are thinking; but I was not prepared for this débâcle. I was so sure that we should return to Berlin that I left my luggage there.

At 6 p.m. Churchill ordered drinks and cigars to be brought in for the war-room staff. He then left – never to return to the war-room – for Buckingham Palace.

George VI, 26 July 1945:

I saw Winston at 7.0 p.m. and it was a very sad meeting. I told him I thought the people were very ungrateful after the way they had been led in the war. He was very calm and said that with the majority the socialists had got over the other parties (153) and with careful management they could remain in power for years. He would be Leader of the Opposition. I asked him if I should send for Mr Attlee to form a government and he agreed. We said goodbye and I thanked him for all his help to me during the five war years.

After seeing Attlee, the King wrote a personal letter to Churchill.

... Your breadth of vision and your grasp of the essential things were a great comfort to me in the darkest days of the war. I like to think that we have never disagreed on any really important matter. For all those things I thank you most sincerely. I feel that your conduct as Prime Minister and Minister of Defence has never been surpassed. You have had many difficulties to deal with both as a politician and as a strategist of war but you have always surmounted them with supreme courage...

Churchill returned to 10 Downing Street (at that time there was still sufficient courtesy in public life not to require a premier to pack his bags and depart in the moment of defeat). His two daughters, Sarah and Mary, changed into their smartest dresses, and they and some young friends, including Robin Maugham, endeavoured to 'cheer up papa'. (Mrs Churchill had retired to bed.) Churchill gave the impression of being gay and unmoved. It was said to him: 'But you won the race, sir.' He replied, 'Yes, and in consequence I've been warned off the turf.'[1]

Sometime during the course of that hectic and agonizing day at Storey's Gate, Churchill had found the spirit and concentration to compose what is perhaps the most gracious acceptance of democratic defeat in the English language: 'The decision of the British people has been recorded in the votes counted today. I have therefore laid down the charge which was placed upon me in darker times. I regret that I have not been permitted to finish the work against Japan ... It only remains for me to express to the British people, for whom I have acted in these perilous years, my profound gratitude for the unflinching, unswerving support which they have given me during my task, and for the many expressions of kindness which they have shown towards their servant.'

Not all Labour men accepted victory with as good a grace as Churchill accepted defeat. That night the victorious Labour Party held an ill-considered victory rally at Central Hall, London. Harold Laski, chairman of the Labour Party, who had been

---

[1] G. Paule, *The War and Colonel Warden*. On the strength of such slim evidence some writers have come forward with the curious idea that Churchill, certain that he would be unable to solve post-war problems, actually contrived to lose the election. Churchill seldom wept unless he was happy.

EPILOGUE: LOSER

coarsely attacked by Churchill and the *Express* during the election said:

At long last we have made possible full friendship with the Soviet Union ... May I, as the temporary head of the Socialist Gestapo, say that not all of us have been treated with generosity in this election ...

Laski, however, was not unready to show his own generosity:

But on this day his rule as Prime Minister draws to a close I want in the name of the British Labour Party, to thank Mr Churchill for the great service he has rendered to this nation.

Others found political maturity less easy. On the night of victory Herbert Morrison issued a statement lacking in the very magnanimity which Churchill himself always prized.

Mr Churchill has joined in the stunts, cultivated the red herrings, and was as good as anybody in inventing irrelevancies, as was shown by his statement about the Gestapo. The truth was that the Prime Minister was a bad leader of his party.

The Times, 27 July 1945:

It [is] necessary to seek the explanation of the Conservative defeat largely in the circumstances and conduct of the election itself. Mr Churchill himself introduced and insisted upon emphasizing the narrower animosities of the party fight. As a result the great national programme was allowed to slip into the background; the Prime Minister's own stature was temporarily diminished.

Daily Telegraph, 27 July 1945:

The result of the election was attributed last night to a revulsion of feeling against the government rather than to an excess of support to the Socialist policy. There was strong evidence of this trend in Mr Churchill's own constituency, Woodford, where his Independent opponent, Mr A. Hancock, polled what was regarded as the remarkable total of 10,488 votes against Mr Churchill's 27,688. Mr Hancock's vote is not thought to be in any sense justified by the degree of support for his policy in the constituency.

Mr Hancock had virtually no policy. His vote was indeed remarkable.

New York Times, 27 July 1945:

In one of the most stunning election surprises in the history of democracy, Great Britain swung to the left today in a landslide that smothered the Conservatives and put Labour into power with a great majority ... The world, which looked to Britain for a guiding trend has had its tremendous answer. Today and tomorrow and for months or years to come, the Left is the dominating power in global politics... The people went about their business as the Churchill Government swiftly disintegrated. Tonight there were fewer persons at Buckingham Palace for the changing of the Government than there usually are for the changing of the guard. In the centre of London, Trafalgar Square, site of many political rallies, was a concrete desert. Leicester Square, where crowds had danced on VE Day, was as sleepy as a village green. The only gathering that could be called a crowd consisted of several dozen persons in Downing Street... Two or three dozen persons were gathered behind the barbed-wire barrier gazing at the door of 10, Downing Street.

It is perhaps the natural reaction of a nation sick of war and the symbols of war and moved above every other impulse by the desire for change. This war weariness goes very deep in Britain, as deep as the desperate longing for the first signs of peace. All through the steadfast struggle with bombs and blackouts and privations, the people have been promised great rewards at the end. They have been promised new homes, security, a far-reaching program of social reform. Now they want to see this dream fulfilled. They have voted for the party pledged to the quickest and fullest realization of the peace program and against the party whose long tenure of power has coincided with the grimmest period in English history. Mr Churchill chose to fight his inept campaign on domestic issues, and it is clear that these issues have decided the election.

Of the Big Three of six months ago, only Stalin remains. Two of the chief actors in the greatest drama have made place for untried men. The two voices that spoke for the democratic hosts as the war moved to its climax will not be heard in the peace conference.

The election left two questions. Would the promises of Labour, for a Utopian reward for the common man and woman, be as easy to fulfil in the coming peace as they had been to make – or would they get lost in the web of difficulties that man seemed to spin around himself as he progressed through history? And would the loss of the two giants of the war prove a disaster – or would it really make much difference at all?

H. V. Kaltenborn, political commentator, N.B.C., New York, 27 July 1945:

There is a feeling here, justified or not, that the Churchill government represented old-time British Imperialism. There is also a feeling, justified or not, that the Labour Party has a more constructive attitude towards the aspirations of the under-privileged people of the world.

EPILOGUE: LOSER   311

Attlee, having disposed of rival claimants to the premiership with brusque efficiency, returned to Potsdam to take Churchill's chair. With him was Ernest Bevin, whose blunt talking to both Russians and Americans caused some consternation among the latter, but was the only ruffle on the settlement which, almost with relief, acknowledged the presence of the former in Poland, the Balkans, and much of central Europe.

Churchill moved into Claridge's Hotel.

Harold Nicolson, diary, 1 August 1945:

Robin Maugham rings me up. He had been round to No. 10 on July 26. Winston was in magnificent form and took his defeat with humour.

B.B.C., Home Service, six o'clock News, 6 August (Bank Holiday), 1945:

Here is the news: President Truman has announced a tremendous achievement by allied scientists. They have produced the atomic bomb. One has already been dropped on a Japanese army base. It alone contained as much explosive power as two-thousand of our great ten-tonners. The President has also foreshadowed the enormous peace-time value of this harnessing of atomic energy. At home, it's been a Bank Holiday of thunderstorms as well as sunshine. A record crowd at Lord's has seen Australia make 265 for 5 wickets.

At the end of the Japanese war, Churchill was not there to speak to the people as he had at the end of the German conflict. Attlee was dry and uninspiring. The people wanted something else. Fortunately, George VI was there – by now the most-loved monarch the nation had known – and his speech, the finest of his career, rose to the occasion, and was not indeed without some Churchillian flavour:

We have our part to play in restoring the shattered fabric of civilization. It is a proud and difficult part, and if you carry on in the years to come as you have done so splendidly in the war, you and your children can look forward to the future, not with fear, but with high hopes of a surer happiness for all. It is to this great task that I call you now, and I know that I shall not call in vain. In the meantime, from the bottom of my heart, I thank my people for all that they have done, not only for themselves but for mankind.

But would the British people ever be quite the same again? Had the war, following so soon on the previous one, sapped them at last of the indefinable spirit for which they were known?

The following day saw the first speeches in the new Parliament. Churchill devoted his speech to a defence of the use of the atom bomb. He did not, as well he might have done, place sole responsibility on President Truman. He said it had avoided the sacrifice of 1,000,000 American and 250,000 British lives. 'This revelation of the secrets of nature, long mercifully withheld from man, should arouse the most solemn reflections in the mind and conscience of every human being capable of comprehension. We must, indeed, pray that these awful agencies will be made to conduce to peace among the nations, and that instead of wreaking measureless havoc upon the entire globe they may become a perennial fountain of world prosperity.' As so often, Churchill could be relied on to put the matter better than anyone else.

On 2 September the Japanese forces formally capitulated to Douglas MacArthur, who finished a splendidly brief address with the words, 'These proceedings are closed.' It was six years less one day since the Admiralty had flashed to its ships at sea, 'Winston is back.'

One in every eighty people in the world in 1939 had been killed in the war.

A British soldier, having served over five years away from home in the Second World War, Woolwich, October 1945:

At last, about four o'clock, the shout from the inner room of 'Next, please' meant me. Inside was a rather surprisingly (perhaps not so surprisingly) old-looking major ... The upshot was that I was given unofficial – indefinitely – extended leave and a further sheaf of papers to take to various other officers. In one of these the clerk said: 'I'll just see if we have your card, Sir.' He went over to an enormous filing cabinet and scrabbled about in an enormous index. Suddenly, with a shock, I saw, *Guest, J.*, 187517, and a few details which I hadn't time to read ... Outside I found Gypsy again, and we walked along the edge of the parade ground. The leaves were blowing from the half-bare trees in the grey evening light. It was slightly misty, autumnal. Beyond the parade ground, on an open stretch of grass, there was a football match going on – the shouts reached us faintly. Nearer at hand were squads of men being marched up and down by N.C.O.s. : 'Pick those feet up ... Left ... Left ... Swing those arms' – and another squad, formed into a square, was learning to present arms. Lights were being switched on in uncurtained rooms ... Gypsy said what we both felt: 'So this is the end. I didn't expect the war to end this way.' It was just petering out.

There was no excitement, no farewells and – I felt then – nothing to look forward to. We had come full circle.

Churchill finished the Second World War not with personal triumph, but with personal defeat on two fronts: as a politician; and as a statesman. He was out of office. His work to secure a peace worthy of the war had failed.

He was beaten at Westminster and at the Big Three conferences.

As the greatest leader in war Britain had ever known, Churchill was successful in the wide context. Britain won the war – although, through no fault of his, the tools were by no means enough for her to do the job alone. But in the context of his own policies, 1945 was in reality less of a great victory for the man himself than an appalling tragedy. For the first part of the war he had struggled desperately to order military events, determined to avoid the strategic indolences of the earlier war: when he had succeeded in thus dominating the professionals, he had often been wrong and they had been right. In the latter part of the war, he alone had seen the dangers of the ensuing peace, and had striven to prepare for them – although he may have underestimated the fears and suspicions of the Russians: his allies had often been wrong and he had been right. But none would heed him. It was a noble victory: and a fateful defeat.

George Bernard Shaw, just after the war:

What I want Churchill to tell us is whether if he had his life to live over again he would waste it in the British House of Commons as it has been wasted by the Party System. He could have done far more as Mayor of one of the provincial cities . . . His real career has been as a soldier and an author.

That summer Churchill, at his home in Kent, read piles of newspapers; pondered on the vast sums offered him for his memoirs; cursed the taxes that would take his earnings from them; begged old colleagues, like Alex, to come again soon when they visited him at his home in Kent. Only weeks before, he could have commanded them to come at his will – could have flown out to Alex, when he needed encouragement, at a few hours notice. Now Alex was too busy to return.

For Winston Churchill the old war had already ended months before MacArthur's signature: he was temporarily demobilized from the new one. He had served his part, and served it the best way he knew.

Lord Moran, 1945:

'It's no use, Charles, pretending I'm not hard hit. I can't school myself to do nothing for the rest of my life. It would have been better to have been killed in an aeroplane, or to have died like Roosevelt. After I left Potsdam, Joe did what he liked ... I get fits of depression. You know how my days were filled; now it has all gone. I go to bed about twelve o'clock. There is nothing to sit up for ... '.

Churchill had taken office in 1939, as an elderly backbench rebel. Now he was leader of the Conservative opposition. It had been a long story.

Sources

Details of publication are given at first mention only. Pages are for the beginning of the extract.

1. PROLOGUE: PROPHET, PART I.

The true tragedy – *The Tragedy of Winston Churchill*, V. W. Germains (Hurst & Blackett, 1931), p. 278.

A few misguided – *The English: Are They Human?*, G. J. Renier (Williams & Norgate, 1931), p. 153.

If indeed – *The Observer*, article, R. Rhodes-James, 1966 (quoted in).

Winston Churchill is trying – *Churchill and Beaverbrook*, K. Young (Eyre & Spottiswoode, 1966), p. 116.

Nobody in British politics – *Churchill by his Contemporaries*, ed. C. Eade (Hutchinson, 1953), p. 121.

He has held – *Churchill and Beaverbrook*, p. 120.

We have heard – *Quotemanship*, ed. P. F. Boller (Southern Methodist University Press, 1967) (quoted in).

I think Winston – *Churchill and Beaverbrook*, p. 121.

War is now inevitable – *John Anderson*, J. W. Wheeler-Bennett (Macmillan, 1962), p. 280.

His greatest love – *Cavalcade*, article, W. J. Brittain, 1936 (quoted, *Time & Tide*, 1965).

Germany is arming – *Step by Step*, W. S. Churchill (Odhams, 1939), p. 13.

Mr Baldwin knew – *The Gathering Storm*, W. S. Churchill (Cassell, 1948), p. 157.

The flotsam – *A Diary With Letters*, T. Jones (Oxford, 1954), p. 324.

In face of such problems – *Life of Neville Chamberlain*, K. Feiling (Macmillan, 1946), p. 347.

We had an excitement – *Diaries and Letters: 1930–1939*, H. Nicolson (Collins, 1966), p. 341.

I fully realize – *Life of Neville Chamberlain*, p. 360.

SOURCES (PAGES 8–18)

I was in Rouen – *The Last Enemy*, R. Hillary (Macmillan, new ed., 1950), p. 33.
At about 11.30 – *Diaries and Letters: 1930–1939*, p. 363.
Personally I believe – *Old Men Forget*, Viscount Norwich (Hart-Davis, 1953), p. 235.
He showed it – *The Thirties* (Collins, new ed., 1967), p. 324.
Our group decide – *Diaries and Letters: 1930–1939*, p. 375.
Mr Churchill's castigation – *Sunday Times*, article, M. Gilbert, 1965 (quoted in).
I am fully aware – *Second World War*, D. Cooper (later Viscount Norwich) (Cape, 1939).
After all – *Churchill by his Contemporaries*, p. 209.
I went to a hush-hush meeting – *Diaries and Letters: 1930–1939*, p. 377.
The country has learnt – *New Statesman & Nation*, article, K. Martin, 7 January 1939.
I was in London – *Two Cheers for Democracy*, E. M. Forster (Arnold, 1951), p. 35.
It is interesting – *How War Came*, R. G. Swing (Nicolson & Watson, 1940), p. 20.
Goering is too free – *New Statesman & Nation*, article, R. H. S. Crossman, 1939.
As always – *Life of Neville Chamberlain*, p. 401.
The nearer we get – *Life of Neville Chamberlain*, p. 406.
Dine with Kenneth – *Diaries and Letters: 1930–1939*, p. 403.
I saw – *Richard Stafford Cripps*, C. Cooke (Hodder, 1957), p. 242.
There was handclapping – *Daily Express*, article, T. Driberg, 24 June 1939.
The *Daily Telegraph* joined in the hue and cry – *Geoffrey Dawson and Our Times*, Sir E. Wrench (Hutchinson, 1955), p. 393.
Why is the definite – *News Chronicle*, article, J. B. Priestley, 10 July 1939.
War today – *Into Battle*, W. S. Churchill (Cassell, 1941), p. 125 (quoted in).
If the international situation – *Old Men Forget*, p. 256.
Now let me call – *How War Came*, p. 118.
Gas Helmets – *The Phoney War*, E. S. Turner (M. Joseph, 1961), p. 55 (quoted in).

Groping along – *The Thirties*, p. 338.
It's a strange face – *The High Cost of Hitler*, J. Gunther (H. Hamilton, 1939), p. 106.
I think I see – *My Political Life*, Vol. III, L. S. Amery (Hutchinson, 1955), p. 326.

2. 1939: NAVAL PERSON

Office-girl – *War Begins at Home*, ed. T. Harrison, C. Madge (Chatto, 1940), p. 39.
There was no bravura – *The Oaken Heart*, M. Allingham (M. Joseph, 1941), p. 84.
It would be unjust – *The Gathering Storm*, p. 322.
On the last Wednesday – *Men, Martyrs, and Mountebanks*, B. Baxter (Hutchinson, 1940), p. 251.
Winston ... Brendan – *The Portsmouth Letters*, W. M. James (Macmillan, 1946), p. 12.
Just heard the B.B.C. – *Berlin Diary*, W. L. Schirer (H. Hamilton, 1941), p. 183.
[He] thought – *Richard Stafford Cripps*, p. 251.
Why should this war – *International Conciliation* (Carnegie Endowment for International Peace, 1939) p. 501 (quoted in).
There is no compromise – *K–H News – Letter Supplement 166A*, 1939.
To say that democracy – *Why England Slept*, J. F. Kennedy (Hutchinson, 1940), p. 234.
As I am a born coward – *New Statesman & Nation*, letter, 1939.
The emergence – *For What Do We Fight?*, Sir N. Angell (H. Hamilton, 1939), p. 2.
His mind is receptive – *Reynolds News*, article, 'Cameronian', 29 October 1940.
I have led – *Proceedings of the International Military Tribunal at Nuremberg* (H.M.S.O., 1946).
I claim that – *Time*, 1939 (quoted in).
Winston has been through – *Nine Troubled Years*, Viscount Templewood (Collins, 1954), p. 410.
In conferences – *Memoirs*, Vol. II, Sir B. H. Liddell Hart (Cassell, 1965), p. 264.

When the fascinating – *Right Honourable Gentlemen*, V. Adams (H. Hamilton, 1939), p. 102.

Two days ago – *The Portsmouth Letters*, p. 30.

The difference between – *The Ironside Diaries*, ed. R. Macleod and D. Kelly (Constable, 1962), p. 208.

One morning very early – *War Reporter*, B. Gray (Hale, 1942), p. 45.

Mr Winston Churchill ... stood – *War Reporter*, p. 44.

Last night to the Admiralty – *Trumpets From the Steep*, Diana Cooper (Hart-Davis, 1960), p. 37.

Mr Churchill also – *Concerning W. S. Churchill*, Sir G. Arthur (Heinemann, 1940), p. 194.

The colonel shook his head – *European Spring*, C. B. Luce (H. Hamilton, 1941), p. 158.

Between these two – *What of the Night?*, V. Adams (H. Hamilton, 1940), p. 120.

I would rather – *Life of Neville Chamberlain*, p. 422.

Winston is back – *The Ironside Diaries*, p. 247.

The whole of northern Norway – *The Gathering Storm*, p. 480.

To the House – *Diaries and Letters: 1939–1945*, H. Nicolson p. 70.

It must mean – *My Political Life*, p. 357.

One of the fallacies – *The Ironside Diaries*, p. 260.

Winston was a bit – *The Ironside Diaries*, p. 282.

One of the costliest – *Chicago Daily News*, 1940.

Winston demurred – *The Ironside Diaries*, p. 287.

The tapers – *Diaries and Letters: 1939–1945*, p. 74.

Most pessimistic – *Stafford Cripps*, E. Estorick (Heinemann, 1949), p. 239.

We are fighting today – *The War That Churchill Waged*, L. Broad (Hutchinson, 1906), p. 26 (quoted in).

One hundred and forty years – *Hansard*, Vol. 360, 1940.

Exception has been taken – *Hansard*, Vol. 360. 1362, 1940.

The P.M., Winston, David – *Life of Lord Halifax*, Earl of Birkenhead (H. Hamilton, 1965), p. 454.

Mr Chamberlain's early resignation – *News Chronicle*, report, 10 May 1940.

Mr Ambassador – *Proceedings of the International Military Tribunal at Nuremberg*, 1946.

SOURCES (PAGES 38–51) 319

L.G. realizes – *Tempestuous Journey*, F. Owen (Hutchinson, 1954), p. 748.
The P.M. told me – *Life of Lord Halifax*, p. 455.
I saw the Prime Minister – *King George VI*, J. W. Wheeler-Bennett (Macmillan, 1958), p. 443.

3. 1940: EMERGENCY PREMIER

The substitution – *Ciano's Diaries*, ed. M. Muggeridge (Heinemann, 1947), p. 248.
Feeling rather lonely – *Geoffrey Dawson and Our Times*, p. 415.
I cannot get – *King George VI*, p. 446.
In regard to Belgium – *News Chronicle*, article, Captain B. H. Liddell Hart, 11 May 1940.
You ask, what is our policy – *Into Battle*, p. 208.
When Chamberlain enters – *Diaries and Letters: 1939–1945*, p. 85.
May I – *Hansard*, Vol. 360. 1510, 1940.
I do not desire – *Hansard*, Vol. 360. 1512, 1940.
I cannot see – *Hansard*, Vol. 360. 1508, 1940.
As the guns – *England's Hour*, V. Brittain (Macmillan, 1941), p. 35.
Quite a good little – *Geoffrey Dawson and Our Times*, p. 419.
The coming of Winston – *A Diary With Letters*, p. 460.
Naturally the appointment – *Dynamic Democracy*, F. Williams (Macmillan, 1941), p. 18.
Mr Winston Churchill arrived – *Private Diaries of Baudouin*, P. Baudouin, ed. Sir C. Petrie (Eyre & Spottiswoode, 1943), p. 32.
Tall, clean-shaven – *Assignment to Catastrophe*, Vol. I, Sir E. L. Spears (Heinemann, 1945), pp. 90, 184.
On May 19 Winston – *England's Hour*, p. 39.
If ever we needed – *The Portsmouth Letters*, p. 15.
No plan – *The Ironside Diaries*, p. 321.
If we have made errors – *Private Papers of Hore-Belisha*, R. J. Minney (Collins, 1960), p. 289.
I was more than horrified – *Trenchard*, A. Boyle (Collins, 1962), p. 718.
Winston completely lost his temper – *Trenchard*, p. 719.
Winston Churchill is sixty-five – *Winston Churchill: The Struggle for Survival*, Lord Moran (Constable, 1966).

Perhaps Winston – *Bridge Into the Future: Letters of Max Plowman* (Dakers, 1944), p. 710.
It is as clear as daylight – *Life of Neville Chamberlain*, p. 446.
No one could say – *War at the Top*, J. Leasor and Sir L. Hollis (M. Joseph, 1959), p. 60.
At 7.30 p.m. – *Private Diaries of Baudouin*, p. 57.
This meeting was affecting – *Private Diaries of Baudouin*, p. 69.
Tens of thousands – *The Observer*, report, 2 June 1940.
This evening Churchill made – *Diary of a Diplomatic Correspondent*, G. Bilainkin (Allen & Unwin, 1942), p. 99.
The full gravity – *News Chronicle*, 5 June 1940.
I have heard Mr Churchill – *This Is London*, E. R. Murrow (Cassell, 1941), p. 136.
Mr Churchill is the unchanging – *The Oaken Heart*, pp. 169, 189.
French Embassy staff – *Diary of a Diplomatic Correspondent*, p. 102.
England had decided – *Private Diaries of Baudouin*, p. 99.
After a short night's sleep – *Private Diaries of Baudouin*, p. 101.
In any case there shall be – *Private Diaries of Baudouin*, p. 104.
My hero, Churchill – *Diary of a Diplomatic Correspondent*, p. 112.
I then heard – *Private Diaries of Baudouin*, p. 115.
At this most fateful – *Their Finest Hour*, W. S. Churchill (Cassell, 1949), p. 183.
The weather – *England's Hour*, p. 60.

4. 1940: INSPIRED LEADER

How I wish Winston – *Diaries and Letters: 1939–1945*, p. 97.
Their confidence – *Strictly Personal*, W. S. Maugham (Heinemann, 1942), p. 130.
The fighting spirit – *Ciano's Diaries*, p. 274.
He does not have – *Benito Mussolini*, C. Hibbert (Longmans, 1962), p. 256.
I was ushered into the presence – *Publish and Be Damned*, H. Cudlipp (Dakers, 1953), p. 144.
Even Churchill's eloquence – *Daily Mirror*, article, 20 June 1940.
Hear curious story – *Diary of a Diplomatic Correspondent*, p. 127.
I said, 'Is there nothing – *Diary of a Diplomatic Correspondent*, p. 104.
I had finished my lunch – *Private Diaries of Baudouin*, p. 156.

De Gaulle seems – *A French Officer's Diary*, D. Barlone (Cambridge, 1942), p. 79.
Great news – *A French Officer's Diary*, p. 102.
I said I feared – *Diary of a Diplomatic Correspondent*, p. 147.
Maisky's and Churchill's – *Diary of a Diplomatic Correspondent*, p. 145.
On Wednesday – *A Diary with Letters*, p. 464.
The war is to go on – *Sunday Pictorial*, article, D. Lloyd George, 1940.
Mr Churchill has just – *The Prime Minister*, P. Paneth (Alliance Press, 1943), p. 61.
The invasion of Britain – *Hitler and his Admirals*, A. Martienssen, (Secker & Warburg, 1948) (quoted in).
The press campaign – *Berlin Diary*, p. 360.
I've proved that – *Inside Hitler's Headquarters*, W. Warlimont, (Weidenfeld & Nicolson, 1964), p. 452.
I was summoned – *The Ironside Diaries*, p. 387.
Just by ourselves – *The Turn of the Tide*, Sir A. Bryant (Collins, 1957), p. 199.
Found Wavell – *The Reckoning*, Earl of Avon (Cassell, 1965), p. 131.
We are in danger – broadcast, C. Lindbergh, 1940.
Kennedy, in morning dress – *Diary of a Diplomatic Correspondent*, p. 180.
Kennedy in good spirits – *Diary of a Diplomatic Correspondent*, p. 195.
Several members of parliament – *News Chronicle*, article, A. J. Cummings, 18 August 1940.
The creation of an army – *Private Papers of Hore-Belisha*, p. 290.
When I look round – *Their Finest Hour*, p. 567.
The local papers – *Berlin Diary*, p. 403.
Told that P.M. – *The Turn of the Tide*, p. 212.
When the barrage – *Outside Information*, N. R. Smith (Macmillan, 1941), p. 41.
Still no move – *The Turn of the Tide*, p. 216.
There are some things – *Secret Session Speeches*, W. S. Churchill (Cassell, 1946), p. 17.
We are very disturbed – *Their Finest Hour*, p. 645.
Remember we shall never – *Their Finest Hour*, p. 453.
In September '38 – *Life of Neville Chamberlain*, p. 457.
He did not have – *The Observer*, article, Sir I. Jacob, 1964.

Cudlipp learned at dinner – *Publish and Be Damned*, p. 150.
I tried to listen – *Outside Information*, p. 142.
Piecing together today – *Berlin Diary*, p. 430.
The Prime Minister makes a statement – *Diaries and Letters: 1939–1945*, p. 125.
He seems better – *Diaries and Letters 1939–1945*, p. 128.
There is occurring – *This is London*, p. 231.
I have not often assisted – *Life of Lord Halifax*, p. 469.
What I am trying – *The Public Papers and Addresses of Franklin D. Roosevelt* (Macmillan, New York, 1941).
Winston was tired – *The Reckoning*, p. 182.
Churchill is the same man – *Churchill by his Contemporaries*, p. 211.
It is the will – *This is Pearl!*, W. Millis (Morrow, 1947) (quoted in).
Whatever might – *Annual Register* (Longmans, 1941), p. 97.

5. 1941: OLD SOLDIER

My dear Prime Minister – *King George VI*, p. 553.
I lunched at Holland House – *A Penguin in the Eyrie*, H. Bolitho (Hutchinson, 1955), p. 66.
If Churchill wins this war – *The Reeling Earth*, S. G. Millin (Faber, 1945), p. 103.
Cassandra – *Publish and Be Damned*, p. 162.
There is a spirit – *Publish and Be Damned*, p. 163.
Winston went into – *Publish and Be Damned*, p. 156.
Number 10 Downing Street – *The White House Papers*, Vol. I, ed. R. Sherwood (Eyre & Spottiswoode, 1943), p. 238.
Dear Mr President – *The White House Papers*, p. 244.
Your 'former Navy person' – *The White House Papers*, p. 257.
I have an interesting day – *The Portsmouth Letters*, p. 99.
His conversation was – *Only the Stars are Neutral*, Q. Reynolds (Cassell, 1942), p. 20.
I am told by the Navy – *The White House Papers*, p. 262.
Whenever we are alone – *The Struggle for Survival*.
Churchill is an obstinate – *The Prime Minister*, p. 54 (quoted in).
It is a tragedy – *The Prime Minister*, p. 54 (quoted in).
All the books – *The Prime Minister*, p. 55 (quoted in).

SOURCES (PAGES 104-17)

Gloriously sunny day – *Off The Record*, C. Graves (Hutchinson, 1946), p. 115.
On Sunday – *Trumpets from the Steep*, p. 73.
Will there be reprisals – *The Reeling Earth*, p. 104.
It is in the interest – *Sunday Times*, article, D. Thompson, 1941.
So long as Winston – *This is London*, p. 266.
The British people – *The Public Papers and Addresses of Franklin D. Roosevelt*.
Now that President Roosevelt – *The Prime Minister*, p. 70 (quoted in).
There is a growing feeling – *Behind the Battle*, J. de Courcy (Eyre & Spottiswoode, 1942), p. 198.
He gave his countrymen – *Time*, article, March 1941.
We can hardly be – *The Business of War*, Sir J. Kennedy and B. Fergusson (Hutchinson, 1957), p. 84.
Detachments – *With Rommel in the Desert*, H. W. Schmidt (Harrap, 1951), p. 9.
Dill asked me – *The Business of War*, p. 90.
We had to wait – *The Turn of the Tide*, p. 253.
Italy's entry – *Testament of Adolf Hitler* (Cassell, 1961; Icon edition), p. 82.
At present, the efforts – *Wavell in the Middle East*, H. Rowan-Robinson (Hutchinson, 1941), p. 227.
The government has not – *The Nature of Modern Warfare*, C. Falls (Cambridge, 1941).
A series of defeats – *But for Britain*, H. Fyfe (Macdonald, 1943), p. 144.
Mr Churchill is not only – *Sunday Times*, article, 27 April 1941.
That the Prime Minister is bearing – *New Statesman & Nation*, article, 3 May 1941.
Mr Churchill's own position – *Sunday Times*, article, 4 May 1941.
Churchill is the most bloodthirsty – *Churchill by his Contemporaries*, p. 212.
In my lifetime – *Hansard*, Vol. 371. 757, 1941.
The army must have – *Hansard*, Vol. 371. 774, 1941.
There never was any apparent need – *Hansard*, Vol. 371, 784, 1941.
We have a very terrible task – *Hansard*, Vol. 371. 881, 1941.

I think that what the right hon. Gentleman is doing – *Private Papers of Hore-Belisha*, p. 291.
On the immediate questions – *New Statesman & Nation*, article, 10 August 1941.
As vividly as at any hour – *The Observer*, article, J. L. Garvin, 1941.
We have been – *Daily Mail*, article, 2 June 1941.
Our first reaction – *Daily Herald*, article, 4 June 1941.
It would be helpful – *Private Papers of Hore-Belisha*, p. 292.
The right hon. member for Devonport – *Private Papers of Hore-Belisha*, p. 293.
The Prime Minister was good – *Orders of the Day*, Earl Winterton (Cassell, 1953), p. 272.
There is a murmuring campaign – *Off the Record*, p. 194.
After the war – *Wavell*, J. Connell (Collins, 1964).
General Wavell was in the public estimation – *Behind the Battle*, p. 174.
Trenchard admires Winston – *Diaries and Letters: 1939–1945*, p. 172.
Molotov professes to believe – *The Scotsman*, article, 22 June 1941.
Hitler went to war – *Ciano's Diaries*, p. 371.
Mr Churchill is a statesman – *The Prime Minister*, p. 60.
[Churchill] had also attacked Dill – *The Business of War*, p. 142.
Everyone is terribly depressed – *Londoner's Life*, C. Graves (Hutchinson, 1942), p. 164.
Everyone is very gloomy – *Londoner's Life*, p. 165.
There was – *Victory From the Air*, 'Auspex' (Bles, 1941), p. 230.
The House of Commons has never listened – *The Observer*, article, 13 July 1941.
Asked to name the likeliest successor – *The Prime Minister*, p. 64 (quoted in).
The man in the street – *The Wounded Don't Cry*, Q. Reynolds (Cassell, 1941), p. 180.
Last Saturday – *Auchinleck*, J. Connell (Cassell, 1959), p. 267.
To say a few words – *The Turn of the Tide*, p. 251.
Our Chiefs of Staff – *The White House Papers*, p. 314.
We dined in high spirits – *Atlantic Meeting*, H. V. Morton (Methuen, 1943), p. 30.
Although Mr Churchill was not always visible – *Atlantic Meeting*, p. 60.

Then the first of the hymns – *Atlantic Meeting*, p. 100.
Considering all the tales – *The Grand Alliance*, W. S. Churchill (Cassell, 1950), p. 386.
I remembered – *Atlantic Meeting*, p. 128.
The Prime Minister came to lunch – *King George VI*, p. 529.
To celebrate this – *The Reckoning*, p. 276.
I found that the only other guest – *The Turn of the Tide*, p. 262.
A fission bomb – *This is Pearl!*
Mussolini was discouraged – *Ciano's Diaries*, p. 396.
He then went on to say – *The Turn of the Tide*, p. 265.
This produced the most awful outburst – *The Turn of the Tide*, p. 298.
England has had – *What They Said at the Time*, ed. K. Freeman (Muller, 1945), p. 376 (quoted in).
He is today – *Sunday Times*, report, 30 November 1941.
Was there perhaps a new race – *The Last Enemy*, p. 174.
Maybe Winston thinks – *Trumpets from the Steep*, p. 121.
I confess – *The Grand Alliance*, p. 522.
A naval attack – *Sunday Times*, article, 7 December 1941.
I can see one plane – *Daily Express*, report, 12 December 1941.
There is absolutely no escape – *Someone Had Blundered*, B. Ash (M. Joseph, 1960).
Raffles Hotel – *Suez to Singapore*, C. Brown (Random House, 1942).
He is a different man – *The Struggle for Survival*.
I am not worried – *With Prejudice*, Lord Tedder (Cassell, 1966), p. 688.

6. 1942: POLITICAL PREY

Then Churchill walked – *Daily Express*, report, 2 January 1942.
Proud of their English heritage – *Ramparts of the Pacific*, H. Aberd (Bodley Head, 1942).
The Australians are extremely angry – *The Goebbels Diaries*, ed. L. P. Lockner (H. Hamilton, 1948).
Talked with the Chief of Staff – *The Stilwell Papers*, J. W. Stilwell, ed. T. H. White (Macdonald, 1949), p. 43.
Where is there one place – *Daily Express*, article, 5 January 1942.
There were, and still are – *Behind the Battle*, p. 216.

Bungling and mismanagement – *Daily Mirror*, article, 12 January 1942.
Meeting of the National Labour Executive – *Diaries and Letters: 1939–1945*, p. 205.
As the train carried – *The Struggle for Survival*.
The question is beginning – *Tribune*, article, 23 January 1942.
The British people's love – *The Prime Minister*, p. 76.
Even though, in my opinion – *The Goebbels Diaries*, p. 9.
How united is – *Hitler's Reich and Churchill's Britain*, S. Laird and W. Graebner (Batsford, 1942), p. 44.
That twaddler – *The Prime Minister*, p. 47.
In the last war – *The Prime Minister*, p. 62.
The whole people – *The Times*, letter, Sir W. Beveridge, 26 January 1942.
We have had a great deal – *Hansard*, Vol. 377. 593, 1942.
I would almost say – *Hansard*, Vol. 377. 620, 1942.
I cannot vote for the government – *Hansard*, Vol. 377. 639, 1942.
There is a growing – *Hansard*, Vol. 377. 756, 1942.
The English are making – *The Goebbels Diaries*, p. 251.
[Churchill] says – *Diaries and Letters: 1939–1945*, p. 208.
Let the Prime Minister choose – *Hansard*, Vol. 377. 870, 1942.
I think that all of us – *Hansard*, Vol. 377. 965, 1942.
The country requires – *Hansard*, Vol. 377. 995, 1942.
Wardlaw-Milne makes – *Diaries and Letters 1939–1945*, p. 208.
As the P.M. prepared – *The Struggle for Survival*.
I have read – *Ciano's Diaries*, p. 428.
We were very much impressed – *Immortal Years*, Sir E. Wrench (Hutchinson, 1945), p. 127.
It would be an excellent thing – *Tribune*, article, 30 January 1942.
It is time the country – *Tribune*, article, 6 February 1942.
Churchill's preparations – *The Goebbels Diaries*, p. 33.
It is indeed a total war – *Tribune*, article, Sir S. Cripps, 6 February 1942.
There seems to be a lack – *Stafford Cripps*, p. 291.
The Fuehrer regards – *The Goebbels Diaries*, p. 42.
I must ask the House – *Hansard*, Vol. 377. 1683, 1942.
I should like to know – *Ciano's Diaries*, p. 436.

SOURCES (PAGES 161-78) 327

The House of Commons – *Chips*, ed. R. Rhodes-James (Weidenfeld & Nicolson, 1967), 19 February 1942.
What once appeared – *Ciano's Diaries*, p. 436.
Ribbentrop prophesies – *Ciano's Diaries*, p. 437.
The way of freedom – *Daily Express*, report, 1942.
It is doubtful – *The Portsmouth Letters*, p. 167.
I have become aware – *Personal Experience*, Lord Casey (Constable, 1962), p. 123.
We are asking that – *Hansard*, Vol. 378. 122, 1942.
When this Prime Minister – *Hansard*, Vol. 378. 143, 1942.
When the downfall of France – *Hansard*, Vol. 378. 158, 1942.
The *Manchester Guardian* now admits – *The Goebbels Diaries*, p. 67.
Mr Chamberlain took the office – *The Times*, report, 26 February 1942; and *War at the Top*, p. 228.
In the United States – *The Goebbels Diaries*, p. 55.
Found P.M. had drafted – *The Turn of the Tide*, p. 338.
Winston is very touchy – *The Business of War*, p. 209.
The debate in England – *The Goebbels Diaries*, p. 2.
Winston dresses night and day – *Trumpets From the Steep*, p. 153.
The last day of the first quarter – *The Turn of the Tide*, p. 342.
The accepted tip – *Daily Mirror*, article, 1942.
The crime – *Hansard*, Vol. 378. 2235, 1942.
The press today – *Hansard*, Vol. 378. 2242, 1942.
I do not like – *Hansard*, Vol. 378. 2248, 1942.
I resent allusions – *Hansard*, Vol. 378. 2284. 2290, 1942.
A very busy day – *The Turn of the Tide*, p. 354.
Back to Downing Street – *The Turn of the Tide*, p. 355.
We are addressed – *Diaries and Letters 1939–1945*, p. 222.
Malcolm had been lunching – *Diaries and Letters: 1939–1945*, p. 223.
Secret Session – *Diaries and Letters 1939–1945*, p. 223.
Ever since my journey – *Daily Express*, article, 23 April 1942.
The winter months in Russia – *Ciano's Diaries*, p. 461.
There is something to be said – *Tribune*, article, 1 May 1942.
The tanks and troops – *Tribune*, article, 8 May 1942.
The Prime Minister made his great – *A Village in Piccadilly*, R. Henrey (Dent, 1942), p. 160.
For three weeks – *Tribune*, article, 15 May 1942.

On Sunday, Churchill – *Tribune*, article, 15 May 1942.
Why Mr Churchill – *Tribune*, letter, 15 May 1942.
Leadership? – *Hansard*, Vol. 380. 141, 1942.
I had a letter – *Hansard*, Vol. 380. 149, 1942.
I said eighteen months ago – *Hansard*,Vol 380. 178, 1942.
I do not think – *Hansard*, Vol. 380. 257, 1942.
If the Prime Minister butts – *Hansard*, Vol. 380. 262, 1942.
No one, not even – *Hansard*, Vol. 380. 288, 1942.
The House is in a bad mood – *Diaries and Letters: 1939–1945*, p. 226.
Churchill's conduct – *The Goebbels Diaries*, p. 166.
History will say – *New York Times*, 21 May 1942.
The Prime Minister's position – *Churchill and Beaverbrook*, p. 246.
The parliamentary debates – *The Business of War*, p. 233.
The Prime Minister has said – *National News-Letter*, No. 307, 1942.
Never was so much withheld – *Lest We Regret*, D. Reed (Cape, 1943), p. 97.
Mr Churchill said – *The Call to Honour: Documents*, C. de Gaulle (Collins, 1955), p. 356.
I found it difficult – *The Turn of the Tide*, p. 414.
These remarks of mine [note 1] – *The Turn of the Tide*, p. 415.
Went to the White House – *The Struggle for Survival*.
Winston's buoyant temperament – *The Struggle for Survival*.
If, whenever we have – *Hansard*, Vol. 391. 312, 1942.
Every man must – *Hansard*, Vol. 381. 389, 1942.
It is a fact that – *Hansard*, Vol. 381. 433, 1942.
To the House – *Diaries and Letters 1939–1945*, p. 231.
It is the duty – *Hansard*, Vol. 381. 534, 1942.
May I, as a serving officer – *Hansard*, Vol. 381. 570, 1942.
I want to ask the Prime Minister – *Hansard*, Vol. 381. 581, 1942.
I ask no favours – *The End of the Beginning*, W. S. Churchill (Cassell, 1943), p. 147.
The second day – *Diaries and Letters 1939–1945*, p. 231.
It is difficult to tell – *New York Times*, report, 4 July 1942.
It is very encouraging – *The Prime Minister*, p. 56.
We must count – *The Prime Minister*, p. 60.
I dine at Pratts – *Diaries and Letters: 1939–1945*, p. 238.
I think Churchill runs England – *Hitler's Reich and Churchill's England*, p. 68.

If the Russians collapse – *Diaries and Letters: 1939–1945*, p. 235.
In a telegram – *The Business of War*, p. 254.
Winston certainly inspires – *The Business of War*, p. 255.
Is it not essential – *Hansard*, Vol. 381. 1404, 1942.
Last night the Prime Minister – *The White House Papers*, p. 616.
Determined at last – *The Turn of the Tide*, p. 475.
Back to the Embassy – *The Turn of the Tide*, p. 477.
I am tired – *The Sound of the Trumpet*, S. G. Millin (Faber, 1947), p. 9.
The P.M. is perfectly nonchalant – *Three Years With Eisenhower*, H. C. Butcher (Heinemann, 1946), p. 64.
The C.G. got to bed – *Three Years With Eisenhower*, p. 68.
In England, now – *The Sound of the Trumpet*, p. 8.
Well played, Churchill – *The Prime Minister*, p. 110.
Brendan Bracken: 'I want you, – *The Struggle for Survival*, p. 72.
If we have reached – *The Prime Minister*, p. 112.
Churchill agrees – *Three Years With Eisenhower*, p. 75.
As Ike and Clark – *Three Years With Eisenhower*, p. 82.
I know Churchill – *The Rommel Papers*, ed. B. H. Liddell Hart (Collins, 1953), p. 290.
Guy Burgess – *Diaries and Letters: 1939–1945*, p. 241.
In my view – *Richard Stafford Cripps*, p. 298.
Many troublesome things – *The Turn of the Tide*, p. 505.
Brendan Bracken came – *The Struggle for Survival*, p. 76.
Aneurin Bevan stands – *Diaries and Letters: 1939–1945*, p. 244.
Churchill remains predominant – *Churchill and Beaverbrook*, p. 249.
You have not convinced – *Richard Stafford Cripps*, p. 300.
Except for three days – *The Sound of the Trumpet*, p. 80.
During the morning – *Memoirs*, Viscount Montgomery (Collins, 1958), p. 132.
Dearest Lu – *The Rommel Papers*, p. 310.
He ... was specially nice – *The Turn of the Tide*, p. 513.
Marshal Smuts asked – *Unity: Documents*, C. de Gaulle (Weidenfeld & Nicolson, 1959), p. 73.
The elimination of Churchill – *Memorandum* for Chiefs of Staff, 1942.
P.M. delighted – *The Turn of the Tide*, p. 516.

Midnight – *Drive: A Chronicle of Patton's Army*, C. Codman (Little, Brown, 1957).
Ministerial changes – *Daily Mail*, article, 23 November 1942.
The dawn of 1943 – *The End of the Beginning*, p. 243.
Cabinet meeting from 5.30 – *The Turn of the Tide*, p. 529.
We finished off – *The Turn of the Tide*, p. 535.
At 6 p.m. – *The Turn of the Tide*, p. 535.
Roosevelt has sent – *The Turn of the Tide*, p. 536.
I had no part – *The End of the Beginning*, p. 255.

7. 1943: PROUD STRATEGIST

One little bomb – *Sunday Dispatch*, 11 January 1943.
[Churchill's] villa was guarded – *The Blast of War*, H. Macmillan (Macmillan, 1967).
General, I have heard – *Crusade in Europe*, D. Eisenhower (Heinemann, 1949), p. 153.
For what it is worth – *As He Saw It*, E. Roosevelt (Duell, Sloan & Pearce, New York, 1946), p. 117.
It has been – *The Turn of the Tide*, p. 555.
When a man tells me – *Ego 6*, J. Agate (Harrap, 1944), p. 133.
The all-round depreciation – *The Portsmouth Letters*, p. 154.
The P.M. sent for me – *The Turn of the Tide*, p. 586.
It is a curious fact – *The Goebbels Diaries*, p. 251.
The Combined Chiefs of Staff – *I Was There*, W. D. Leahy (Gollancz, 1950), p. 190.
With Wavell in command – *The Stilwell Papers*, p. 198.
The P.M., General Marshall – *Three Years With Eisenhower*, p. 266.
Before dinner – *Three Years With Eisenhower*, p. 268.
Some time during the dinner – table conversation – *Three Years With Eisenhower*, p. 270.
Tonight at Chequers – *Personal Experience*, p. 166.
Trees three feet thick – *The War 1939–1945*, ed. D. Flower, J. Reeves (Cassell, 1960), p. 568 (quoted in).
The overheated air – *Bomber Offensive*, Sir A. Harris (Collins, 1947).
Would not the proper answer – *Hansard*, Vol. 395. 338, 1943.
The key to common sense – *Watchwords*, J. F. C. Fuller (Skeffington, 1944), p. 30.
left threequarters or more – *The Times*, report, 29 June 1945.

W.S.C. in Cabinet – *Personal Experience*, p. 167.
Interesting Cabinet – *Personal Experience*, p. 167.
We sat on the veranda – *Three Years With Eisenhower*, p. 317.
He has had some late – *The Business of War*, p. 297.
American troops steamed into – *They Left the Back Door Open*, L. S. B. Shapiro (Jarrolds, 1945), p. 62.
The Quebec conference – *The Turn of the Tide*, p. 722.
The truth was that we – *Eclipse*, A. Moorehead (H. Hamilton, 1945), p. 18.
The Duce will enter – *The Goebbels Diaries*, p. 349.
The invasion and taking – *Once There was a War*, J. Steinbeck (U.S., 1943; Heinemann, 1959), p. 160.
Smuts is not happy – *King George VI*, p. 594.
Returned from leave – *The Business of War*, p. 305.
Concern as a political leader – *Crusade in Europe*, p. 213.
Madame – *The Struggle for Survival*, p. 131.
When I saw the P.M. – *The Struggle for Survival*, p. 136.
Churchill was sixty-nine – *I Was There*, p. 250.
The P.M. has become – *The Struggle for Survival*.
Our luck is out – *The Struggle for Survival*.
I went, on waking – *The Struggle for Survival*.
It was left – *The Struggle for Survival*.
I think we have – *The Struggle for Survival*.
The news that Winston – *The Portsmouth Letters*, p. 245.
That a man of sixty-nine – *Spectator*, article, 31 December 1942.

8. 1944: STRUGGLING STATESMAN

Clemmie and Sarah – *Old Men Forget*, p. 318.
Later, after the review – *Trumpets from the Steep*, p. 180.
This was an exciting day – *Diaries and Letters 1939–1945*, p. 344.
I fear that Winston – *Diaries and Letters 1939–1945*, p. 347.
The Bishop of Chichester – *The Times*, report, 10 February 1944.
Within the past – *And Yet I Like Americans*, J. L. Hodson (Gollancz, 1945), p. 296.
Vast energy – *The Business of War*, p. 323.
When the conference started – *The Business of War*, p. 326.
Within the country – *The Waiting Year*, R. Dimbleby (Hodder, 1944), p. 153.

Be brave! – *The Diary of a Young Girl*, A. Frank (Vallentine, Mitchell, 1952).
Ed. Stettinius told me – *Three Years With Eisenhower*, p. 443.
If you live in Sussex – *Voices From Britain*, P. Smithers (Allen & Unwin, 1947), p. 201.
A fact which Mr Churchill – *New Statesman & Nation*, article, 6 May 1944.
We are not taking – *The Times*, report, 25 May 1944.
The government should tell – *The Times*, report, 25 May 1944.
Mr Churchill made – *The Times*, report, 26 May 1944 (quoted in).
The bulk of Mr Churchill's speech – *New Statesman & Nation*, article, 27 May 1944.
I understand, sir – *Memoirs*, p. 238.
At the end of the inspection – *Eclipse*, p. 80.
I asked W. – *King George VI*, p. 601.
Lascelles came to me – *King George VI*, p. 602.
My dear Winston – *King George VI*, p. 602.
I said – *King George VI*, p. 604.
Ike received a phone call – *Three Years With Eisenhower*, p. 477.
Ismay sent me – *King George VI*, p. 604.
I received a letter – *King George VI*, p. 606.
Some of the men – *From the City, From the Plough*, A. Baron (Cape, 1948).
The Speaker took the chair – *Daily Express*, report, 7 June 1944.
Anthony begins – *Diaries and Letters: 1939–1945*, p. 385.
He is less certain – *The Struggle for Survival*, p. 161.
Experience of the past – *Crusade in Europe*, p. 309.
Ike is in England – *Three Years With Eisenhower*, p. 548.
Ike has been – *Three Years With Eisenhower*, p. 549.
I think I am beginning – *The Struggle for Survival*.
The situation in Europe – *The Stilwell Papers*, p. 289.
We didn't have – *The War 1939–1945*, p. 921 (quoted in).
[Churchill] did his best – *Triumph in the West*, Sir A. Bryant (Collins, 1959), p. 277.
After breakfasting – *The Struggle for Survival*.
When he stands – *The Struggle for Survival*.
Temperamental buoyancy – *New Statesman & Nation*, article, 23 September 1944.

SOURCES (PAGES 255-71)   333

At two minutes past ten – *The Listener*, report, 1944.
Lord Dunglass said – *The Times*, report, 29 September 1944.
When he gets through – *The Initials in the Heart*, L. Whistler (Hart-Davis, 1964), p. 108.
London has been under fire – *New York Times*, report, 1944.
This morning – *The Struggle for Survival*.
I am delighted to learn – *Triumph and Tragedy*, W. S. Churchill (Cassell, 1954), p. 211.
He is at Forward Headquarters – *Triumph in the West*, p. 334.
The very unsatisfactory – *Triumph in the West*, p. 338.
At 12.30 – *Triumph in the West*, p. 340.
Went to see Winston – *Triumph in the West*, p. 345.
During our discussion – *Triumph in the West*, p. 346.
I have just finished – *Triumph in the West*, p. 351.
I was very depressed – *Triumph in the West*, p. 352.
Much as I prefer – *Daily Telegraph*, report, 9 December 1944.
[Tom] Driberg thought – *Daily Telegraph*, report, 9 December 1944.
Our purpose – *Daily Telegraph*, report, 9 December 1944.
Poor old England – *The Dawn of Liberation*, W. S. Churchill (Cassell, 1945), p. 277.
This was the day – *Diaries and Letters: 1939–1945*, p. 416.
Must we be schoolmasters – *Manchester Guardian*, article, 1944.
The British government – *The Times*, article, 1944.
The parliament is definitely to the right – *The White House Papers*, p. 831.
On Saturday night – *The White House Papers*, p. 832.
Either this war – *Tribune*, article, H. G. Wells, 15 December 1944.
Due to the Greek situation – *The White House Papers*, p. 834.
No one knows – *The White House Papers*, p. 835.
As I was waiting – *The Struggle for Survival*, p. 214.
He was ... taken in – *The Blast of War*.

9. 1945 PROPHET, PART II

I am greatly indebted – *Hansard*, Vol. 407. 426, 1945.
Mr A. Bevan said – *The Times*, report, 20 January 1945.
Hopkins arrived – *Three Years With Eisenhower*, p. 634.

SOURCES (PAGES 271-89)

Churchill seems – *Testament of Adolf Hitler*, p. 37.
Dined next to Portal – *The Struggle for Survival*.
All morning the P.M. – *The Struggle for Survival*.
Maisky stated – *Frankly Speaking*, James F. Byrnes (Heinemann, 1947), p. 27.
The peace of the world – *Frankly Speaking*, p. 36.
Winston is puzzled – *The Struggle for Survival*.
Found the P.M. moody – *The Struggle for Survival*.
At this point, Stalin – *Frankly Speaking*, p. 30.
The discussion of the proposal – *Frankly Speaking*, p. 31.
Churchill, I thought – *I Was There*, p. 377.
The P.M. – *The Struggle for Survival*, p. 231.
I am sorry – *Hansard*, Vol. 408. 1267-1676, 1945.
We spent Monday – *Three Years With Eisenhower*, p. 649.
Tonight we dined – *Triumph in the West*, p. 424.
We had a visit – *So Few Got Through*, M. Lindsay (Collins, 1946), p. 220.
When I heard – *The Times*, report, 1945.
As regards the P.M.'s proposals – *Triumph in the West*, p. 430.
As regards the P.M. – *Triumph in the West*, p. 431.
Tomorrow I start off – *Triumph in the West*, p. 432.
After lunch – *Triumph in the West*, p. 432.
We then went into the caravan – *Triumph in the West*, p. 433.
Churchill stood – *Eclipse*, p. 204.
Winston then became a little – *Triumph in the West*, p. 434.
We got into a tank-landing – *Triumph in the West*, p. 437.
He was determined – *Triumph in the West*, p. 440.
May I point out – *Crusade in Europe*, p. 438.
The British blast – *Top Secret*, R. Ingersoll (Partridge, 1946), p. 248.
I woke up – *Diaries and Letters: 1939-1945*, p. 447.
Ike returned – *Three Years With Eisenhower*, p. 673.
Zones of occupation – *I Was There*, p. 410.

10. 1945: VICTOR

Is that you – *Year of Decisions*, H. Truman, (Hodder, 1955), p.92.
German men – *Proceedings of the International Military Tribunal at Nuremberg*, 1946.
The Mission – *The American Treasury*, (Harper, 1955).

This is VE Day – *Daily Telegraph*, report, 8 May 1945.
Our thoughts – *Daily Telegraph*, article, 8 May 1945.
With a mind – *The Times*, 8 May 1945.
Proved itself the strongest – *Victory*, W. S. Churchill (Cassell, 1946), p. 127.
The Prime Minister was given – *The Times*, report, 9 May 1945.
Thus a heroic – *The Listener*, report, 17 May 1945.
On the continent – *Triumph and Tragedy*, W. S. Churchill (Cassell, 1954), p. 672.
Perhaps the best guarantees – *The Listener*, article, 17 May 1945.
It seems years – *The Portsmouth Letters*, p. 280.

11. EPILOGUE: LOSER

At 6.50 p.m. – *The Private Papers of Hore-Belisha*, p. 299.
Parliament is already – *Richard Stafford Cripps*, p. 329.
Mr Churchill is now – *Daily Telegraph*, report, 25 May 1945.
People feel – *Diaries and Letters: 1939–1945*, p. 465.
When Winston Churchill – *Manchester Guardian*, 1945.
I declare to you – *Victory*, p. 189.
Well, it seems – *Daily Mirror*, letter, 7 June 1945.
You know – *Diaries and Letters: 1939–1945*, p. 472.
My husband won't – *Daily Mirror*, letter, 25 June 1945.
Tomorrow the future – *Daily Mirror*, article, 4 July 1945.
The greatest task – *The Times*, report, 4 July 1945.
There can be – *News-Letter*, No. 469, 5 July 1945.
I think that Churchill – *Diaries and Letters: 1939–1945*, p. 475.
[The election] might have been – *News-Letter*, No. 471, 19 July 1945.
There is not much comfort – *Year of Decisions*, p. 112.
I said that frankly – *I Was There*, p. 441.
One conclusion – *I Was There*, p. 442.
In consideration – *Year of Decisions*, p. 226.
Now, in British eyes – *Top Secret*, p. 271.
'I'm very depressed' – *The Struggle for Survival*, p. 257.
The P.M. disclosed – *The Struggle for Survival*, p. 262.
There is some indignation – *Old Men Forget*, p. 356.
The Prime Minister has sent – *Old Men Forget*, p. 357.
On the opening day – *Frankly Speaking*, p. 77.

SOURCES (PAGES 306–14)

Stalin opened – *I Was There*, p. 466.
He had absorbed – *Triumph in the West*, p. 477.
I flew to London – *I Was There*, p. 486.
I walked down – *The Struggle for Survival*, p. 286.
I saw Winston – *King George VI*.
Your breadth of vision – *King George VI*.
The decision of – *Triumph and Tragedy*, p. 584.
At long last – *The Times*, report, 27 July 1945.
Mr Churchill has joined – *The Times*, report, 27 July 1945.
It [is] necessary – *The Times*, article, 27 July 1945.
The result – *Daily Telegraph*, report, 27 July 1945.
In one of the most stunning – *New York Times*, 27 July 1945.
There is a feeling – *The Times*, 27 July 1945 (quoted in).
Robin Maugham rings me – *Diaries and Letters: 1939–1945*, p. 479.
Here is the news – *Sunday Telegraph*, 1945 (quoted in).
We have our part – *The Times*, report, 16 August 1945.
This revelation – *The Times*, report, 17 August 1945.
At last – *Broken Images*, J. Guest (Longmans, 1949), p. 230.
What I want – *Churchill by his Contemporaries*, p. 464.
'It's no use, Charles, – *The Struggle for Survival*, p. 289.

Index

Abdication Crisis, 6, 161
Abyssinia, 110, 112, 139
Acland, Sir Richard, 232, 271
Adams, Vyvyan, 28, 32
Agate, James, 213
Alamein, 207–8, 224
Alanbrooke, Viscount, see Brooke, Sir Alan
Albery, Sir Irving, 170
Alexander, A. V. later Viscount Alexander of Hillsborough, 41, 75
Alexander, Field-Marshal Earl, 211, 273, 280–1, 313; Italian campaign, 197, 199, 204, 206, 229, 247, 249–51, 252, 257; Greek campaign, 268
Alexandria, 173, 203, 241, 277
Algeria, 208, 213, 217–19
Amery, L. S., 4, 7, 10, 11, 19, 34, 45, 135; denounced Chamberlain, 36, 37
Anderson, Sir John, illus. 137; 42, 86, 185, 225
Angell, Sir Norman, 26
Anglo-U.S. relations, 93, 100, 143, 145, 173, 189, 216, 231, 259, 262–73 pass., 280–1
Annual Register, 96
Anzio, 236, 239, 247
Ardennes, 94, 267, 269, 272, 280
Army Bureau of Current Affairs, 153–4
Arnhem, 255
Arnold, General Henry, 212, 250, 306
Astor, Lord, 183
Atlantic Charter, 128–31, 174, 175, 243, 266, 278, 305
Atom Bomb, 133, 211, 253, 305–6, 311–12
Attlee, Clement, illus. 137; in War Cabinet, 41, 45, 87, 204, 222, 295; on victory, 54; meeting with

Mirror on criticism and censorship, 88–9, 99; as poss. P.M., 157, 185; deputy P.M., 161–2; enemy of Beaverbrook, 162; election campaign, 300–1; victory, 307–8; Potsdam, 311; other mentions, 135, 144, 230
Auchinleck, General Sir Claude, 121, 127–8, 133, 167–8, 191, 197, 205
Australia, 84–5, 141–2, 152, 160–1, 163, 186, 205, 207

Baldwin, Stanley, 4, 5, 6, 17, 52, 85, 151, 295
Balkans, Italian invasion, 109–10; Hitler, 112–13; Commons debate, 115–18; *Tribune*, 177; proposed invasion and link-up with Russia, 222; Russia against, 226; Imperialist intentions, 227–9, 302; Teheran conference, 229; Churchill strategy, 249–50; Potsdam, 311
Barham, H.M.S., 156
Battle of Britain, 64, 75, 78, 81, 95, 175, 241

Battle of the River Plate, 28
Baudouin, Paul, 46–8, 53–4, 59–61, 69–71
Baxter, Beverley, 22, 182
Beaverbrook, Lord, illus. 49; on W.S.C., 2, 3, 4, 163, 183, 205; 'splendid isolation', 6; Min. of Aircraft Production, 42, 81, 124, 125; at meeting with French, 59, 61; intimate of W.S.C., 87; meeting with *Mirror*, 88–9; on invasion, 101; Ministry of Supply, 125; supporter of Russia, 132, 162, 174; friend of Bevan, 144; campaign for Second Front,

z

338 INDEX

Beaverbrook, Lord—*cont.*
  145, 172, 183; Nicolson on Beaverbrook, 146; refuted, 184; Cripps offered Min. of Supply, 148; as poss. P.M., 157; Cripps on B——, 157; W.S.C. on duties of B——, 158; Min. of Production, 159; resigned and went to U.S., 162; protests loyalty to W.S.C., 174; supported Munich, 183; supported W.S.C. as Min. of Defence, 188; campaign for General Election, 196–7; in Marrakesh with W.S.C., 232–4; election campaign, 296–8, 304, 307; control of *Express* policy, 299
Belgium, 29, 38, 41, 53, 252, 257
Bellenger, Fred, M.P., 56, 192
Benghazi, 156
Bevan, Aneurin, illus. 136; expelled from Labour Party, 15; *Tribune*, 144; critic of W.S.C., 151–2, 158–60, 204–5, 270–1, 282–3; *Daily Mirror*, 171; vote of censure debate, 190, 192; Greek debate, 261
Beveridge, Sir William, 151, 279, 307
Beveridge Report, 214, 254–5
Bevin, Ernest, War Cabinet, 42, 87, 125, 222, 295; influence of Labour Party and Bevin, 45–6; W.S.C. supporter, 126, 145, 267; on Press criticism, 145, 170; possible P.M., 157, 185; Beaverbrook, 125, 162, 183; Election, 297; Foreign Sec. at Potsdam, 311
Big Three conferences, 228, 266, 295, 310, 313; Teheran, 228; Yalta, 272–8; Potsdam, 305–6
Billotte, General G. H., 50
Birkenhead, Lord, 132
Bismarck (German ship), 119
Blackett, Professor, P. M. S., 168
Blitz, 81–3, 87, 91, 95, 175, 205
Bodensee Rundschau, 150
Bolitho, Hector, 97
Bomber Command, 168–9, 202, 221, 241, 282–3
Bombing Policy, 81, 168–9, 193, 198, 202, 215, 219–21, 237, 282–4
Bonham-Carter, Lady Violet, 21, 37

Boothby, Robert, 7, 10, 11, 67, 126, 155, 190
Bracken, Brendan, illus. 137, 3, 7, 10, 23, 99, 127, 201–2, 204, 296, 307
Bradley, General, 240, 258–60, 286–7
Brest, 160, 165
Brooke, Sir Alan (later Lord Alanbrooke) replaces Gen. Ironside, 76; German invasion, 82–3, 89; C.I.G.S., 134, 209; W.S.C., 77, 128, 132–3, 135, 167, 209; poss. loss of war, 169; W.S.C./U.S. strategy, 172, 186–7, 195–6, 212, 217; Africa campaign, 199, 207–8; strategy, 210, 215; Casablanca, 212; Quebec, 252–3; not to lead Allied invasion, 223–4; Montgomery–Eisenhower controversy, 257–61, 286; W.S.C. visit to crossing of Rhine, 284–6; victory lunch, 291; on A-bomb, 306; other mentions, extracts, 111, 197, 206, 214, 245
Brown, W. J., 279–80
Burgess, Guy, 203
Burma, 188, 209, 216, 222–3, 238, 252, 254
Butcher, Captain H. C., 200–3, 217–18, 222, 240–1, 250, 271, 280–1, 287
Butler, Harold, 102
Butler, R. A., 221, 237
Byrnes, James F., 273–6, 305, 306

Cabinet War Room, 52, 306–7
Cairo, 163, 197, 200, 203, 213, 227, 229
Canadian Troops, 58, 207, 224, 252
Canning, George, 8
Caretaker Government, 296
Cartland, Ronald, 10
Casablanca conference, 210, 211, 212, 240
Casey, R. G., 163–4, 206, 211, 219, 221, 238
Cassandra (Connor, William), 88, 98, 146, 171
Chamberlain, Austen, 3

INDEX

Chamberlain, Neville, Prime Minister, 6, 17, 26, 27; rearmament, 7, 8, 12, 22, 52; Munich agreement, 9, 10, 13; on Churchill, 14; joins War Cabinet, 18, 21; appeasement, 15–16; war declared, 20; on bombing, 168; aims of war, 25; dismissed Hore-Belisha, 29; successor as P.M., 32, 36–9; illness, 33; Norway, 35; denounced by Amery, 36; fall, 36–40, 149; in War Cabinet, 41, 45; Lloyd George, 53; W.S.C. on Chamberlain, 67; pressure for removal, 67–8; retired from Gov., 85; death, 86; other mentions, 43, 44, 61, 69, 88, 126, 151, 175, 255

Channon, Sir Henry, 161

Chartwell, 5, 313

Chatfield, Admiral of the Fleet, Lord, 166

Cherwell, Lord (formerly Frederick Lindemann) 132, 168–9

Chichester, Bishop of (G. K. A. Bell), 236

Chigwell Unionist Assoc., 11

China, 136, 138, 161, 216, 227, 238, 252

Churchill,
  Mrs., C., 28, 230, 232, 234, 307, 308
  Mary, 28, 308
  Randolph, 155
  Sarah, 232, 308, illus. 137

Churchill, Winston, illus. 32, 33, 137;
  as inventor, 29, 33, 248
  as orator, 31, 91, 118, 194
  as soldier, 251
  as dictator, 194, 201, 213, 265–6
  as political outcast, 1–3, 6, 45
  as imperialist, 227–9, 238, 241–3, 265, 267, 302, 304
  on bombing, 81
  on the Army, 75–7
  on the House of Commons, 194
  on India, 7
  on rearmament, 12
  on Kennedy's defeatism, 14–15
  on making speeches to the House, 271
  on France, 273
  on post-war Europe, 250, 255, 268–70, 293
  on his democratic tenure of office, 277

Churchill, Winston, attacks defence policy, 3; joins Chamberlain's cabinet, 18; appointed P.M., 39; Press conferences, 127; criticism: Pacific, 138; Greece, 112–20; see also House of Commons; disinterest in domestic matters, 150, 203, 214, 221; pneumonia, 229–31; relations with U.S., 212, 262–3, 266, 269; Iron curtain, 301; Anti-Russian, 249, 302; General Election, 295–8, 300; defeat, 306–8; speech on Stalin's requests at Potsdam, 305; defends use of A-bomb, 312; evaluation, 95, 313; 'to have died like Roosevelt', 314; see also: Minister of Defence Speeches; Anglo–U.S. relations

Ciano, Count, 40, 66, 123, 133, 156, 161, 174, 233

Clark, General, 200, 202–3

Clark, Kenneth, 14

Clark-Kerr, Sir Archibald, 210

Cocks, Seymour, 261

Commonwealth Party, 232

Connor, William, see Cassandra

Cooper, Lady Diana, illus. 48; 30–1, 105, 127, 136, 169, 234–5

Cooper, Duff, illus. 48; Hitler influence over Chamberlain, 9; Munich debate, 10; resignation, 11; anti-Chamberlain group, 12; rearmament, 13; letter to Baldwin on becoming P.M., 17; attacks Lloyd George, 24; Norway debate, 36; in War Cabinet, 42, 45, 126–7; sent to Far East, 127, 136; in Marrakesh, 232, 233–4; de Gaulle, 304–5

Cranborne, Lord, 8, 10, 237

Crete, 112–14, 119, 175, 177, 181, 188, 194, 226

Cripps, Sir Stafford, illus. 137; expelled from Labour Party, 15; meeting with W.S.C., 15, 24; calls

Cripps, Sir Stafford—*cont.*
for coalition, 35–6, 43; ambassador to Moscow, 45; poss. P.M., 146, 157, 184; return from Moscow to Parl., 147–8, 157; critic, 158; friend of Russia, 147, 157, 159; Goebbels, 160; Leader of House, 161, 181–2, 191; War Cabinet, 161, 162; mission to India, 163; returns, 173; debate on progress of war, 181–2; increasing opposition to W.S.C., 200, 203, 204–5; resigned from War Cabinet, 208; Min. of Aircraft Prod., 208–9; critic of area bombing, 220; in coalition, 222; election speech, 296
Crossley, Anthony, 10
Crossman, R. H. S., 14, 283
Cudlipp, Hugh, 88, 171
Cudlipp, Percy, 126
Cummings, A. J., 80
Cunningham, Admiral Sir Andrew, 128, 260, 291
Cunningham Reid, Capt., A., 192
Current History and Forum, 125
Curtin, John, 142
Czechoslovakia, 7, 8, 9, 14

D-Day, 245–7
Dagens Nyheter, 148
Daily Express, W.S.C. in U.S.A., 141, campaign for Second Front, 144, 160, 183, 188; support for W.S.C., 145, 174, 188; General Election, 196, 299, 304, 309; report of announcement of D-Day in House, 246–7
Daily Herald, 46, 114, 119, 126, 129, 145
Daily Mail, 36, 104, 114, 119, 126,
Daily Mirror, supported W.S.C., 66–7; potential enemy, 68; critic of war effort, 88; poss. censorship of criticism, 88–9, 98–9, 146, 170–1; attack on Generals, 170; Bevan, 171; Election campaign, 298–300
Daily Sketch, 145
Daily Telegraph, 16, 291, 309
Daily Worker, 170
Dakar, 84–5, 119, 188
Damaskinos, Archbishop, 268

Daniel, Raymond, 193
Dardanelles, 1, 161, 195, 222, 227, 236
Darlan, Admiral, 69, 70
Das Reich, 103, 193
Davies, Clement, 165, 189, 192
Davies, Joseph E., 302
Dawson, Geoffrey, 16, 45
Defence, Minister of, Churchill as, 32–4, 42, 75–6, 95–6, 109, 119, 134, 135, 140, 141, 146–7, 154, 159, 160, 165, 166, 176, 180, 183, 184, 188, 191, 291, 308
De Gaulle, General Charles, illus. 136; proposed union of France and England, 62–3; in England, 71; Dakar, 84; support for England, 135; resistance movement, 207; relations with W.S.C., 185–6, 206–7, 218–19, 232–4, 253, 304–5; on D-Day, 248; refuses to meet Roosevelt, 277; French troops in Stuttgart, 287
De Guingand, Maj.-Gen. Sir Francis, 206, 281
De la Bere, Sir Rupert, 196–7
Denmark, 288, 289
Derby, Lord, 16
De Valera, President Eamonn, 138–9, 290, 291
Dieppe, 199, 207
Dill, General Sir John, 76, 109–11, 120–1, 123–4, 127, 134, 224
Dimbleby, Richard, 240
Doenitz, Admiral von, 290
Douglas-Home, Sir Alec, see Lord Dunglass
Dowding, Air Chief Marshal Lord, 48
Dresden raid, 282–4
Driberg, Tom, 16, 262
Duncan, Sir Andrew, 56, 87
Dunglass, Lord (later Sir Alec Douglas-Home), 242–3, 255–6, 277–9, 293
Dunkerque (French cruiser), 70, 71
Dunkirk, 53–6, 68, 77, 114, 124, 176, 185
Dutch East Indies, 136, 167, 175

INDEX 341

Eden, Anthony, illus. 48; resigned as Foreign Sec., 6, 13; rebel group, 7, 11, 15, 37; abstained on Munich, 10; Hitler, 11; in War Cabinet, 41, 45; at C.O.S. meetings, etc., 51, 76, 77, 111, 127, 135, 202, 210, 268; Greek campaign, 109–10; 'dark days' of war, 94; criticisms of war effort, 98; on W.S.C., 132; poss. P.M., 157, 185, 195; de Gaulle, 248; W.S.C. on delivering speech to House, 271; Greek debate, 262–3; Polish elections, 279

Education Act 1944, 221–2, 237

Egypt, 110, 111, 123–4, 188, 193, 199, 203, 277

Eighth Army, 197, 199, 213, 235

Eisenhower, General, Commander U.S. landing in Africa, 200, 202; Casablanca: Second Front, 212; W.S.C. on Med. campaign, 217; as committee man, 222; European strategy, 222; appointed Supreme Cdr. Allied invasion, 224; against S. France invasion plan, 227; took up Command, 235; visits troops, 240; de Gaulle, 248; S. France landings, 249–50; takes command of forces in France, 252; Montgomery questions command, 257–61; Ardennes, 267, 280; in Germany, 286; Berlin disagreement, 286–7; German zones, 288; Allied mission completed, 290; zone control, 303

Elizabeth I, speech at Tilbury, 57

Elliot, Walter, 192

Emrys-Evans, P. V., 10

Epping Conservative Association, 11

Europe, Churchill on collective security, 21; Goebbels 214, and Hitler on co-operation, 271–2; self-determination, 242–3, 255; post-war, 258, 264, 266, 267; British 'power politics', 268, 269, 270

Evening Standard, 64, 126, 145, 175, 299

Falls, Cyril, 113

Far East, 143, 152, 154, 184, 191

Flying Bombs, 247–8, 257

Foot, Michael, 126, 144, 170, 183

Forster, E. M., 13

France, (see also Second Front), German invasion, 46–50, 110, 166, 176, 188, 270; Armistice debate, 59–64, 68; proposed union with England, 62–3; scuttling of Fleet, 69–72; de Gaulle on France, 185–6; French resistance, 207; operation 'Overlord', 224, 226, 235; post-war govt., 242; Anvil U.S. landings in South supported by French troops, 249–51; U.S. forces enter Paris, 251; W.S.C. on France, 273; not invited to Yalta, 277; in Syria, 110, 304

Francis-Williams, Lord, 46

Frank, Anne, 240

Free Europe, 123

French West Africa, 196, 202, 208

Fuller, J. F. C., 221

Gallacher, William, 118, 261

Gallipoli, 227, see also Dardanelles

Gamelin, General, 30, 47, 176

Gandhi, 3

Garvin, J. L., 73, 118, 183

General Election, 196–7, 269, 295–301, 306–10

George, VI King, illus. 33; Chamberlain resignation, 39–40; message to W.S.C., 97; on W.S.C. talks with F.D.R., 131; interview with Smuts, 226; prevented W.S.C. sailing with fleet on D-Day, 245; VE Day, 291; Election results, 307; letter to W.S.C., 308; VJ Day, 311

Gerbrandy, Professor, 123

Germany, rearmament, 5; as aggressor, 13; peace overtures, 73; enters Italy, 224; Allied invasion strategy, 260, and disagreement, 286–7; E. territory to Poland, 266; zoned, 280; race for Berlin, 280, 284, 286; crossing of the Rhine, 281, 284–6; Stuttgart taken by French, 287; concentration camps, 288; meeting

Germany,—*cont.*
on the Elbe, 288; surrender negotiations, 289; last-ditch battle in Berlin, 290; broadcast to German people, 293; withdrawal U.S. troops from Russian zone, 302-3
Gestapo, 14; 'Socialist Gestapo', 297, 300, 309
Giraud, General Henri, 218
Gneisenau (German ship), 160, 165, 188
Godesberg Ultimatum, 10
Goebbels, as propagandist, 103-4, 240; on Churchill, 103; on Australia, 143; G.B. govt. crisis, 148, 182; G.B. war aims, 154; East Asia, 159; morale in G.B., 166; U.S. criticism of W.S.C., 167; G.B. strategy, 168; European co-operation, 214; Mussolini, 224
Goering, Hermann, 5, 14, 30, 81
Gort, Lord, 16, 30, 50, 185
Graebner, Walter, 148-50, 194
Graf Spee, 28
Greece, Italian invasion, 109; decision on British aid, 109; German and British troops enter Greece, 110; campaign disaster, 112, 114, 119, 181, 188; Balkan debate, 115-18; *Tribune*, 177, political unrest, 241-2; Commons debate on Greece, 261-3; U.S. interest, 262, 264-7; British troops, 262; in Athens, 264, 265; compromise agreement, 267-8; W.S.C. visit, 277; other mentions, 100-1, 257, 271
Greenwood, Arthur, 26, 41, 44, 45, 163, 255, 278
Griffiths, James, 165
Grigg, Edward, 3, 7
Grigg, Sir James, 163, 246
Gunther, John, 18

Haig, Earl, 75, 120, 134
Halifax, Lord, Foreign Sec., 6; Grand alliance, 7; poss. P.M., 17, 32, 35-40; critic of Norwegian campaign, 34; in War Cabinet, 41, 45; mission to France, 53, 59, 61; recommended W.S.C. as leader of Conservative Party, 86; replaced by Eden—sent as ambassador to U.S., 93-4; Greek campaign, 264-5
Hamburg raid, 219-20
Hankey, Lord, 167
Harding, Field-Marshal Lord, 112
Harriman, Averell, 198
Harris, Sir Arthur, 'Bomber', 168-9, 219-21, 241, 283
Harris, Sir Percy, 154
Hart, Sir B. H. Liddell, 12, 27, 36, 41
'Haw-Haw, Lord,' 89
Herbert, A. P., 152, 171, 182
Herbert, Sidney, 10
Hewitt, Admiral, 264-5
Hillary, Richard, 8, 136
Himmler, 289-90
Hitler, Adolf, Chancellor, 3; seized Austria and Czechoslovakia, 8; Munich agreement, 9, 13; invasion of Poland, 18; French campaign, 54; 'in London', 65; failure of Battle of Britain, 81; peace with G.B. before attack on Russia, 90; Lend-lease signed, 107; fighting on two fronts, 122; meeting with Mussolini, 174; attempt on life, 248; suicide, 290
Speeches: 11, 24, 26-7, 74, 75, 95, 96; on Italian role in war, 112-13; on Churchill, 115, 150; Europe, 271-2
Hoare, Sir Samuel (1st Lord Templewood), 27, 73, 143
Hobart, Percy, 76
Holland, 38, 46
Hollis, General Sir Leslie, 52
Holt, R. D., 107-8
Home Defence (Security) Executive, 79
Hong Kong, 17, 139-40, 185, 188
Hood, H.M.S., 118, 188
Hopkins, Harry, 99-103, 127-9, 172-3, 195, 212, 264-7, 271
Hore-Belisha, Leslie, 16, 27-8; War Minister, 21; dismissal, 29; critic of organization of war effort, 80-1, 116-20, 124, 151, 155, 176, 181,

INDEX 343

Hore-Belisha—*cont.*
182; on Press censorship, 171; censure debate, 191-2; in caretaker govt., 295-6
Horobin, T. L., 170
House of Commons Debates:
on Munich, 10-11
on Norway, 36-7
on Churchill coalition, 42-4
on Secret sessions, 68, 83, 173
on scuttling French Fleet, 72
on Home Defence (Security) Executive, 79-80
on Balkans, 115-18
on production, 124-5
on progress of war, 80, 152-6, 161, 180-2, 255
on Singapore, 164
on Press censorship, 170-1
on vote of censure, 188-92
on Greece, 261-3, 269-71
on Russia-Poland, 264-6
on Yalta, 277
House of Commons, White Paper on concentration camps, 288; stood in memory of Jews, 288; receives Churchill on V-Day, 292
House of Lords, debate on progress of war, 166
Hull, Cordell, 61, 168
Huxley, Julian, 14

Ibn Saud of Arabia, 277
Iceland, 131
Illustrious, H.M.S., 101
Imperialism, British aims in: Med. and Balkans, 215, 227-9, 267; India, 238; Greece, 241-2; Italy, 262; Asia, 267; general, 269; Churchill refutes charge, 270
India, W.S.C. on India, 2-3, 7, 161; Wavell C-in-C, 121, 122; reaction to Vote of Confidence, 156; Cripps in India, 163; campaign, 172, 222-3, 252; U.S. criticism of campaign and imperialist intent, 238; famine, 218
Indian Ocean, 172, 173, 218
Indo-China, 136

Ingersoll, Ralph, 303
Inskip, Sir Thomas, 17, 67
Invasion of England, 65, 74, 82-4, 89-91, 101, 109, 123, 132, 207, 215
Iraq, 110
Ironside, General Sir Edmund, on Churchill, 29, 33; decorated by French, 30; on Norway, 34-5; on French campaign, 50; replaced, 76
Ismay, General, Hastings, 48, 102, 194, 217, 245, 260
Isolationism, 106-8
Italy, aggressor, 13; negotiations with, 53; invaded France, 58; Desert campaign, 92-3; invaded Greece, 109; Hitler on failure of Italian role, 112-13, 272; ships destroyed in Med., 133; plan to push Italy out of war, 210, 215; invasion plan, 212, 215, 216, 217; Quebec conf., 223-4; Allied landing and Armistice, Germans enter, 224; declared war on Germany, 226; landing at Anzio, 236; 'Overlord', 239; post-war govt., 242; allies enter Rome, 245, 247; Churchill visit, 249-51; Sforza, 262-3; Alexander advance, 287

James, Admiral Sir W. M., 23, 164, 213, 294
Japan, 17, 18, Pearl Harbor, 137, 175; sank British ships, 137-8; invasion of Malaya, 137, 139; W.S.C. underestimation of Japan, 127, 136, 138, 161; Philippines, 139, 143; brought U.S. into war, 140; threat to Australia, 142-3; British failure in Far East and need for Anglo-U.S. command, 143; debate in House, 155, 156; Dutch East Indies, 167; threat to India, 172; *Tribune* attack on W.S.C., 175; atrocities, 207; domination in Pacific broken, 210; U.S. strategy, 212 and criticism, 216; ultimate defeat, 215-16, 254; value of Burma campaign, 252; remoteness of Japan, 293; A-bomb, 306, 311; capitulation, 312
Jews, 193, 207, 288

Jodl, General, 291
Jones, Dr Thomas, 45, 72-3
Jowitt, Lord, 296

Kaltenborn, H. V., 310
Keitel, General, 75
Kelmsley, Lord, 104
Kennedy, Maj.-Gen. Sir John, 109-11, 113, 123, 168, 184, 195, 196, 222-3, 226, 238-9
Kennedy, John F., 25, 79
Kennedy, Joseph, 14-15, 16, 68-9, 78-9, 100, 101, 104, 108
Keyes, Sir Roger, 10, 36, 189, 192
Keynes, Maynard, 294
King, Cecil, 66, 88-9, 98-9
King, Admiral (U.S. Navy), 212, 250, 252, 264
King-Hall, Stephen, 25, 146, 166, 184, 300-1

Labour Party, refusal to serve under Chamberlain, 32, 149; dislike of W.S.C., 3; Cripps and Churchill, 15; coalition, 39, 221-2; conference, 38; value, 45; welcome to W.S.C., 72, 236; critics of W.S.C., 81, 151, 194; cabinet members against *Herald* criticism, 145; Greenwood, 163; tribute to W.S.C., 180; Beveridge report, 214; General Election, 295-300; victory, 308-9; future, 310
Laird, Stephen, 148-50, 194
Lang, Archbishop, 237
Laski, Harold, 79, 308-9
Lattre de Tassigny, General de, 232
Laval, Pierre, 69, 70
Law, Richard, 7, 10, 67
Lawrence, T. E., 76, 102, 122
League of Nations, 242, 243
Leahy, Admiral, 215, 228, 265, 276-7, 302, 305, 306
Leathers, Lord, 211
Leigh-Mallory, Air Chief Marshal, Sir Trafford, 240
Lend-Lease, 93-4, 100, 107, 128, 131, 252

Ley, Dr Robert, 103
Libya, 117, 122, 124, 135, 146, 154, 168, 175, 188, 213
Lindbergh, Charles, 78, 107
Lindemann, Frederick (later Lord Cherwell), 132, 168-9
Lindsey, Kenneth, 146
Lippmann, Walter, 3, 14
Listener, 294
Lloyd George, peace move, 24, 73; Halifax for P.M., 35; attack on govt., 37; as poss. P.M., 38, 183, 194; speech to W.S.C. on becoming P.M., 43; refused Cabinet post, 53, 205; on Army, 76; declined U.S. ambassadorship, 93; as First War P.M., 73, 114, 120, 132, 134, 165, 182, 189, 213; speech on production, 117-18; congratulates W.S.C. on D-Day, 247; beginnings of Welfare State, 296
Lloyd, Lord, 8
London conference, 196
Longhurst, Henry, 171
Lothian, Lord, 27, 93
Low, David, 64
Luce, Clare Booth, 31, 37
Luce, Henry, 37, 183
Lyttleton, Oliver, 87, 114, 122, 163, 211

MacArthur, General Douglas, 143, 167, 252, 257, 312, 313
Macaulay, Rose, 170
Macdonald, Malcolm, 173
Macdonald, Ramsey, 4
Macmillan, Harold, 8, 10, 11, 32, 67, 124, 162, 211, 212, 268, 307
Maginot Line, 176, 190, 204
Maisky, Ivan, 72, 145, 273-4
Malaya, 137, 139, 142, 155, 165, 175, 223
Malta, 133, 226
Manchester Guardian, 148, 166, 263-4, 297
Margesson, David, 94, 159, 163, 304
Markham, Frank, 146
Marlborough, Duke of, 4, 5, 32, 125, 177, 179, 187

INDEX

Marshall, George, General, 143, 172; Second Front, 195; relations with F.D.R., 186–7; on invasion of Italy, 215; on Pacific war, 212; visits Algiers, 217; Quebec, 222; as leader of Allied landings, 224, 226; defer to Eisenhower on Europe, 250; Eisenhower–Montgomery controversy, 260; race to Berlin, 286–7; A-bomb, 306
Martel, Lt.-Gen., G. le Q., 175
Martin, J. H., 165
Martin, Kingsley, 12
Maugham, Lord, 11
Robin, 308, 311
Maugham, Somerset, 65
Maxton, James, 44, 155
McGovern, John, 181, 189
Mediterranean, danger to shipping, 91, 101; campaign, 132–3, 190; 'soft underbelly of France', 198; defeat Italy thro' Med., 210, 217, 226; effect on India, 218; British interests, 215, 218, 227
Melbourne Herald, 142
Menzies, Robert, 84–5, 113, 142
Middle East, 109, 114, 121–3, 128, 136, 152, 163–4, 167, 172, 173, 197, 206, 208, 226
Military Co-ordination Committee, 5, 17, 32–4
Ministry of Production, 125, 153, 157, 159, 162, 163
Ministry of Supply, 46, 125, 157, 158
Molotov, 122, 198
Montgomery, Field-Marshal Viscount, 8th Army, 197, 199; offensive delay, 203; opens, 205–6; Alamein, 207–8; Tobruk, 208; 'Overlord', 235, 239, 243; visits troops, 240, 244–5; command U.S. forces, 249, Eisenhower takes over, 252; questions Eisenhower's command, 257–61; Ardennes, 267; plan to race to Berlin disagreement with U.S., 286; reaches Baltic, 288; accepted surrender of German forces, 290; zone control, 303
Moorehead, Alan, 224, 244

Moran, Lord, formerly Sir Charles Wilson, doctor to W.S.C., 51–2, 103; effect of U.S. entry on W.S.C., 139; criticism of W.S.C., 147, 156, 201–2; and need for a victory, 167, 204; fall of Tobruk, 187; China, 227; W.S.C. pneumonia, 229–30, 234; W.S.C. on Anzio, 236; W.S.C. on Russian threat, 249; on Italy and Alexander, 251; F.D.R. illness, 275; General Election, 304, 307; 'There is nothing to sit up for', 314; other extracts: 162, 228, 229, 253, 254, 257, 268, 273, 275, 277
Morocco, 208
Morrison, Herbert, illus. 137; in War Cabinet, 42, 45, 46, 86, 87, 209, 222; as P.M., 37, 157; warning to Press, 170, 171; General Election, 296, 297, 309
Mortimer, Raymond, 300
Morton, H. V., 129–31
Mosley, Sir Oswald, 171
Mountbatten, Lord Louis, 229, 238
Muggeridge, Malcolm, 9, 18
Mulberry Harbour, 248
Munich Agreement, 8, 9, 10, 11, 13, 79, 96, 149, 175
Munichites, 42, 45, 66, 87, 94, 126, 151, 155, 183, 255, 278
Murrow, Ed., 56, 91, 107
Mussolini, 66, 133, 160, 174, 224, 287

Nachtausgabe, 81
National Government, 4, 6, 11, 15
News Chronicle, 38, 55, 148
Newspaper Proprietors, Ass., 88–9
New Statesman & Nation, 12, 114, 118, 241–2, 243, 254, 288
New York Times, 174, 183, 193, 257, 309
New Zealand, 160–1, 207
Nicolson, Harold, in National Govt., 4, on Chamberlain, 9; Munich debate, 10; rebel group, 11; on Kennedy defeatism, 14–15; on Norway, 33, 35; on W.S.C., 7, 43, 65, 91, 122, 154, 155, 173, 204, 236; as minister, 126; meeting Nat. Labour

Nicolson, Harold—*cont.*
  Ex., 146; report of debate on war, 155; secret session, 173; censure debate, 192; Russia, 195; Cripps, 203; Churchill homecoming, 236; self-determination for Europe, 242; de Gaulle, 248; Greek debate and Sforza, 263; Polish elections, 279; death of F.D.R., 287; General Election, 297, 311
North African Campaign, Wavell attacks Italians, 92–3; 95, 100–1; Hitler to aid Italians, 109; Rommel lands, 110; diffusion of Army, 112; Wavell counter-attack failure, 120, 124, 132, 135, 152; Rommel counter-attack, 167–8; need for Allied control and fall of Tobruk, 187; Montgomery 8th Army, 197; plans for offensive, 199, 200, 201; Cripps opposition, 201, 203; P.M. against delay, 204; offensive launched, 205–6; Rommel defeated at Alamein, 207–8; Tobruk recaptured, 208; base for assault on Europe, 209–10, 212, 215; push back Germans, 214–15; Axis collapse, 216
Norway expedition, 33–6, 50, 112, 114, 116, 149, 176, 188
Nuremberg rally, 8

Observer, The, 37, 54, 125, 183
Operation Anvil, 250
Operation Overlord, see also Second Front, 224, 226, 235, 238–9, 240
Oran, 69–72
Owen, Frank, 126, 144, 175–7, 180, 183

Pacific Ocean, 188, 210, 212, 216, 257, 293
Papandreou, George, 268
Peace moves, 24, 26, 73, 104, 161
Pearl Harbor, 137, 175
Pétain, Marshal, 59, 63, 118
Petherick, Maurice, 279
Pethick-Lawrence, Lord, 152
Philippines, 139, 143, 257

Phillips, Admiral Sir Tom, 137
Pile, General Sir Fredk., 158
Plowman, Max, 52
Poland, invasion, 17, 18; G.B. ultimatum to Germany, 19; Govt.-in-exile, 105; Russians reach Warsaw, 252; British commitment, 256–7, 270; Russian-Polish debate, 264, 266; Russians in Warsaw, 269; Yalta discussions, 272; Elections, 275–8; W.S.C. letter to Stalin, 301; Potsdam, Stalin asks for transfer of Polish property, etc., 305; Churchill defended Polish forces, 305; Potsdam, 311
Popular Front, 15, 16
Portal, Sir Charles, illus. 137; 75, 89, 95, 135, 260, 273, 291
Portes, Comtesse de, 48
Potsdam conference, 303, 305–6, 311, 314
Pound, Sir Dudley, 75, 196
Press Censorship, 88–9, 99, 170–2
Priestley, J. B., 16
Prince of Wales, H.M.S., 119, 130, 137–8, 173, 188
Prinz Eugen (German ship), 160
Pritt, D. N., 118
Profumo, John, 191

Quebec conference, 1st, 223–5; 2nd 252–4
Queen Elizabeth, H.M.S., 173

R.A.F., 48, 50, 75–6, 78, 81, 83, 94, 95, 143, 177, 219, 282
Rainboro', Thomas, *pseudonym*, see Owen, Frank
Regulation 18B, 171
Reparations, 272–4
Repulse, H.M.S., 137, 173, 188
Reynaud, Paul, 46–8, 52–4, 59–63
Reynolds News, 26
Reynolds, Quentin, 102, 126, 127
Rhine Crossing, 281, 284–6
Rhineland, 4
Rhodes, Island of, 226
Ribbentrop von, 24, 123, 161, 174–5
Roberts, Wilfrid, 170

Robertson, Sir William, 195
Rollo, Charles, 125
Rommel, General, 110, 112, 124, 133, 167–8, 193, 199, 203, 204, 206, 207–8, 210, 235, 247, 248
Roosevelt, Franklin D., appeal to U.S. to enter war, 59–60, 61, 78; Lend-Lease, 94, 107; sent Hopkins to W.S.C., 99–101; W.S.C.'s pills, 103; peace rumours, 104; Atlantic conference and Charter, 128–31; W.S.C. visit, 138; friendship established, 147, 148; de Valera, 139; told of Alamein 208; Second Front, 172, 186–7, 216, 222, 226, 228; Casablanca conference, 210, 211, 213; Washington conference, 215–16; de Gaulle, 219; rebuffs W.S.C., 225; Cairo conference, 227; Teheran conference, 228; Churchill and Eden view of F.D.R. 248; accepts control of British fleet, 252; in control of war, 253; help for Alexander and proposed meeting, 257; supported Eisenhower in Montgomery quarrel, 260; strained relations with Churchill, 263, 266; at Yalta 272–7; ill, 275; last meeting with W.S.C., 277; de Gaulle refuses meeting, 277; Dresden raid, 283–4; disagreement with W.S.C. over German defeat, 287; death, 287; strategy of campaign of criticism, 294
Rothermere, Lord, 67
Roumania, 242
Rowan-Robinson, Maj.-Gen. H., 113
Royal Oak, H.M.S., 27
Rundstedt, General von, 54, 247
Russia, see also Stalin, Cripps as Ambassador, 45 and appeal for aid, 157, 159; Bessarabia, 72; Germans prepare, 90, 112, and launch attack, 122, 123, 124, 168, 172, 175, 177, 194, 195, 210; appeal for Second Front, 131–2, 135, 144, 145, 147, 149, 152, 172, 182, 210, 215; support from Beaverbrook, 162, 163, 174, 225; Anglo-Russian relations, 189, 199; 'Balance of power' in Balkans, 226; Roumania, 242; Europe, 243, 249, 286, 313; German withdrawal, 215; Kiev retaken, 227; Roumania released, 242; enter Bucharest, 252; reach Warsaw, 252, 269; Douglas-Home on Poland, 256; to annex E. Poland, 266; Yalta conference, 272; troops enter Vienna, 287; meeting on the Elbe, 288; German peace negotiations, 289; fighting in Berlin and Soviet flag over Reichstag, 290; possible war with Britain, 303; U.S. troops out of Russian zone and Russians out of Austria, 302–3; A-Bomb, 306; Potsdam: Italy and Poland, 305; Potsdam: Poland and Balkans, 311

Sackville-West, Vita, 298
Salerno, 224–5
Salter, Dr A., 118
Samuel, Herbert, 2
Sandys, Duncan, 7, 10, 81, 158
Savory, Professor, 115
Scapa Flow, 27
Scharnhorst (German ship), 160, 165, 188
Scotsman, The, 122
Scribner's Commentator, 107
Second Front, 123; Stalin view, 131–2, 210; individuals' views: 155, 158, 169, 203, 226, 235, *Daily Express* and Beaverbrook: 141, 144, 149, 160, 162, 174; 'Second Front Now' campaign, 172, 179, 183, 188, 225; *Tribune*, 179; postponement, 195, 197–8, 209, 212, 215, 216; supported by S. France invasion, 198, 215, 229, 239, 249, 250; British aims in Med., 218; Washington conference, 143, 187, 215, date fixed, 216–17; Casablanca conference, 212; Algiers conference, 222; Quebec conference, 223; Teheran conference, 228; 'Overlord' commander, 223–4; preparations, 235,

Second Front—*cont.*
238, 239, 240, 243–5; D-Day, 245–7; W.S.C. visit, 248; U.S. criticism of campaign, 249
Sforza, Count, 262–3
Shapiro, Lionel, 223
Shaw, George Bernard, 25–6, 313
Shinwell, Emanuel, illus. 136; 3, 116–18, 146, 151, 155, 157, 183, 202, 261, 279, 297
Sicily, 212, 216, 217, 222, 223–4
Sikorski, President, 105
Silverman, Sydney, 192
Simon, Sir John, 143
Sinclair, Sir Archibald, 8, 42, 75, 220, 282
Singapore, 127, 136–9, 142, 155, 156, 159, 160, 164, 165, 173, 175, 181, 185, 188
Slim, General, 301
Smuts, General, 122; friend of W.S.C., 87, 225, 229; on W.S.C., 97–8, 200, 201, 205; on bombing, 105; approval of Greek campaign, 109; post-war world, 140; Lloyd George, 205; de Gaulle, 206–7; Italian campaign strategy, 224; 'Overlord' strategy, 226
Southampton, H.M.S., 101
Southby, Sir Archibald, 154, 165, 246
Spaak, Paul Henri, 38
Spaatz, General Carl Andrew, 240
Spears, E. L. 8, 10, 11, 48
Spectator, 231
Speeches; 'Blood, toil, tears, and sweat,' 42–3, 1st speech as P.M., 49; 'We shall fight on the beaches', 55–6; 'This was their finest hour', 63–4; 'The few', 78; Unity of Government, 82–4; to French, 85; 'Give us the tools', 94; air war over Germany, 124–5; 'It only remains for us to act', 155–6; reply to vote of Censure, 191; Broadcast, 29.11.42., 209; ... 'Let us get back to our job', 214; lessening in effect, 256–7; 'we stood alone', 269–70; Yalta debate, 278; Victory broadcast, 291; victory speech to House, 292; 'We will never surrender', 294; Election: Socialist Gestapo, 297; accepting defeat at election, 308; on use of A-bomb, 312
Stalin, younger than W.S.C., 41; Kennedy on Stalin, 79; German attack, 122; asked for Second Front, 131, 210, 222, 228–9; postponed, 196; first meeting with W.S.C. on Second Front and general strategy, 197–9; Alamein, 208; W.S.C. in Moscow, 257; at Yalta, 272–7; on Poland, 275–6; race for Berlin, 280, 284; area bombing, 283; German peace negotiations, 289; rule without criticism, 294; need to contain, 295; Polish question, 301; trusteeship of Italian colony, 305; and transfer of Polish property, 305, 314
Stanley, Oliver, 34
Steinbeck, John, 225
Stettinius, Ed., 240, 265, 266
Stilwell, General Joe, 143, 216, 238, 251
Stimson, Henry, 216, 222, 227, 306
Stokes, Richard, illus. 49; 144, 151, 165, 181, 255; against area bombing, 220, 282–3; unconditional surrender, 271
Strasbourg (French ship), 70
Suez Canal, 77, 188
Sumatra, 216, 223
Sunday Dispatch, 211
Sunday Express, 183
Sunday Pictorial, 73, 88, 89
Sunday Times, 114, 119, 136
Swinton, Lord, 7, 79–80
Syria, 110, 304

Tedder, Lord Arthur, 77, 240, 258, 260, 261, 280–1
Teheran conference, 227–9
Thailand, 136
Thomas, J., 10
Thompson, Commander, 217
Thompson, C. V. R., 141
Thompson, Dorothoy, 106–7
Time, 108

Times, The, 6, 10–11, 19, 27, 114, 147, 151, 183, 203, 236–7, 255–6, 264, 270–1, 291, 300, 309
Tizard, Professor Sir Henry, 168–9
Tobruk, 110–11, 123, 185, 187–8, 191, 208
Trade Unions, 46, 118, 201, 264, 267
Trenchard, Lord, 50–1, 122, 202
Tribune, 126, 141, 144, 147, 158–9, 175–80, 183, 265–6
Tripoli, 110, 177, 213, 224
Truman, President: president, 287; German zoning, 288; possible German surrender, 289; letter from W.S.C. on Iron Curtain, 301; relations with Stalin, 302; withdrawal of troops from Russian zone, 302–3; Potsdam atom bomb decision, 305; A-bomb used, 311–12
Tunisia, 177, 208, 213, 215, 224, 226
Turkey, 210, 213, 215, 226

Unconditional Surrender, 212, 240, 269, 271, 290, 292
United Nations Organization, 144, 272, 274–5
United States of America, see also Anglo-U.S. relations, Roosevelt: U.S. boat searched by British, 29; fall of France, plea for U.S. aid, 59–60; refusal, 61; agreed to sell arms, 68–9; Atlantic Charter signed, 131; Pearl Harbor, 137; Philippines campaign, 143; Washington conference, 143; relations with Australia, 160–1; relations with Vichy, 186; criticism of W.S.C., 167, 237, 243, 267, 204; criticism of Burma campaign, 238; criticism of Montgomery, 249; criticism of use of U.S. in British intervention in Greece, 264–5; U.S.A.F., 198, 219, 282; Second Front, 172, 195, 196, 207, 212; Indian Ocean and Middle East, 172; operation 'Torch' landings in N.W. Africa, 196, 200, 208; report on bombing of Germany, 221; U.S. took control of war, 224, 253; death of Roosevelt, Truman President, 287; German peace negotiations, 289; A-bomb, 305–6

Valiant, H.M.S., 173
Vansittart, Lord, 67
Vichy Government, 69, 71, 84, 110, 186, 208
Voroshilov, Marshal, 198
Vote of Censure, 188–92, 203
Votes of Confidence, 42–4, 115–18, 149, 152–7, 193, 237, 264

Warden, Colonel, code name for W.S.C., 233
Wardlaw-Milne, Sir John, 125, 155, 160, 180, 188–9
Washington conferences, 1, 143; 2, 215–17; 3, 225
Wavell, General, 77–8, 92–3, 109–12, 114, 117, 120–2, 139, 167, 193, 197, 216, 235, 243
Wells, H. G., 265
Westdeutscher Beobachter, 103
Weygand, General, 49, 59, 60, 69
Whistler, Laurence, 256
White, Graham, 153
Wigram, Ralph, 4
Wilkie, Wendell, 139
Williams, Sir Herbert, 153–4
Wilson, Sir Charles, see Lord Moran
Winant, John G., 104, 264, 306
Wingate, Orde, General, 76
Winterton, Lord, 3, 120, 188, 189, 190
Wolmer, Viscount, 10
Wolstencroft, Frank, 201
Wood, Sir Kingsley, 67, 163, 225
Woodford, 300, 309
Wrench, Sir Evelyn, 156

Yalta conference, 272–8, 303
Yugoslavia, 242, 250, 289

Zec, Philip, 170
Zuckermann, Professor S., 168

For Product Safety Concerns and Information please contact our EU representative GPSR@taylorandfrancis.com
Taylor & Francis Verlag GmbH, Kaufingerstraße 24, 80331 München, Germany

www.ingramcontent.com/pod-product-compliance
Lightning Source LLC
Chambersburg PA
CBHW071148300426
44113CB00009B/1122